Research and Technological Innovation

D1229263

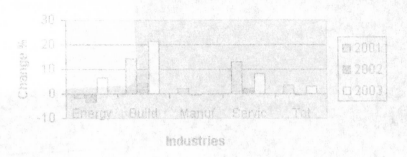

Fig 1. Turnover Yearly Variation in Different Industries (%)
Source: Mediobanca, 2004

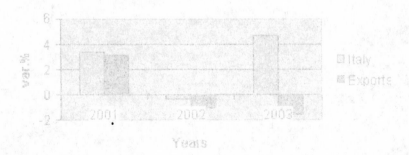

Fig 2. Turnover Variation Italy vs Exports, Years 2001-2003 (%)
Source: Mediobanca, 2004

S9732

Alberto Quadrio Curzio · Marco Fortis
(Editors)

Research and Technological Innovation

The Challenge for a New Europe

With 66 Figures and 19 Tables

Université d'Ottawa
BIBLIOTHÈQUES
Université d'Ottawa
LIBRARIES
University of Ottawa

Physica-Verlag

A Springer Company

b 28216830

Professor Alberto Quadrio Curzio
Research Centre CRANEC
Università Cattolica
Via Necchi, 5
20123 Milano
Italy
alberto.quadriocurzio@unicatt.it

Professor Marco Fortis
Edison S.p.A.
Foro Buonaparte, 31
20121 Milano
Italy
marco.fortis@edison.it

HC
240.9
.T4
R47
2005

ISBN-10   3-7908-1594-2 Physica-Verlag Heidelberg New York
ISBN-13   978-3-7908-1594-8 Physica-Verlag Heidelberg New York

Cataloging-in-Publication Data applied for
Library of Congress Control Number: 2005929963

This work is subject to copyright. All rights are reserved, whether the whole or part of the material is concerned, specifically the rights of translation, reprinting, reuse of illustrations, recitation, broadcasting, reproduction on microfilm or in any other way, and storage in data banks. Duplication of this publication or parts thereof is permitted only under the provisions of the German Copyright Law of September 9, 1965, in its current version, and permission for use must always be obtained from Physica-Verlag. Violations are liable for prosecution under the German Copyright Law.

Physica is a part of Springer Science+Business Media

springeronline.com

© Physica-Verlag Heidelberg 2005
Printed in Germany

The use of general descriptive names, registered names, trademarks, etc. in this publication does not imply, even in the absence of a specific statement, that such names are exempt from the relevant protective laws and regulations and therefore free for general use.

Cover-Design: Erich Kirchner, Heidelberg

SPIN 11496908   43/3153-5 4 3 2 1 0 – Printed on acid-free paper

Preface

This volume contains some essays of two international conferences both organized by Fondazione Edison under the aegis and with the scientific collaboration of the Accademia Nazionale dei Lincei.

The first conference is "Districts, Pillars, Network Facilities" held in Rome, in the siege of Lincei at Palazzo Corsini, on 8th and 9th April, 2003. The Organizing Committee of this conference was composed by Giacomo Becattini, Sergio Carrà, Marco Fortis, Giorgio Lunghini, Luigi Pasinetti, Umberto Quadrino, Alberto Quadrio Curzio, Alessandro Roncaglia and Edoardo Vesentini.

The second conference is "New Science, New Industry – The Challenges for the New Europe" held in Rome in the siege of Lincei at Palazzo Corsini, on 13th and 14th October, 2004. The Organizing Committee of this conference was composed by Arnaldo Bagnasco, Patrizio Bianchi, Sergio Carrà, Marco Fortis, Augusto Graziani, Alberto Quadrio Curzio, Edoardo Vesentini and Giovanni Zanetti.

Both were international conferences with the participation of a total of 48 speakers coming from 9 different countries.

We publish in this volume only some essays of the two Conferences as the decision to edit a book in English was taken only after the two conferences were over. Therefore not all the speakers were able to contribute with a paper.

Some information are useful to know the two organizing Institutions.

Accademia Nazionale dei Lincei was founded in Rome in 1604 by Federico Cesi and had among its founding members Galileo Galilei who published under the aegis of the Academy his famous *Istoria e dimostrazioni intorno alle macchie solari* (1613). Lincei is one of the oldest and most famous national academies of science in the world and has its siege in Rome at Palazzo Corsini and Villa Farnesina where there are also paintings by Raphael.

Fondazione Edison is much younger having been founded in 1999. It encourages research and dissemination of knowledge about social, economic, cultural and civil issues. It promotes research and innovation related to local production systems and industrial districts. Up to now it has published seven books in an Italian series of the Editor Il Mulino, one book with Accademia Nazionale dei Lincei and two books with Springer.

The editors of this volume, personally and on behalf of Fondazione Edison, wish to extend their heartfelt thanks to all those who have contributed to the success of the conferences and particularly to all of the speakers, whose papers are presented in this volume. Many thanks are due to Valeria Miceli who gave her valuable contribution to the editing of this volume and to Beatrice Biagetti who gave her valuable contribution to the secretarial activities for the organization of the conferences.

Milan, March 2005   Alberto Quadrio Curzio
                                                    Marco Fortis

tion, still working in agricultural or craft sectors, ready to feed the development of a mass industry able to attract a working class with low qualifications. Along with this working class there also was a little group of technicians (mostly engineers) that managed the operations in the large firms, but excluded from property and control, and also a class of professionals (doctors and lawyers) that run local communities, but taking no part in production activities.

In those years the demand for education typical of a growing country added up to the needs of local and technical elites. This phenomenon determined, even if through different adjustments, a continuous increase in the number of enrolled students catching up the levels of developed countries. Nevertheless the number of students graduating within the course legal duration has remained, in absolute terms, similar to that of the 60's. In 2001 the number of students graduating within the course legal duration was 4%, while more than 63% of students graduated with a delay of three or more years.

The direct consequence of this situation is that, in 1999, the yearly cost for each student in Italy was the same as in Spain, Portugal and Greece, the less developed countries in Europe ($ 7,500 against an EU average of $ 9,700). Nevertheless the cost for each student cumulated for the average duration of the degree course was in 1999 of $ 41,000, above France and UK levels (Avveduto, 2003).

The percentage of population with a university degree appeared to be incompatible, in Italy, with the country level of development. In 2001, only 12% of the population aged between 25 and 34 years and only 10% of the population aged between 25 and 64 years had a university degree against European percentages of respectively 29% and 23%. For the Doctorates, the Italian average was only 0.4% for the population aged between 25 and 34 years, placing Italy at the bottom of European rankings, well below Spain and Portugal levels (OCSE, 2002).

University structure was made up, in 2001-2002, by 74 Universities and postgraduate technical colleges and 515 faculties.

Italian universities can be divided into two groups: the 9 biggest universities collect 38% of the enrolled students, while the remaining 62% is spread among the other 65 universities. The first 9 institutes have an average of 70,000 students while the others have an average of 16,000 students. At the beginning of the 80's the first 9 universities counted 57% of the students and the others the remaining 43%. It has therefore taken place a reallocation of students in the territory due to the creation, in the last twenty years, of new academic entities.

Permanent lecturers were 55,000 plus about 15,000 lecturers on contract. In 2001 only 5% of the teachers is younger than 34 years, 24% is between 35 and 45, 33% is between 45 and 54, and 38% is above 55 years. This profile is very different from the European average (CNVSU-MIUR, 2003). The following block in the recruitment has frozen the situation, worsening the comparison in terms of teachers' and researchers' age with the rest of Europe.

The ageing of the University structure in Italy comes out evidently from the age profile of teachers and researchers (Figure 6). In 1985 nearly 50% of the teachers was between 35 and 44 years old. In 1993 the same group is between 45 and 55. In 2001 it is above 55 years.

Contents

Introduction - Research, Technology, Innovation: Analysis and Cases

Alberto Quadrio Curzio[a], Marco Fortis[b]

[a] Research Centre CRANEC, Università Cattolica, Milan, Italy
alberto.quadriocurzio@unicatt.it
[b] Fondazione Edison, Foro Buonaparte 31, Milan, Italy
marco.fortis@edison.it

1. Foreword

We begin this book, which contains some essays of the international conferences described in the preface, with a brief reflection on the two institutions that promoted them: Fondazione Edison, which organized the conferences, and Accademia Nazionale dei Lincei, which gave the scientific sponsorship to them.

Both these institutions are important for their different traditions in the fields of scientific and technological research.

Fondazione Edison is closely associated with the historical roots of Edison, founded in 1884 and of Montecatini, founded in 1888. The two firms later on merged in a new firm named Montedison.

The two companies were able to build on their 'local' civil and economic base and then expand nationally and internationally by constantly focusing on technological innovation. It is a well-known fact that the discovery of polypropylene, for which Giulio Natta received the Nobel Prize in 1963, was made possible by the support of Montecatini in an outstanding example of collaboration between industry and research. Many other remarkable personalities throughout Montecatini's and Edison's histories deserved mention for their ability to combine entrepreneurial spirit and scientific and technological innovation, most notably Guido Donegani, Giacomo Fauser and Giuseppe Colombo[1].

Accademia Nazionale dei Lincei, which honoured the mentioned conferences with its trust and scientific sponsorship, was founded in 1603, making it the oldest Academy in the world. It is worth mentioning that its founding members included

---

[1] Quadrio Curzio A, Fortis M, Pavese C (2003), Il Gruppo Edison: 1883-2003. Profili economici e societari, Vol I-II, Il Mulino, Bologna.

Galileo Galilei, who in 1613 published his *Historia e Dimostrazioni Intorno alle Macchie Solari* as part of the Academy's proceedings. This is not the place for a lengthy and detailed presentation of the extraordinary scientific merits of the Accademia dei Lincei and of its contributions to Italian and international scientific history. Interestingly, Giulio Natta, Nobel Prize, was a member of the Academy in 1947, as were Giuseppe Colombo, member since 1888 and Giacomo Fauser, member since 1948[2].

It seems to us, then, that the holding of these international conferences and the publication of this book provide an historical perspective linking these two institutions, which share a complementary vision, even though their objectives are different. And this vision is that science and technology must cooperate and this means for us that industry can not prosper without research.

The same vision is also shared in this volume whose purpose is to explain the importance of scientific research and technological innovation to improve or to maintain economic leadership.

The volume is organized into 11 chapters many of which are rich of data, tables and figures. It is divided into two sections: the first one providing a historical and theoretical perspective on scientific-technological innovation and its importance for industrial growth.

The second section presents some national success stories to confirm the theoretical perspective and provide examples of how public policies and private incentives can combine fostering research and innovation and consequently attracting investments and generating growth.

Let us consider briefly some of the main points of the essays and of the book. The selection will be highly personal and therefore we apologise with the authors if they do not agree with our choices, even if we quote them extensively

2. Historical and Theoretical-Applied Perspectives

From the previous foreword, it should be clear that for us history matters very much. This is also the reason why we asked *Joel Mokyr* to provide an historical perspective to the whole conference and he done that in a very satisfactory way around the concept of 'useful knowledge' in its essay "The intellectual origins of modern economic growth: knowledge and technological change in the industrial revolution".

According to Mokyr the Industrial Revolution was the result of two phenomena: on one hand the increase in the relative contribution to economic growth of technological progress compared to other elements; and on the other one the transformation of the institutional basis supporting this progress.

Mokyr asks how it is possible to explain such change and suggests that "the change in the rate and nature of economic growth in the West must be explained

---

[2] Among the many publications on Lincei see D Freedberg (2002) The eye of the Lynx, The University of Chicago Press, London, Chicago.

through developments in the intellectual realm concerning this 'useful knowledge'." This is the center of what we like to call its rational interpretation that can be spelt out as follows: "The short answer as to why the West is so much richer today than it was two centuries ago is that as collectives, these societies 'know' more. This does not necessarily mean that each individual on average knows more than his or her great-great grandparent (although that is almost certainly the case given the increased investment in human capital), but that the social knowledge, defined as the union of all pieces of individual knowledge, has expanded. Greater specialization, professionalisation, and expertisation have meant that the total amount of knowledge that society controls is vastly larger than ever before. The effective deployment of that knowledge, scientific or otherwise, in the service of production is the primary – if not the only – cause for the rapid growth of western economies in the past centuries".

In his paper Mokyr develops what we call a historical-theoretical approach, based largely on the experience of the Western economies in the eighteenth century. This is the centre of what we like to call its historical interpretation that can be spelt out as follows: "The Enlightenment in the West is the only intellectual movement in human history that owed its irreversibility to the ability to transform itself into economic growth. It did so by fuelling the engine of economic growth through the sustained supply of useful knowledge and the ability to apply this knowledge eventually to the nitty gritty of production in the fields and workshops where the GDP is ultimately produced."

On these two foundations (Rational and Historical) Mokyr develops all his analysis. We consider here only two points. The first one is institutional, the second one relates to access costs.

From the institutional point of view, Mokyr points out that we had long term growth also by "providing the economies with institutional steering wheels that on the whole prevented them from crashing the vehicle of economic growth into the trees of rent-seeking, war, and other forms of destructive behaviour."

From the access costs point of view, Mokyr argues that the irreversibility of the accumulation of useful knowledge was due to ever-falling access costs. "As long as knowledge was confined to a small number of specialists with high access costs for everyone else, there was a serious risk that it could be lost. Many of the great inventions of China and Classical Antiquity in fact were no longer available to subsequent generations. The decline in access costs meant that knowledge was spread over many more minds and storage devices, so that any reversals in technological progress after the Industrial Revolution were ruled out."

The volume continues with three essays which we call theoretical and applied as they explain with different, but complementary models, the process of innovation also with specific references to effective cases of today experience. One essay deals with the territorialisation of innovation; the second one with the interplay of agglomeration economies and diseconomies in the growth process of a high-tech cluster; the third one with the dynamic features of many high-technology clusters that increase the division of labour and the fragmentation of production.

Territorialisation of innovation: **Christian Longhi**'s paper "Local systems and networks in the globalization process" puts at its centre the innovation both as an engine for the evolution of productivity, economic growth and regional development and a key to explain the reinforcement of the concentration of activities in Europe.

Longhi explains that "As innovation can be considered as the key of competitiveness and of evolution of disparities, the contemporaneous economy can be best characterized as simultaneously globalised and knowledge-based, and deeply shaped by the spatial distribution of competences. Indeed, innovation is a collective process that implies a set of formal and informal relations. Its socio-economic dimension, the importance of intangible elements, of tacit knowledge – largely person-embodied and context dependent – suggest that territorialisation of activities is a basic element of the understanding of the working of the economies. According to this approach, technology is no longer given, and easily transferable across space, but is the result of a process of creation of new resources within firms, between firms, and between firms and other institutions, and highly specific to local areas. These institutional structures, which define the process of innovation, are indeed deeply embedded in particular territories. Global and local are, apparently paradoxically, the two faces of the same process."

In our opinion this is a remarkable application of the more general Mokyr's statement on the role of knowledge. Among the many interesting aspects of Longhi's reasoning let us point out to the following two.

The first one is the meaning of 'glocal': "The deepening of globalisation, from mere relocations to a complex integration of the multinational firms or networks at the world level has shown the increasing importance of the local, of the 'context' as the key of competitiveness and economic development. Different systems of production highly embedded in their region, as industrial districts, have even reinforced during these phases. Far from leading to a 'new geography', the contemporaneous process of globalisation would in fact sustain a cumulative process of reinforcement of existing disparities, of the centres of economic development and wealth creation, in short some sort of lock-in regarding the territorial characteristics of economic activities. The paper will show on the contrary that this apparent stability of the location of economic activities and of the ongoing trends regarding disparities hides in fact deep changes and reorganisation of the whole economic system. It will focus on local systems, as they are apparently the locus of the previous contradiction: when places and locations seem stable, the contemporaneous process of globalisation has in fact induced a deep 'revolution' in their internal and external relationships".

The second aspect is the transformation of linkages among European regions: "Particularly within the economic integration occurring in Europe, the increasing number of linkages of regions with other locations within or across different geographic boundaries is often underlined. In fact the problem is not the quantitative increases of linkages, but their qualitative transformation. The understanding of these transformations is a key to the understanding of the ongoing economic changes and to the definition of coherent strategies of development or related public policies."

Mario Maggioni's paper aim is "to apply an original theoretical framework, derived from population ecology, to the analysis of the development of high-tech clusters in order to underline the interplay of agglomeration economies and dis-economies in their growth process and to stress the complex and different (i.e. synergic, competitive, etc.) interactions which exist between different high-tech industries, within the same area, and between different areas within the same in-dustry".

Population ecology is concerned with how populations interact with the envi-ronment and how these interactions give rise to the larger patterns of communities and ecosystems. Population ecology deals with the study of how natural elements and other organisms interact in competition and in co-operation.

Maggioni translates this suggestion in the field of industrial economics by studying the development of local systems of productions (and in particular of high-tech clusters) as the outcomes of "two distinct but interrelated processes: an inner dynamics (driven by the number of firms already located in the cluster) and an external dynamics (driven by the spatial and industrial interaction between and within clusters)". These models describe the growth process of an industrial clus-ter (i.e. the agglomeration in a given area of a number of firms belonging to a cer-tain industry) as a function of the size of the local population of firms, a ceiling level – which takes into account the limit imposed by the available amount of re-sources (inputs and local infrastructure); and the size of interacting populations (i.e. the number of firms of other industry located in the same area and of the same industry but located in other areas).

The process of internal development is represented within a stock-flow which, according to Maggioni, is able to "take into account a series of typical processes and stylized facts which characterize the clustering phenomenon ...: often new firms in a cluster are started either by people which were previously employed by other local firms willing to try the entrepreneurial venture (spin-off) or by local resident willing to emulate successful entrepreneurs (imitation); in an uncertain environment – where there are information asymmetries between insiders (resi-dent firms) and outsiders (external and "potential" firms) – the number of located firms signals to the potential entrant the profitability of the location; the location of a new firm into an already established cluster signals his quality to potential customers by showing it's ability to survive to harm's length competition in in-puts markets". Moreover the role of agglomeration economies and diseconomies in shaping the growth path of a cluster refers to the fact that "each new entrant in-creases the locational benefits to each and every incumbents (agglomeration economies, which develop through the marshallian externalities channels: labour market pooling, specialized intermediate inputs, technological externalities and knowledge spillovers) only up to a point, then it decreases them (agglomeration diseconomies) when congestion and competition prevail".

The paper shows also some interesting empirical application to the US case, by investigating the development of a number of high-tech industries within several US States. The mix of econometric estimation and phase diagrams allows Maggioni to identify the existence of long-run equilibria of inter-sectorial a/o in-ter-state interactions and to suggest possible future industrial dynamics.

Peter Swann deals with one of the most interesting dynamic features of many high-technology clusters: the increase in the division of labour, and hence the so-called fragmentation of production. "One striking example of this is in the manufacture of personal computers (PCs), where it has become almost meaningless to ask in what country a PC is manufactured. The various components of a PC are manufactured in many different countries, assembly may be done in more than one country, and the final 'badge' may be added somewhere else again. Particular companies (and indeed particular clusters) may become specialized in just one particular activity within the overall process of PC manufacture. This specialization and fragmentation of production depends on interaction between the different activities, and hence on cost-effective communication and transportation."

The objective of Swann's paper is to describe and analyze a simple model of the comparative efficiency of several different industrial structures. At one end the author examines the co-location of all production phases with final consumption; at the other one the emergence of specialized clusters each focusing on just one stage of production. The model shows "how this comparative efficiency depends on economies of scale and scope, economies of agglomeration and congestion costs, and on costs of communication and transportation." The model also explains "how the degree of codification of the production process influences this comparative efficiency, and hence explains why the ICT revolution may cause a relevant change in the clustering pattern of given industries over the product life cycle."

As Swann aptly underlines "while many have focused on the good side of clustering, there is also inevitably a bad side". The role of transportation and communication infrastructure becomes therefore crucial in determining the level and the evolution of regional disparities: without infrastructures "either the cluster do not form or all activity tends to pile into the most concentrated clusters leading to high congestion in the biggest cities and decline of other regions."

In this sense the policy implications of the paper are very important both at the national and European level, as stressed by the author: "the paper is relevant to the process of clustering in many European countries, but especially relevant to issues arising in the United Kingdom. The British government has adopted clustering as a major instrument of industrial policy, and believes it has a role in helping to revive the economies of poorer regions. Unfortunately however, much of the clustering observed in practice is a further concentration of activity into the over-heated South East of England."

The paper concludes by showing that a careful industrial policy must take into serious account the role of transportation infrastructure: a fragmented/specialized cluster structure (which is less congestion-prone) "would be more plausible if the public transportation infrastructures were in better condition and cheaper."

3. European Union, National and R&D Cases

This section of the volume can be divided into two parts. The first one (David, Andreta, Lindberg) deals mainly with the situation in the EU even if it presents (mainly David) a wider paradigm. The second part (Feldman, Eatwell, Braunherjelm, Bianchi-Ramaciotti) deals with national and/or sectorial cases.

Paul David's essay, being paradigmatical and applied, is the best link with the previous section. The starting point is a response to the February 2003 *Communication on the role of the universities in the Europe of knowledge*, issued by the Commission of the European Communities which ,after having assessed Europe's critical needs in the epoch of 'knowledge-driven economic growth', identifies the university as the institution suited to meet those needs. The Communication called for debate on the changes in the European universities needed to meet the mentioned needs. "Reduced to its essence, this presented a view of Europe's institutions of higher education as possessing the potential to be more effective than its industry at the business of technological innovation. But, it also faulted the university researchers and administrators for failing to make the realization of that potential a priority. What is being advocated, therefore, is tantamount to a program of institutional reforms intended to mobilize of that capability in order to meet a dual societal problem: financing the rising costs of public education and research, and enlarging the share of EU gross domestic product that is devoted to public and private investment in R&D."

David suggests that "the likely costs, as well as the promised benefits of this proposal deserve more careful consideration than they have been receiving from enthusiasts for the grand goal."

With regard to the costs, "it is apparent that many of the features of universities that have rendered them particularly effective when called upon to perform in their historical societal role as 'nodes' in the international dissemination of knowledge and, since Humboldt, as generators of fundamental advances in scientific understanding, might have to be sacrificed in order to effectively carry through the institutional reforms suggested by the EC's *Communication*. Within the familiar context of academic, 'open science' norms and governance structures, the comparative advantage of university-based researchers' lies in conducting inquiries that may provide the foundations for valuable commercial innovations. But the best way to do this is precisely not the closely managed, tightly-coupled search for discoveries and inventions that fires the imaginations of many political leaders, policy-advisors and financially hard-pressed university administrators who are seeking predictable and readily identifiable near-term payoffs."

With regard to the benefits "it is equally apparent that the EC's *Communication* (and many similar policy pronouncements of national government ministries) has failed to show that there is an adequate evidentiary basis for supposing that the envisaged societal gains will be substantial enough to justify attempting to transform Europe's most prestigious academic institutions into 'knowledge-management enterprises.' It is not plausible to suppose that more than a few among Europe's research universities would, by exploiting the intellectual property created by the people who study and work there, be enabled to contribute materially to the costs of their own upkeep."

David continues by analyzing in details the pros and cons of taking into account the US university-industry relations. "Ideas for European institutional reform and regeneration along those lines clearly have been inspired by perceptions of vigorous university-industry research partnerships, rising patenting activity and the flourishing of academic entrepreneurship in the U.S. during the two closing decades of the past century". He considers the effects of Bayh-Dole Act (1980) concluding that "the highly decentralized approach of the Bayh-Dole Act, in giving every university and public research institute the responsibility for securing and exploiting its intellectual property portfolio, has imposed significant 'learning costs' on the system as a whole and brought into existence a new professional group – university technology managers – who have personal and collective interests in the perpetuation of these arrangements. Concomitantly, there are few if any large, R&D intensive firms in the U.S. that now express general enthusiasm for the Bayh-Dole regime, and, many of their executives now speak in very critical terms about the performance of most of the universities' technology licensing offices."

David's conclusion is sharp and simple as he stresses that there is not a single best recipe for all situations: "European policy-makers concerned with the scientific and technological foundations for business innovation and economic growth should be considering reforms and revitalizing measures that build upon the region's own rich and diverse institutional foundations, rather than risking doing damage to them by blindly imitating a dubious American experiment."

Ezio Andreta in his paper discusses the Lisbon Strategy and the reasons why certain tools have been set in the EU. He takes into account, at least, two aspects: the first one is that of industrial mutation; the other one is that of R&D and innovation.

Industrial mutation, he says, is a central point also in the Agenda of European Councils and in the worries of European Ministers on three grounds: 1) the loss of foreign markets; 2) the loss of jobs; 3) an excessive automation of the production system. Industrial mutation can be exemplified through the existence of "two perfectly active economic systems that, though with different basic characteristics, do co-exist and our challenge is exactly the change-over from one to the other. It is the change-over from traditional industry to a new industry, i.e. from a resources-based to a knowledge-based economy. The traditional industry is overwhelming in Europe, where 80% of industry is traditional, therefore old, suitable for an old pattern that is now changing."

Regarding R&D and innovation, Andreta's worries are due to the fact that: "Europe invests only 2%, or 170 billion euro/year, vs. 280 of the US, which means an absolute-value gap of 110 billions, or a 33% difference, and the absolute value is important because of the critical mass it moves,... in the US 70% of the investment is private and industrial and 30% public. In Europe 55% is private and 45% public. In Japan 80% is private and very little public. In the research sector Europe has 5.7 researchers per 1000 workers, vs. 8 in the US and as many as 10 in Japan. However, what is interesting inside these indicators is the public-to-private relationship: Europe has 1 private vs. almost 5 public, the US exactly the opposite, 1 public vs. 7 private researchers, same as in Japan."

To this scenario, UE reacted with the Lisbon strategy: "In the year 2000 the heads of State took a turn in Lisbon and decided to make Europe the most dynamic economy in the world, but based on knowledge, by 2010 (in 10 years). The turn pivots not on 'most dynamic' but on 'based on knowledge'. The goal, therefore, is to transform a resources-based economy into a knowledge-based one...After a few months the Lisbon Declaration was completed with the set-up of the European Research Area."

"The interesting point is that there is a convergence of tools because, beyond this European Area, there is immediately a 3% target, but this 3% is a difficult target, because in order to reach 3% of the GDP by 2010 an annual incremental growth of 8.5% is required, of which 9.9% from the private sector – which is behind schedule – and 6.5% public. The efforts should therefore be concentrated more in the private than in the public sector, because it is the private sector that needs to change. The public administration should also change through an intelligent targeting of its resources. However, even if we reached 3%, we would still face a gap: the number of research workers. Europe has 960 thousand researchers. 700 thousand more are required to reach 3% of the GDP, but they must have a new, not an old profile. 400 thousand European researchers are working in the US, 120 thousand in research and the others in industry."

Andreta concludes that "The knowledge-based society is our society [is..] the driver of development, the driver of a new type of system and values". The EU "picture is not good [but] there are recovery signs toward a positive mutation, which is necessary and above all urgent, and, what is even more important, is linked to research and innovation". "The critical point [is the connection between] research/innovation, because innovation without research is likely to be not only insufficient, but even harmful."

Uno Lindberg's essay is the useful connection between the more general analysis on the UE situation and some national/sectorial cases: that on Finland (and Sweden) considered by Lindberg; that on biotechnology; that at micro-macro level on Sweden; that on Cambridge in England; that on Italy's University.

Lindberg's essay has two aspects: one refers to the subject that carried out the study, EASAC; the other one to the object of the study which is the Barcelona 3% target and the situation in Finland and Sweden.

EASAC(European Academies Science Advisory Council) received from one Committee of the European Parliament the task to undertake a case study of R&D expenditure trends in Sweden and Finland, the two countries which have the highest and most rapidly growing R&D spends in the EU. Some words on EASAC are important also for the connection with Lincei. "EASAC provides a means for the national Academies of Europe to work together to inject high quality science into EU policy-making.[the aim] is building science into policy at EU level by providing independent, expert, credible advice about the scientific aspects of public policy issues to those who make or influence policy for the European Union. EASAC ultimate target is being recognized by EU policy-makers ...[and] combines ease and speed of operation, with the unrivalled prestige and authority of the national Academies of science and with the opportunities that come from ready access to the networks of members and colleagues that constitute Academies."

The case study elaborated by EASAC was presented in 2004 with the final aim "to identify possible instruments that might be valuable in the process of strengthening R&D in Europe." We consider only the case of Finland because Sweden is also dealt out, even if with a different approach, in Braunerhjelm's essay.

"In terms of the size of the economy, structure of industry, educational level and other variables, Finland and Sweden are quite similar, although there are significant differences in tax load and in many indicators measuring the size of the economy. There are also differences in soft indicators."

In Finland in particular there is the "trust that the business sector has in the economic policy and knowledge infrastructure. This trust would seem to be related to the functioning of a Science and Technology Policy Council (STPC)... Clearly, this council is playing a major role in shaping the economic policy of Finland, where Nokia has been of particular importance. The success of Nokia, with its positive effects on literally thousands of other companies, has influenced the entire economic policy in a favourable way. The telecom and IT businesses owe their success to the economic policy, which has built on ideas of cluster formation and innovation systems... As a complement to the STPC, the technology development centre (The National Technology Agency of Finland, TEKES) was established in 1983 to finance applied and industrial R&D."

"The lesson learnt from the Finnish case is that it is favourable if different ministries, public and private research institutes, companies and consumer organizations can cooperate, and keep a close contact also with higher education in universities and research institutes...Horizontal communications between business, research and authorities have the capacity to identify the weakest links in the system rapidly, to initiate a broad debate, and to take immediate actions. With the rather wide fluctuations that can occur in the competitive business world today, it is important to be able to react swiftly."

Maryann Feldman's purpose is to demonstrate that "The development of firms within regions is fundamental to our understanding of economic development, technological change, industrial evolution and economic growth. Firms located in geographically bounded knowledge rich environments are expected to realize higher rates of innovation, increased entrepreneurial activity, and increased productivity due to the localized nature of knowledge creation and deployment."

To this aim she analyzes the biotechnology sector because "it presents an opportunity to study the emergence and growth of a new industry. Biotechnology is the commercialization of scientific discoveries related to genetic engineering... Biotech, however, is still at an early stage of development and there are many competing hypotheses about its future development."

Feldman's paper provides an analysis of the development of the biotech industry using the 'Anchor-tenant' hypothesis which offers some interesting insights about the effect of a cluster composition (and in particular on the relationships between small and large firms) on its development path. "The concept of a regional anchor – a large firm that provides both stability and traffic in ideas – is related to the number of start-ups and their growth and provides a more detailed examination of the forces of agglomeration with implications for development of emerging industries and regional specialization…The ability of firms to derive economic value from knowledge is dependent on the firms' capabilities and strategic use of resources but the local environment shapes the firm's competencies, ability to absorb and utilize knowledge in the development of new products. Thus, the capabilities of firms and regions weave a tapestry of knowledge creation and commercial success."

"In its earliest years, the biotech industry grew up around university star scientists who licensed innovations to companies. Today, there are many initiatives that attempt to build biotechnology clusters around universities using formal technology transfer mechanisms. Yet universities appear not to be a sufficient condition to promote an industrial cluster. Further, as biotechnology moves out of the lab, out of small single technology based start-ups and into new commercial applications, the location dynamics of the industry are evolving."

According to Feldman, the presence of a number of Anchor Firms may explain the success of the US biotechnology sector, thus suggesting that large and small firms may well cooperate in generating value added and jobs both in traditional and in innovative industries.

John Eatwell in his paper analyses another success story: the Cambridge phenomenon. "Over the past 30 years the economy of the City of Cambridge and of the surrounding area (Greater Cambridge) has been transformed by the growth of predominantly high-technology industry. This transformation… has produced the largest concentration of high-technology research and production in Europe (the leading rival being, probably, Munich). This essay examine the history of that phenomenon, its impact on the British economy, and the changing nature of the technological basis of that phenomenon as the engine of growth moves from electronics towards biotechnology. Emerging constraints on the growth of new industries in Cambridge are also considered in the light of policies now being developed to attempt to overcome those constraints. Some comparisons are made with other concentrations of high-technology industrial growth (in a global context the competition to Cambridge), such as Silicon Valley, Munich or Sophia Antipolis, seeking lessons from the policies that have been adopted there, and assessing their relevance for the Cambridge region."

A rather different success story –at national level – is presented by *Pontus Braunerhjelm* who focuses his analysis on Sweden.

"Sweden is often taken as an example of a knowledge driven economy: a leading R&D spender since at least a couple of decades, top rankings in scientific publications, universities with a solid international reputation … In addition, Swedish industry endorses a disproportional large share of successful multinational corporations (MNCs) with a strong global position: AstraZeneca, Atlas Copco, Ericsson

Gambro, Sandvik, Scania and Volvo, to mention a few. In the latter part of the 1990s, when Sweden seemed to be on the brink of entering the so called 'new economy', these established and well-known MNCs were complemented by a seemingly vibrant technology-based entrepreneurship, foremost in the information- and communication technologies (ICT)…According to contemporary growth theory, such comparatively strong knowledge endowment should show up in strong growth performance."

However Braunerhjelm shows that, once more, reality is often different from theory: "Based on knowledge endowments Sweden's growth rate could be expected to outpace most other countries…[on the contrary] A striking, and intriguing, feature of the Swedish economy is the relatively poor growth performance in recent decades, and a marked slowdown …Swedish growth picked up in the latter part of the 1990s, however, largely driven by catch-up effects after the recession in 1991 to 1993. Hence, the relatively strong growth recorded since then is not primarily driven by knowledge…Knowledge is a necessary but not sufficient condition for growth."

Braunerhjelm highlights the evolutionary contradiction between these two paths: "on the one hand an impressive augmentation of the knowledge stock but on the other a growth pattern that has remained below the OECD-average for a long time. How do we explain 'growth-less' knowledge augmentation in an economy? To resolve this puzzle we have to examine the extent to which economic policies are designed to foster accumulation and upgrading of knowledge, as compared to creating incentives to exploit and convert knowledge into commercial products and services. Sweden has been successful in knowledge creation; however, less attention has been directed towards the mechanisms that promote knowledge exploitation. Doubtlessly Swedish economic policies have managed to provide a more stable macroeconomic setting; rather the weaknesses seem to pertain to microeconomic policy failures in providing a business environment predominantly geared towards knowledge intensive production."

The paper suggests that a supplementary set of incentive policies focusing on enhancing the conduits of knowledge spill-over also plays a central role in promoting economic growth, such as entrepreneurship and labour market policies. This implies that "it is unlikely that Sweden is in the wake of entering a sustainable, knowledge driven, growth path [until…] there is too much emphasis on systems, [and] too little on incentives."

Patrizio Bianchi and *Laura Ramaciotti* deal with the role of University in the Italian context and, in particular, they present the successful case of Emilia Romagna region.

The authors are convinced that "The essential link between new science and new industry is represented by university. The latter must consist of a network of public universities to be strengthened in their autonomy and capacity. In this context a possible development path is based on the creation of knowledge networks where firms and universities can work together to project new industrial districts."

Bianchi-Ramaciotti make reference to a number of interesting examples of good policy instruments promoted by regional governments in Italy. The regional government of "Emilia Romagna has presented its proposal of industrial policy that favours the creation of new districts where public universities work as 'scaffold' to promote new network associations based on the knowledge produced in the universities themselves...Emilia Romagna region has developed in the last years a new approach aimed at promoting the creation of research and technological transfer networks. In the 70's the region helped the development of industrial districts through the establishment of service centres for firms, the support to the cooperation between firms and local institutions, the promotion of funds to enhance innovation intended, in those years, only as machinery purchase. After 30 years, Emilia Romagna proposes different tools to create new high-tech districts. In 2001 the regional government, the four public universities (Bologna, Ferrara, Modena and Reggio, Parma) and the research institutes based in the region (CNR and ENEA), signed an agreement to realize a regional network for industrial research, innovation and technological transfer...[and] other initiatives followed with a remarkable success."

4. Conclusions

This volume represents a step forward in the understanding of how scientific and technological research impacts on innovation and economic growth. In the above presented analysis there are both positive and negative judgments on the EU situation and strategies, even if this is not the core of the volume itself. But on this topic we want to conclude. From one side the EU has perfectly understood, at institutional level, that R&D is fundamental and on this basis has defined the Lisbon strategy. From another side the EU has not yet been able do develop fully such strategy especially because the National States are still slow to fully cooperate. We also have considered in many other studies such problems[3] but we are sure that this book adds quite a lot to the strategies which must be realized in Europe and in its member countries. It is good that 'Lisbon 2'[4] has been approved but this is not enough if the programmes are not translated with adequate speed into reality.

---

[3] See, Quadrio Curzio A (2004), Paradigmi di ricerca, sviluppo e innovazione: l'Italia in Europa, in Garonna P, Gros-Pietro GM (eds.), *Il Modello Italiano di competitività*, Il Sole 24 Ore, Milano, pp. 69-122; Quadrio Curzio A (2003), Ricerca e Innovazione: futuro dell'Europa, in *Il futuro dell'Europa. La ricerca motore dello sviluppo*, Proceedings of "II Giornata della Ricerca", Confindustria, Roma 1° ottobre 2003, SIPI, Roma, pp.59-85; Quadrio Curzio A (2003) Il Rapporto Sapir. Un'agenda per la crescita europea, in «Il Mulino», LII, n.409, 5/2003, Bologna, pp. 933-943; Quadrio Curzio A, Fortis M, Galli G (2002), La competitività dell'Italia. I. Scienza, Ricerca, Innovazione, Ricerca del Centro Studi Confindustria, Il Sole 24 Ore, Milano.
[4] European Commission (2005), *Working together for growth and jobs - A new start for the Lisbon Strategy*, Communication to the Spring European Council - COM (2005) 24, Brussels, 2 February 2005. See http://europa.eu.int/growthandjobs/index_en.htm

journals (*Economics Letters, Weltwirtschaftliches Archiv, Applied Economics, Journal of Evolutionary Economics, Small Business Economics* etc.) and also contributed to several books internationally published. In 2000 he participated in the CEPR Monitoring European Integration report (with co-authors R. Faini, V. Norman, F. Ruane and P. Seabright). Pontus Braunerhjelm is presently heading two larger research projects. One on endogenous growth and entrepreneurship (other participants are David Audretsch, Zoltan Acs, etc.), one on the emergence of agglomerated production structures; clusters (together with Maryann Feldman). Pontus Braunerhjelm has presented papers at the ASSA/AEA-, CEPR-, EEA-, EARIE-, IEA-, WEA-meetings, and also acted referee for EER, EJ, JEBO, JICS, JIO, WWA, etc. Presently Pontus Braunerhjelm share his time between The Center for Business and Policy Studies (SNS), Stockholm, where he is Research Director, and Linköping University.

Paul A. David. He is Professor of Economics and Senior Fellow of the Institute for Economic Policy Research at Stanford University, where he has been a member of the faculty continuously since 1961 and was formerly (in 1977- 1994) the William Robertson Co Professor of American Economic History. From 1994 until 2002 he held a Senior Research Fellowship at All Souls College, Oxford, where presently he is an Emeritus Fellow. Since November 2002 he has been Senior Fellow of the Oxford Internet Institute announced in the University of Oxford.
David is known internationally for his contributions in American economic history, economic and historical demography, and the economics of science and technology. He is the author of more than 145 journal articles and contributions to edited books and several more volumes due to appear under his own name during 2005. He is a founding editor of the international journal *Economics of Innovation and New Technology*, and currently serves on the editorial boards of different scientific-economic journals.
He has been elected as a Fellow of the International Econometrics Society (1975), Fellow of the American Academy of Arts and Sciences (1979), Ordinary Fellow of the British Academy (1995), and Member of the American Philosophical Society (2003). In 1996 the University of Oxford conferred upon him the title of Professor of Economics and Economic History, "in recognition of distinction." He holds a Doctorate *Honoris Causa* from the University of Torino (2003). He has served as elected Vice-President, and President of the Economic History Association (1988-89), and was a Member of Council of the Royal Economics Society (1996-2002).
David has served as a consultant to U. S. government agencies and foundations including the National Academy of Sciences' National Research Council, the National Science Foundation, and the Departments of Commerce, and of Energy, the Rockefeller Foundation, the Sloan Foundation and numerous other public and private organizations.

John Eatwell. He is the President of Queens' College, Cambridge, Director of the Cambridge Endowment for Research in Finance, and Professor of Financial Policy in the Judge Institute of Management, University of Cambridge.

I. Scientific-Technological Innovation and Industrial Growth

The Intellectual Origins of Modern Economic Growth[1]

Joel Mokyr

Departments of Economics, Northwestern University,Evanston, Illinois (USA)
j-mokyr@northwestern.edu

1. Introduction

Economic growth was not a novelty in 1800. In a celebrated passage, Adam Smith had noted that the "annual produce of land and labor" had been growing in Britain for a long time.[2] Yet there is something distinctive in the changes that occurred in the economies of the West after the Industrial Revolution, that seem to confirm our intuition that something genuinely important had happened. To be sure, technological innovations, institutional reforms, and fresh ideas do not affect the aggregate level of economic activity abruptly: they need to diffuse from region to region, from activity to activity, cross boundaries and seas, be evaluated, adapted, and refined. Their promoters have to dislodge the entrenched, persuade the skeptic, and reassure the fearful. It is not surprising, therefore, that whatever we identify precisely as the Industrial Revolution after 1760 took its sweet time to start affecting GDP per capita in the West in earnest.[3]

---

[1] Presentation address to the Economic History Association, San Jose, CA, 11/11/04. Suggestions of Kenneth Alder, Maristella Botticini, Margaret Jacob, Edward Muir, Cormac Ó Gráda, Avner Greif and Richard Unger are acknowledged. I am indebted to Fabio Braggion, Chip Dickerson, Hillary King, and Michael Silver for research assistance.

[2] Smith, *Wealth of Nations*, pp. 365-66. Modern economic historians have reached different conclusions. While none of those methods are uncontroversial, their unanimity seems to indicate that the "assumption" of modern economists such as Robert Lucas and Oded Galor that there was no economic growth before 1800 is a gross oversimplification. See for instance Clark, *Secret History*; Snooks, *New Perspectives*.

[3] There is a substantial literature that asks with Jeffrey Williamson "why was economic growth so slow during the Industrial Revolution?" although the answers tend to be dif-

Modern economic growth differs from the processes that Smith identified and that made Britain and the rest of Western Europe so much richer in 1700 than it had been in 1066. To the hard nosed scholar who insists that "it was all only a matter of degree," one response is that "in economic history degree is everything." There is a qualitative difference between an economy in which GDP per capita grows at 1.5 percent and one in it which grows at 0.2%. The other is that it was not just a matter of degree. It was qualitatively different in at least three fundamental aspects. First, growth gradually ceased to be a niche phenomenon. Before 1750 growth had been limited to relatively small areas or limited sectors, often a successful city state, a capital of a powerful monarchy, or a limited agricultural region. These niches had to spend much of their riches to protect their possessions against greedy neighbors, real-life manifestations of Mancur Olson's "roving bandits" who often killed entire flocks of golden-eggs-laying geese. After the Industrial Revolution it became a more aggregative phenomenon, with a substantial number of economies becoming members of the much-coveted "convergence club." Second, pre-1750 growth, such as it was, was dominated by institutional change, in its widest sense: law and order, the establishment of commercial relations, credit, trust, and enforceable contracts created the preconditions for wealth to expand through more efficient allocation, exchange and investment.[4] Technological change, while never quite absent, was usually too slow and too localized to assume the dominant role it was to take later. Third, pre-modern growth was normally not sustainable and remained vulnerable to set-backs and shocks, both man-made and natural. The economic glories of the Dutch Republic and Venice had melted away by 1800, just as those of early sixteenth century Spain had vanished by the death of Philip II.[5] In the late eighteenth century the relative contribution of technological progress to economic growth compared to other elements began to increase, and the institutional basis supporting this progress was transformed. The result was the Industrial Revolution. It may have been slow, it may have been not all that industrial and even less revolutionary, it may not even have been wholly British, but it was the taproot of modern economic growth.

How do we explain this change? What has been missing, so far, is a full appreciation of the importance of useful knowledge. Economic decisions are made by individuals on the basis of certain beliefs they hold and knowledge they possess. In recent years, it has once again become "kosher" if not quite de rigueur to speak of "cultural beliefs" following Avner Greif's path-breaking work on the emergence of institutions that made trade possible in stateless and even largely lawless societies.[6] Douglass North refers to shared cultural beliefs and as the "scaffolds" on which institutions are built.[7] But Greif and North are primarily interested in the

---

ferent from the ones given by him. See Williamson, *Why Was British Growth So Slow?*, pp. 687-712. For some suggested answers see Mokyr, *Editor's Introduction*, pp. 12-17.

[4] See Greif, *Institutions*.

[5] De Vries and Van Der Woude. *First Modern Economy;* Drelichman, *American Silver*.

[6] Greif, *Cultural beliefs;* Temin, *Is it Kosher?* pp. 267-87.

[7] See North, *Understanding the Process*.

kind of beliefs that people hold about one another, how others will behave under certain circumstances. My interest here is about the beliefs people held about their physical milieu. In my "Gifts of Athena" I refer to these beliefs as "useful knowledge," but of course they are but beliefs about the physical environment and natural phenomena, held with higher or lower degrees of unanimity and confidence ("tightness"). Yet all societies have consensus-shaping mechanisms, which determine what kind of beliefs will predominate. I suggest in what is to follow that the change in the rate and nature of economic growth in the West must be explained through developments in the intellectual realm concerning this "useful knowledge."

The short answer as to why the West is so much richer today than it was two centuries ago is that as collectives, these societies "know" more.[8] This does not necessarily mean that each individual on average knows more than his or her great-great grandparent (although that is almost certainly the case given the increased investment in human capital), but that the social knowledge, defined as the union of all pieces of individual knowledge, has expanded. Greater specialization, professionalization, and expertization have meant that the total amount of knowledge that society controls is vastly larger than ever before. The effective deployment of that knowledge, scientific or otherwise, in the service of production is the primary – if not the only – cause for the rapid growth of western economies in the past centuries. The huge literature that has accumulated on the topic in recent years has been ably summarized by Helpman's recent book.[9] In what follows, I propose a slightly different approach, based largely on the experience of the Western economies in the eighteenth century.

2. The Intellectual Roots of the Industrial Revolution

Economic historians like to explain economic phenomena with other economic phenomena. The Industrial Revolution, it was felt for many decades, should be explained by economic factors. Relative prices, property rights, endowments, demand factors, fiscal and monetary institutions, investment, savings, exports, and changes in labor supply have all been put forward as possible explanations.[10] Between the presence of coal, the glorious revolution, a mobile and open society, the control of a colonial empire and a powerful navy, a greedy middle class, a productive agriculture, an unusually high supply of skilled artisans and mechanics serving the private sector, and assorted other stories, a veritable smorgasbord of explanations for Britain's success has been offered. The reader is invited to pick and choose, or just pile them one on top of the other and the explanations may be satisfactory by sheer quantity. Yet these approaches have all suffered from the "en-

---

[8] For a more detailed statement on this, see Mokyr, *Gifts of Athena*.

[9] Helpman, *The Mystery*.

[10] For a full survey, see Mokyr, *Editor's Introduction*, pp. 1–127.

dogenous growth problem": none of them can carry the weight of the explanandum without relying on technological change. If technology was at the heart of the Industrial Revolution, why was it changing at a rate more rapid and on a scale more widespread than ever before and why did it accelerate in the nineteenth century instead of fizzle out?

One possible reason why this literature has been inconclusive is that many scholars have sought the causes for the economic change in the West as something particular to *Britain*. Yet this approach might be misleading. The Industrial Revolution was a *Western* phenomenon. It was more than just a British affair, if less than a "European" affair. The causes for the differences in technological patterns and rates of development between the several European economies that by 1914 constituted the core of the convergence club is a source of a fascinating and instructive debate, but may not hold the keys to the riddle of the Industrial Revolution. Britain's position as the lead car in the Occident Express that gathered speed in the nineteenth century and drove away from the rest of the world is of tremendous interest, but it does not tell us much about the source of power. Was Britain the engine that pulled the other European cars behind it, or was the Western world like an electric train deriving its motive power from a shared source of energy? If so, what was this source?

One answer, I submit, that thus far has not received nearly enough attention from economic historians involves the intellectual changes that occurred in Europe before the Industrial Revolution. These changes affected the sphere of useful knowledge, and its interaction with the world of production. In some sense, this statement is so obvious as to be almost trivial, but the insight has been clouded by the somewhat tedious debate on the role of science in the Industrial Revolution. As economic historians have known for many years, it is very difficult to argue that the scientific revolution of the seventeenth century we associate with Galileo, Descartes, Newton, and the like had a direct impact on the pivotal technological breakthroughs of the Industrial Revolution. To be sure, a few important inventions, especially before 1800, can be directly attributed to great scientific discoveries or were dependent in some way on scientific expertise.[11] Yet the bulk of the advances in physics, chemistry, biology, medicine, and other areas occurred too late to have an effect on the industrial changes of the last third of the eighteenth century. The scientific advances of the seventeenth century, crucial as they were to the understanding of the universe, were largely peripheral to the main thrust of eighteenth-century technology that we think of as the Industrial Revolution. During the age of Enlightenment, and especially the decades after 1750, much of Europe witnessed a flourishing of interest in the application of useful knowledge to the arts and crafts, as well as to agriculture. Yet, as Charles Gillispie has remarked, in the eighteenth century, whatever the interplay between science and

---

[11] The *opus classicus* on this topic remains Musson and Robinson, *Science and Technology.* For the best recent statement, see Jacob, *Scientific Culture.*; id., *Cultural Foundations*, pp. 67–85.

production may have been, "it did not consist in the application of up-to-date theory to techniques for growing and making things."[12]

True enough: in the early stages of the Industrial Revolution many of the important advances owed little to science in a direct way. However, had technological progress been independent of what happened at the loftier intellectual level, had it consisted purely of disseminating best-practice existing procedures, standardize them, and hope for learning-by-doing effects, the process would eventually have run into diminishing returns and fizzled out. What was it that prevented that from happening in the decades following the burst of macroinventions we identify with the classic Industrial Revolution? In part, it is our own thinking of "science" that is at fault, since we tend to think of science as more "analytical" than descriptive. The eighteenth century, however, spent an enormous amount of intellectual energy on describing what it could not understand. The three "C's" — counting, classifying, cataloguing — were central to the Baconian program that guided much of the growth of useful knowledge in the century before the Industrial Revolution. Heat, energy, chemical affinities, electrical tension, capacitance, resistivity and many other properties of materials from iron to bricks to molasses were measured and tabulated before they were, in some sense, "understood." Measurement itself was not novel in the eighteenth century; the accuracy, thoroughness, and reliability, the scope of phenomena and quantities being measured, and the diffusion of this knowledge surely were.

In the nineteenth century, the connection between science and technology became gradually tighter, yet is sufficiently gradual and heterogeneous to make any dating very hazardous. Scholars such as Nathan Rosenberg and Derek Price have argued for the causality running mainly from technology to science rather than the reverse.[13] Arguably, however, science and technology were both endogenous to a third set of factors that determined the direction and intensity of the intellectual pursuits that led to advances in both. In what follows, I shall try to identify what this set consists of, document it in some detail, and then consider to which extent these factors may be regarded as "exogenous." I propose that one source of the success of the Industrial Revolution must be found in the developments in the area of the generation and diffusion of useful knowledge that occurred in Europe before and around 1750, and specifically in the Enlightenment.

The confusion surrounding the role of science in the eighteenth century on economic developments and the rather tiresome debate regarding the merits and shortcomings of the so-called "linear model" (in which science supposedly "leads"

---

[12] Gillispie, *Science and Polity*, p. 336. For canonical statements on the "unimportance of science" see Hall, *What Did the Industrial Revolution?*; Neil McKendrick, *The Role of Science*; Mathias, *Who Unbound Prometheus?*. John R. Harris has been even more skeptical of the importance of science relative to "tacit" skills and has even argued that France's backwardness in steelmaking was in part due to its reliance on scientists, who at first gave misleading and later rather useless advice to steel makers; compare Harris, *Industrial Espionage*, pp. 219-21.

[13] Price, *Notes towards a Philosophy*. Rosenberg, *Perspectives on Technology*; id. *How Exogenous is Science?*

to technology) stem from the narrow and possibly anachronistic definitions of the concept of useful knowledge. In addition to what the eighteenth century called "natural philosophy," it consisted of catalogs of facts, based on experience and experiment rather than on understanding or careful analysis and testing. Many of these facts were organized compilations about what worked: the right mixture of materials, the right temperature or pressure in a vessel, the correct fertilizer in a given type of soil, the optimal viscosity of a lubricant, the correct tension on a piece of fabric, the shortest way to sail across the sea while using the right trade winds and avoiding reefs, and not-so-basic facts of nature used in productive activities from medicinal herbs to cattle breeding to glass blowing to marling. It involved not only the work of people whom we regard today as scientists but also those who collected data and practices, botanists, zoologists, geographers, mineralogists, instrument-makers, and other highly skilled artisans and placed this knowledge in the public realm. For that reason I prefer the much wider category of propositional knowledge.[14]

3. The Enlightenment and Eighteenth-Century Technology

The Enlightenment of the late seventeenth and eighteenth centuries bridges the Scientific and the Industrial Revolutions. Definitions of this amorphous and often contradictory historical phenomenon are many, but for the purposes of explaining the Industrial Revolution we need only to examine a slice of it, which I have termed the Industrial Enlightenment, a belief in the possibility and desirability of economic progress and growth through knowledge.[15] The idea of *improvement* involved much more than economic growth or technological change; it included moral and social improvement, alleviating the suffering of the poor and the unfortunate, and more generally such matters as justice and freedom. Yet the idea that production could be made more efficient through more useful knowledge gradually gained acceptance. Scotland, again, showed the way, but the idea diffused throughout Britain and the Western world.[16]

---

[14] For more details, see Mokyr, *Gifts,* ch. 2 and id., *Long-term Economic Growth.*

[15] One of the most cogent statements is by McNeil, *Under the Banner,* pp. 24-25, who notes the importance of a "faith in science that brought the legacy of the Scientific Revolution to bear on industrial society ... it is imperative to look at the interaction between culture *and* industry, between the Enlightenment and the Industrial Revolution." As Spadafora has noted, the belief in the possibility (if not the inevitability) of progress was necessary if the West was to actually experience anything like it. Spadafora, *The Idea of Progress in Eighteenth-Century Britain.*

[16] The Scottish philosopher George Campbell (1719-96) noted for example in 1776 that "for some centuries backwards, the men of every age have made great and unexpected improvements on the labours of their predecessors. And it is very probable that the subsequent age will produce discoveries and acquisitions which we of this age are as little capable of foreseeing as those who preceded us in the last century were capable of con-

It surely is true that not all Enlightenment philosophers believed that material progress was either desirable or inevitable or were persuaded that the rise of a commercial and industrial society was a desirable end. And yet the cultural beliefs that began to dominate the elites of the eighteenth-century West created the attitudes, the institutions, and the mechanisms by which new useful knowledge was created, diffused, and put to good use. Above all was the increasingly pervasive belief in the Baconian notion that we can attain material progress (that is, economic growth) through controlling nature and that we can only harness nature by understanding her in order, as he himself put it, to bring about "the relief of man's estate." Francis Bacon, indeed, is a pivotal figure in understanding the Industrial Enlightenment and its impact. "Lord Bacon" as he was referred to by his eighteenth-century admirers was cited approvingly by many of the leading lights of the Enlightenment, including Diderot, Lavoisier, Davy, and the astronomer John Herschel.[17] Modern scholars seem agreed: Bacon was the most influential mind to regard knowledge as subject to constant growth, as an entity that continuously expands and adds to itself.[18] As such his influence helped inspire the Industrial Enlightenment.[19] The understanding of nature was a collective project in which the

---

jecturing the progress that would be made in the present" (cited by Spadafora, 1990, p. 56).

[17] Sargent, ed. *Francis Bacon,* pp. 27-28. In a wonderful piece of doggerel entitled *Ode to the Royal Society,* written by the now (deservedly) neglected poet Abraham Cowley (one of the Society's co-founders) and reprinted as a preface to Thomas Sprat's celebrated *History of the Royal Society of London*, the gratefulness of the scholars of the time to Bacon was well-expressed: "From these and all long Errors of the Way; In which our wandring Predecessors went; And like th' old Hebrews many Years did stray; in Desarts but of small Extent; Bacon, like Moses, led us forth at last; The barren Wilderness he past; Did on the very Border stand; of the blest promis'd Land; And from the Mountain's Top of his exalted Wit; Saw it himself and shew'd us it."

[18] As always, there were earlier expressions of such ideas, not always wholly acknowledged by Bacon. One example is the sixteenth century French theologian Pierre de la Ramée (Peter Ramus), with whom Bacon would have agreed that "the union of mathematics and the practice of scholarly arts by artisans would bring about great civic prosperity" (Smith, *The Business*, p. 36).

[19] Farrington, *Francis Bacon.* Vickers, *Francis Bacon. Journal of the History of Ideas*, pp. 493-518. Bacon's influence on the Industrial Enlightenment can be readily ascertained by the deep admiration the encyclopédistes felt toward him, exemplified by a long article on Baconisme written by the Abbé Pestre and the credit given him by Diderot himself in his entries on *Art* and *Encyclopédie*. The *Journal Encyclopédique* wrote in 1756 "If this society owes everything to Chancellor Bacon, the philosopher does not owe less to the authors of the *Encyclopédie*" (cited by Kronick, *History*, p. 42). The Scottish Enlightenment philosophers Dugald Stewart and Francis Jeffrey agreed on Baconian method and goals, even if they differed on some of the interpretation (Chitnis, *Scottish Enlightenment*, pp. 214-15). A practical enlightenment scientist such as Humphry Davy had no doubt that Bacon was "....the first philosopher who laid down plans for extending knowledge of universal application; who ventured to assert, that all the science could be nothing more than expressions or arrangements of facts... the pursuit of the new method of investigation, in a very short time, wholly altered the face of every department of natural

division of knowledge was similar to Adam Smith's idea of the division of labor, another enlightenment notion. Smith realized that such a division of knowledge in a civilized society "presented unique and unprecedented opportunities for further technical progress."[20] The more pragmatically inclined thinkers of the Industrial Enlightenment concurred.[21] Bacon's idea of bringing this about was through what he called a "House of Salomon" – a research academy in which teams of specialists collect data and experiment, and a higher level of scientists try to distill these into general regularities and laws. Such an institution was the Royal Society, whose initial objectives were inspired by Bacon.[22] A finer and more extensive division of knowledge could not have been attained without improved access that made it possible to share the knowledge, and then apply and adapt it to solve technical problems. Access to useful knowledge created the opportunities to recombine its components to create new forms that would expand its volume of knowledge at an ever faster rate. Bacon, indeed, placed a high value on compiling inventories and catalogues of *existing* knowledge and techniques, and some of these ideas are reflected in the interest the Royal Society displayed in the "useful arts" in its early years.[23] In subsequent decades, the Royal Society allowed in amateurs and dilettantes and thus became less of a pure "Baconian" institution than the French *Académie Royale*.

Of course, the eighteenth century still saw a lot of efforts that were purely epistemic or metaphysical in motivation, but the emphasis slowly changed. The message that the Industrial Revolution inherited from the seventeenth century concerned the very purpose and objective of propositional knowledge. The result was a change in the *agenda* of research in which the "useful arts" began to assume an equal, and eventually dominant, place alongside the liberal arts. This "Baconian Program" assumed that the main purpose of knowledge was to improve mankind's condition rather than the mere satisfaction of that most creative of human characteristics, curiosity, or demonstrating some metaphysical point, such as illustrating

---

knowledge. Davy, *Sketch of the Character*, pp 121-122. Across the channel, the French minister of the Interior, Nicolas-Louis François de Neufchâteau invoked the spirit of Francis Bacon when opening the 1798 French industrial exhibition. See Jacob, *Putting Science*.

[20] Rosenberg, *Adam Smith*, p. 137.

[21] A typical passage in this spirit was written by the British chemist and philosopher Joseph Priestley: "If, by this means, one art or science should grow too large for an easy comprehension in a moderate space of time, a commodious subdivision will be made. Thus all knowledge will be subdivided and extended, and *knowledge* as Lord Bacon observes, being *power*, the human powers will be increased ... men will make their situation in this world abundantly more easy and comfortable." Priestley, *Essay,* p. 7.

[22] McClellan III, *Science Reorganized*, p. 52.

[23] As Musson and Robinson stress in *Science and Technology*, p. 16, "Bacon's influence can be perceived everywhere among men of science in the seventeenth and eighteenth centuries, constantly encouraging them to comprehend workshop practices."

the wisdom of the creator.[24] Studying and extending useful knowledge, it was increasingly felt, was respectable and suitable to a gentleman.[25] Natural philosophy, its prestige hugely enhanced by the insights of Newton, was marketed as being useful to economic improvement.[26] Farmers, manufacturers, sailors, engineers, merchants, miners, bleachers, and army officers asked questions, and the community of learned persons, the *savants*, were more and more pressured to provide them with answers. The "business of science," John T. Desaguliers noted in the 1730s, was "to make Art and Nature subservient to the Necessities of Life in joining proper Causes to produce the most useful Effects."[27] The great Lavoisier worked on assorted applied problems, including as a young man on the chemistry of gypsum and the problems of street lighting. Perhaps no area or propositional knowledge showed as much promise to application as mathematics, which made enormous strides after the seminal works of Descartes, Huygens, Newton and Leibniz. Mathematical techniques following the development of calculus were applied to questions of motion and the challenges of mechanics, although these were initially not the mechanics of engineers and architects as much as those of "rational mechanics," which analyzed idealized properties, rather than actual day-to-day problems loaded with ugly characteristics such as friction and resistance. Many of the leading *philosophes* of the Enlightenment, including Diderot, were pessimistic of the ability of mathematics to advance beyond its current state and contribute much to material progress.[28] Yet mathematicians were asked to solve practical problems. Leonhard Euler, the most talented mathematician of the age, was concerned with ship design, lenses, the buckling of beams, and (with his less famous son Johann) contributed a great deal to hydraulics.[29] Naturalists and bota-

---

[24] Calvin in the sixteenth century still followed St. Augustine's condemnation of curiosity as a "vanity." By way of contrast, in the 1660s, Thomas Sprat felt that what gentlemen were suitable to research precisely because they were "free and unconfined."

[25] Thus in 1710 the *Tatler* wrote that "It is the duty of all who make philosophy the entertainment of their lives, to turn their thoughts to practical schemes for the good of society, and not pass away their time in fruitless searches which tend rather to the ostentation of knowledge than the service of life." Cited by Shapin, *Scholar and a Gentleman*, p. 309. In a similar vein, *The Gentleman's Magazine* wrote in 1731 that "our knowledge should be in the first place that which is most useful, then that which is fashionable." Cited by Burke, 2000, p. 111.

[26] Cohen, *Inside Newcomen's*, p. 127 points out that the Baconian ideology "went under the sainted name of Newton."

[27] Desaguliers, *Course*, vol. 1, p. 3.

[28] Furbank, *Diderot*, p. 110. Hankins, *Science*, p. 45. Hankins add that "Diderot was wrong...in the years between 1780 and 1840... mathematics and mechanics found a place precisely where Diderot thought they had no place."

[29] See above all, Reynolds, *Stronger*, pp. 233-50. Another example of such an application of mathematical knowledge to a mundane problem is Colin MacLaurin's ingenious solution (1735) to the problem of measuring the quantity of molasses in irregularly shaped barrels by the use of classical geometry. Not only did he solve the rather difficult mathematical problem with uncommon elegance, he also provided simple formulas, tables, and

nists, in very different ways, were equally regarded as contributing to the wealth of their nations. Linnaeus's belief that skillful naturalists could transform farming was widely shared and inspired the establishment of agricultural societies and farm improvement organizations throughout Europe. By the second half of the eighteenth century, botany, horticulture, and agronomy were working hand-in-hand through publications, meetings, and model gardens to introduce new crops, adjust rotations, improve tools and better management.[30]

Many of the answers that mathematicians and natural philosophers gave to engineers, industrialists, and farmers were, of course, useless, misleading, or wrong. The eighteenth century was nothing at all like a steady progress of better understanding of nature and its application to agriculture and manufacturing. The alleged "usefulness" of knowledge was often an attempt by scholars to secure financial support and patronage from wealthy individuals and official sponsors.[31] But no matter how self-serving and pretentious the claims of those who controlled propositional knowledge were, the Industrial Enlightenment did not waver in its belief that economic growth through better and more knowledge was possible. Progress through more and better knowledge had also moral and political implications; it was believed that better-informed and more enlightened individuals would be more ethical and better-behaved citizens. "Useful knowledge" in the eighteenth century thus meant something more than it does to our, wiser and sadder, age.

4. Access Costs: Some Reflections

The Industrial Enlightenment was in part about the expansion of useful knowledge. Knowledge exists in the final analysis within the mind of an individual, but for it to be socially productive it needs to be shared and distributed. If a vital piece of knowledge is discovered but only one individual possesses it and keeps it se-

---

algorithms for the customs officers, that were used for many years. See Grabiner, *Some Disputes*, pp. 139-168.

[30] One source of confirmation of the belief in the possibility of economic progress may have been perceptions of agricultural progress. As John Gascoigne has recently noted, "as the land bore more, better, and increasingly diversified fruits as a consequence of patient experiment with new techniques and crops, so, too, the need to apply comparable methods to other areas of the economy and society came to seem more insistent." Gascoigne, *Joseph Banks*, p. 185.

[31] A good early example of such hope was the work of the Scottish botanist and physician, Sir Robert Sibbald (1641-1721), whose widespread interests, extensive correspondence network, and continental education were harbingers of things to come in the eighteenth century. Sibbald was extremely active in reforming the University of Edinburgh and helped establish the Royal College of Medicine as well as an early botanical garden in town. Yet as Paul Wood remarks, much of Sibbald's work failed to bear fruit in his lifetime and he failed in his dream to turn learning into human benefit. See Wood, *Science*. For the importance of claims for usefulness to obtain patronage, see especially, Spary, *Utopia's Garden*, p. 127.

cret, it is by definition part of social knowledge, but has little economic value. What counted for useful knowledge to play a role in generating economic growth was therefore *access costs*, the marginal cost involved in acquiring knowledge possessed by someone else in society. The concept is in line with recent thinking about the Enlightenment which regards it as above all "as a system of communication creating a public of rational individuals."[32] The economic significance of *access costs* has three dimensions. One is the obvious one that access made it possible for producers to learn of best-practice techniques and emulate them. Needless to say, *access costs* are not the only wedge between best- and average practice techniques, but it is safe to assume that ignorance will make such wedges both larger and more permanent. Secondly, technological progress depended on the knowledge of other techniques already in use. As has often been noted, much invention took the form of the "recombination" of existing techniques.[33] Moreover, technological progress often depended on "analogical" thinking, in which inventors, consciously or subconsciously, transform an idea they have already seen into something novel.[34] Furthermore, knowledge of what techniques exist will alert original and creative individuals to gaps and opportunities in the existing set of techniques, and prevent potential inventors of misspending their resources by reinventing the wheel. Thirdly, as I have stressed in my *Gifts of Athena*, lower access costs made it possible for inventors to tap the propositional knowledge on which the new technique rests — insofar as such knowledge was available and effective.[35] Understanding why and how a technique works at some level of generality made it easier to clean up bugs, adapt it to new uses and different environments, and unleashed the cumulative stream of microinventions on which nineteenth-century productivity growth rested. It streamlined the process of invention by reducing the likelihood of blind alleys such as searches for perpetual motion machines and the like. All of these suggest that the easier the access to existing propositional knowledge and to practices in use, the more likely inventions were to emerge and result in sustained economic growth. Contemporaries became

---

[32] Censer, *Journals*, p. 311, though he should have added "informed" to the "rational."

[33] The classic example of such an invention during the Industrial Revolution is surely Cort's patent for the second half of his puddling and rolling process, in which the common rolling mill was used to weld together pieces of scrap iron at a sufficiently high temperature. His invention "clearly inspired" a naval contractor named William Forbes who used grooved rollers to produce improved copper bolts for naval ships (Harris, *Copper*, p. 183). For a theoretical discussion of recombination in technological change, see Weitzman, *Hybridizing*, pp. 207-13.

[34] McGee, *Rethinking Invention*.

[35] I use the term "effective" rather that "correct" because terms like "true" or "correct" are irrelevant and inappropriate here. The best we can do is to say that a piece of knowledge held in the past was "right" or "wrong" in the sense that it is inconsistent with our beliefs. By "effective" I mean such knowledge on which certain techniques rest that perform better than techniques based on some other base according to some pre-specified criterion. For instance, bloodletting might have been effective simply because it did help patients if only through a placebo effect.

slowly aware of the possibilities of bringing to bear science on production.[36] As one assiduous collector of facts remarked in 1772, "before a thing can be improved it must be known, hence the utility of those publications that abound in fact either in the offer of new or the elucidation of old ones."[37] Whether in agriculture, pottery, steam-engine construction, or chemical industry, leading manufacturers eagerly sought and found the advice of scientists. In and of itself this does not prove that this knowledge was instrumental in technical advances and productivity growth, since these progressive industrialists may have been successful for other reasons. But in the nineteenth century such input becomes more and more prominent.[38]

The level of *access costs* can be decomposed into four separate components. First, there was the cost involved in establishing that this knowledge actually existed, that is, that there was at least one individual in society who possessed it. Second, there was the cost of finding out who the lowest-cost supplier of this knowledge was and where it could be found. Third, there was the actual cost of acquiring it, which could range from a simple search through a library or catalog to the need of reading a scientific article, visiting a site, or hiring a consultant or expert who could convey it. Fourth, there was the cost of verifying the knowledge and establishing the extent of its "tightness," that is, to what extent was this a consensus view among the experts or authorities on certain propositions and how certain were they of its truthfulness?

What determined *access costs*? One obvious determinant is technological: how costly it was to code, store, transmit, and receive useful knowledge and what was the best-practice technology through which it was transmitted and in what language and terminology it was expressed? Another is social and cultural: to what extent were individuals who made a discovery willing to share such useful knowledge (for example as part of "open science" that awards credit for priority), and allow inventions to be used freely (for instance in processes of collective invention or "open source" development)? Did organizations exist that channeled knowledge from those who knew useful things to those who could and were willing to exploit such knowledge? Finally, there are economic factors: did markets for useful knowledge exist? Economists know that such markets (and the intellectual property on which they rest) will be deficient and incomplete, yet *some* of them clearly did exist and others emerged during the Industrial Revolution.

---

[36] As Voltaire noted in his *The Age of Louis XV*, written late in his life in 1770: "pure natural philosophy has illustrated the necessary arts; and these arts have already begun to heal the wounds of the state caused by two fatal wars. Stuffs manufactured in a cheaper manner, by ingenuity of the most celebrated mechanics" (Vol. 2, pp. 369-70).

[37] Young, *Political Essays* p. v. Emph. in original.

[38] One telling example is Neilson's hot blast (1828), a fuel-saving innovation from the "second stage" of the Industrial Revolution. Neilson had learned of Gay-Lussac calculation of the rate of expansion of oxygen and nitrogen between $0°$ and $80°$ C and used laboratory experiments to persuade Scottish ironmasters to apply it, which proved "the salvation of the Scottish iron industry" (Clow and Clow, *Chemical Revolution* p. 356).

4.1. Access Costs: Technical Factors

The decline in access costs in the century or so before the Industrial Revolution cannot be attributed to a single factor. There is no question that the cost of transmitting information was declining already before the arrival of the railroad. Abstracting from homing pigeons and the semaphore telegraph, knowledge moved as fast and as far as people did. People and carriages carried books, periodicals, and other storage devices. All the same, much of the knowledge that counted was not written down or depicted in the (increasingly detailed and sophisticated) technical drawings of the age, but embodied in implicit forms we would call "skills," "dexterity," and other synonyms for what is known as tacit knowledge. The ratio of codified knowledge to tacit knowledge was itself a function of the technology and costs of codification and the payoff to efforts to do so, although tacit knowledge inevitably remained an essential part of knowledge.[39] Access to knowledge thus depended not only on written records but also on personal transmission and training. Much of the tacit and practical useful knowledge in eighteenth-century Europe moved about through itinerant skilled artisans who taught the tricks of their trade to local craftsmen, or the normal human proclivities for observation and imitation did their work.[40] Industrial espionage, both within an economy and across borders, became an important part of technological diffusion.[41] In Enlightenment Europe, people — including skilled craftsmen — moved about more often and further than ever, despite the undeniable discomforts of the road. While the great breakthroughs in transport technology were still in the future, the decline in the cost and speed of moving about in Europe in the eighteenth century are too well-documented to require elaboration here.[42] Transportation improvements also speeded up the mail; a great deal of scientific communication depended on personal correspondence between individuals.

---

[39] For a more detailed analysis of the economics of tacit knowledge, see Cowan and Foray. *Economics*, pp. 595–622.

[40] Harris, *Skills*. Epstein, *Knowledge Sharing*, esp. pp. 15-20. Eighteenth century Europe was criss-crossed by a variety of technological informants and spies such as Gabriel Jars (studying metalmaking) and Nicolas Desmarest (papermaking) (Gillispie, *Science and Polity.Old Regime*, pp.429-37, 444-54). For a discussion of the importance of geographical mobility on the diffusion of artisanal skills in Italy, see Belfanti, *Guilds*. The effect of traveling was also notable in the improved access to agricultural knowledge, as attested by the many Frenchmen who visited Britain after 1750, and studied farm methods and techniques. See Bourde, *Influence*.

[41] Harris, *Industrial Espionage*, pp. 164-175. Id., *Industrial Espionage*. British legislation to prevent the outflow of skilled craftsmen and certain kinds of machinery were in the long run doomed to failure, though it is hard to disagree with Harris's assessment that they raised access costs and had a retardative effect on the diffusion of technology.

[42] In Britain, better-built roads and coaches sharply reduced internal travel time in the eighteenth century: the coach from London to Edinburgh still took 10-12 days in the mid 1750s, whereas in 1836 (just before being replaced by a railroad) it could cover the distance in 45 ½ hours. In France, travel times were halved or better on many routes between 1765 and 1785. See data reported by Szostak, *The Role*, p. 70.

The eighteenth century also witnessed the improvement of the transfer of formerly tacit knowledge. Part of it was simply the improvement of the language of technology: mathematical symbols, standardized measures, more universal scales and notation added a great deal to the ease of communication of codified technological information. Diagrams and illustrations became more sophisticated.[43] Above all, there was printing, but in and of themselves printing was not decisive, or else the Industrial Revolution might have occurred in the sixteenth century. Paper had been introduced into Europe in the thirteenth century, and as an access-cost and storage-cost reducing material it must have had few substitutes. The paper industry grew remarkably in the seventeenth century culminating in the invention of the Hollander (1670), a device that applied wind- or water power to the difficult process of ripping up the rags needed for pulping.[44] The effect of printing and paper was, as Eric L. Jones has noted, constrained in that only widespread literacy could realize its full effect throughout society. It also mattered, of course, whether the literate actually read, and what kind of texts they chose. In Enlightenment Europe, the printing press finally lived up to its full potential. It may still have been that, as Jones points out, "published ideas flowed through narrow channels bounded by limited literacy and unlimited poverty," and that the bulk of the population had little or no access to libraries and could not afford to buy books and (highly taxed) newspapers. But technical knowledge had a way of seeping through to those who needed it and could find a use for it.[45] Reading became increasingly common, as literacy rates edged upward and books became cheaper and more widely available through lending libraries and the reading rooms attached to learned societies and academies. The first free public library in Britain, Chetham's in Manchester, was founded in 1653 and prospered in the eighteenth century.[46] Coffee houses and booksellers often offered magazines to be browsed by customers.[47] Many of the Scientific and Scholarly societies that emerged in the eighteenth century built up their own libraries. The idea was to make useful knowledge ac-

---

[43] Thomas Newcomen surely must have seen Papin's sketches of his models of proto-engines and pumps, published in various issues of *Philosophical Transactions* between 1685 and 1700. One example of a book that codified a great deal of formerly tacit knowledge was Bernard de Bélidor's famed *Architecture Hydraulique*, published in four volumes in 1737. It discussed almost all fields of civil engineering, and the great British engineers John Smeaton, John Rennie, and Thomas Telford all owned copies. Charles Plumier (1646-1704) wrote a book on the art of using a lathe (*l'Art de Tourner*), which - whether of use to craftsmen or not - was sufficiently regarded to be translated into Russian, the translation attributed to the Emperor Peter the Great himself.

[44] For a study of Pierre Montgolfier, one of the most progressive paper manufacturers of eighteenth century France, see Rosenband, *Papermaking*.

[45] Jones, *Culture*, p. 13

[46] Musson and Robinson, *Science and Technology*, p. 113. In 1697, the rev. Thomas Bray [1697, (1967)] called for 400 lending libraries to be established throughout Britain, believing that making knowledge more accessible would "raise a Noble Spirit of Emulation in those Leaned Societies and would excite more of the members thereof to exert themselves in being serviceable to the world" (p. 11).

[47] See Outram, *Enlightenment*, p. 21.

cessible. Furthermore, in the century between Newton's Principia and Lavoisier's Traité Elementaire Latin disappeared as the language in which books were published.[48]

A telltale sign of the changing age were the scientific and other technical magazines that began appearing all over Europe. Many of these periodicals were derivative popularizations and intended to summarize and review the existing literature, and thus directly reduced access costs even if their respect for intellectual property left a lot to be desired. To be sure, only a minority of the population read, and that of those the bulk read novels, romantic potboilers turned out by hacks in what Darnton has called "Grub Street," scandalous pamphlets and religious tracts. Books on the useful arts, science, and mathematics were without doubt of interest to only a small minority.[49] Even within science, the majority of publications was concerned with the kind of knowledge that was not often directly concerned with the technical problems of the early stages of the Industrial Revolution.[50]

Useful knowledge was thus transmitted in codified form through "storage devices." John R. Harris, an authority on British eighteenth century technology, has doubted the extent that codified knowledge mattered in the early stages of the Industrial Revolution. As far as skills and workmanship were concerned, it is possible to exaggerate the importance of books and periodicals as means through which technical knowledge was accessed. It surely was less important in the metal trades or mining than in medicine, agriculture, instrument-making, electricity, astronomy, or chemistry. It changed over time, with much of the volume of technical and scientific publishing concentrated in the last third of the eighteenth century.[51] Yet Harris's judgment is also affected by his narrow focus on the transmission of the techniques themselves, without fully realizing that what mattered in many industries is the diffusion of the propositional knowledge on which the techniques rested, so that they could be adapted, refined, and tweaked by the select few who accessed these knowledge bases. Moreover, artefacts and instruments were storage

---

[48] The Swedish metallurgist, Tobern Bergman published his major work, *De Praecipitatis Metallicis* (a major theoretical essay on the nature of steel) in Latin as late as 1780. An English translation, by no less a scholar than William Withering, a founding member of the Lunar Society, came out in 1783.

[49] A study of the contents of French private libraries (probably unrepresentative) shows only about 3.2 percent of all books devoted to what we may call useful knowledge, more than half being novels and 32 percent being devoted to history or theology. See Mornet, *Enseignements*, p. 457.

[50] The *Natural Science* section of J.D. Reuss's *Repertorium* (Index of scientific literature) published between 1801 and 1821 — and which covers only a small part of the scientific journals — indicates that astronomy accounted for 19 percent of the scientific papers published between 1665 and 1800 and zoology for 18 percent, while mechanics accounted for 4 percent and chemistry for 6 percent. See Gascoigne, *A Historical Catalogue*, p. 100.

[51] Harris, *Skills* pp. 21-23. It might be added that Harris writes specifically about mining and coal-using technology, and that outside geology and the adoption of steam-powered pumps, there was actually little technological progress in the mining sector.

devices as much as descriptions and illustrations. In the eighteenth century an international market in scientific and industrial instruments had emerged, with British instrument makers buying and selling instruments from and to all over Europe.[52] These instruments were used for scientific experimentation as well as for industrial improvement; in the eyes of the men of the Industrial Enlightenment, there was little difference between the two. Capital goods such as steam engines and spinning machines were moving about, various prohibitions on the export of machinery notwithstanding.

It could be objected that, this knowledge, whether codified or tacit, was shared by only a minute percentage of the population. However, the technological thrust during the Industrial Revolution was not the result of the action of the majority of population; in the hurry of the economic history profession to get away from the absurd hero-worship of a few key inventors as having carried the Industrial Revolution, it has tended to go too far in the other direction by asserting that unless much or most of the population had access to technical knowledge, the spread of new techniques was limited. The truth is somewhere in between; it is undeniable that technological progress during the Industrial Revolution was an elite phenomenon, carried not by a dozen or two of big names who made it to the *National Dictionary of Biography*, but by the thousands of trained engineers, capable mechanics, and dexterous craftsmen on whose shoulders the inventors could stand.

Yet when all is said and done, we are talking about thousands, perhaps a few tens of thousands, not hundreds of thousands or millions of people in industrializing Europe; democratic instincts notwithstanding, what the large majority of workers knew mattered little as long as they did what they were told by those who knew more.[53] Technological advance in the period of the Industrial Revolution was a minority affair; most of the entrepreneurs of the time were not like Boulton and Wedgwood and had no knowledge of or interest in science or even innovation, just as most landowners were not improvers. But the dynamics of competition are such that in the long run the few drag along the many.

---

[52] Thus the Portuguese instrument maker Jean Hyacinthe de Magellan – who had worked with Priestley in the 1770s — bought thermometers from Wedgwood, and sold the needed instruments to Alessandro Volta. Volta in turn used these to construct his eponymous pile (reputedly upon hints received from William Nicholson in London). See Stewart, *Laboratory*, p. 13.

[53] Adam Smith expressed this kind of elitism in his *Early Draft*, in which he noted that "to think or to reason comes to be, like every other employment, a particular business, which is carried on by very few people who furnish the public with all the thought and reason possessed by the vast multitudes that labour." The benefits of the "speculations of the philosopher... may evidently descend to the meanest of people" if they led to improvements in the mechanical arts. Smith, *Lectures on Jurisprudence*, pp. 569-72. Soame Jenyns, a mid-eighteenth century writer, advocated ignorance for the poor as "the only opiate capable of infusing the insensibility which can enable them to endure the miseries of poverty and the fatigues of the drudgeries of life." See Jenyns, *Free Inquiry*, pp. 65-66. As Rosenberg points out, such a division of knowledge was increasingly pertinent to a sophisticated ("civilized") society in which specialized "philosophers" would account for technological progress. Cf. Rosenberg, *Adam Smith*, pp. 134-36.

The exact composition of who these "few" were changed during the period in question. Late in the seventeenth century and in the first decades of the eighteenth, it was clearly the political elite that felt that new knowledge and the rejection of age-old sacred cows were the keys to social progress. Over the eighteenth century, conservative elements slowly gained the upper hand, especially when liberal and progressive elements were allied with both the American rebels and the French Jacobins. Especially in Britain, anti-Enlightenment sentiments flared up in the 1790s. But whatever happened in the center of power in London, it could not stop the Industrial Enlightenment from spreading into provincial society. In the European provincial societies of Manchester, Liverpool, Newcastle, Leeds, Antwerp, Lyons, Marseilles, Nantes, and Milan, J.H. Plumb has noted, we do not find Diderots and Humes, but neither do we find [reactionary thinkers] such as Samuel Johnson or Edmund Burke. Instead, "we find knots of enlightened men with a passionate regard for empirical knowledge, secular in their intellectual attitudes, although often muddled, uncertain and tentative, with ... rational and irrational beliefs combined in the same man." Their religious feelings were quite diverse and many thoughtful and well-read minds of the enlightenment still fell for bogus and faddish ideas put out by charlatans.[54] On the whole, not all important eighteenth-century thought was enlightened and the Enlightenment itself was a complex and often self-contradictory movement, in which many different streams competed. Some scholars have found the differences between thinkers *within* the Enlightenment more important than their common denominator.[55] As J.H. Plumb put it in his inimitable style, "between the stars of the first magnitude are vast spaces of darkness."[56] Yet these spaces of "darkness" are often revealed, at closer inspection, to be filled with interesting material and some beliefs and axioms that were shared across the regions where the influence of the Enlightenment was palpable. In the end, the belief in advances in knowledge and their capability to improve the human lot was the one intellectual heritage that was critical to material progress.

4.2. Access Costs: Cultural and Social Factors

In addition to the technology of access there was culture. The culture of "open science" that evolved in the seventeenth century meant that observation and experience were placed in the public domain and that credit was assigned by priority. Its open-ness manifested itself in two dimensions, both in the full disclosure of findings and methods and in the lack of barriers to entry for competent persons willing to learn the language. Scientific knowledge became a public good, communicated

---

[54] Well-known examples were the wondrous Dr. John Brown (1735–88), whose popularity was based on his insistence that all diseases could be cured by either alcohol or opium, and the notorious fraud Alessandro Cagliostro (1743-95) who peddled elixirs of youth and love powders to the high and mighty, and whose séances had become the rage of fashionable society in Paris by 1785 till he found himself in the Bastille.

[55] For example, von Hayek, *Legal and Political Philosophy*, p. 106.

[56] Plumb, *Reason and Unreason*, pp. 5, 23.

freely rather than confined to a secretive exclusive few as had been the custom in medieval Europe. Open-ness, as Paul David and others have pointed out, had major benefits in that validation was made easy, duplication reduced, and spillover effects could be augmented. It increasingly closed down research roads that led to *cul de sacs* and bogus knowledge. Magic, occult, mystical beliefs, and simple charlatanery, while still alive and often well in the eighteenth century, found themselves on the defense against an increasingly skeptical community that demanded to reproduce their results or refute them.

Access costs depend crucially on the culture and social customs of useful knowledge. The rhetorical conventions in scientific discourse changed in the seventeenth century. Authority and trust, of course, remained essential to the pursuit of knowledge as they must, but the rules of the discourse and the criteria for "what was (believed to be) true" or "what worked" shifted toward a more empirical and verifiable direction. The community of those who added to useful knowledge demanded that it be tested, so that it could be trusted.[57] Verification and testing meant that a deliberate effort was made to make useful knowledge "tighter" and thus, all other things equal, more likely to be used.[58] This tightness is what makes modern science a strategic factor in economic growth. Inevitably, the skepticism of experts of each others' findings and the careful testing reinforced the trust of the potential users, who could assume that this knowledge had already been vetted by the very best and if it had been accepted by them, the likelihood of an error was minimized.[59] In science, as in commercial transactions, trust is an information-cost saving device and as such it was essential if useful knowledge was not only to be diffused but also verified and accepted and — most important for our purposes — acted upon.[60] The sharing of knowledge within "open science" required systematic

---

[57] Steven Shapin has outlined the changes in trust and expertise in Britain during the seventeenth century, associating expertise, for better or for worse, with social class and locality. While the approach to science was ostensibly based on a "question authority" principle (the Royal Society's motto was *nullius in verba*—on no one's word), in fact no system of shared useful (or any kind of) knowledge can exist without some mechanism that generates trust. The apparent skepticism with which scientists treated the knowledge created by their colleagues increased the trust that outsiders could have in the findings, because they could then assume —as is still true today—that these findings had been scrutinized and checked by other "experts."see Shapin, *Social History*.

[58] By "tight," I mean knowledge that is believed to be true by a consensus, and that this consensus is based on considerable confidence.

[59] As Hilaire-Pérez put it, "the value of inventions was too important an economic stake to be left to be dissipated among the many forms of recognition and amateurs: the establishment of truth became the professional responsibility of academic science." (Hilaire-Pérez, *Invention technique*, p. 60).

[60] In the scientific world of the late seventeenth and eighteenth centuries, a network of trust and verification emerged in the West that seems to have stood the test of time. It is well described by Polanyi; the space of useful knowledge is divided in small neighboring units. If an individual B is surrounded by neighbors A and C who can verify his work, and C is similarly surrounded by B and D and so on, the world of useful knowledge

reporting of methods and materials using a common vocabulary and consensus standards, and was the major component in the decline in access costs, making propositional knowledge, such as it was, available to those who might find a use for it.

This trend was reinforced by a redefinition of fact and experience: seventeenth century and early enlightenment scientific thought became more interested in cataloguing specific events, to be reassessed and reformulated into general principles based, in the best Baconian tradition, on hard empirical facts and the results of experiment. Yet there are facts and there are facts. In the second half of the eighteenth century, those in charge of augmenting the set of propositional knowledge increasingly relied on quantification and formal mathematical methods. The increasing reliance on mathematics and graphical representation in the writing of technical works supported this need for precise and effective communication. As Rider puts it, "mathematics was eminently rational in eighteenth century eyes, its symbols and results were truly international ... in an age that prized the rational and the universal, mathematics ...offered inspiration and example to the reformers of language."[61] Formal methods and quantification are access-cost reducing devices, in that they are an efficient language to communicate facts and relationships, and that the rules are more or less universal (at least within the community that counted for the processing and application of useful knowledge). Computation and formal methods were necessary because they were an efficient way of communicating and because they lent themselves more readily to falsification. A rhetoric of precision, through meticulous procedures and sophisticated equipment emerged that facilitated scientific consensuses, if not always in straightforward manner.[62] Heilbron submits that in the seventeenth century most of "learned Europe" was still largely innumerate, but that in the second half of the eighteenth century propositional knowledge, from temperature and rainfall tables, to agricultural yields, the hardness and softness of materials, and economic and demographic information was increasingly presented in tables and expected its readers to be comfortable with that language or at least be willing to learn.[63] Tables not only made the presentation of information more efficient, they organized and analyzed it by forcing the author to taxonomize the data. A booklet such as Smeaton's famous *Treaty on Water and Wind Mills* used tables lavishly to report his experiments, but already four decades earlier, in 1718, Henry Beighton had published a table entitled *A Calculation of the Power of the Fire (Newcomen's) engine shew-*

---

reaches an equilibrium in which science, as a whole, can be trusted even by those who are not themselves part of it. Polanyi, *Personal Knowledge,* pp. 216-22.

[61] Rider, *Measure of Ideas*, p. 115.

[62] The triumph of Lavoisier's chemistry over its British opponents in the later 1790s is a good example. See Golinski, *The Nicety of Experiment.*

[63] Heilbron, *Introductory Essay*, p. 9. These methods soon were applied to mundane purposes. An example is John Dougharty, *The General Gauger: or, the Principles and Practice of Gauging Beer, Wine, and Malt*. The sixth edition, corrected by the author. London, 1750. The first half or so of the book lays out the basic arithmetic manipulations, starting from the basics.

ing the Diameter of the Cylinder, for Steam of the Pump that is Capable of Raising any Quantity of Water, from 48 to 440 Hogsheads an Hours; 15 to 100 yards.[64] Tables of astronomical, legal, historical, literary, and religious information appeared in many eighteenth-century books, but some of it was practical and mundane. John H. Desaguliers in 1734 published a (bi-lingual) set of 175 tables from which Jewellers could determine the value of diamonds.[65] Later in the eighteenth century tables were complemented by graphs, and the growing sophistication of information was enhanced by visual means. William Playfair pioneered the display of data in graphical form, defending their use explicitly on the basis of a reduction in access costs.[66] This idea caught on but slowly, and oddly enough faster on the Continent than in Britain, which seems on the whole to have preferred tables.[67] That even with formal notation and well-organized data there will still be plenty of ambiguity left is something that most economists – and surely all economic historians – are all too keenly aware of.

Precisely because the Industrial Enlightenment was not limited to be a national or local phenomenon, it became increasingly felt that differences in language and standards were an impediment and increased access costs. Watt, James Keir, and the Derby clockmaker John Whitehurst, worked on a system of universal terms and standards, that would make French and British experiments "speak the same language."[68] In the eighteenth century access costs fell in part because national and geographic barriers were easily crossed.[69] The Enlightenment movement as a whole was cosmopolitan, with the typical scientist or philosopher more a citizen of the Republic of Letters than of his own country.[70] Many of the central figures

---

[64] Smeaton, *Experimental Enquiry*. Beighton's Table is reproduced in Desaguliers, *Course of Experimental Philosophy*, p. 535. Desaguliers remarked that "Mr. Beighton's table agreed with all the experiments made ever since 1717." For more details on Beighton, a remarkable early example of the Industrial Enlightenment, see Stewart, *Rise of Public Science*, pp. 242-51.

[65] Desaguliers, *Jewellers Accounts*.

[66] Playfair, *The commercial and political atlas*. "As knowledge increases amongst mankind, and transactions multiply, it becomes more and more desirable to abbreviate and facilitate the modes of conveying information." Cited byHeadrick, *When Information came of Age*, p. 127. This text does not appear in the 1786 original edition. Playfair's book was concerned with economic data, not science and technology.

[67] James Watt, Playfair's employer, advised him "that it might be proper to give in letter press the Tables from which the Charts have been constructed." Cited by Spence, *Invention and Use of Statistical Charts*, p. 78.

[68] Uglow, *The Lunar Men*, p. 357.

[69] For an excellent discussion of the growing mobility of scientific and technological knowledge in the eighteenth century, see Inkster, *Mental Capital*.

[70] Darnton, *The Unity of Europe*. The idea of the *Respublica Litteraria* goes back to the late middle ages, and by the eighteenth century had extended to mechanical and technical knowledge. John R. Harris has noted that as early as the 1720s the development of the early steam engine was the center of intense interest in the European scientific community, and "international intelligence about the engine diffused with great speed, the speed

of the Industrial Enlightenment were well-travelled, none more than Franklin and Rumford and realized the importance of reading in foreign languages (language differences is a component of access costs).[71] Books on science and technology were translated quickly, even when nations were at war with one another. P.J. Macquer's encyclopedic textbook on chemistry was translated (with considerable additions) by James Keir, a member of the Lunar society, and the works of Lavoisier and Berthollet were translated in Britain within a short time of their first appearances. The British knew all too well that Continental chemists were superior to their own. In return, the French translated scientific works published in Britain, and here too, the translators were often leading experts themselves, such as the Comte de Buffon translating Stephen Hales's influential *Vegetable Staticks* in 1735 and John T. Desaguliers translating the leading Dutch Newtonian Willem 's Gravesande's *Mathematical Elements of Natural Philosophy* (1720), studied later by James Watt whose father owned the book. Chaptal's *Elements of Chemistry* (1795) was translated into English by William Nicholson, a distinguished chemist.[72] Honor and prestige crossed national boundaries as easily as knowledge. Lavoisier was a fellow of the Royal Society, and corresponded among others with Josiah Wedgwood about the use of refractory clays.[73] In 1808, James Watt, Edward Jenner, and the chemist Richard Kirwan were elected foreign associates of the French Academy of Sciences (then known as the *Institut National*), war or no war. Statements such as that knowledge was supranational and that "the sciences were never at war" (as Lavoisier claimed in 1793) are of course an overidealization. Reality, especially after 1793, deviated from the ideals of the Enlightenment, and political and military considerations increasingly got in the way of the free flow of useful knowledge.[74] Useful knowledge, it was realized, could be valuable to the State when engaged in combating another.

Access costs consisted in great measure on knowing what was known, and to facilitate access, knowledge had to be classified. This turned out to be an involved project and much intellectual capital was spent on taxonomy and the organization

---

of correspondence between the scientific luminaries of Europe of that period." See Harris, *Industrial Espionage*, p. 296.

[71] Robert Hooke taught himself Dutch to read Leeuwenhoek's famous letters on microscopy, and a century later John Smeaton taught himself French to be able to read the papers of French hydraulic theorists such as de Parcieux and traveled to the Netherlands to study their use of wind power firsthand.

[72] Uglow, *Lunar Men*, p. 27. The movement of translations was symmetrical. In 1780, a French publisher published a whole bundle of *Ouvrages sur l'économie politique et Rurale, traduit de l'Anglais* including work by Arthur Young and John Arbuthnot (who had written an important work on ploughs). Bourde, *Influence*, p. 97. In agriculture, as Gillispie correctly points out, the impact of such information flows "beyond the circle of persons who wrote, printed and read the books," was probably small. See Gillispie, *Science and Polity*, p. 367.

[73] Schofield, *Lunar Society*, p. 378.

[74] De Beer, *Sciences*.

of knowledge.[75] Access to knowledge required search engines. The new search engine of the eighteenth century was the encyclopedia, exploiting that miracle of organizational technology, alphabetization. To be sure, Diderot and d'Alembert's *Encyclopédie* did not augur the Industrial Revolution, it did not predict factories, and had little or nothing to say about mechanical cotton spinning equipment or steam engines. It catered primarily to the landowning elite and the bourgeoisie of the ancien régime (notaries, lawyers, local officials) rather than specifically to an innovative industrial bourgeoisie, such as it was. It was, in many ways, a conservative document.[76] Moreover, the idea of such a search engine was not altogether new, and attempts to sum up all that is known in some fashion can be found in China and in medieval Europe. However, the drive to organize knowledge in a way that made it accessible at a high level of detail yet easy to use was very much a product of the eighteenth century.[77] The *Encyclopédie* and similar works of the eighteenth century symbolized the very different way of looking at technological knowledge: instead of intuition came systematic analysis, instead of tacit dexterity came an attempt to attain an understanding of the principles at work, instead of secrets learned from a master came an open and accessible system of training and learning. It also insisted on organizing knowledge in user-friendly compilations, arranged in an accessible way, and while subscribers may not have been mostly artisans and small manufacturers, the knowledge contained in it dripped out and trickled down through a variety of leaks to those who could make use of it.[78] Encyclopedias allowed not only for faster searches, but also underlined the agnosticism of the project to biased taxonomies of knowledge. As pragmatic and heuristic documents, and while it may be an overstatement that they were a starting point toward a new concept of knowledge, they reflected an intellectual innovation that deliberately sought to reduce access costs.[79]

Furthermore, then as now, works that have an "encyclopedic" nature are instinctively trusted. It is believed - perhaps too optimistically - that such synthetic works reflect authority and best-practice knowledge, and that any statements reflecting baseless speculation and personal bias have been excised by conscientious encyclopedia editors. As such, the emergence of encyclopedias as an accessible source of useful knowledge reduced access costs on another front, namely the costs of verification. Many other works of useful knowledge were sponsored by the French Royal Academy, the British Royal Society, or similar formal institu-

---

[75] Burke, *A Social History*, ch. 5.

[76] Darnton, *Business of Enlightenment*, p. 286.

[77] Heilbron, *Introductory Essay* p. 20 notes that Diderot and d'Alembert were but indolent in comparison with the massive (64 volumes) work published by J.H. Zedler, *Grosses vollständiges Universal-Lexikon aller Wissenschafte und Künste,* published 1732-54.

[78] Pannabecker points out that the plates in the *Encyclopédie* were designed by the highly skilled Louis-Jacques Goussier who eventually became a machine designer at the Conservatoire des arts et métiers in Paris. They were meant to popularize the rational systematization of the mechanical arts to facilitate technological progress. Pannabecker, *Diderot*, pp. 6-22 and id., *Representing*.

[79] Broberg, *Broken Circle*, pp. 45-71.

tions. Such quasi-official imprimaturs were intended to make them look more believable and tighter.[80] The age also witnessed the rise of bibliographical guides and handbooks, that helped readers find their way to the knowledge they sought.

Encyclopedias and "dictionaries" were supplemented by a variety of textbooks, manuals, compendia, gazettes, and compilations of techniques and devices that were in use somewhere, none more detailed than the over thirteen thousand pages of the 80 volumes of the *Descriptions des Arts et Métiers* compiled in France before the Revolution — in Gillispie's judgment the largest body of technological literature ever produced.[81] Much more modest and affordable were the multitudinous "dictionaries" of useful arts, published all over Europe.[82] In agriculture, meticulously compiled data collections looking at such topics as yields, crops, and cultivation methods were common.[83] Engineering manuals, meticulous descriptions of various "useful arts" were published, translated, pirated, and — one presumes — read at a wider scale than ever before. One of the most impressive and best-organized of such textbooks was P.J. Macquer's *Dictionnaire de Chimie* published in 1766 and, as noted, translated into English in 1771 by the chemist James Keir.[84] It contained over 500 articles on practical chemistry, arranged alphabetically. Keir supplemented his translation with the most recent discoveries made by Dr. Black, Mr. Cavendish and others. It was the finest and most accessible compilation of pre-Lavoisier chemical knowledge, and indicative of the great

---

[80] The *Philosophical Transactions* published by the Royal Society and the *Histoire et Mémoires* published by the *Académie Royale des Sciences* were among the most influential publications of their time. They were routinely reported on in the wide-circulation *Gentleman's Magazine* and abridged, abstracted, and translated all over the Continent.

[81] Cole and Watts, *Handicrafts of France*. Gillispie, *Science and Polity*, p. 344.

[82] For instance, Jaubert, *Dictionnaire Raisonné*, Hall, *New Royal Encyclopedia;* Society of Gentlemen, *New and Complete Dictionary*.

[83] William Ellis's *Modern Husbandman or Practice of Farming* (1731) gave a month-by-month set of suggestions, much like Arthur Young's most successful book, *The Farmer's Kalendar* (1770). Summaries of this information often took the form of frequently-updated dictionaries and compendia, such as Society of Gentlemen, *Complete Farmer* first published by the Society of Arts in 1766.. Most of these writings were empirical or instructional in nature, but a few actually tried to provide the readers with some systematic analysis of the principles at work. One of those was Francis Home's *Principles of Agriculture and Vegetation* (1757). One of the great private data collection projects of the time were Arthur Young's famed *Tours* of various parts of England and William Marshall's series on *Rural Economy* (Goddard, 1989). They collected hundreds of observations on farm practice in Britain and the continent, although at times Young's conclusions were contrary to what his own data indicated . See Allen and Ó Gráda, 1988. In France, Duhamel de Monceau's *Traité de la Culture des Terres* (1753) found a wide readership and was translated into English and published in 1759. His textbook *Élements d'agriculture (1762)* was also widely translated and reprinted. The French repaid the honor in 1801-02, by publishing an 18 volume translation of Arthur Young's works on agriculture and politics under the title *Le Cultivateur Anglais*.

[84] Macquer, *Dictionary of Chemistry*. Originally printed in 1771, a fifth edition had already been published by 1777, indicating the success of the work.

value placed on access to knowledge believed to be potentially useful. There were other such volumes. Richard Watson, elected Professor of Chemistry at Cambridge in 1764 wrote a popular text, *Chemical Essays,* which sold thousands of copies and went through eleven editions. Elementary mathematical knowledge, especially arithmetic and geometry, had to be made accessible cheaply and reliably to a host of craftsmen and skilled artisans, from instrument makers to surveyors to accountants. Here the classic book was Francis Walkingame's *Tutor's Assistant,* which, between its first publication in 1751 and the death of its author in 1783, went through 18 editions, each consisting of between five and ten thousand copies.[85] Formal knowledge was also made more accessible by logical systematization and organization, as illustrated by the detailed indexes that became standard on works of useful knowledge, but also epitomized by the work of Carl Linnaeus, whose classificatory schemes were arguably the most influential scientific endeavor between Newton and Lavoisier, his binomial nomenclature reducing communication- and access costs to natural history and botanical knowledge.

Furthermore, access costs had a strictly social dimension. Technological communication inevitably often took the form of personal contact, and such exchanges on knowledge were more effective when the two sides trusted one another. Historically, one of the great sources of technological stagnation had been the social divide between those who knew things ("*savants*") and those who made things ("*fabricants*"). The relationship between those who possessed useful knowledge and those who might find a use for it was changing in eighteenth-century Europe and points to a further reduction in access costs. To construct pipelines through which those two groups could communicate was at the very heart of the movement.[86] These pipelines, or *passerelles* as Hilaire-Pérez has called them, ran both ways; they served as a mechanism through which practical people with specific technical problems to solve could air their needs and absorb what best-practice knowledge had to offer which, of course, at most times was rather little. At the same time, knowledge of crafts and manufactures could influence the research agenda of the scientists, as the Royal Society, at least in its first decades, stressed, by posing focused and well-defined problems. The movement of knowledge was thus bi-directional, as seems natural to us in the twenty-first century. In eighteenth-century Europe, however, such exchanges were still quite novel and it only slowly dawned on people that it would benefit and direct science as much as it

---

[85] Walkingame, *Tutor's Assistant.* By the end of the century, student guide-books to the *Tutor's Assistant* had appeared. See Wallis, *Early Best-seller,* pp. 199-208. Walkingame included mathematical methods employed by glaziers, painters, plasterers and bricklayers, pointing to the applied and pragmatic nature of the mathematics he taught.

[86] This point was first made by Edward Zilsel in 1942, who placed the beginning of this movement in the middle of the sixteenth century. While this may be too early for the movement to have much economic effect, the insight that technological progress occurs when intellectuals communicate with producers is central to its historical explanation. Compare Zilsel, *Sociological Roots of Science,* pp. 544—60. For a recent restatement, see Jacob, *Scientific Culture.*

would influence industry.[87] By the 1760s in much of Europe the social gap between natural philosophers and entrepreneurs had begun to close, though only very slowly, far too slowly for those who recognized its importance.[88] Social contacts between *savants* and *fabricants* were sufficiently close for Joseph Priestley to marry the sister of the great ironmonger John Wilkinson, and the doyen of British science and president of the Royal Society, Joseph Banks, corresponded with many of the leading industrialists of the time.

Open science and the sharing of useful knowledge meant, of course, that the persons created this knowledge could not extract the rents it created. Those who added to propositional knowledge would be rewarded by honor, peer recognition, and fame, not a monetary reward proportional to their contribution. For most of the truly great scientists of the era, from Newton to Linnaeus to Lavoisier, the honor and recognition was usually enough if a certain reservation comfort constraint was satisfied. Even those scientists who discovered matters of significant importance to industry, such as Claude Berthollet, Joseph Priestley, Benjamin Franklin, and Humphry Davy, often wanted credit, not profit.

4.3. Access Costs: Institutional Factors

The Industrial Enlightenment consisted in large part of the emergence of institutions devoted to the flow of ideas. Among those, it would seem, Universities should have played a major role. This was surely true for Scotland, where such leading lights as Colin McLaurin, William Cullen, Joseph Black, John Robison and many others taught courses of considerable technical significance. At the University of Glasgow many of these courses were opened to artisans and other townspeople interested in studying chemistry and other applied fields. The course taught by Joseph Black in Edinburgh was attended by 200 listeners, while his suc-

---

[87] Thomas Sprat recognized this in the 1660s when he wrote that no New Atlantis (Bacon's ideal scientific community) was possible unless "Mechanick Labourers shall have Philosophical heads; or the Philosophers shall have Mechanical hands." See Sprat, *History of the Royal-Society of London,* p. 397. In its early days, the Royal Society invested heavily in the study of crafts and technology and commissioned a History of Trades, but this effort in the end failed. Cf. Hunter, 1989.

[88] Humphry Davy felt in 1802 that "in consequence of the multiplication of the means of instruction, the man of science and the manufacturer are daily becoming more assimilated to each other." Davy, 1802, vol. 2, p. 321. Not all agreed at the time: William Thompson, Count Rumford, noted in 1799 that "there are no two classes of men in society that are more distinct, or that are more separated from each other by a more marked line, than philosophers and those who are engaged in arts and manufactures" and that this prevented "all connection and intercourse between them." He expressed hope that the Royal Institution he helped found in 1799 would "facilitate and consolidate" the union between science and art and to direct "their united efforts to the improvement of agriculture, manufactures, and commerce, and to the increase of domestic comfort." See Thompson (1876), pp. 743-45.

cessor, Thomas Charles Hope occasionally addressed over 500 auditors.[89] In Germany a wave of new Universities, included that in Göttingen, were founded in the 1740s, training future bureaucrats in agricultural science, engineering, mining, and forestry.[90]

Yet, oddly enough, the role of formal educational institutions in the reduction of access costs was quite modest in the first century of the Industrial Revolution.[91] English Universities were rather ineffective in teaching applied science and mechanics in this period, although the gap was made up in part by the Scottish Universities, and in part by sixty or so dissenting academies, which taught experimental science, mathematics, and botany among other subjects. Among those, Warrington Academy was one of the best, and the great chemist Joseph Priestley taught there for a while, though surprisingly he was made to teach history, grammar, and rhetoric.[92] These institutions reached only a thin elite, though apparently that was enough. In the early nineteenth century, there were some attempts to close the educational gap between classes by means of the so-called Mechanics Institutes, inspired by George Birckbeck, which supplied adult education in the evening, with the purpose of bridging the gap between the working class and science.[93] Contemporaries noted that these institutes by and large failed in their objective to spread scientific knowledge to the masses and mostly provided remedial education to laborers, as well as scientific knowledge to members of the skilled labor aristocracy.[94]

The other institutional mechanism emerging during the Industrial Enlightenment to connect between those who possessed prescriptive knowledge and those who wanted to apply it was the emergence of meeting places where men of industry interacted with natural philosophers. Many of these meetings were ad hoc lec-

---

[89] Wood, *Science*, p. 109.

[90] Outram, *Enlightenment* p. 60.

[91] Oxford and Cambridge have been given little credit for teaching much of value to a vibrant economy, and their enrollments declined in the eighteenth century. Adam Smith in a famous sentence remarked sarcastically that at Oxford the dons had "long ago given up all pretence of teaching," and Priestley compared them to "pools of stagnant water. "There were a few exceptions, especially in Cambridge where Richard Watson was "chiefly concerned with manufacturing processes rather than with the advancement of pure science" and John Hadley who showed a "noticeable interest in industrial-chemical processes " (Musson and Robinson, *Science and Technology*, pp. 168, 36). His colleague in Magdalene College, John Rowning, was a mathematician who wrote a popular *Compendious System of Natural Philosophy* that went through seven editions between 1735 and 1772. Birse has collected data that show that out of 498 applied scientists and engineers born between 1700 and 1850, 91 were educated in Scotland, 50 at Oxbridge, and 329 (about two-thirds) had no university education at all. See Birse, *Engineering*, p. 16. Over the eighteenth century, moreover, the number of engineers and applied scientists who received a formal institutionalized education declined.

[92] Schofield, *Lunar Society*, p. 195

[93] Inkster, *Social Context*, pp. 277-307.

[94] Roderick and Stephens, *Education and Industry*, pp. 54-60.

tures and demonstrations by professional lecturers and popularizers.[95] Musson and Robinson, who were among the first to recognize the significance of these lecturers point out that only a few of them were of national significance, while others were "mostly local" figures.[96] Much of the improved access to useful knowledge took place through informal meetings of which we have but poor records, in coffee houses and pubs, improvised lectures, private salons.[97] By 1700 there were 2000 coffeehouses in London, many of which were sites of learning, literary activity and political discussions. Perhaps the most famous of these coffee house societies was the London Chapter Coffee House, the favorite of the fellows of the Royal Society, whose membership resembled (and overlapped with) the Birmingham Lunar Society.[98] Masonic lodges, too, proved a locus for the exchange of

---

[95] Of the itinerant lecturers, the most famous was John T. Desaguliers. Desaguliers, a leading proponent of Newton with an international reputation (he lectured in the Netherlands) received a royal pension of £ 70 per annum as well as a variety of patents, fees, and prizes. His *Course of Mechanical and Experimental Philosophy* (1724) was based on his hugely popular lectures on science and technology. William Whiston, one of Newton's most distinguished proponents and successor at Cambridge "entertained his provincial listeners with combinations of scientific subjects and Providence and the Millennium." James Jurin, master of the Newcastle Grammar School, gave courses catering to the local gentlemen concerned with collieries and lead-mines. (See Stewart, *Rise of Public Science,* p. 147). Other British lecturers of note were Peter Shaw, a chemist and physician, the instrument maker Benjamin Martin, Stephen Demainbray who lectured both in France and England and later became Superintendent of the King's Observatory at Kew, and the Rev. Richard Watson at Cambridge whose lectures on Chemistry in the 1760s were so successful that he drew a patronage of £ 100 for his impoverished chair. In France the premier lecturer and scientific celebrity of his time was Abbé Jean-Antoine Nollet, whose fame rests on early public experiments with electricity (he once passed an electrical charge from a Leyden jar through a row of Carthusian monks more than a mile long). Nollet also trained and encouraged a number of his disciples as lecturers, as well as some of the most celebrated scientists of his age, such as Lavoisier and Monge. Similarly, Guillaume-François Rouelle's lectures on chemistry in the Jardin du roi drew an audience that included Rousseau, Diderot and even Lavoisier himself. Compare Stewart, *Laboratory and Manufacture.* In Napoleonic France, the "best scientific minds of the day" were lecturing to the public about steam engines, and it became common to regard some scientific training as a natural prelude for entrepreneurial activity (Jacob, *Putting Science to Work*).

[96] For a magisterial survey, see Musson and Robinson, *Science and Technology,* pp. 87-189.

[97] In the closing years of the seventeenth century, the Marine Coffee House in Birchin Lane behind the Royal Exchange in London was the first location for an organized set of lectures on mathematics given by the rev. John Harris, to be followed by series on experimental philosophy. See Stewart, *Selling of Newton,* p. 180. Among the best-known private eighteenth century Paris *salons* were those of Mme de Tencin and Mme l'Espinasse.

[98] Levere and Turner, *Discussing Chemistry and Steam.* Its membership reads like a veritable list of the *Who's who* of the British Industrial Enlightenment of the 1780s. Needless to say, many of these lecturers structured their lectures around topics that had no immediate or even remote applicability, presented theories that were bogus even by the stan-

scientific and technological information even if that was not their primary mission.[99] Lecturers performed entertaining public experiments, in which electricity and magnetism played roles disproportionate to their technical significance. Needless to say, there are other explanations for the popularity of scientific lectures, not all of them persuasive.[100]

After 1750 informal meetings started to slowly dwindle in importance, as they were replaced by more formal organizations, but the demand for useful knowledge remained strong. The establishment of the Royal Society in 1662 was one of the first signs of what was to come. There had, of course, been precedents, such as the *Accademia dei Lincei* founded in 1603 in Rome and disbanded in 1630. Formal academies were founded and bankrolled by states or local governments, whereas spontaneous societies, often specialized, were organized by its participants. It is striking to what degree this phenomenon in the eighteenth century becomes a *provincial* phenomenon; small towns increasingly found they had the critical mass of interested persons to form a formal club devoted to scientific and technological discourse. Of those, a few have attained fame as the kind of organizations that were instrumental in bringing about the Industrial Revolution, none more than the Birmingham Lunar Society.[101] Knowledge exchange was the very raison d'Etre of the Birmingham Lunar Society, which provided routine contact between scientists such as Priestley and Keir, mechanics such as Whitehurst and Watt, and entrepreneurs such as Boulton and Wedgwood.[102]

In France, great institutions were created under royal patronage, above all the *Académie Royale des Sciences*, created by Colbert and Louis XIV in 1666 to dis-

---

dards of the time, and at times they showed a bias toward the flashy and dramatic experiment over the strictly useful. Schaffer, *Natural Philosophy*, pp. 1-43. Desaguliers himself admitted that " a great many persons get a considerable knowledge of Natural Philosophy by way of amusement" (cited by Schaffer, *Machine Philosophy*, p. 159). But as Stewart (*The laboratory*, p. 8) remarks, "a sense of practical consequence was not immediately excluded by the spectacular."

[99] On the significance of Masonic Lodges, see Jacob, *Living the Enlightenment*; Hoff, *The Enlightenment*, pp. 139-45.

[100] Elliott, *The Birth of Public Science*, p. 96, apparently influenced by notions of the "Habermasean public sphere," thinks that their attractiveness came from their being intellectually challenging, morally uplifting, and that they enhanced polite education while not being socially disruptive and offering no threat to peace and stability. This would equally apply to lectures on classical sculpture or cooking classes.

[101] This is most eloquently expressed by Uglow, *Lunar Men*. See also the classic Schofield, *Lunar Society*.

[102] In 1776, Josiah Wedgwood consulted his fellow Lunar Society member, the chemist James Keir, on matters of heating vitreous substances and together they discovered a way to reduce the veins and streaks that disfigured glass at the time. See Schofield, *Lunar Society*, p. 172. Henry Cort, whose invention of the puddling and rolling process was no less central than Watt's separate condenser, also consulted Joseph Black during his work. Compare Clow and Clow, *Chemical Revolution*.

seminate information and resources.[103] Yet the phenomenon was nationwide: McClellan estimates that 33 official learned societies were functioning in the French provinces during the eighteenth century counting over 6,400 members and that overall during the eighteenth century perhaps between 10,000 and 12,000 men belonged to learned societies that dealt at least in part with science.[104] The *Académie Royale* exercised a fair amount of control over the direction of French scientific development and acted as technical advisor to the monarchy. By determining what was published and exercising control over patents, the *Académie* became a powerful administrative body, providing scientific and technical advice to government bureaus.[105] French academies had a somewhat different objective than Britain: it is often argued that the *Académie* linked the aspirations of the scientific community to the utilitarian concerns of the government, creating not a Baconian society open to all comers and all disciplines but a closed academy limited primarily to Parisian scholars. French science was in some ways different from British science, both in its agenda and its methodology. Yet the difference between France and Britain was one of emphasis and nuance, not of essence: they shared a utilitarian optimism of man's ability to create wealth through knowledge. French science, as the old truism has it, was more formal, deductive, and abstract than British science, which had a pragmatic and more experimental bend.[106] But instead of a source of weakness, this diversity ultimately provided the Enlightenment project with strength through, as it were, a division of labor between various societies specializing in the areas of their comparative advantage. Rather than a set of competing players or a horse race, we should regard the European Enlightenment as a joint project in which collective knowledge was produced, increasingly accessible to the participants.

Elsewhere on the Continent, too, there was a growing recognition of the importance of the creation of new useful knowledge and improved access to the entire stock. In the Netherlands, rich but increasingly technologically backward, heroic efforts were made to infuse the economy with more innovativeness.[107] In Ger-

---

[103] Its membership included most of the distinguished scientists of France in the eighteenth century including d'Alembert, Buffon, Clairaut, Condorcet, Fontenelle, Laplace, Lavoisier, and Reaumur. It published the most prestigious and substantive scientific series of the century in its annual proceedings *Histoire et Memoires* and sponsored scientific prize contests such as the Meslay prizes. It recognized achievement and rewarded success for individual discoveries and tried to enhance the social status of scientists by granting salaries and pensions. A broad range of scientific disciplines were covered, with mathematics and astronomy well represented, and botany and medicine not less prominent.

[104] McClellan III, *Academie Royale des Sciences*, p. 547.

[105] Hilaire-Pérez, *L'invention technique,* pp. XXX. Gillespie, *Science and Polity*, pp. 81-99, 461-63.

[106] For a recent statement, see Jacob and Stewart, *Practical Matter*, p. 119.

[107] The first of these was established in Haarlem in 1752, and within a few decades the phenomenon spread (much like in England) to the provincial towns. The Scientific Society of Rotterdam known oddly as the *Batavic Association for Experimental Philosophy* was the most applied of all, and advocated the use of steam engines (which were purchased in

many, provincial academies to promote industrial, agricultural, and political progress through science were founded in all the significant German states in the eighteenth century. The Berlin Academy was founded in 1700 and in its early years directed by the great Leibniz, and among its achievements was the discovery that sugar could be extracted from beets (1747). Around 200 such societies appeared in Germany during the half-century spanning from the Seven Years War to the Napoleonic occupation of Germany, such as the Patriotic Society founded at Hamburg in 1765.[108] Many of the German societies were dedicated to political economy, emphasizing what they believed to be the welfare of the population at large and the country over private profit. Local and provincial societies supplemented and expanded the work of national academies.[109] Publishing played an important role in the work of societies bent on the encouragement of invention, innovation and improvement, reflecting the growing conviction that through the diffusion of useful knowledge somehow the public good was enhanced. At the level of access to propositional knowledge, at least, there is little evidence that the *ancien régime* was incapable of generating sustained progress.

Some of these societies fit perfectly into the idea of an Industrial Enlightenment. One such was the Society of Arts, founded in 1754, made a point of encouraging invention by awarding prizes, publicizing new ideas, and facilitating communication between those who possessed useful knowledge and those who could use it. The Royal Institution, founded by Count Rumford and Joseph Banks in 1799, provided public lectures on scientific and technological topics. Its stated purpose in its charter summarizes what the Industrial Enlightenment was about: it was established for "diffusing the knowledge, and facilitating the general introduc-

---

the 1770s but without success). The Amsterdam Society, known as *Felix Meritis*, carried out experiments in physics and chemistry. These societies stimulated interest in physical and experimental sciences in the Netherlands, and they organized prize-essay contests on useful applications of natural philosophy. A physicist named Benjamin Bosma for decades gave lectures on mathematics, geography, and applied physics in Amsterdam. A Dutch Society of Chemistry founded in the early 1790s helped to convert the Dutch to the new chemistry proposed by Lavoisier (Snelders, 1992). The Dutch high schools, known as *Athenea,* taught mathematics, physics, astronomy, and at times counted distinguished scientists among their staff.

[108] Lowood, *Patriotism, Profit, and the Promotion of Science,* pp. 26-27.

[109] Lowood, *Patriotism* has argued that the German local societies were predominantly private institutions, unlike state-controlled academies, which enabled them to be more open, with few conditions of entry, unlike the selective, elitist academies. They broke down social barriers, for the established structures of Old Regime society might impede useful work requiring a mixed contribution from the membership of practical experience, scientific knowledge, and political power. Unlike the more scientifically-inclined academies, they were open to a wide circle of occupations, including farmers, peasants, artisans, craftsmen, foresters, and gardeners, and attempted to improve the productivity of these activities. Prizes rewarded tangible accomplishments, primarily in the agricultural or technical spheres. Their goal was not to advance learning like earlier academies, but rather to apply useful results of human knowledge, discovery and invention to practical and civic life.

tion, of useful mechanical inventions and improvements; and for teaching, by courses of philosophical lectures and experiments, the application of science to the common purposes of life."[110] In Britain, most of these societies were the result of private initiatives and funds, whereas on the Continent they were usually supported by local or national government. Yet these were differences of degree, not of essence, and certainly not of ideology.[111]

What did these scientific societies do to further economic development in Europe? They organized lectures, symposia, public experiments, and discussion groups, and published "proceedings" of a variety of nature. Many of them had prize essay contests. Much of the material discussed by these organizations was of course quite remote from economic applications. Many of them were meant to standardize languages, or were engaged in discussing issues of archaeology and local history. Others discussed music, the arts, poetry, and the theatre. A substantial number of them were either the drinking clubs of a bored leisure class or the pet projects of local nobles, magistrates, or bourgeois busybodies to show off the next town or county.[112] But in the course of the eighteenth century "natural history" and "experimental philosophy" increasingly started to play a role in these learned societies. Agriculture, chemistry, botany, mineralogy, geology, and medicine became topics around which entire organizations pivoted.[113] They were without any question an elite phenomenon, and as such their direct impact was limited. However, as Habermas has maintained, at least the theory - if not the practice - of formal and informal meeting places in the eighteenth century was for members to disregard status and wealth treat one another as equal in status, recognizing only

---

[110] The lectures given by Humphry Davy were so popular that the carriages that brought his audience to hear him so clogged up Albermarle Street in London that it was turned into the first one-way street of the City.

[111] Allan, *The Society*, pp. 434-452.

[112] For a good summary see McClellan III, *Learned Societies*, pp. 371-77. See also the six entries under *academies* in id., Vol. 1, pp. 4-17.

[113] The first agricultural "improvement society" in Britain was the *Scottish Honorable Society of Improvers of the Knowledge of Agriculture* (founded in 1723 and disbanded in 1745 after the rebellion). Ireland followed suit in 1731 with the Dublin Society "to promote the development of agriculture, arts, science and industry in Ireland." The 1750s and 1760s witnessed the founding of such agricultural societies as the Scottish *Gordon's Mill Farming Club*, founded in 1758, by Thomas Gordon of Aberdeen University on the idea that "agriculture ought to be considered as a noble & important branch of natural Philosophy." The Continent was not far behind. The idea of agricultural progress on the eighteenth-century Continent was personified in the work of Duhamel du Monceau, a French *agronome* and "specialist in things English" and that of the German Albrecht Thaer. The Florence *Accademia dei Georgofili* (1753) and the *Société d'Agriculture, de Commerce et des Arts de Bretagne* (1757) in Rennes were followed by the *Académie d'Agriculture de la France* (1761), the Royal Danish agricultural society (1769) and many others. Terms like "useful knowledge" start cropping up increasingly after 1750, in the names and charters of institutions such as the *Akademie Gemeinnütziger Wissenschaften zu Erfurt* and the British *Society for the Encouragement of Arts, Manufactures and Commerce* (both founded in 1754).

the authority of a "better argument."[114] To be sure, the bulk of their work - as in all creative processes - was wasteful, wrong-headed, and ineffective.[115] But the membership shared a desire to make useful knowledge more accessible, an important trend in the intellectual development of Europe that helped to create the foundation of sustained technological progress in the nineteenth century through reduced access costs.

4.4. Access Costs: Economic Factors

The economic issue of the endogeneity of access costs must be confronted head-on. The decline in access costs was not, of course, a purely supply-driven process. The demand for such technical knowledge by the inventors of the time is exemplified by the rise in technical publications and technical essays in general-purpose periodicals which popularized and summarized best-practice research, which did not publish original findings but popularized and summarized (and often plagiarized) best-practice research published elsewhere. The influence of the Industrial Enlightenment came from both sides, the desire of the *savants* to give and the desire of the *fabricants* to take. The only attempt to date to try to estimate the impact of exogenous variables such as population and relative prices on the diffusion of knowledge in agriculture is an important and neglected paper by Simon and Sullivan.[116] Thinking of it in a supply and demand framework may, however, not be the only way to think of the mechanisms leading to the Industrial Enlightenment. An alternative view would regard it as an evolutionary process, in which elements in an entity called "useful knowledge" increased and were "selected" for in an environment conducive to growth and diffusion of knowledge that eventually became economically productive.

In any event, in the closing decades of the seventeenth century and the first half of the eighteenth, a market for "commodified" useful knowledge starts to emerge and became a hallmark of the Industrial Enlightenment. Professional scientists such as John Harris, James Hodgson, William Whiston, and John T. Desaguliers made money by lecturing, consulting, and publishing.[117] Larry Stewart has re-

[114] Habermas, *The Structural Transformation*, p. 36.
[115] This was well expressed by Eric Jones twenty years ago: "Much of the activity of the science subculture, the club meetings, the flooding exchange of information by mail, fell by the wayside as far as material gain was concerned at the hands of tired or dilettantish or unlucky individuals... Nevertheless there was so very much activity... that some seeds from hobby science and technological curiosity were almost certain not to fall on stony ground." Jones, *Subculture and Market*, p. 877.
[116] Simon and Sullivan, *Population Size*, pp. 21-44. They find the growth of publications and patenting to depend on population size and the relative price of food products. The problem of course is that if the relative price of agricultural goods explains publication of tracts on farming technology, how can we explain the increase of works in chemistry, mechanics, and mathematics?
[117] For details on their careers, see Jacob and Stewart, *Practical Matter,* pp. 61-92

ferred to these men as "entrepreneurs of science" who found that they had a commodity to sell that people with money found attractive.[118] During the Industrial Revolution, these markets for consultants expanded and became more formal.[119] Intellectual property rights in useful knowledge tend on the whole to enhance such markets, since by taking out a patent, the inventor placed the invention in the public realm and had an incentive to publicize it rather than keep it secret.

Some Enlightenment figures made a career (and often a good living) out of specializing in building such bridges between propositional and prescriptive knowledge and might therefore be called access-cost reducers or facilitators. Among them was William Shipley, famous for founding the Society of Arts, but also the Maidstone Society, which was expanded later into the Kentish Society for Promoting Useful Arts. Not a very creative or original individual himself, he was highly active in the management of the Society of Arts and in agricultural improvements in Kent where he had a country home, a hotbed of farm innovation. His credo is summed up in his "plan" for the establishment of the Society of Arts: "Whereas the Riches, Honour, Strength and Prosperity of a Nation depend in a great Measure on Knowledge and Improvement of useful Arts, Manufactures, Etc... several [persons], being fully sensible that due Encouragements and Rewards are greatly conducive to excite a Spirit of Emulation and Industry have resolved to form [the Society of Arts] for such Productions, Inventions or Improvements as shall tend to the employing of the Poor and the Increase of Trade."[120] A second was John Coakley Lettsom, famous for being one of London's most successful and prosperous physicians and for liberating his family's slaves in the Caribbean. He corresponded with many other Enlightenment figures including Benjamin Franklin, Erasmus Darwin, and the noted Swiss physiologist Albrecht von Haller. He wrote a book about the natural history of tea and was a tireless advocate of the introduction of mangel wurzel into British agriculture.[121]

---

[118] Stewart, *The Selling*, p. 181.

[119] Such markets often concerned technical consultants such as the great John Smeaton and the "Smeatonian" engineers that followed his example. Soho-trained engineers traveled widely through Britain, dispensing expertise. The clock- and instrument maker John Whitehurst, a charter member of the Lunar Society, consulted for every major industrial undertaking in Derbyshire, where his skills is pneumatics, mechanics, and hydraulics were in great demand; Joseph Priestley worked as a paid consultant for his fellow "lunatics" Wedgwood and Boulton. See Elliott, *Birth*, p. 83. Schofield, *The Lunar Society of Birmingham*, pp. 22, 201. Another striking example is the emergence of so-called coal viewers who advised coal mine owners on the optimal location and structure of coal mines, the use of equipment, and similar specific issues. Sidney Pollard recounts that these consultants were often called to check on one another, which clearly enhanced their credibility, and that they were generally the "fountain-head" of managerial and engineering talent in the engineering industry. Pollard, *Genesis*, p. 153.

[120] Allan, *William Shipley*, p. 192.

[121] Lettsom, *The Natural History of the Tea-tree*. Lettsom was only one of many who translated experimental and empirical data about tea into positive medical recommendations. See MacFarlane, *The Savage Wars of Peace*, pp. 146-47.

Another was William Nicholson, the founder and editor of the first truly scientific journal, namely *Journal of Natural Philosophy, Chemistry, and the Arts* (more generally known at the time as *Nicholson's Journal*), which commenced publication in 1797.[122] It published the works of most of the leading scientists of the time, and functioned much like today's *Nature* or *Science*, that is, to announce important discoveries in short communications.[123] Or consider Richard Kirwan, the living spirit behind the London Chapter Coffee House Society in the 1780s, an Irish lawyer, chemist, and mineralogist, trained in France and close to many French scientists, who brought together scientists, instrument makers, and industrialists, to discuss how science could be applied. Like other facilitators he was an ardent letter writer, corresponded with all the leading *savants* of Europe, even the Russian Empress Catherine. He wrote the first systematic treatise on Mineralogy (1784), which soon was translated into French, German, and Russian. Elected president of the Royal Irish Academy from 1799 to 1812, he contributed to the introduction of chlorine bleaching into Ireland. Kirwan, too, despite being one of the most respected chemists of his age, was no pioneering scientist and fought a doomed rear-guard action against the anti-phlogiston chemistry imported from France.[124] A fifth Briton who fits this description as a mediator between the world of propositional knowledge and that of technology was Joseph Banks, one of the most distinguished and respected botanists of his time whose life was more or less coincident with the Industrial Revolution. Wealthy and politically-well connected, Banks was a co-founder (with Rumford) of the Royal Institution in 1799, a friend and scientific consultant to George III, and president of the Royal Society for forty-two years. Banks labored tirelessly to help bring about the social and economic improvement the Baconian program advocated, corresponded with many people, supported every innovative branch of manufacturing and agriculture, and was the dominant political figure in Britain's world of science for much of his life. Among his close friends were the agricultural improvers John Sinclair and Arthur Young as well as two pillars of the Industrial Revolution, Matthew Boulton and

---

[122] Nicholson was also a patent agent, representing other inventors. Around 1800 he ran a "scientific establishment for pupils" on London's Soho square. The school's advertisement announced that "this institution affords a degree of practical knowledge of the sciences which is seldom acquired in the early part of life," and promised to deliver weekly lectures on natural philosophy and chemistry "illustrated by frequent exhibition and explanations of the tools, processes and operations of the useful arts and common operations of society."

[123] In it, leading scientists including John Dalton, Berzelius, Davy, Rumford, and George Cayley communicated their findings and opinions. Yet it also contained essays on highly practical matters, such as an *Easy Way of churning Butter* or a *Description of a new Lamp upon M. Argand's Principle*.

[124] His *Essay on Phlogiston* was translated by none other than Mme. Lavoisier herself, with adverse commentaries appended by her husband, as well as Berthollet, Monge, and Morveau. In 1791 Kirwan admitted his conversion to the anti-phlogistonist position. Lever and Turner, *Discussing Chemistr.*. See also Reilly and O'Flynn, *Richard Kirwan*, pp. 298-319.

Josiah Wedgwood. He was associated among others with the Society for the Arts, before taking over the Royal Society, which he ruled with an iron if benign hand.[125] He was every inch an enlightenment figure, devoting his time and wealth to advance learning and to use that learning to create wealth, "an awfully English *philosophe*" in Roy Porter's memorable phrase.[126]

Britain had no monopoly on such facilitators, The same traditions can be observed on the Continent, although after 1789 some talented persons were distracted by and diverted into political or military careers. Among the more notable of them was Henri-Louis Duhamel de Monceau, a noted *agronome* and the chief editor of the massive *Descriptions des Arts et Métiers*.[127] François Rozier (1734-1793), another *agronome* and scientific entrepreneur, "a clergyman whose vocation was the enlightenment" in Gillispie's succinct characterization, publisher of the *Observations sur la Physique, sur l'Histoire Naturelle, et sure les Arts,* widely regarded as the first independent periodical to be concerned wholly with advances in cutting-edge science.[128]   Jean-Antoine Chaptal, a noted chemist, successful entrepreneur, and Minister of the Interior early in the rule of Bonaparte, played a major part in the founding of the *Societé d'Encouragement pour l'Industrie Nationale* and "sought to instill a new scientific ideology to educate entrepreneurs in applied science and engineers in business savvy."[129] His *Chimie appliqée aux arts,* published in four volumes in 1807, became the standard work in industrial chemistry in the early decades of the nineteenth century. Another was Alexandre Vandermonde, a mathematician who was deeply attracted to machinery and technology and collaborated with the famed French inventor Jacques Vaucanson. His most famous contribution was to be the "principal organizer" behind the research project that resulted in the first major industrial application of Lavoisier's new chemistry, namely the "mémoire sur le fer" published jointly with the more famous Gaspard Monge and Claude Berthollet in 1786.[130] Less well-known was Henri de Goyon de la Plomanie, who in 1762 published a two-volume work, *La*

---

[125] Drayton, *Nature's Government,* ch. 4. Gascoigne, *Joseph Banks.*

[126] Porter, *The Creation of the Modern World,* p. 149.

[127] For details see Bourde, *Agronomie et Agronomes,* pp. 253-76, 313-68. Gillispie, who also studied Duhamel in some detail summarized his intellectual persona: "his hallmark was neither style nor wit but usefulness." Condorcet, in his eulogy, wrote of him that in his writings he expected little prior knowledge of his readers and composed his works, not for scientists but for persons who would put what they had learned to use. See Gillispie, *Science and Polity.Old Regime,* p. 338.

[128] McClellan III, *Scientific Journals,* pp. 45-46. Gillispie, *Science and Polity.Old Regime,* p. 188.

[129] Jacob, *Putting Science to Work.* An excellent survey of Chaptal's career and importance is contained in Horn and Jacob, *Jean-Antoine Chaptal,* pp. 671-98. See also Gillispie, *Science and Polity.Napoleonic Years,* pp. 611-34.

[130] The paper established beyond any doubt the chemical differences between cast iron, steel, and wrought iron and attributed the differences in physical properties to differences in carbon content without the use of phlogiston. See Gillispie, *Science and Polity,* pp. 438-44.

France Agricole et Marchande, popularizing a number of inventions in the field of farm implements and hydraulics.[131] In Germany an early figure in this tradition was Johann Joachim Becher (1635-1682), an alchemist, engineer, mathematician, physician, and courtier.[132] On the Continent, courts played a far more central role in this process than in Britain, where this intellectual arbitrage was largely carried out by the private sector.

As might be expected, in some cases the bridge between propositional and prescriptive knowledge occurred within the same mind: the very same people who also were contributing to science made some critical inventions (even if the exact connection between their science and their ingenuity is not always clear).[133] In doing so, they not only facilitated the bi-directional flows of knowledge, but also created hybrid practices in which the standards and methods of one sphere were applied to the other. The spheres were always overlapping, but during the nineteenth century some specialization did set in.[134] Among the inventions made by people whose main fame rests on their scientific accomplishments were the chlorine bleaching process, first suggested by Lavoisier's most illustrious student, Claude Berthollet, the invention of carbonated (sparkling) water and rubber erasers by Joseph Priestley, and the "miners friend," the safety lamp to be used in collieries invented by the leading scientist of his age, Humphry Davy (who also wrote a textbook on agricultural chemistry and discovered that a tropical plant named catechu was a useful additive to tanning). As noted already, many of those "dual" career minds seemed uninterested in making money from their inventions, presumably applying the ethics of open science to the diffusion of technology.[135] Incentives were, as always, central to the actions of the figures of the Industrial Enlightenment, but we should assume that these incentives were the same for all. Nor were they necessarily the same in the age of Enlightenment and in the modern

---

[131] De La Plombanie, *La France Agricole,* pp. 342-462. In Bourde's assessment, he combined beauty with truth in his description and depiction of these tools.

[132] Smith, *The Business* characterizes his career as "halfway between the world of artisans and that of scholars, he became an intermediary — both physical and intellectual — between them" (p. 5, see also pp. 71-77).

[133] Kranakis, *Hybrid Careers,* pp. 177–204. One of her examples is the French engineer and mathematician Claude-Louis Navier (1785-1836), who, among others, used the recently developed Fourier analysis to analyze the vibration in suspension bridges, and did pioneering work in fluid dynamics for which he is still famous. His work, and that of other *polytechniciens,* was highly abstract and mathematical, and of long-term rather than immediate applicability.

[134] As I have argued elsewhere, the adoption of the scientific *method* by inventors and engineers in the eighteenth century, was central to the acceleration of technological progress. See Mokyr, *Gifts of Athena,* pp. 36-38.

[135] Richard Kirwan was "philosophically indifferent to money," and William Nicholson was "continually occupied in useful work but failed to derive any material advantages from his labour." (Dictionary of National Biography, Vol XI, p. 229; Vol. XIV, p. 475. Not all scientists eschewed such profits: the brilliant Scottish aristocrat Archibald Cochrane (Earl of Dundonald) made a huge effort to render the coal tar process he patented profitable, but failed and ended up losing his fortune.

age. In our own post-Schumpeterian world, in which most R&D is carried out by corporate entities, the financial bottom line may well be the dominant motive; in an earlier day, when the decisions were made largely by independent individuals, ambition, curiosity, and altruism may have had a larger role relative to naked greed.

5. The Industrial Enlightenment and Economic Growth

The Industrial Enlightenment, thus, had two dimensions. One was to expand the body of propositional knowledge and to steer it in those directions that might turn out to be useful, that is, both to increase research and to adjust its agenda to make it more likely for discoveries to have useful applications. The second was a deliberate effort to reduce access costs to *existing* knowledge. As noted, those two objectives were not independent, but neatly complemented one another. While they were, of course, like the rest of the Enlightenment, confined to a small elite in the West and never constituted a mass-movement, that elite was pivotal in igniting the processes that brought about the Industrial Revolution. Natural philosophers, physicians, engineers, skilled mechanics, and entrepreneurs combined to change the rate and direction in which new useful knowledge was accumulated and diffused.

How much did all this matter? To dwell on one example of the effect of the improved access to knowledge, consider the development of steam power. There is little doubt that the scientific milieu of Glasgow in which Watt lived was indispensable to his technical abilities. He maintained direct contact with the Scottish scientists Joseph Black and John Robison, and as Dickinson and Jenkins note in their memorial volume, "one can only say that Black gave, Robison gave, and Watt received."[136] Whether or not Watt's crucial insight of the separate condenser was due to Black's theory of latent heat, there can be little doubt that the give-and-take between the scientific community in Glasgow and the creativity of men like Watt was essential in smoothing the path of technological progress.[137] Much the same can be observed in Cornwall a bit later.[138] Decades later, the work of Mancunians Joule and Rankine on thermodynamics led to the development of the two

---

[136] Dickinson and Jenkins, *James Watt and the Steam Engine*, p. 16

[137] Hills explains that Black's theory of latent heat helped Watt compute the optimal amount of water to be injected without cooling the cylinder too much. More interesting, however, was his reliance on William Cullen's finding that in a vacuum water would boil at much lower, even tepid temperatures, releasing steam that would ruin the vacuum in a cylinder. In some sense that piece of propositional knowledge was essential to his realization that he needed a separate condenser. Hills, *Power from Steam*, p. 53.

[138] Richard Trevithick, the Cornish inventor of the high pressure engine, posed sharp questions to his scientist acquaintance Davies Gilbert (later President of the Royal Society), and received answers that supported and encouraged his work. See Burton, *Richard Trevithick*, pp. 59-60.

cylinder compound marine steam engine.[139] The growth of a machine culture in eighteenth century involved a close collaboration and interaction between natural philosophy and highly skilled craftsmen, grappling with difficult mechanical issues such as heat, power, inertia, and friction, recently described by Larry Stewart.[140] The same is true in many other key industries, especially chemical and engineering, and while it is not nearly as obvious in textiles, access to developments in one industry inspired and stimulated inventors elsewhere.[141]

Nothing of the sort, I submit, can be detected at this time in the Ottoman Empire, Japan, India, Africa, or China. Floris Cohen, indeed, has argued flat-out that Francis Bacon was a typically European figure, who could not possibly have come from anywhere else.[142] The Enlightenment touched lightly (and with a substantial delay) upon Iberia, Russia, and South America, but in many of these areas it encountered powerful resistance and retreated. Science, ingenuity, and invention, as many scholars have rightly stressed, had never been a European monopoly, and much of their technological creativity originated with adopting ideas and techniques the Europeans had observed from others. But by discovering the fundamental processes through which knowledge can create more knowledge and creating the institutional environment that facilitated these processes, the Industrial Enlightenment unlocked the path to cumulative growth in the West. The hard question that needs to be answered is not so much why this movement emerged at all, but what explains its triumph in the societies we now associate with "the West." That victory was at times attained through violent revolution imposed by foreign occupiers, but in Britain the success of the Enlightenment, on the whole, met little determined opposition, and as a result has tended to be underrated by historians of the Eighteenth Century.[143] With the success of the Enlightenment

---

[139] Thermodynamics not only made essential contributions to the design of steam engines, such as pointing to the advantages of compounding and steam-jacketing but also created an entirely new way of thinking about what thermal efficiency was and how to measure it. Most important, the widening of the understanding of power technology in this direction pointed to what could *not* be done, and for example that John Ericsson's caloric engine (1853) based on the idea that energy could be "regenerated" (that is, used over and over again) was impossible. See Bryant, *Role of Thermodynamics*.

[140] Stewart, *A Meaning for Machines*.

[141] In Leeds, for instance, both the flax-spinner John Marshall and the woollen manufacturer Benjamin Gott had wide ranging interests in hydraulics, bleaching, mechanics, and related topics. In Manchester, M'Connell and Kennedy, one of the most successful early cotton manufacturers were highly technologically "literate" and closely involved with the Manchester Philosophical and Literary society.

[142] Cohen, *Causes of the Transformation*. In a similar vein, Mark Elvin, *Some Reflections*, p. 58 notes whereas Giambattista Dellaporta, who dominated the *Accademia dei Lincei* in its early days, can be compared to Chinese intellectual of that time, he was replaced by Galileo, who can not.

[143] As J.H. Plumb has noted, "Too much attention ... is paid to the intellectual giants, too little to their social acceptance. Ideas acquire dynamism when they become social attitudes, and this was happening in England," compare Plumb, *Reason and Unreason*, p. 24.

program came rising living standards, power, comfort, and wealth in the societies where it was victorious. The stationary state was replaced by the steady state. It is Europe's intellectual development rather than its coal or its colonial ghost acreage that answers Pomeranz's query of why Chinese science and technology – which did not "stagnate" – "did not revolutionize the Chinese economy."[144]

The Industrial Enlightenment insisted on asking not just "which techniques work" but also "why techniques work" (that is, what natural regularities explain their success). The search for higher levels of generality and encompassing natural regularities were inherent in the massive intellectual heritage of Isaac Newton. The influence of the Newtonians grew steadily through Western Europe in the first half of the eighteenth century, often overlapping with the Enlightenment. Access costs to Newton's work was high because, as Voltaire said, to read Newton the student must be deeply skilled in mathematics and many Enlightenment thinkers worked hard to make his thought more accessible.[145] Newton's philosophy of Nature went far beyond his mathematics and physics; it was an essentially empirical approach in which facts and phenomena were primary and any generalizations and principles were constrained by them rather than true *a priori* as the Cartesians held.[146]

The men and women of the Industrial Enlightenment increasingly felt that a research program based on an empirical-experimentalist approach held the key to continuing economic and social progress. Physicists, engineers, chemists, botanists, medical doctors, and agricultural improvers made sincere efforts to generalize from the observations they made, to fit observed facts and regularities (including successful techniques) to the formal propositional knowledge of the time. The bewildering complexity and diversity of the world of techniques in use was to be reduced to a finite set of general principles governing them. The success of such attempts varied enormously with the complexity of the matter at hand.[147]

Posing the question *why* and *how* a technique worked was of course much easier than answering it. In the longer term, however, raising the questions and developing the tools to get to the answers were essential if technical progress was not to

---

[144] Pomeranz, *The Great Divergence,* p. 48.

[145] Repr. in Jacob, *The Enlightenment,* p. 104. Voltaire himself did as much as anyone to popularize Newton's work on the Continent, including his *Elémens de la philosophie de Neuton,* donnés par Mr de Voltaire. Nouvelle edition. Londres [i.e. Paris]: no publisher, 1738. An interesting case in this regard is the career of Voltaire's companion, the Marquise de Châtelet (1706-49), one of the most remarkable female Enlightenment figures, who published one of the more user-friendly translations of Newton's work into French. In a touching preface, Voltaire dedicated his work to this "vaste et puisante génie, Minerve de la France, immortelle Emilie, disciple de Neuton & de la Verité."

[146] Cassirer, *The Philosophy of Enlightenment* pp. 51-56.

[147] Thus Erasmus Darwin, grandfather of the biologist and himself a charter member of the Lunar Society and an archetypical member of the British Industrial Enlightenment, complained in 1800 that Agriculture and Gardening had remained only Arts without a true theory to connect them. For details about Darwin, see especially McNeil, *Under the Banner of Science,* and Uglow, *Lunar Men.*

fizzle out.[148] The way to phrase the question was set out by Newton: he never explained *why* gravity existed, but its generality was the explanation of a bewildering host of real-world phenomena. Priestley and Lavoisier followed the same methodology. It is interesting that the late Enlightenment was willing to concede the depth of understanding for greater effectiveness. The Standard Model of physics, formulated by Laplace at the end of half a century of research was something that gave reasonable and workable approximations rather than had any claims to the "truth." As Heilbron puts it, quantifying chemists and physicists surrendered their claims to "Truth" in exchange for convenience of thought and ease of computation.[149] An instrumentalist approach to propositional knowledge looked for exploitable empirical relations between natural forces and phenomena without wondering too deep and too hard about the metaphysics. As Gillispie has noted, if science was of any help to production, it was descriptive and experimental rather than analytical science. The triumph of that approach was in the revolution that Antoine Lavoisier brought about in chemistry. His *Élements*, complemented by Dalton's atomic weights, created a pragmatic and useable set of tricks and techniques that soon enough found industrial and other applications, yet did not hypothesize about the deep structure of matter and why the observed regularities were in fact true.[150]

Once such knowledge had been established and found to be helpful, it needed to be made available to the men in the workshops. From the widely-felt need to rationalize and standardize weights and measures, the insistence on writing in vernacular languages, to the launching of scientific societies and academies, to the construction of botanical gardens by enthusiasts such as Georges-Louis Buffon and Joseph Banks to teach the knowledge of plants, to that most paradigmatic Enlightenment triumph, the *Grande Encyclopédie*, the notion of the diffusion and accessibility of shared knowledge found itself at the center of attention among intellectuals.[151] Taxonomies and classifications were invented to organize and systematize the new facts gathered, and new forms of mathematical and chemical no-

---

[148] George Campbell, an important representative of the Scottish Enlightenment noted that "All art [including mechanical art or technology] is founded in science, and practical skills lack complete beauty and utility when they do not originate in knowledge" (cited by Spadafora, *The Idea of Progress*, p. 31).

[149] Heilbron, *Introductory Essay*, p. 5. This tradition, of course, goes back in a sense to Newton and is central to the methodologies of mid-eighteenth century chemists like William Cullen and Joseph Black, who insisted on separating empirical knowledge and theoretical explanation — and often did little of the latter.

[150] Lundgren, *The Changing Role*, pp. 263–64.

[151] See especially Headrick, *When Information,* pp. 142-43. Daniel Roche (*France in the Enlightenment,* pp. 574-75) notes that "if the *Encyclopédie* was able to reach nearly all of society (although peasants and most of the urban poor had access to the work only indirectly), it was because the project was broadly conceived as a work of popularization, of useful diffusion of knowledge." The cheaper versions of the Diderot-d'Alembert masterpiece, printed in Switzerland, sold extremely well; the Geneva (quarto) editions sold around 8000 copies and the Lausanne (octavo) editions as many as 6000.

tation were proposed to standardize the languages of science and make propositional knowledge more accessible. To understand these languages, it was realized that increased technical and mathematical education was required, and mathematics teaching and research expanded from the establishment of chairs in mathematics in the Scottish universities in the late seventeenth century to the founding of the école polytechnique in 1794.[152]

To summarize, then, the *philosophes* realized that, in order for useful knowledge to be economically meaningful, low access costs were crucial and useful knowledge should not be confined to a select few but should be disseminated to those who could put it to productive use. Some Enlightenment thinkers believed that this was already happening in their time: the philosopher and psychologist David Hartley believed that "the diffusion of knowledge to all ranks and orders of men, to all nations, kindred and tongues and peoples... cannot be stopped but proceeds with an ever accelerating velocity."[153]

Diffusion needed help, however, and much of the Industrial Enlightenment was dedicated to making access to useful knowledge easier and cheaper.[154] Intellectual factors never operate alone; institutional change was equally necessary. The importance of property rights, incentives, factor markets, natural resources, law and order, market integration, and many other economic elements is not in question. But without an understanding of the changes in attitudes and beliefs of the key players in the growth of useful knowledge, the technological elements will remain inside a black box.

6. Quantifying the Enlightenment

To quantify the Enlightenment seems to violate Einstein's dictum that not everything that counts can be counted anymore than that not everything that can be counted counts. Yet it would be useful to get a measure of the quantitative dimensions of the growth of the Enlightenment as an intellectual movement and to get a

---

[152] See Jacob, *Putting Science*.

[153] Hartley, a deeply religious man, made this point in the context of the diffusion of Christian beliefs, but then added that "the great increase in knowledge, literary and philosophical, which has been made in this and the two last centuries... must contribute to promote every great truth ... the coincidence of the three remarkable events, of the reformation, the invention of printing, and the restoration of letters... deserves particular notice here." See Hartley, *Observations on Man*, p. 528.

[154] The best summary of this aspect of the Industrial Enlightenment was given by Diderot in his widely-quoted article on *Arts* in the *Encyclopédie*: "We need a man to rise in the academies and go down to the workshops and gather material about the [mechanical] arts to be set out in a book that will persuade the artisans to read, philosophers to think along useful lines, and the great to make at least some worthwhile use of their authority and wealth."

sense of the degree to which this was a local or a continent-wide phenomenon.[155] It also might be useful to examine the argument that the Industrial Revolution and technological progress were independent of the Enlightenment because of the widely repeated belief that France was the locus classicus of the Enlightenment whereas Britain was the cradle of the Industrial Revolution, and the two were separate, perhaps even orthogonal, historical developments.[156] The Enlightenment, unlike the Middle Ages, was not a concept invented by historians many centuries later, and while in 1784 Kant could note that the "age of Enlightenment" in which he lived was not yet "an Enlightened age", it was a concept that contemporaries were aware of. Nonetheless, historians today are better positioned to assess where the Enlightenment was of substantial importance. To derive a measure of this, I have relied on the recently published *Encyclopedia of the Enlightenment*. To count the importance of the Enlightenment, every geographical item (country, city, region, etc.) in the index was compiled and weighted by the number of lines devoted to it.[157] In Table 1 below, I include two measures of the Enlightenment: an exclusive measure that counts only the number of lines that mention a country (e.g. "England") and an inclusive measure that counts both measures of a country and of regions in it (e.g., includes both "Italy" and "Tuscany"). The latter count has the advantage including areas that would be under-represented otherwise because they were only geographical and not political concepts in eighteenth century Europe, but it contains some measure of double counting. The data in no way represents a scientific measure of anything except the editorial judgment of a group of modern enlightenment scholars (mostly Americans), but as such it provides us with at least a rough estimate of the regional distribution.[158]

---

[155] A few quantitative assessments exist, though it is not clear how they were arrived at. Thus Richard Herr has estimated that less than 1 percent of the Spanish population "welcomed" the Enlightenment, a tenth as many as in France. See Herr, *Eighteenth-Century Revolution*, pp. 198-200.

[156] For a devastating rebuttal to the first of these two statements, see Porter, *Creation*. For a qualification of the latter, see Mokyr, *Long-term Economic Growth*.

[157] Kors, ed., *Encyclopedia of the Enlightenment*. The procedure followed the extensive index in vol. 4. If an essay on a general topic mentioned a country or region, we counted the lines that discussed that area only. If an article was devoted to a geographical concept (e.g., "Scandinavia in Vol. 4, pp. 20-25) we counted all the lines in that article. The article on "academies" includes a subheading on "Scandinavia" (Vol. 1, pp. 18-19) which was then counted in its entirety. The article on "Education, reform" (Vol. 1, p. 385) has a three line sentence that mentions Scandinavia, as well as France, England and Scotland; those three lines then were entered for all four countries.

[158] Of the nine members of the board of editors, six are affiliated with universities in the US, one in Canada, one in Ireland and one in France. The composition of the board, however, cannot be accused of anti-French bias, as two of its American members are noted experts on eighteenth century France and the French revolution. In that limited sense it is a more unbiased source to study the spread of the enlightenment than Delon, ed., *Encyclopedia of the Enlightenment*, which is written by a preponderant majority of French scholars. The Delon volumes, in any case, did not have an index that was useful for our purpose, so no direct comparison could be made.

Table 1. Geographical Distribution of Enlightenment Concepts as Reflected in the *Encyclopedia of the Enlightenment* (lines per million of 1750 population)

Country	Lines counted (exclusive)	Lines counted (incl. regions)	Lines counted (incl. regs. and urban)	Enlight. Index (exclusive)	Enlight. index (incl. regions only)	Enlight. index (incl. regions & towns).
France	2065	2085	3145	86	86.8	131
England	2348	2362	3138	391.3	393.7	523
Scotland	701	709	1207	701	709	1207
Ireland	210	210	224	70	70	75
Germany	1618	1863	2389	107.9	124.2	159
Netherlands	1042	1066	1236	245.2	250.8	291
Switzerland	471	471	716	314	314	477
Scandinavia	344	436	789	116.3	208	210
Italy	503	700	1600	33.5	46.7	106
Spain	689	689	706	72.5	72.5	74
Portugal	264	264	264	117.3	117.3	117
Austria	391	407	483	142.2	148	175
Hungary	253	253	253	126.5	126.5	126
Poland	435	435	435	62.2	62.2	62
Russia	762	817	831	29.3	31.4	32
Balkans	17	17	17	2.1	2.1	2.1
Greece	282	282	282	161.1	161.1	161
Latin America	448	608	611	32.6	44.2	44.4
N. America	712	1717	1903	323	780.4	865
Ottoman Emp.	182	235	238	7.6	9.8	9.9

The striking thing about Table 1 is, of course, that France's alleged supremacy in the enlightenment movement is not confirmed. Leaving out North America (which may well be biased by the fact that so many of the contributors are North Americans and the publisher is in New York), the image of Table 1 is that Britain and the Low Countries represent a higher level of the Enlightenment than a group of Western Continental countries that includes Germany, Scandinavia, Central Europe, and in which France occupies a less than overwhelming middle position. The importance of France is reflected in the fact that Paris (991 lines) is more heavily mentioned than any other town, but British towns between them covered more lines (London, Glasgow, and Edinburgh alone had 1168), and France's population was three times Britain's in 1750. Adding the mentions of cities does change the numbers a bit (and worsens double counting if we add lines that mention a town to those that mention a country), but does not seriously change the picture.

The Encyclopedia index is of course biased and flawed in many other ways; the many references to "Greece" clearly refer to ancient Greece rather than indicate a hitherto unknown flourishing of the enlightenment in Ottoman-occupied

Greece.[159] It is in no case an index that makes any claims to cardinality. It would be absurd to claim that just because Scotland has nine times the index that France had, it in any shape or form could claim to be nine times more enlightened than France. But even if we do not deflate by population (a process that appreciably weakens France's relative position), the ordinal values of the index suggest that a Franco-centrist position in the Enlightenment seems untenable: even in *absolute* terms (which is what may have counted) Britain still exceeds France, and Germany is but a hair behind. Perhaps, however, the real objection to this measure is that it pertains to the *Enlightenment* as commonly used, and thus obviously does not deal with the *Industrial* enlightenment as defined above. For the purposes of technological change, we may be less concerned with the philosophical or political concerns that dominated much Enlightenment thinking and instead focuses on the growth of science and other forms of useful knowledge, its application to industry and agriculture, and the diffusion of best-practice techniques among the population of artisans and farmers.

To capture at least the first of these, we can look at the geographical incidence of scientific and technological periodicals, the publication of which became increasingly associated with the European enlightenment in the eighteenth century.[160] A useful source is the list of all scientific and technical journals published in Europe between 1600 and 1800. David Kronick meticulously compiled this difficult and often confusing source, and whereas some aspects of his work and conclusions bear re-examination, much of what is to follow is indebted to his data collection.[161] An analysis of these journals is inevitably deficient in that it pays no heed to the number of readers of these periodicals, the number of copies printed and circulated, and does not assess the content beyond Kronick's label.[162] Yet it allows us to measure publication dates, place, and the general topic of the periodical. As such, it gives us a rough but instructive indicator of the "degree" of industrial enlightenment prevalent.[163] As Kronick notes, "by far the largest part of this literature represented not original research or contributions but a derivative form

---

[159] Some of these towns reflect topics of classical rather than eighteenth century interest, e.g. the 174 lines devoted to Pompeii and Herculanum or the 31 devoted to Sparta. Neither of those were included.

[160] See especially McClellan, *Scientific Journals*

[161] Kronick, *Scientific and Technical Periodicals;* Id., *History*

[162] At times, periodical titles could be misleading. The *Ladies' Diary* edited by the engineer, surveyor, and mathematician Henry Beighton was full of essays on mathematical and physical topics including his famous 1718 table on the capacity of the Newcomen engine cited above. The *Gentleman's Diary* edited by Thomas Peat between 1756 and 1780 was similarly largely devoted to the solution of mathematical problems See Musson and Robinson, *Science and Technology*, p. 47; *Dictionary of National Biography*, Vol. XV, p. 625.

[163] The analysis here differs somewhat from the one Kronick conducts himself in that I make no distinction between "substantive" journals, "society proceedings" and journals of abstracts and reviews. My main purpose here is to illustrate the decline in access costs, and journals that published abstracts and reviews served a similar purpose.

of journalism which served the purpose of the dissemination of information."[164] That kind of publication is of course precisely descriptive of an activity that was primarily aimed at a reduction of access costs. There can be little doubt that the importance of periodicals as a means of access to useful knowledge underwent a revolution during the age of Enlightenment.[165]

There are three major findings to report. The first, unsurprisingly, is that the number of new journals published accelerates rapidly after 1650; indeed, the new journals published in the last three decades of the eighteenth century account for 68 percent of all journals published in this period. This is demonstrated in fig. 1.

Second, the distribution by topic, roughly defined, shows some interesting changes during this period. On the whole, Science and Medicine account for about 30 percent each of all journals, and this total remains fairly stable over the entire period (fig. 2). What is remarkable is the steep rise in the journals devoted to political economy and social science from essentially nil to a substantial number in the second half of the eighteenth century, especially in Germany where interest in political economy and the science of government was substantial. The same is true for journals dedicated to technology and engineering (incl. agriculture). This increase comes at the expense of more general and philosophical journals, whose share declines despite an increase in absolute numbers.

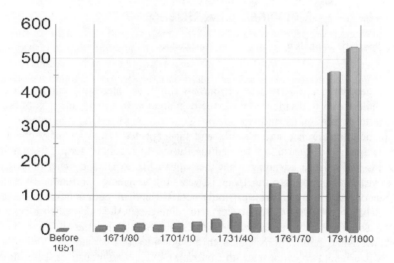

Fig 1. Scientific Periodicals by Year of First Appearance

---

[164] Kronick, *History,* p. 239

[165] Gascoigne's sample of the most important scientists born in the period 1665-1780 shows that a full 65 percent of them published in scientific journals, though there is no real way of telling whether such journals were their main channel. The percentages rises steeply over time: for scientists born in 1600-09 it is 17 percent, for those born in 1700-09 it is 65 percent and for those born in 1770-79 is 85 percent. These statistics entirely exclude engineering, medical and agricultural journals. See Gascoigne, *Historical Catalogue,* p92.

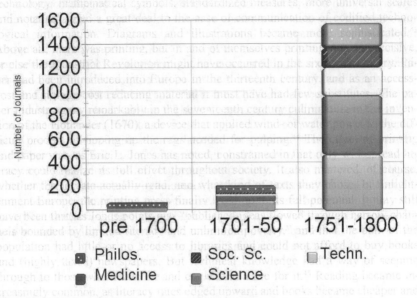

Fig 2. Scientific Journals by Year of First Appearance

The geographical distribution of journals shows an interesting pattern. Europe as a whole seems to divide into three regions: areas with a high rate of publication relative to population (Scandinavia, Low Countries, Switzerland), an intermediate group including France and Britain, and the expectedly low-intensity countries such as Spain and Austria, not to mention Russia. In absolute terms, German periodicals had a large advantage, but their mean life expectancy was only about seven years, as opposed to the 16 or 17 years of the average periodical in Britain or France.[166] Some areas do surprisingly poorly: Scotland counts only ten periodicals, Belgium only seven. This reflects, to some extent their dependence on periodicals coming in from elsewhere. All the same, Scotland outranks France in per capita weighted publications, but both are considerably behind the Netherlands and Switzerland, two countries with flourishing publishing industries (catering no-doubt in part to foreign markets). The distribution of new journals by subject matter does not show Britain as in any way unusual; the only odd phenomenon is the very high proclivity of Scandinavian countries for science and the high frequency

---

[166] This is pointed out by Kronick, *History*, pp. 86-87. Elsewhere (p. 160) he notes that in Germany "the lack of political centralization was reflected in the large number of regional journals, every intellectual center or University town in Germany had its own journal of learned and scholarly news."

of medical and social science journals in Germany. As far as technology, agriculture and engineering are concerned, remarkably enough France was in the lead. None of these results are materially different whether we count journals by first appearance only or whether we weight them by years of survival, except that German periodicals become less important as average periodical life in Germany was substantially shorter.

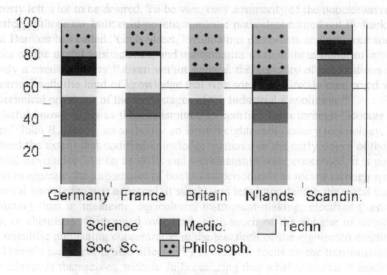

Fig 3. Subject Area of New Periodicals by Country and Subject (in Percent, Weighted)

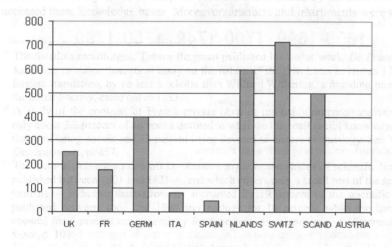

Fig 4. Number of Periodicals per Capita (by First Appearance, Weighted by Years)

Finally, to get a better quantitative handle on the development of the formal institutions that were meant to reduce access costs, I utilize a database that relies heavily on the website "Scholarly Societies" collected by the University of Waterloo.[167] The Waterloo database used covers 200 years (1600-1799) and contains 236 societies founded in Europe in those years. Since the database is still incomplete, it was supplemented by a set of standard works that deal with scientific academies and societies, yielding a total of 349 societies.[168] There is no presumption that the database is complete, though it is likely that any omitted formal societies were of tertiary importance. Counting such organizations without weighting is of course a crude procedure. Yet the movement over time between 1600 and 1800 and the differences in cross section display three trends, all of which are indicative of the impact of the Industrial Enlightenment on European intellectual life.

First, as shown by fig. 5, there is a clear time trend: after an efflorescence in the 1650 and 1660's there is a slowing down of the founding of these learned societies until the 1730s, after which the phenomenon takes off.

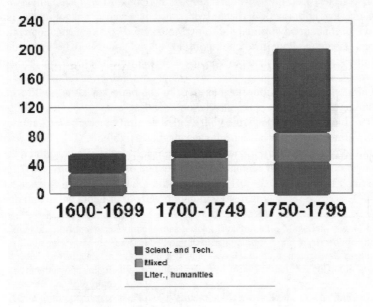

Fig 5. Scientific Societies by Period and Purpose

---

[167] http://www.scholarly-societies.org. The database was put together by its editor Jim Parrott. I am grateful to Mr. Parrott for his advice and assistance.

[168] Among those are Lowood, *Patriotism*, McClellan, *Science Reorganized;* Daniel Roche, *Le Siecle des Lumieres,* and Cochrane, *Tradition and Enlightenment*

Secondly, as fig. 6 shows, learned academies and societies were a Continent-wide phenomenon. Indeed, the advantage of the British Isles in learned societies is not particularly striking by comparison with economically backward Italy and Germany: in the two centuries before 1800, Britain accounted only for 30 societies whereas France had 54 and Germany and Italy counted 31 each. Yet in the second half of the eighteenth century Britain experienced a flourishing of intellectual life as measured by the number of formal learned societies established there. At the same time a veritable explosion occurred in the "small countries" of Europe (Iberia, Scandinavia, Low Countries and Switzerland).

Deflating by population, as in Fig. 7, yields a somewhat different picture. Western Europe's small country and Germany clearly took the lead in this kind of intellectual activity after 1750, with Italy and to a lesser extent France falling behind. Within the "small countries," the literate nations in Scandinavia and the Netherlands experience a veritable outburst of such societies after 1750.

Third, as fig. 6 shows, there is a considerable growth in the number of societies interested primarily in applied and science-oriented nature after 1750, although all three categories experience considerable growth in the second half of the eighteenth century. As can be seen from fig 6, Britain has perhaps a slight advantage in terms of the relative importance of societies classified as "scientific," but this difference is far from overwhelming.

Such numbers, taken at face value, are misleading. In Italy and Germany many of the local societies reflect the political fragmentation of the countries, in which local aristocrats or magistrates had to display their independence, accounting for some provincial societies in small towns such as Cortona, Palermo, and Rovereto. Yet similar provincial institutions are found in France and Spain. It is also true that some societies were of an ephemeral nature and duplicated others.[169] One interesting finding is that fig. 7 shows, oddly, that the number of societies was higher in the second half of the eighteenth century than in the previous century and a half except in Italy; this may indicate the growing importance of private, spontaneously founded scientific societies in the later period: Italian societies were predominantly established by local authorities.

---

[169] A good example is the *Societas Disputatoria Medica Haunienis* (Medical Debating Society of Copenhagen), founded in 1785 as the result of a disagreement between two Danish physicians. It folded two years later.

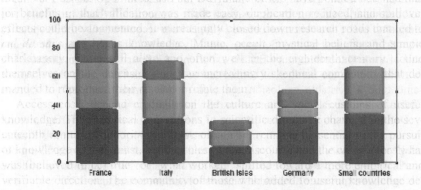

Fig 6. Scientific Societies by Country and Purpose; 1600-1800
Legenda: Grey: Liter and Human; Dark Grey:Science and Technology; Light Grey: Mixed

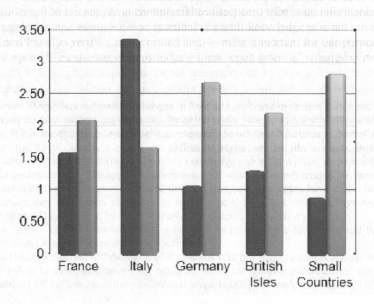

Fig 7. Per Capita Number of Societies and Academies; 1600-1800
Legenda: Dark Grey:1600-1750; Light Grey: 1750-1800

To summarize these findings, two things stand out. The first is that the eighteenth century found a variety of mechanisms to reduce access costs, and that all measures we can find point to a rapid acceleration in the institutions that brought this about. Second, differences among the national styles and emphases among the main societies that later were to constitute the "convergence club" can be discerned, but most of them were secondary to their partaking in the more general movements of the Industrial Enlightenment. There is little in the quantifiable evidence to single out the Enlightenment movement in Britain as being unusual or particularly conducive to economic success. The historical factors that explain the rise of the Industrial West are thus not the same as the one that explain Britain's leadership.

7. Conclusions

The Enlightenment in the West is the only intellectual movement in human history that owed its irreversibility to the ability to transform itself into economic growth. It did so by fueling the engine of economic growth through the sustained supply of useful knowledge and the miraculous ability to apply this knowledge eventually to the nitty-gritty of production in the fields and workshops where the GDP is ultimately produced. It did so also by providing the economies with institutional steering wheels that on the whole prevented them from crashing the vehicle of economic growth into the trees of rent-seeking, war, and other forms of destructive behavior.[170] It is safe to say that the vehicle had a few fender-benders and near misses on the way, and here and there had to swerve had to avoid the semi-trailers of total war and totalitarianism.

The Industrial Enlightenment produced technological progress, but there was no guarantee that it would have resulted in sustained economic growth. In addition to the Baconian program, the Enlightenment produced what might best be called a doctrine of *economic reasonableness*, which became embodied in the tenets of political economy, and eventually influenced policy makers in most of the Western economies. Economic reasonableness concerned issues of political economy such as free trade, improved infrastructure, law and order's effect on commerce, and more efficient, less distortionary taxes. Above all is the Enlightenment idea that when individuals work for their own good, they normally also contribute to the welfare of society, the exception being re-distribution and rent-seeking. It redefined the role of the public sphere in the economic game, pointing to the delicate balance between those who lubricate the wheels of economic activity and those who manipulate them for their own private profit. It recognized the possibility of what we might call today coordination failures and suggested policies to rectify them.

---

[170] On this see Mokyr, *Mercantilism*.

Without institutional progress to complement the technological progress, the sustainability of economic improvement would have been limited and in the end might have been frittered away and eliminated by the relentless erosion of rent-seeking. Needless to say, the growth of economic reasonableness was far less monotonic and irreversible than technological progress. Opportunistic and selfish behavior did not go away simply because Enlightenment intellectuals denounced it. The cosmopolitan, internationalist subtext of the most progressive wings of the Enlightenment was constantly struggling with the traditions of mercantilism and the instincts of economic rivalry and political hostility between the major European powers. As long as the Enlightenment was a movement of elites, who saw themselves as members of the Republic of Letters, it could maintain a cosmopolitan character. By its own logic, however, as it spread to larger and larger circles, nationalist and romantic sentiments inevitably clashed with the enlightened internationalist instincts of the *philosophes*, threatening the great synergy between institutional and technological elements of the Enlightenment.

The interactions between these elements are of course complex and makes positive identification of causal factors difficult. The impact of enlightenment thought on institutional reforms took place with long lags and over a very long period of time.[171] Moreover, such economic liberalization - not to be confused with political liberalization and franchise extension - took a long time till it affected output growth. In any event, its impact was largely in what it prevented, not what it caused. As such the exact effects may be hard to trace with much accuracy. Indeed, the great irony of the European Enlightenment is that the attempts by France to adopt more "enlightened institutions" led to a prolonged military conflicted with the nation that had already adopted many of those. In the process, enlightenment ideas were put on the back burner. After 1815, however, the *Pax Britannica* heralded in a new culture of peace and trade. It, too, was not to last. In the best Hegelian traditions, it created forces that challenged it. Nationalism, protectionism, and economic étatism were responses to the Enlightenment, not an inevitable corollary. The Enlightenment itself can by no stretch of the imagination be held responsible for the twentieth-century horrors that Adorno and Horkheimer and their modern-day postmodern epigones such as John Gray blame them for.[172] One of the oddest phenomena in modern historiography, indeed, are the vitriolic and nasty attacks on the Enlightenment, which perversely is being blamed for modern-day Barbarism but never credited for bringing about modern-day prosperity.[173]

---

[171] Indeed, John Nye has argued that the impact of political economy on trade liberalization in Britain has traditionally been misdated and took place much later than hitherto supposed. Nye, *Wars*.

[172] Horkheimer and Adorno, *Dialectic*. Gray, *Enlightenment's Wake*.

[173] This revulsion has deep philosophical roots in the works of Nietzsche and Heidegger, but the usefulness of the critique to historians interested in economic progress is doubtful. Even left-wing historians are embarrassed by notions that the Enlightenment inevitably led in some way to male-domination, imperialism, totalitarianism, environmental degradation, and exploitation. Eric Hobsbawm notes with some disdain that this literature describes the Enlightenment as "anything from superficial and intellectually naive to a

The central fact of modern economic growth is the ultimate irreversibility of the accumulation of useful knowledge paired to ever-falling access costs. As long as knowledge was confined to a small number of specialists with high access costs for everyone else, there was a serious risk that it could be lost. Many of the great inventions of China and Classical Antiquity were no longer available to subsequent generations. The decline in access costs meant that knowledge was spread over many more minds and storage devices, so that any reversals in technological progress after the Industrial Revolution were ruled out. If the continued growth of the West was ever in danger, it came from the imbalance between rapid progress in the accumulation of useful knowledge and the more halting and ambiguous changes in supporting institutions.

Such an approach to modern growth would imply that the differences between the nations of the West should be less important than their basic commonalities. The point is not so much that there were no national difference in the institutions and culture that generated useful knowledge in France, Germany or Britain, as that when the knowledge was accepted, it was readily diffused within the world in which the Enlightenment had taken root, through periodicals, translations, international exhibitions and conferences, and personal communications. Emphasizing national differences in style and emphasis within the West is to miss the fundamental unity of the world affected by this intellectual movement. In this view of the Industrial Revolution, Britain had a first-mover advantage that was extended by the political upheavals of the Revolutionary and Napoleonic era, but the convergence of technology and income in the later nineteenth century was inherent in the nature of the movement that generated economic growth.

All this leaves in the middle what explains the Enlightenment itself. It surely was no autonomous shock like the Black Death or a Mongol invasion that altered the course of European history without requiring an explanation itself. The Enlightenment had roots in the commercial capitalism of the later middle ages and the sixteenth century. Many of the elements of a progressive society — such as individualism, man-made formal law, corporatism, self governance, and rules that were determined through an institutionalized process (in which those who were subject to them could be heard and have an input) already existed in late medieval Europe.[174] Pre-1750 economic growth created the economic surpluses that made it possible for a considerable number of people to move to urban areas and non-agricultural occupations, including to become full-time intellectuals. Yet despite the stimuli of the Great Discoveries and the technical advances of the fifteenth century, Renaissance Europe did not generate anything like modern growth. Many highly commercial societies of the past, for one reason or another, failed to switch from trade-based growth to technology-based growth. Even the great Dutch prosperity of the seventeenth century in the end dissipated and petered out.

---

conspiracy of dead white men in periwigs to provide the intellectual foundation for Western Imperialism." See Hobsbawm, *Barbarism*, pp, 253-65.

[174] Greif, *Institutions*, ch. XIII-17.

In order for commercial expansion and Smithian growth to transform them-selves into a self-sustaining process of rapid growth something more was required. The ultimate economic significance of the Enlightenment was to bring this about. But what was the Industrial Enlightenment itself? Understanding its intellectual origins is a daunting task. Of the many explanations that have been proposed, it is worth mentioning a powerful argument made by the late B.J.T. Dobbs that when a period of relative stability settled on Europe's social and political life in the later seventeenth century, hopes for an imminent millennium were becoming dimmer, and open useful knowledge with utilitarian purposes (inspired by Bacon) replaced the more mystical and secretive activities of the late Renaissance alchemists. It is also plausible that an impulse to the Industrial Enlightenment came from below, from artisanal writers writing about mechanical arts such as mining and architec-ture in the previous centuries.[175]

Yet such purely intellectual explanations need to be complemented by institu-tional ones. In coming to grips with the oversimplified question of "why there was a European Enlightenment," a starting point is to ask not so much why some peo-ple emerged who elucidated ideas and policies we now consider to be "enlight-ened"as much as why these people succeeded. It is highly probable that men and women with novel ideas emerged outside the West, and would have been part of an Islamic Enlightenment or a Chinese Enlightenment, had these grown to become movements of historical importance.[176] Europe differed in that the seeds of inno-vation sprouted and flourished. In part, therefore, the triumph of the Enlighten-ment was contingent, the result not of sheer accident or random variables as much as of a set of political and social struggles that could have gone the other way. The counter-reformation led by the reactionary forces of Spain was defeated in a set of

[175] Dobbs, *From the Secrecy*. Long, *Openness*.

[176] It could well be argued that seeds of an Enlightenment were sown by Fang Yi-Chih (1611-1671), the author of a book meaningfully entitled *Small Encyclopedia of the Prin-ciples of Things*, which discussed potentially useful forms of propositional knowledge such as meteorology and geography. He was a harbinger of the eighteenth century school of *kaozheng* or school of "evidentiary research," which sounds promising until we realize that they were primarily interested in linguistics and historical studies "confident that these would lead to greater certainty about what the true words and intentions of China's ancient sages had been and, hence, to a better understanding of how to live in the pre-sent" (Spence, *Search for Modern China*, p. 103). Similarly, the great scholar Tai Chen who was "a truly scientific spirit ...whose principles hardly differed from those which in the West made possible the progress of the exact sciences. But this scientific spirit was applied almost exclusively to the investigation of the past" (Gernet, *History*, p. 513). The vast efforts of the Chinese Ch'ing emperors in publishing encyclopedias and compila-tions of knowledge under K'ang Chi and Qian Long, above all the massive *Gujin tushu jicheng* compiled by Chen Menglei and published in 1726 (one of the largest books ever produced with 10,000 chapters, 800,000 pages and 5,000 figures) indicate an awareness of the importance of access cost. It is meaningful, however, that Chen was arrested and deported (twice), and his name was removed from the project and that the entire project was done under imperial auspices. Altogether about 60 copies were made of it, a number that pales in comparison with the 25,000 copies sold of the *encyclopédie*.

wars, that left Europe bleeding and divided but that marked a sizeable part of the Continent that was open for fresh ideas to be introduced in the competitive intellectual market-place.[177]

If so, there was nothing inevitable or inexorable about modern economic growth. Much like the emergence of *homo sapiens sapiens* in the Pleistocene after some 60 million years of mammal development, and not, say, in the long period (50 million years) between the Eocene and the end of the Miocene, a long period of "pre-history" occurred before the dramatic phase transition that changed the face of the planet forever. There is nothing in evolutionary theory that makes the rise of homo sapiens inevitable or its precise timing an explicable phenomenon. While metaphors may mislead, the parallel points to the possibility that radical and irreversible historical change may occur as a contingency. That does not absolve us from the possibility of thinking about its causes — contingency does not mean randomness.

To understand the origins of the triumphs of Enlightenment thought, we must understand the victory of skepticism and rebellion against authority in the centuries of early modern Europe. Aside from the obvious cases of Luther and his fellow reformers, we may point to the growing proclivity of Europeans to question traditions that had ruled during centuries in which original scholarship had rarely consisted of more than exegesis and commentary on the classics.[178] Of course, Francis Bacon himself was a leader among those skeptics.[179] Criticism of authority was prevalent in every society, no matter how reactionary and repressive, but the question of essence must be what explains the survival and success of this movement. Here part of the answer must be sought in the system of political fragmentation and countervailing power in which those who contested the "truth" as perceived by the status quo could normally find protection against the inevitable

---

[177] See Lebow, Parker, and Tetlock, eds., *Unmaking the West.*

[178] Illustrative of this inclination is the career of Lorenzo Valla (1407-1457). Humanist, philologist and professional rebel, most famous for his demonstration that the "Donation of Constantine" was a forgery, he attacked other sacrosanct icons such as Cicero's style, Livy's history, and St. Thomas's theology. He seemed to "delight in challenging established authorities" and his work was "an attempt by a humanist intellectual to change rhetorical study from a process that involved the 'passive' acquisition of erudition into an 'active' discipline that would be capable of engaging practical problems" (Connell, *Introduction*, pp. 1, 6).

[179] In an unpublished work, oddly entitled *The Masculine Birth of Time,* Bacon launched a sharp and severe attack on Aristotelian philosophy. The entire canon of classical thought, from Plato to Hippocrates and from Thomas Aquinas to Peter Ramus were denounced. Their sin was, above all, moral: they were, in Bacon's view, indifferent to the mastery of man over nature, which was the only way to alleviate the plight of mankind "with new discoveries and powers." See Farrington, *Francis Bacon,* pp. 62-68. Ramus (1515-72) himself, an influential Calvinist philosopher, had been similarly disrespectful of accepted orthodoxy, but had the bad fortune to find himself in Paris on St. Bartholomew's Day in 1572, where he was murdered.

persecution they could face.[180] What is unique in the European experience is not what happened to Jan Hus and Giordano Bruno, but that the same fate was not ordained for the many others who shamelessly slaughtered sacred cows in natural philosophy and metaphysics.[181] Skepticism, rebelliousness, and disrespect were the as much taproots of innovation as economic incentives. In the European environment, these sentiments survived largely because their propagators were able to play different political units, as well as spiritual and temporal authorities, against one another. Multicentrism made it possible for original thinkers to move between different regions and spheres of influence, to seek and change protectors and patrons. When some centers were destroyed by political events, the center of gravity shifted elsewhere.[182] Moreover, competition by courts and patrons of science for the "superstars" led to informational and reputational difficulties that in the end may have helped bring about the system of open science.[183] Political fragmentation had its costs, of course, and it was not a sufficient condition for intellectual innovation. All the same, what made the European Enlightenment succeed, was the combination of political multicentricity and sharpening intellectual competition thanks to falling access costs. It did not succeed everywhere, but it did not have to. By 1680 or so this skepticism, though by no means unchallenged, had become sufficiently widespread to become irresistible. It evolved into an intellectual *movement*.

In the end, the Enlightenment delivered perhaps less than what the more naive idealists of the Enlightenment had hoped for. The more ambitious and optimistic schemes of such *philosophes* as Condorcet or David Hartley are not to be confused with the whole of Enlightenment thought and work in the eighteenth century.[184] Humphry Davy, by 1802, had no more illusions that we should "amuse ourselves with brilliant though delusive dreams concerning the infinite improva-

---

[180] Valla himself was protected by King Alphonso of Naples from the recriminations of Pope Eugenius V and the Naples Inquisition. So fragmented were the politics of Europe at the time that Eugenius's successor, Nicholas V, appointed him Papal secretary.

[181] The most outspoken example was the pugnacious German physician Paracelsus (1493-1541), sometimes referred to as a "medical Luther," who in 1527 publicly burned the books of Galen and Avicenna, the medical authorities he despised.

[182] Britain's supremacy in the late eighteenth century may well have benefited from the adventitious events that spared it the fate that befell the scientific and intellectual center of pre-1620 Prague. It seems not unreasonable to speculate that had the Czech Renaissance not been destroyed by the Thirty-years War, it might have evolved into a center of a Central European Enlightenment and the innovative thrust of the eighteenth century might have had a different locational pattern. For a discussion of the intellectual glories of the Habsburg court around 1600, see Evans, *Rudolf II*. The Moravian religious leader and educational reformer Jan Amos Comenius, fleeing his native Czech lands from the Imperial forces, repeatedly found himself in politically uncomfortable circumstances and spent time in Poland, London, Paris, Sweden, and Amsterdam.

[183] David, *Patronage*.

[184] Broadie has noted that the optimism of most Enlightenment "literati" was guarded and that there was no serious streak of utopianism in the Scottish Enlightenment. Broadie, *Scottish Enlightenment*, p. 39.

bility of man, the annihilation of labour, disease, and even death... we consider only a state of human progression arising out of its present progression" and then added prophetically, "we look for a time that we may reasonably expect, for a bright day of which we already behold the dawn."[185] The optimists may have overestimated the ability of people to reason in many social settings, they may have been naive about the objective function that rulers and people of power and wealth were maximizing, and surely even the more cynical political thinkers such as Hume and Smith did not fully realize how strategic behavior and collective action in non-repeated settings could lead to Pareto-dominated equilibria. The hyper-rational assumptions about the perfectability of the human environment and the re-structuring of institutions may seem ingenuous to us.

And yet the Baconian program succeeded beyond the wildest dreams of the natural philosophers and engineers who made the Industrial Enlightenment. The Enlightenment believed that human improvement could be attained through reason and knowledge. But as belief in reason has become more and more qualified in the centuries after Davy, the notion that the growth of useful knowledge is the main-spring of economic growth has proven to be an overwhelming truth. The result has been what Robert Darnton has termed "progress with a little p," distinct from the ambitious utopianism and political sentimentalism characteristic of some Enlightenment thinkers, but it conforms to the economist's prosaic and sober notion that economic growth is not an undivided blessing but the best we can hope for in a second best world.[186] It consists of the modest and incremental gains of pleasure over pain, of health over sickness, of abundance over want, of comfort over physical misery. It is what the history of economic growth is all about.

References

Allan DGC (1974) The Society of Arts and Government, 1754-1800: Public Encouragement of Arts, Manufactures, and Commerce in Eighteenth-century England. In *Eighteenth-century Studies* 7, No. 4: 434-452.

Allen RC, Ó Gráda C. (1988) On the Road Again with Arthur Young: English, Irish, and French Agriculture During the Industrial Revolution. In *Journal 38*: 93-116.

Birse RM (1983) Engineering at Edinburgh University: A Short History, 1673-1983. Edinburgh: School of Engineering, University of Edinburgh.

Belfanti CM (2004) Guilds, Patents, and the Circulation of Technical Knowledge. In *Technology and Culture* 45 (July 2004): 569-89.

Bourde AJ (1953) The Influence of England on the French Agronomes, 1750-1789. Cambridge: Cambridge University Press.

Bray T (1697) An Essay toward Promoting Necessary and Useful Knowledge. London: E. Holt. Repr.1967.

Broadie A (2001) The Scottish Enlightenment. Edinburgh: Birlinn Press.

---

[185] Davy, *Discourse*, Vol. II, p. 323.

[186] Darnton, *Case for the Enlightenment*, p. 23.

Broberg G (1990) The Broken Circle. In *The Quantifying Spirit in the 18th Century,* edited by Tore Frängsmyr, J. L. Heilbron, and Robin E. Rider, 45-71. Berkeley: University of California Press.

Bryant L (1973) The Role of Thermodynamics in the Evolution of Heat Engines. In *Technology and Culture* 14, No. 2 (April 1973).

Burke P (2000) A Social History of Knowledge. Cambridge: Polity Press

Burton A (2000) Richard Trevithick: Giant of Steam. London: Aurum Press

Cassirer E (1955) The Philosophy of Enlightenment. Boston: Beacon Press

Censer JR (2003) Journals, Newspapers, and Gazettes: France In *Encyclopedia of the Enlightenment* 2, edited by Allen Kors, 311. New York: Oxford University Press

Chitnis A (1976) The Scottish Enlightenment. London: Croom Helm

Clark G (2001) The Secret History of the Industrial Revolution. Unpublished Manuscript, University of California, Davis.

Clow A, Clow NL (1952) The Chemical Revolution: A Contribution to Social Technology. London: Batchworth. Repr. New York: Gordon and Breach, 1992.

Cochrane EW (1961) Tradition and Enlightenment in the Tuscan academies, 1690-1800. Chicago: University of Chicago Press

Cohen HF (2001) Causes of the Transformation, and what was Specifically European about it. Unpublished Manuscript: University of Twente, the Netherlands

Cohen HF (2004) Inside Newcomen's Fire Engine: the Scientific Revolution and the Rise of the Modern World. In *History of Technology* 25, pp. 111-132.

Cole AH, Watts, George B (1952) The Handicrafts of France as Recorded in the Descriptions des Arts et Métiers 1761–1788. Boston: Baker Library

Connell WJ (1996) Introduction to Lorenzo Valla: a Symposium. In *Journal of the History of Ideas* 57, No. 1: pp 1, 6.

Cowan R, Foray D (1997) The Economics of Codification and the Diffusion of Knowledge. In *Industrial and Corporate Change* 6, no. 3: pp 595–622.

Darnton R (1979) The Business of Enlightenment. Cambridge: Harvard University Press.

Darnton R (2003) The Case for the Enlightenment. In *George Washington's False Teeth*, New York: W.W. Norton.

Darnton R (2003) The Unity of Europe. In *George Washington's False Teeth*. New York: W.W. Norton.

David PA (2004) Patronage, Reputation, and Common Agency Contracting in the Scientific Revolution. Unpublished, Stanford University

Davy H (1802) A Discourse Introductory to a Course of Lectures on Chemistry. In *The Collected Works of Sir Humphry Davy* 2, edited by John Davy: 321.

Davy H (1840) Sketch of the Character of Lord Bacon. In *The Collected Works of Sir Humphry Davy, Bart. 7,* edited by John Davy, 121-122. London: Smith, Elder & Co.

De Beer G (1960) The Sciences were Never at War. London: Thomas Nelson

Delon M (2001) Encyclopedia of the Enlightenment. 2 vols. Chicago: Fitzroy-Dearborn.

Desaguliers JT (1763) A Course of Experimental Philosophy, third edition, Vol. 2. London.

Desaguliers JT (1724) Course of Mechanical and Experimental Philosophy. XXX.

Desaguliers JH (1734) Jewellers Accounts made Easy. London: printed for the author.

De Vries J, Van Der Woude The First Modern Economy: Success, Failure and Perseverance of the Dutch Economy, 1500-1815. Cambridge: Cambridge University Press.

Dickinson HW, Jenkins R (1927) James Watt and the Steam Engine. London: Encore editions.

Dictionary of National Biography, Oxford: Oxford University Press, 1963, entries for "Richard Kirwan," "William Nicholson," and "Thomas Peat."

Dobbs BJT (1990) From the Secrecy of Alchemy to the Openness of Chemistry. In *Solomon's House Revisited: The Organization and Institutionalization of Science,* edited by Tore Frängsmyr, 75-94. Canton, MA: Science History Publications.

Dougharty J (1750) The General Gauger: or, the Principles and Practice of Gauging Beer, Wine, and Malt. London

Drayton R (2000) Nature's Government: Science, Imperial Britain, and the 'Improvement' of the World. New Haven: Yale University Press

Drelichman M (2003) American Silver and the Decline of Spain. Ph.D. thesis, Northwestern University.

Elliott P (2000) The Birth of Public Science in the English Provinces: Natural Philosophy in Derby, 1690-1760. In *Annals of Science* 57: 61-101.

Elvin M (2004) Some Reflections on the Use of 'Styles of Scientific Thinking' to Disaggregate and Sharpen Comparisons between China and Europe. In *History of Technology,* Vol. 25, pp. 53-103.

Epstein SR (2004) Knowledge-Sharing and Technological Transfer in Premodern Europe, C. 1200 - C. 1800. Unpublished manuscript presented to the EHA Annual Conference, San Jose, Sept. 2004.

Evans RJW (1997) Rudolf II and his World. London: Thames & Hudson

Farrington B (1979) Francis Bacon: Philosopher of Industrial Science. New York: Farrar, Straus and Giroux.

Furbank PN (1992) Diderot: a Critical Biography. New York: Knopf.

Gascoigne J (1994) Joseph Banks and the English Enlightenment. Cambridge: Cambridge University Press

Gascoigne RM (1985) A Historical Catalogue of Scientific Periodicals 1665-1800. New York: Garland.

Gernet J (1982) A History of Chinese Civilization. Cambridge: Cambridge University Press.

Gillispie CC (1980) Science and Polity in France at the end of the Old Regime. Princeton: Princeton University Press.

Gillispie CC (2004) Science and Polity in France: The Revolutionary and Napoleonic Years. Princeton: Princeton University Press

Goyon Henri de la Plombanie (1762) La France Agricole et Marchande. 2 vols. Avignon: no publisher.

Golinski J (1995) The Nicety of Experiment: Precision of Measurement and Precision of Reasoning in Late Eighteenth-century Chemistry. In Norton Wise, ed., *The Values of Precision,* pp. 72-91. Princeton: Princeton University Press.

Grabiner JV (1998) Some disputes of Consequence: MacLaurin among the Molasses Barrels. In *Social Studies of Science* 28, No 1.: 139-168.

Gray J (1995) Enlightenment's Wake: Politics and culture at the close of the modern age. London; New York: Routledge.

Greif A (1994) Cultural beliefs and the organization of society: a historical and theoretical reflection on collectivist and individualist societies. In *Journal of Political Economy* 102, no. 5: 912-941.

Greif A (2005) Institutions: Theory and History. Cambridge: Cambridge University Press. Forthcoming.

Habermas J (1991) The Structural Transformation of the Public Sphere. Cambridge: MIT Press.

Hall AR (1974) What Did the Industrial Revolution in Britain Owe to Science? In *Historical Perspectives: Studies in English Thought and Society in Honour of J.H. Plumb*, edited by Neil McKendrick. pp. 129-151. London: Europa Publications.

Hall WH (1788) The New Royal Encyclopedia; or, Complete Modern Dictionary of Arts and Sciences. 3 vols. London: C. Cooke.

Hankins TL (1985) Science and the Enlightenment. Cambridge: Cambridge University Press.

Harris JR (1992) Copper and Shipping in the Eighteenth century. In *Essays in Industry and Technology in the Eighteenth Century*. Ashgate: Variorum.

Harris JR (1992) Industrial Espionage in the Eighteenth century. In *Essays in Industry and Technology in the Eighteenth Century*. Ashgate: Variorum.

Harris JR (1992) Skills, Coal and British Industry in the Eighteenth century. in *Essays in Industry and Technology in the Eighteenth Century*. Ashgate: Variorum.

Harris JR (2001) Industrial Espionage and Technology Transfer. Aldershot, Eng.: Ashgate.

Hartley D (1791) Observations on Man, his Duty and his Expectations. London: J. Johnson.

Headrick D (2000) When Information came of Age. New York: Oxford University Press.

Heilbron JL (1990) Introductory Essay. In *The Quantifying Spirit in the 18th Century*, edited by Tore Frängsmyr, J. L. Heilbron, and Robin E. Rider. Berkeley: University of California Press.

Helpman E (2004) The Mystery of Economic Growth. Cambridge, MA: Harvard University Press.

Herr R (1958) The Eighteenth-Century Revolution in Spain. Princeton, New Jersey: Princeton University Press.

Hilaire-Pérez L (2000) L'invention technique au siecle des lumieres. Paris: Albin Michel.

Hills RL (1989) Power from Steam: a History of the Stationary Steam Engine. Cambridge: Cambridge University Press.

Hobsbawm E (1997) Barbarism: a User's Guide. In *On History*, 253-65. New York: New Press.

Horkheimer M, Adorno TW (1976) Dialectic of the Enlightenment. New York: Continuum.

Horn J, Jacob MC (1998) Jean-Antoine Chaptal and the Cultural Roots of French Industrialization. In *Technology and Culture* 39, no. 4: 671-98.

Hunter M (1989) Establishing the New Science : the Experience of the Early Royal Society. Woodbridge, Suffolk, and Wolfeboro, N.H.: Boydell Press

Im Hoff U (1994) The Enlightenment. Oxford: Blackwell.

Inkster I (1997) Mental Capital: Transfers of Knowledge and Technique in Eighteenth century Europe. In *Scientific Culture and Urbanization in Industrialising Britain*. Aldershot: Ashgate Variorum.

Inkster I (1997) The Social Context of an Educational Movement: a Revisionist Approach to the English Mechanics' Institutes, 1820-1850. Reprinted in *Scientific Culture and Urbanisation in Industrializaing Britain, 277-307*. Aldershot: Ashgate Variorum.

Jacob MC (1991) Living the Enlightenment: Freemasonry and Politics in eighteenth-century Europe. New York: Oxford University Press.

Jacob MC (1997) Scientific Culture and the Making of the Industrial West. New York: Oxford University Press.

Jacob MC (1998) The Cultural Foundations of Early Industrialization. In *Technological Revolutions in Europe*, edited by Maxine Berg and Kristin Bruland, 67–85. Cheltenham: Edward Elgar

Jacob MC (2004) Putting Science to Work. Unpublished paper, presented to the History of Science meetings in Halifax, NS, July 2004.

Jacob MC, Larry S (2004) Practical Matter: Newton's Science in the Service of Industry and Empire, 1687-1851. Cambridge, MA: Harvard University Press

Jaubert A (1773) Dictionnaire Raisonné Universel des Arts et Métiers. 4 vols. Paris: P. Fr. Didot.

Jenyns S (1761) A Free Inquiry into the Nature and Origin of Evil. Fourth edition, with an additional preface, and some explanatory notes. London: R. and J. Dodsley, pp. 65-66.

Jones EL Culture and the Price of Information. Unpublished Manuscript.

Jones EL (1984) Subculture and Market. In *Economic Development and Cultural Change* 32, No. 4: 877.

Kors AC ed. (2003) Encyclopedia of the Enlightenment. 4 vols. New York: Oxford University Press.

Kranakis E (1992) Hybrid Careers and the Interaction of Science and Technology. In *Technological Development and Science in the Industrial Age*, edited by Peter Kroes and Martijn Bakker, 177–204. Dordrecht: Kluwer.

Kronick DA (1991) Scientific and Technical Periodicals of the Seventeenth and Eighteenth centuries: A Guide. Metuchen, N.J.: Scarecrow Press.

Kronick DA (1962) A History of Scientific and Technical Periodicals, New York: Scarecrow Press.

Lebow RN, Parker, Geoffrey, and Tetlock, Philip eds.. Unmaking the West. Working Paper, University of Michigan.

Lettsom JC (1772) The Natural History of the Tea-tree, with Observations on the Medical Qualities of Tea, and Effects of Tea-drinking. London: Edward and Charles Dilly.

Levere TH, Turner GLE (2002) Discussing Chemistry and Steam: The Minutes of a Coffee House Philosophical Society 1780-1787. Oxford: Oxford University Press.

Long PO (2004) Openness, Secrecy, Authorship: Technical Arts and the Culture of Knowledge from Antiquity to the Renaissance. Baltimore: Johns Hopkins Press.

Lowood H (1991) Patriotism, Profit, and the Promotion of Science in the German Enlightenment: the economic and scientific societies, 1760-1815. New York: Garland Pub.

Lundgren A (1990) The Changing Role of Numbers in 18th Century Chemistry. In *The Quantifying Spirit in the 18th Century*, edited by Tore Frängsmyr, J. L. Heilbron, and Robin E. Rider, 363-64. Berkeley: University of California Press.

MacFarlane A (1997) The Savage Wars of Peace. Oxford: Blackwell's.

Macquer PJ (1771) A Dictionary of Chemistry. Containing the Theory and Practice of that Science. London: printed for T. Cadell and P. Elmsly.

Goddard N (1989) Agricultural Literature and Societies. In G.E. Mingay, ed., *The Agrarian History of England and Wales*, Vol. VI, 1750-1850. Cambridge: Cambridge University Press, pp. 361-83.

Mathias P (1979) Who Unbound Prometheus? in *The Transformation of England*, 45-72. New York: Columbia University Press.

McClellan JE (1981) The Academie Royale des Sciences, 1699-1793: A Statistical Portrait. In *Isis* 72, No. 4: 547.

McClellan JE (2003) Learned Societies. In *Encyclopedia of the Enlightenment* 3, edited by Alan Charles Kors, 371-77 . New York: Oxford University Press.

McClellan JE (1985) Science Reorganized: Scientific Societies in the Eighteenth century. New York: Columbia University Press.

McClellan JE (2003) Scientific Journals. In *Encyclopedia of the Enlightenment* 4, edited by Alan Charles Kors, 45-46. New York: Oxford University Press.

McGee G (2004) Rethinking Invention: Cognition and the Economics of Technological Creativity. Department of Economics, University of Melbourne.

McKendrick N (1973) The Role of Science in the Industrial Revolution. In *Changing Perspectives in the History of Science*, edited by Mikuláš Teich and Robert Young. London: Heinemann.

McNeil M (1987) Under the Banner of Science: Erasmus Darwin and his Age. Manchester: Manchester University Press.

Mokyr J (1998) Editor's Introduction: The New Economic history and the Industrial Revolution. In *The British Industrial Revolution: An Economic Perspective*, edited by Joel Mokyr. Boulder, Colo.: Westview Press.

Mokyr J (2002) The Gifts of Athena: Historical Origins of the Knowledge Economy. Princeton: Princeton University Press.

Mokyr J (2005) Long-term Economic growth and the History of Technology. In *The Handbook of Economic growth*, edited by Philippe Aghion and Steven Durlauf. Forthcoming.

Mokyr J (2005) Mercantilism, the Enlightenment, and the Industrial Revolution. Presented to the Conference in Honor of Eli F. Heckscher, Stockholm, May 2003, revised, July 2004. Forthcoming in Ronald Findlay, Rolf Henriksson, Hokan Lindgren, and Mats Lundahl (eds), *Eli F. Heckscher (1879-1952): A Celebratory Symposium*. Cambridge, MA: MIT Press.

Mornet D (1910) Les Enseignements des Bibliotheques privées, 1750-1780. In *Revue d'Histoire Litteraire de la France* 17: 457.

Musson AE, Robinson E (1969) Science and Technology in the Industrial Revolution. Manchester: Manchester University Press.

North DC (2004) Understanding the Process of Economic Change. Princeton: Princeton University Press.

Nye J Wars, Wine and Roses. Unpublished Manuscript.

O'Flynn N, Reilly J (1930) Richard Kirwan, an Irish Chemist of the Eighteenth Century. In *Isis* 13, no. 2: 298-319.

Outram D (1995) The Enlightenment. Cambridge: Cambridge University Press.

Pannabecker JR (1996) Diderot, Rousseau, and the Mechanical Arts: Disciplines, Systems, and Social Context. In *Journal of Industrial Teacher Education* 33, no. 4: 6-22.

Pannabecker JR (1998) Representing Mechanical Arts in Diderot's Encyclopédie. In *Technology and Culture* 39, no. 1 (Jan. 1998): 33–73.

Playfair W (1786) The Commercial and Political Atlas; Representing, by Means of Stained Copper-plate Charts, the Exports, Imports, and General Trade of England. London: J. Debret.

Plumb JJ (1972) Reason and Unreason in the Eighteenth century. In *In the Light of History*, 24. New York: Delta Books.

Polanyi M (1962) Personal Knowledge: Towards a Post-Critical Philosophy. Chicago: Chicago University Press.

Pollard S (1968) Genesis of Modern Management. Harmondsworth: Penguin Books.

Pomeranz K (2000) The Great Divergence: China, Europe, and the Making of the Modern World Economy. Princeton, N.J.: Princeton University Press.

Porter R (2000) The Creation of the Modern World: The Untold Story of the British Enlightenment. New York: W.W. Norton.

Price D, J. de Solla (1984) Notes towards a Philosophy of the Science/Technology Interaction. In *The Nature of Knowledge: are Models of Scientific Change Relevant?* edited by Rachel Laudan. Dordrecht: Kluwer.

Priestley J (1768) An Essay on the First Principles of Government and on the Nature of Political, Civil and Religious Liberty. London: Printed for J. Doosley in Pall Mall.

Reynolds TS (1983) Stronger than a Hundred Men: A History of the Vertical Water Wheel. Baltimore: Johns Hopkins Press.

Rider RE Measure of Ideas, Rule of Language: Mathematics and Language in the 18th Century. In *The Quantifying Spirit in the 18th Century,* edited by Tore Frängsmyr, J. L. Heilbron, and Robin E. Rider, 113-140. Berkeley: University of California Press.

Roche D (1998) France in the Enlightenment. Cambridge, MA: Harvard University Press.

Roche D (1978) Le Siecle des Lumieres en Province: Académies et académiciens Provinciaux, 1680-1789. Paris: Mouton.

Roderick GW, Stephens M (1978) Education and Industry in the Nineteenth Century. London: Longman.

Rosenband L (2000) Papermaking in Eighteenth century France. Baltimore: John Hopkins University Press.

Rosenberg N (1965) Adam Smith on the Division of Labour: Two Views or One? In *Economica,* Vol. 32, No. 126: 127-39.

Rosenberg N (1976) Perspectives on Technology. Cambridge: Cambridge University Press.

Rosenberg N (1982) How Exogenous is Science? In *Inside the Black Box: Technology and Economics,* Cambridge: Cambridge University Press.

Sargent RM ed. (1999) Francis Bacon: Selected Philosophical Works. Indianapolis: Hackett Publishing Co.

Schaffer S (1983) Natural Philosophy and Public Spectacle in the Eighteenth century. In *History of Science* 21, No. 1: 1-43.

Schaffer S (1994) Machine Philosophy: Demonstration Devices in Georgian Mechanics.In *Osiris* 9:157-82.

Schofield R (1963) The Lunar Society of Birmingham. Oxford: Clarendon Press.

Shapin S (1994) The Social History of Truth. Chicago: University of Chicago Press.

Simon L, Sullivan RJ (1989) Population Size, Knowledge Stock, and Other Determinants of Agricultural Publication and Patenting: England, 1541-1850. In *Explorations in Economic History* 26: 21-44.

Smeaton J (1760) An Experimental Enquiry concerning the Natural Powers of Water and Wind to turn Mills, and other Machines, depending on a Circular Motion. London.

Smith A (1978) Lectures on Jurisprudence. Edited by R.L. Meek et al. Oxford: Oxford University Press.

Smith A (1976) An Inquiry into the Nature and Causes of the Wealth of Nations. Cannan ed. Chicago: University of Chicago Press. Reprint. Oxford: Oxford University Press.

Smith P (1994) The Business of Alchemy: Science and Culture in the Holy Roman Empire. Princeton: Princeton University Press.

Snooks G (1994) New Perspectives on the Industrial Revolution. In *Was the Industrial Revolution Necessary?* edited by Graeme Donald Snooks, London: Routledge.

Spary EC (2000) Utopia's Garden: French Natural History from Old Regime to Revolution. Chicago: University of Chicago Press.

Spence I (2000) The Invention and Use of Statistical Charts. In *Journal de la Societé Française de Statistique* 141, No. 4: 77-81.

Spence J (1990) The Search for Modern China. New York: W.W. Norton.

Society of Gentlemen (1763-64) A New and Complete Dictionary of Arts and Sciences; comprehending all the Branches of Useful Knowledge. 4 vols. London: W.Owen.

Society of Gentlemen (1793) The complete farmer: or, a general dictionary of husbandry in all its branches; containing the various methods of cultivating and improving every Species of Land. fourth ed., London: T. Longman.

Spadafora D (1990) The Idea of Progress in Eighteenth-Century Britain. New Haven: Yale University Press.

Sprat T (1702) The History of the Royal-Society of London, for the Improving of Natural Knowledge. London: Printed for Rob. Scot, Ri. Chiswell, Tho. Chapman, and Geo. Sawbridge.

Stewart L (1992) The Rise of Public Science. Cambridge: Cambridge University Press.

Stewart L (1986) The Selling of Newton: Science and Technology in Early Eighteenth-century England. In *Journal of British Studies* 25, No. 2: 181.

Stewart L (1998) A Meaning for Machines: Modernity, Utility, and the Eighteenth-century British Public. In *Journal of Modern History* 70, no. 2, pp. 259-94.

Stewart L (2004) The Laboratory and the Manufacture of the Enlightenment. Unpublished Manuscript, University of Saskatchewan.

Szostak R (1991) The Role of Transportation in the Industrial Revolution. Montreal: McGill's-Queen's University Press.

Temin P (1997) Is it Kosher to talk about Culture? In This JOURNAL, 57, no. 2: 267-87.

Thompson, William Count Rumford (1876) The Complete Works of Count Rumford. London: the American Academy of Arts and Sciences, MacMillan & Co.

Uglow J (2002) The Lunar Men: Five Friends whose Curiosity changed the World. New York: Farrar, Strauss and Giroux.

Vickers B (1992) Francis Bacon and the Progress of Knowledge. In *Journal of the History of Ideas* 53, No. 2: 493-518.

Voltaire (1738) Elémens de la philosophie de Neuton. Londres [i.e., Paris]: no publisher.

Voltaire (1770) The Age of Louis XV. Being the sequel of The age of Louis XIV, Vol. 2. London: G, Kearsly.

Von Hayek F (1967) The Legal and Political Philosophy of David Hume. In *Studies in Philosophy, Politics and Economic.* Chicago: University of Chicago Press.

Walkingame F (1751) The Tutor's Assistant: being a Compendium of Arithmetic; and a Complete Question-book. In five parts. London: Dan. Browne.

Wallis PJ (1963) An Early Best-seller: Francis Walkingame's 'Tutor's Assistant'. In *Mathematical Gazette* 47, No. 361: 199-208.

Weitzman M (1996) Hybridizing Growth Theory. In *American Economic Review* 86: 207-13.

Williamson JG (1984) Why Was British Growth So Slow During the Industrial Revolution? In This JOURNAL 44: 687-712.

Wood P (2003) Science in the Scottish Enlightenment. In *The Scottish Enlightenment*, edited by Alexander Broadie.. Cambridge: Cambridge University Press.

Young A (1772) Political Essays concerning the Present State of the British Empire. London: printed for W. Strahan and T. Cadell.

Zilsel E (1942) The Sociological Roots of Science. In *American Journal of Sociology* 47, no. 4: 544-60.

Local Systems and Networks in the Globalisation Process[1]

Christian Longhi

CNRS, 250 Rue A.Einstein, Valbonne, 06560, France
longhi@idefi.cnrs.fr

1. Introduction

The contemporaneous process of globalisation has induced major changes in nearly every economic activity, nearly every region or nation. It has evolved across time, but seems to have steadily deepened. Basically, its impact on the localisation of economic activities and on the strategies of firms has been a major concern from researchers to governments. In Europe, this process started in a general context of high rates of unemployment, of deep processes of industrial restructuring. Growing relocation and internationalisation have so given once the image of a de-territorialized economy, of footloose firms, moving their activities according wage or cost advantages. This 'geography of costs' (Veltz 1993) represents certainly a reality, as the processes of relocation constantly show. Concurrently, the development of the information and communication technologies and the related process of digitalisation have been interpreted as the 'death of geography, reinforcing the previous process (Cairncross 1997). As often underlined the information and communication technologies induce increasing codification of knowledge and allow instantaneous and costless transfers of such knowledge across space, unveiling a spaceless economy. The 'new economy' would in some sense coincide with a 'new geography', a huge transformation of the economic landscape driven by costs and underlain by important transfers towards peripheries. Again, this dimension obviously exists, but finally the reality has appeared somewhat very different. The reinforcement of the existing structures of agglomeration has been on the contrary evidenced. Even in Europe, where economic integration should according to the traditional growth theory have enhanced the emergence of a new geography through a redistribution of economic activities in space,

---

[1] This paper is a reprinting already published in Atti dei Convegni Lincei, *Distretti Pilastri Reti. Italia ed Europa* (Roma, 8-9 aprile 2003), Accademia Nazionale dei Lincei, 2004.

the existing disparities *within* the European economies have increased (Armstrong 1995). Since the late seventies, the speed of the convergence process in Europe is slowing down, or even reversing (Graham and Hart 1999). In fact, innovation has been evidenced as a key issue to explain the reinforcement of the concentration of activities in Europe (Fagerberg et al. 1997). Even the Sixth Periodical Report (1999) of the European Commission evidences innovative activities as one of the most important factors contributing to the evolution of the productivity, economic growth and regional development.

As innovation can be considered as the key of competitiveness and of evolution of disparities, the contemporaneous economy can be best characterized as simultaneously globalised and knowledge-based (OECD, 1996), and deeply shaped by the spatial distribution of competences. Indeed, innovation is a collective process that implies a set of formal and informal relations. Its socio-economic dimension, the importance of intangible elements, of tacit knowledge – largely person-embodied and context dependent (Maskell and Malmberg 1999) – suggest that territorialisation of activities is a basic element of the understanding of the working of the economies. According to this approach, technology is no longer given, and easily transferable across space, but is the result of a process of creation of new resources within firms, between firms, and between firms and other institutions, and highly specific to local areas. These institutional structures, which define the process of innovation, are indeed deeply embedded in particular territories. Global and local are, apparently paradoxically, the two faces of the same process.

The deepening of globalisation, from mere relocations to a complex integration of the multinational firms or networks at the world level have shown the increasing importance of the local, of the 'context' as the key of competitiveness and economic development. Different systems of production highly embedded in their region, as industrial districts, have even reinforced during these phases. Far from leading to a 'new geography', the contemporaneous process of globalisation would in fact sustain a cumulative process of reinforcement of existing disparities, of the centres of economic development and wealth creation, in short some sort of lock-in regarding the territorial characteristics of economic activities. The paper will show on the contrary that this apparent stability of the location of economic activities and of the ongoing trends regarding disparities hides in fact deep changes and reorganisation of the whole economic system. It will focus on local systems, as they are apparently the locus of the previous contradiction: when places and locations seem stable, the contemporaneous process of globalisation has in fact induced a deep 'revolution' in their internal and external relationships. Particularly within the economic integration occurring in Europe, the increasing number of linkages of regions with other locations within or across different geographic boundaries is often underlined. In fact the problem is not the quantitative increases of linkages, but their qualitative transformation. The understanding of these transformations is a key to the understanding of the ongoing economic changes and to the definition of coherent strategies of development or related public policies. Section 2 of the paper will thus focus on the meaning of changes regarding local systems: what does 'revolution' can mean in this context ? what is the sense of these global – local linkages and the general emphasis on local development? A prerequisite to the answer of these questions is an effort of definition of the local which allows changes and thus diversity. Section 3 will analyse the role of globalisation in these changes. Again, globalisation is not simply linked to internationalisation; this aspect is perhaps even not the more important. Globalisation is indeed among other elements more deeply linked to innovation, organisation of the production, privatisation, differentiation that impacts through the firms and institutions on the nature of the territorialisation of economic activities. These different dimensions of globalisation will be analysed and highlighted in turn; it will be shown that these different processes lead in fact to the same conclusion: the 'metropolisation' of economic activities. 'Metropolisation' will be shown to be the territorial side of globalisation, which links the global networks of innovation, and the role of local will have to be interpreted in this setting. The section 4 will illustrate these territorial dynamics through the analysis of a particular local system, the 'sticky places'. According to the expression of Markusen (1996) they will be shown to be those places that have successfully driven recombination of their local systems. Section 5 concludes.

2. From Geography to Local Systems

The local level is today often considered as the pertinent level of analysis to apprehend and implement economic development as such, when since A. Smith nations have always been the essential level of analysis in economic analysis. This fact is the result of different basic and deepening changes that affect the world economies since the seventies, and an important renewal of the economic theory, which has in some sense rationalized the necessity of strategies of local development. The questioning of traditional theories has induced the emergence of new economic policies and institutional arrangements to cope with the new views, corresponding to the rise of regions and local clusters as keystone of economic development.

In fact the questioning of the a priori hypothesis of convergence implicit in the economic theory and the spaceless dimension of economic activity is recent, and rests on the developments of the 'new economic geography' born from the seminal works of Krugman (1991). The reality of economic geography shows indeed a flagrant inequality of the distribution of activities across space. The consideration of externalities – technological or pecuniary – has allowed to characterize the concentration of activities as an emergent property of economic activities and to consider effectively space in the analysis: simple rules of individual behaviours can produce complex aggregated results – concentration – which were not a priori contained in these rules. But still, according to Krugman (1991), location is perfectly reversible for transport costs, wage costs or return of capital differentials, or anticipation of firms on these elements. In fact, in his analysis of Marshallian industrial districts for instance, Krugman (1991) highlights the role of intermediary goods or local markets of labour in agglomeration economies and cumulative processes, but excludes technological externalities, because "they do not leave paper traces by which they may be measured and tracked", and are not theoretically necessary to evidence that concentration and specialisation are emergent properties of the economy. The 'geography of costs', as Krugman (1991) suggests, represents certainly a reality, as the processes of relocation eventually show, but does not capture the foundation of the contemporaneous territorial dynamics, basically oriented towards increasing disparities between leading and lagging regions.

The persistence over time of the concentration of economic activities in space has in fact clearly been identified by Marshall, through externalities which cause firms to agglomerate in industrial districts: a pooled market for skilled workers with industry-specific competences; the availability of non-tradable and specialised intermediate inputs, provided by local suppliers; knowledge spillovers and a supportive industrial atmosphere. Knowledge spillovers are usually highly concentrated at the geographical level, and can explain persistence and deepening of concentration. The recognition of the distinctive role of industrial districts on the economic and technological scene became evident with their rise in the Third Italy and the role of the institutional arrangements set up locally on development evidenced by Becattini (1990) or Brusco (1982). And since the nineties, the debates on regional or local development, and more generally on economic development, have progressively been focused on the concept of 'clusters', which is now widely used by people ranging from theoretical researchers to public policy makers. Why such a sudden fascination, after periods where space was considered as neutral? In fact, when crisis was deeply affecting large industrial firms or regions in the seventies, different specific areas of prosperity emerged, from the Silicon Valley to Prato, or Cambridge, or Bologna often independently of implemented economic policies. Paradoxically, it is a work of Porter (1990) on the Competitive Advantage of Nations which will establish 'clusters' as keys of economic development. For Porter (1990), the dynamical processes of productivity growth underlying the Competitive Advantage of Nations are locally anchored. As he clearly stated, growth can be measured at the level of nations, but nations in some sense never produce nor exchange. Their competitive advantage arises from the strength of regions, cities, districts, which are the locus of production. Competitive industries are not evenly dispersed across space, but concentrated in clusters where specialized resources and organisational routines create specific advantages. Likewise, innovation, the capacity of economies to change and adapt to their environments, are deeply rooted in clusters, and strongly related to the organisation of the industry implemented locally. Thus, building on Marshall's concept of agglomeration, Porter (1990) has done most to impose clusters as the pertinent locus of economic development. More precisely, clusters are defined as "geographic concentrations of interconnected companies, specialized suppliers, service providers, firms in related industries, and associates institutions in a particular field, linked by commonalities and complementarities".

Porter (1990) has thus imposed clusters as the nexus of development, and given an economic dimension to territories; still, he does not define precisely the internal dynamics of the clusters nor consider the different forms the concepts could adopt. The cases considered by Porter (1990) are more often defined as local concentration in a particular industry. In fact it has often been asserted that his clusters stand as statistical artefacts defining the relative structure of the specialisations of the economies. The clusters are indeed equally applied to highly different locations or regions, from metropolitan to restructuring areas, which can be misleading when considering local development, as of an optimal policy, a best practice, could be defined. The risk would be to turn back to the growth poles of F. Perroux, which have been equally developed in their time in theoretical analyses or policy implementations, and to their shortcoming, i.e. an insufficient analysis of the socio-economic context and of the organisational and institutional frameworks necessary to induce development. The problem of local development does not indeed amount to concentration of some specialized industries, but regards more their territorialisation.

Some pieces of the puzzle of economic development and the related role of local in the globalised economies seem missing. Apparently, if it appears evident that clusters are pivotal, "... nobody has yet been able to explain why some clusters lose their way, whereas others, such as Silicon Valley, have so far been able to renew themselves"[2], when the reasons for the success or failure of these complexes appear fundamental to promote development. As stressed by Feldman (2001), despite their potential importance and the public resources devoted to them, we have a limited understanding of how the clusters emerge, growth, and transform the economies. The role ascribed to the factors of development – the diamond – by Porter (1990), seems to lag rather than lead the cluster formation. Clusters, or territories, are thus generic concepts which have to be specified in order to allow understanding of local development and design of coherent policies.

Markusen (1996) has made a first attempt to explain why some places are sticky and able to face changes when other fall with the slippery world created by globalisation. Competitive places are 'sticky' not only because of their firms or industries, but also because of the "regional cooperative system of industrial governance which enables them to adapt and flourish despite globalizing tendencies" (Markusen, 1996). Indeed, technological emphasis and static approach seem to characterize the Porter's clusters (1990), whereas the key feature of territories is that they are dynamic; as suggested implicitly by Markusen (1996). The concept of local systems allow to combine the different aspects of contemporaneous development : Technology-Organization-Territory, the holy trinity defined by Storper (1997).

Clusters or territories will thus be defined as evolving, open complex systems. The 'system' provides a basis for finding connections between various aspects of the territory and for tracing its dynamic. Territories are enacted systems; individual agents, key actors, or institutions are the basic determinants of their trajectories; as such, despite underlying common processes, their trajectories are unique, unpredictable, and non-replicable. The nature of the local development appears as an emergent property of the system, i.e. coherent and unexpected macro behaviour of the whole which is not an attribute of the parts, but results from their micro interactions, and which can go with important discontinuities. The internal as well as external interactions of the local systems are essential to the definition of the dy-

---

[2] *The Economist,* 29th March 1997

namical paths. Changes, 'small events' regarding these interactions can result in crisis or re-configuration of the systems (Garnsey 1998; Garnsey and Longhi 1999).

Regarding globalisation, viable clusters are by definition open systems, external linkages are always constitutive of their existence. The main point is indeed the changes in the nature of their linkages – internal as well as external – and of the internal and external networks they constitute. Local systems have to implement those changes to benefit from or simply face the ongoing evolutions. The local system approach highlights finally that there does not exist an 'optimal' form of local system and local development, but specific forms that co-exist and evolve. Diversity is certainly the most important feature of local systems, as the emergent characteristics of the systems are specific to the organisational settings defined locally and to the coordination processes designed to implement economic activities. Still, this continuum of feasible solution can be arranged somewhat in order to grasp the reality and define some categories allowing to classify the local systems in broad categories. Among others, Markusen (1996) has proposed a taxonomy of local systems built as a taxonomy of interactions. The nature and intensity of the interactions are not related to proximity, but to the organisational structure governing these interactions between (local and external) firms and institutions. The taxonomy of Markusen (1996) is organized along four categories, which she makes explicit as presented in the following:

1. *Industrial districts*: Dominated by small, locally owned firms, substantial intra district trade among buyers and suppliers, key investment decisions made locally, long-term contracts and commitments between local buyers and suppliers, highly flexible labour market internal to the district, workers committed to district, rather than to firms, high rates of labour in-migration, unique local identity, high degree of cooperation among competitors, disproportionate shares of workers engaged in design, innovation, strong trade associations, strong local government.

2. *Hub-and-spokes*: Dominated by one or several large, vertically integrated firms surrounded by suppliers, substantial links to suppliers and competitors outside, key investment decisions made locally, but spread out globally, long-term contracts and commitments between dominant large firm and suppliers, less flexible internal labour market, workers committed to large firm, high rates of labour in-migration, unique local identity, low degree of cooperation among competitors, disproportionate shares of blue-collar workers, absence of trade associations, high degree of public involvement in providing infrastructures.

3. *Satellite platforms*: Dominated by large, externally owned and headquartered firms, minimal trade among buyers and suppliers, key investment decisions made externally, absence of long term commitments to suppliers locally, high degree of cooperation with external firms (parent company), low degree of cooperation among competitors, external labour market (internal to vertically integrated firms), workers committed to firms, high rates of labour in-

migration and out-migration, no trade association that provide shared infrastructure, strong local government role in providing infrastructure.

4. *State-anchored*: Dominated by one or several large government institutions such as military bases, state or national capitals, large public universities, surrounded by suppliers and customers, low rate of turnover, substantial trade among dominant institutions and suppliers, key investment decisions made at various level of government, some internal, other external, short-term contracts and commitments between dominant institutions and suppliers, low degree of cooperation, workers committed to large institutions, unique local identity, weak trade association, high degree of public involvement in providing infrastructures.

According to us, the taxonomy of Markusen (1996) fitted perfectly the organisation of territories or local systems that have prevailed over the "pre-globalised" world, according to the meaning we have given to globalisation supra. The globalisation process, the deepening of the knowledge-based economy and the organisational designs it favours, have induced new territorial arrangements. Organisation of the industry and organisation of the territory are indeed closely related, and new forms have emerged from the previous ones. Two main categories can be defined:

5. *Technological districts*: the concept has first been introduced by Antonelli (1989). To adopt the Markusen (1996) standards to define the different categories, technological districts could be characterized as in the following. Characteristics of the industrial district, with large local firms and small innovative firms, substantial intra district trade among buyers and suppliers, key investment decisions made locally, highly flexible labour market internal to the district, strong external linkages, workers committed to district, rather than to firms, high rates of labour in-migration, unique local identity, high degree of cooperation among competitors, disproportionate shares of workers engaged in design, innovation, strong trade associations, strong local government.

6. *Technopoles*: as defined by Luger (2001); again along the work of Markusen (1996), *technopoles* could be characterized as in the following. Regions developed around several interrelated knowledge elements (including but not limited to science parks or research or technology centres), dominated by small high tech firms and large (technology-leading) firms, public and private institutes of research, universities, internal local labour market, workers committed to the *technopole*, rather than to firms, high rates of labour in-migration, unique local cultural identity, high degree of cooperation among competitors, strong external linkages, among firms and research institutes, highly skilled labour, disproportionate shares of high qualified resources engaged in R&D, design, innovation, strong trade associations, high degree of public involvement in providing infrastructures and subsidies.

In these new arrangements, the 'model' of high technology territorial development which has emerged as the absolute reference point and we have here labelled as *technopole* is Silicon Valley. The internal and external firm relationships prevailing in Silicon Valley enable it to be characterized as a 'network region' or metropolis (Gordon 1996). This regional organizational form has evolved contemporaneously with globalization of the innovation process. The structure of inter-firm relationships in Silicon Valley is distinguished by the prevalence of strategic cooperative alliances, within but mainly outside the region, as the institutional base of technological innovation. Silicon Valley's internal dynamism is well-known, and, in addition to labour market and industry-research relationships, is fed by a continuous process of new firm creation, of spin-offs which are often established by workers from large firms (Storper 1993). These spin-offs are created in an already institutionalized regional economy, not only technologically but also in terms of a specific professional culture, with strong specific competences and tacit knowledge. The emergence of new products and of specialized subcontracting enlarges the vertical and horizontal division of labour and sustains the growth of the local industrial complex and the internal market. Finally, the successful spin-offs usually sell themselves to large firms - to capture the innovative quasi-rents - and contribute to their technological renewal (Storper 1993). These important processes of spin-off and sell-out contribute to the creation of regional collective learning, of specific competences within the local milieu.

To sum up, the two last categories of territorial organisation we have defined – technological districts and *technopoles* – are two forms towards some of the previous arrangements – particularly hub-and-spokes and satellite platforms – should evolve to face the contemporaneous changes and secure the viability of the local systems. As already stated, the organisation of the territory goes hand in hand with the organisation of the industry, and the territorialisation of the activities is an essential element of the viability of the process of creation of resources. Local systems are thus places for co-ordinating industrial activities, linkages between organisational and inter-organisational local firm arrangements and external economic systems (Longhi, Quéré 1993). Territories, as technology besides, are never given a priori, they are always the results of the economic process of production and innovation, and thus their shapes – organisational arrangements, internal and external linkages, supporting networks – evolve to face changes. The viability of the local systems depends on these capabilities of evolution.

3. Globalisation: Stylised Facts and Impact on Local Systems

The contemporary economies are the locus of changes which are reported almost everyday, because they are so fast that they impact quasi-immediately the society. The changes are often reduced to technological changes, the emergence of a new trajectory defined by the technologies of information and communication. Obviously, these developments are important and impact considerably on the economy. But technology is a result, the crucial point is the organisational designs set by the firms to innovate, to transform information into knowledge embodied in new products and services, and to institute them on markets.

Most of contemporary economists agree that this deep and rapid structural change is driven by two main forces: the deepening of the globalisation process and the emergence of a knowledge-based economy (OECD 1996). Indeed the nineties have coincided with the emergence of a new form of globalization of activities, in which these changes have specifically impacted the local systems and the nature of the territorialisation of activities. Mostly, internationalisation of exchanges and markets is no more the dominant dimension of globalisation. The 1980s were characterized by a *multinationalization* driven by market processes, the uniformisation of products and processes, in which firms organized themselves into autonomous regional entities. In this phase, the process of globalization was dominated by corporations aiming at globally standardized production systems with a uniform market approach (Gordon 1996; Veltz 1993). Locational choices were driven by the achievement of the most-efficient and cost-effective condition of production and distribution in a world-wide intra-firm division of labour. Such process of globalization was mainly spaceless, in that corporations were not concerned with the specific competencies or capabilities of regions in choosing their location, but were influenced mainly by general conditions in terms of cost and facilities.

The nature of this process of globalization has however dramatically changed in the 1990s (Gordon 1996; Veltz 1993), towards a more integrated phase of the *multinationalisation* of firms. It is no longer mainly oriented towards manufacturing products or supplying particular markets but towards the production of technological innovations. The innovative process of the global firm becomes the heart of the globalization process, and is driven by a network of complementary activities. The increasing integration of the world economy is no longer spaceless. As the process of innovation depends on diverse specific capabilities and knowledge, locational differences in these specificities become important. Locations are not easily substitutable, and choices of location are not driven by general advantages, but by specific advantages of regions in terms of core competencies. In contrast to the 1980s, it is necessary for the global firms to establish strong regional linkages, to plug-in particular local knowledge to benefit from agglomeration economies, increasingly locate small-scale R&D units in specific local systems to augment their knowledge base through monitoring local knowledge bases, a process in which local high-technology SMEs and local research institutes can thus nowadays represent a driving force.

In short, the product *Globalization = Permanent Innovation * Increased Competition* sums up this context, that has induced an increased territorialisation of activities. In our contemporaneous economies, this context of greatly increased competition and resultant need for continuous innovation means that globalization for large firms no longer signifies unification of markets and fading of territories, but a global, interdependent approach to markets and global management of activities characterised by multiple territorial differentiation (Veltz 2000). Paradoxically, the more the integration of activities has increased, the more the local has gained in importance. And the deeper the changes, the more are restricted the strategic locus of location of activities. The movement from internationalisation, *multinationalisation* of firms, to globalisation is equivalent to the movement from diffusion of innovation to globalisation of the innovation process itself.

Internationalisation is thus not the main feature of the contemporaneous globalisation, at least the strategic one when local systems are considered. Innovation, organisation, tertiarisation, competition or cooperation, deregulation, are more important to understand the nature of the process and what is really at stake for the local systems. These different elements will be shortly considered in turn in the following, and it will appear that often the impact is increased *metropolisation* of activities, as if *metropolisation* was the territorial side of globalization.

The emergence of new generic technologies has led to the emergence of new forms of production organization and the development of innovative systems that go beyond the traditional frontiers of individual industries. In these 'cross-border systems of innovation', creation of resources is the result not of the mere adding of technologies, but of the fusion of different technologies into a new technology (Imai and Baba 1989). The process of innovation is no longer restricted within the boundaries of a single firm but brings together different technological capabilities and implies links between different actors, firms or industries, very often dispersed spatially. The process of globalization results in a globally integrated network, especially where new product conception and the innovation process are concerned. The more firm competitiveness depends on innovation-based production, and thus on different sets of competences and tacit knowledge, the more differences of location become important and meaningful (Gordon 1995). Space is not neutral and the corollary of this process of globalization is the increased importance of localization. Globalisation refers thus mainly to global networks of innovation. These networks shape the landscape of economic activities, and appear endogenously fed by the cumulative positive feedbacks generated across its interdependent nodes. These interdependencies can work as driving cumulative processes, or alternatively as exclusion processes of some regions towards others regarding growth and development, depending their belonging to these networks. They can highlight the causes, and not only the symptoms, of the contrasted dynamics between certain territories that have been able to growth and implement processes of change and adaptation to face new environments versus others that lose their way.

Thus, the innovative process is not spaceless. On the contrary, innovation seems to be an intrinsically territorial, localized phenomenon, which is highly dependent on resources which are location specific, linked to specific places and impossible to reproduce elsewhere. These apparently reasonable propositions are in fact in total contradiction to the orthodox analysis of innovation which refers essentially to the adoption of a new but given technology (born from science) which is immediately efficient and available to every economic agent, and thus placeless. Nevertheless, as already stated, technology is not given but is the result of a process of creation of new resources within firms, between firms, and between firms and other institutions. These institutional structures, which define the process of innovation, are deeply imbedded in particular territories. The problem of economic geography is no longer one of locating activities, but of territorialisation: as stressed by Camagni (1995), space, traditionally considered as mere geographic distance, has to be replaced by territory, or relational space, defined through regional economic and social interactions. In the contemporary context of competition and innovation, the emerging 'leading regions' are those regions which have been able to preserve the viability of their process of innovation, to implement processes of change and adaptation to the new environment. It is interesting to note that even before large firms began to restructure their activities, particular territorially embedded local small firm systems, namely the Italian industrial districts, were able to find enough flexibility to adapt to the new conditions of competition and preserve the viability of their system of innovation. This flexibility 'invented' by the territory has been adopted under different forms by the whole economic system.

The increasing uncertainty induced by increased competition and permanent innovation has led firms to adopt the organizational response of 'externalization-cum-disintegration' (Scott 1988) to favour flexibility and reactivity, and has reshaped the geographical structure of industry. Vertical interactions are increasingly most advantageously organised as external transactions between separate firms, while horizontal interactions with R&D or specialized high technology or service firms are increasing because of the increased complexity of the innovation process, which requires more face to face communication because of problems of tacit knowledge transfer and need for contracting. The development of 'just in time' is gone with 'just in task' (Greffe 1999), and suppose the existence of local networks of subcontractors in which the facilities of large or specialized firms can fit into. So firms have developed new interactive modes which are neither market nor hierarchy, but rather constitute network organizational forms characterized by 'relationship contracting' (Powell 1990).

This organizational change has involved major territorial upheavals and a process of economic development which is increasingly localized. The importance of R&D, the need for specialized innovation services have led firms to favour spaces with strong scientific and technological potential, where relevant information and research capabilities can be found. This dynamic has led to the emergence of metropolitan areas as strategic nodes of the contemporary economy. This trend is reinforced by the existence in these urban spaces of large labour markets with a wide range of specialized qualifications. Firms need access to increasingly specific human resources, as well as to external labour markets and competences derived from training in universities and engineering schools. This trend towards *metropolisation* offers firms a compromise between their need for stability, to secure the viability of the process of change, and their need for reversibility of choices, necessary in permanently innovation-driven economies (Veltz 1993). The search for flexibility is thus a search for the reduction of risks associated with basic resources, mainly highly qualified workers and capabilities of mobility, which are often to be found in the large metropolitan areas.

The tertiarisation of the economy complements the evolution of the organisational design set up by firms. The growth of services is characteristic of the modern economy; significantly, they represent in France roughly half of the intermediate consumption of the sectors. This growth feeds the increasing gap between centres and peripheries, as services are essentially an urban activity. But mostly, the 'externalization-cum-disintegration' strategy developed by firms to face changes has implied important organisational upheavals. The externalisation has affected all the activities which are not directly linked with the core competences of the firms. The growth of specialized services meets this process; R&D, marketing, financial strategies, organisational issues are more and more undertaken in close cooperation with specialized service firms. This movement evidences that services do not growth autonomously, but in close association with industry, and characterizes an economy where inter-sectorial relations are more and more important (de Bandt, Gadrey 1994). In this sense, *metropolisation* do not reflect an eventual substitution manufacturing – services, but are the nodes of these relations.

The emergence of new generic technologies has opened the frontier of the firms and led to the significant development of processes of cooperation between firms in all sectors of activity. The increase of the R&D content of products and the enlargement of the diversity of required knowledge have led the firms to substitute multipolar structures or even integrated networks of R&D to the traditional central laboratories of research, i.e. to locate facilities close to competences required by the innovation process, at the world level. The firms' contemporaneous process of innovation rests on diversified networks of knowledge, often spread over different actors and different territories. A consequence for development is the fundamental change in centre – peripheries relationships. In the literature, metropolitan regions are increasingly seen as regional development engines in a globalising world. The assertion can be misleading; in fact it is true only if the metropolitan region is identically reduced to the metropole itself. On the contrary, the metropolitan area is no more the engine of growth of its close peripheries; given the evolution of transport costs and logistics, this proximity it's not worth anymore. It is the proximity of capabilities able to generate externalities within and between the metropolitan networks which is worth. Given the technological evolution and the cross-border nature of the process of innovation, the coherent merging of different knowledge bases is always involved in the definition of highly complex products: Innovation as a problem-solving activity calls for multiple skills and confrontations of non-formalized knowledge, which continuously reshape the solution. Proximity appears pivotal, and the local systems result more geographically restricted to the metropolitan areas and more interdependent. The increasing territorialisation of the location dynamics has led to an organisation of the activity according to a mosaic or archipelago, and underlines the increasing regional disparities which have emerged in the eighties.

In this context of globalisation, the Foreign Direct Investments have heavily increased, but at a significant higher rate since the nineties. Again, these investments are mainly directed towards the more developed areas: the issue is not low wages, but specialized resources and competences. Some investments are obviously made in green fields, but most are dedicated to merger and acquisitions, alliances, embedded research institutes, to plug-in local specific knowledge or capabilities, to allow increased competitive position through innovation, and feed the global innovative networks.

The development of the information and communication technologies, as they are gone with deregulation and liberalisation of the telecom sector, have even increased these trends. The sector stimulates the demand from firms and institutions large users of communication infrastructures and favours private initiatives promoting the development of infrastructures like metropolitan innovative networks. The result can be the reinforcement of the trends of agglomeration of firms, or the restriction of growth opportunities from the introduction of network technologies in existing structure, in which the firms can aggregate to benefit from strong local externalities. The spontaneous development of the supply of telecommunication traces quasi perfectly the hard networks that 'plug into' the Internet from the soft networks gathering knowledge via global innovative networks. Decisions about the location of this infrastructure are largely in the hands of the private sector, responding to agglomeration economies and other 'imperatives' of the business world; the 'deregulated' telecommunications should thus create a strong structuring effect opposed to a balanced regional development (Malecki 2001).

The process of globalization of the innovation system has established metropolitan areas as preferential and interdependent places of creation of wealth. The non-metropolitan areas associated with this process of wealth creation are those local milieux or even micro-local milieux which have been able to join these global networks through their specific capabilities.

4. Globalisation and Recombination

The globalisation process that we have shortly characterized impacts directly on the local systems as it reshapes continuously the economic landscape. In order to find their way in this slippery space, the local systems have to change the local organisational designs of production and exchange processes, to design solutions able to face increased competition and permanent innovation, and to join the global networks underlying the contemporaneous economy. In this sense, the sticky places of Markusen (1996) have been those places that were enough flexible to recombine and adapt to face change, and where the socio-economic context was strong enough to recombine. Regarding the taxonomy of Markusen (1996) all the original categories have been hurt by the globalization process, from the districts to the satellite platforms, and have moved towards new forms or disappeared as coherent local systems. This section will illustrate in turn the evolution of the Markusen (1996) categories through the analysis of different cases, with a particular emphasis on the French situation.

4.1. Industrial Districts

The paradigmatic category of industrial districts has first been affected by the contemporaneous process of globalisation. The districts have often been described as a localized achievement of the division of labour where the competitive efficiency has been proved to be a consequence of the organizational design set by the industrial firms, i.e. networks of specialized subcontractors in vertically disintegrated processes of production (Brusco 1982). As agents are part of the same production process, collective learning processes favour a progressive division of tasks and a progressive specialization among firms, which is nevertheless compatible with a collective appropriation of the results. In fact, the coherence of the self-contained industrial system and the coherence of the socio-economic system are mutually reinforcing themselves, under the constraints of the viability of the local system of innovation, mainly the external market relationships of the final goods produced in the district.

Some examples can be found in Italy, but also in South Germany (Baden-Württenberg) or in different geographical areas (Cooke et Morgan 1998), if factors like the nature of activities, the average size of firms involved, the nature of cooperation agreements, are considered. When in the Italian districts the inter-enterprise relations are based on mutual trust in socio economic communities, in Baden-Württenberg for example, these relations are mainly backed by intermediary organisations like professional association, unions, chamber of commerce. The local industrial context is specialized in automotive industry, with large international firms (Mercedez, Bosh...), and the horizontal coordination of activities is organized by these firms, in order to promote technological transfer and innovation networks across local SMEs. The organizational design qualifying these cooperation models produces new skills and production capabilities, not only due to firm relationships, but also to the original cooperation between local firms and institutions. As a consequence, local institutions (local government, business associations, services centres...) are also a means of improving the co-ordination of local initiatives and of organizing the synchronic and diachronic complementarity of investments made locally. This interplay between firms and local institutions is the source of an efficient organization of local learning processes, and of a control on the functioning of external markets.

The viability of such a local system of innovation depends on this capability to deal with changes in the external market conditions and to adapt to these new conditions in terms of productive locational links among local firms. This trend seems to be working in the traditional industrial districts; as an example, the Emilian economy does not seem to fit any more the so-called Emilian model. The competition faced by the firms from the districts on external markets has radically changed these recent years as a consequence of the reorganization of external large companies. Indeed, the firms have always been able to face the competition from the emergent economies through changes in the range of products, but have finally met the large international firms and changes in demand. The local institutions have taken a lot of initiatives to preserve the competitiveness of the districts. But mainly some firms have adopted new technologies, new products, or new organisational designs to face changes in the competition on markets as well as change in fashion. In the textile districts for example, some firms have decided to adopt new materials (silk) and have organized the change convincing sub contractors to invest into new equipment against the guarantee of long-term relationships (Lazerson, Lorenzoni 1999). Thus, sub-contracting continues to be the dominant mode of organisation of the production, but the different specializations that co-exist now in the districts have led to the emergence of stable vertically integrated networks dedicated to specific process and articulated by a firm leader, far from the 'impanatore' system.

The new context of competition in the markets has motivated important organizational changes, mainly through processes of acquisitions inside the districts, the constitution of 'groups' whose size allows to face the competition. These internal changes have to be complemented by radical changes in the relations with the environment. Indeed, an important process of restructuring or diversification has been implemented in districts by large external firms or financial groups, through acquisitions or organisation of sub-contracting through long-term relationships. But mainly the local firms have succeeded to find alternative modes of coordination of activities to face the changes, and a large share of the activity has been externalised in other regions. It seems that the strategy adopted a long time ago by Benetton, has diffused in all districts. For a while Benetton, with the global externalisation of its production activities, leaving only its key decision making and design functions in its Italian region of origin in the Veneto, was seen as an anomaly, a rare exception (Bianchi 1989).

The same process seeking to 'hollow out' production activities as a way to face the increased competition can be found in Baden-Württenberg. Herrigel (2000) has shown that the division of labour the local firms were embedded in has been challenged, multiple sourcing has been replaced with long-term contracting with smaller numbers of intimate firms. These firms can be local firms, but they need not be. According Hudson (2002), there are increasing tendencies to 'hollow out' the production structures even in the paradigmatic districts: "responding to growing competitive pressures, and taking advantage of the opportunities offered by technological geo-political changes, established or emergent 'lead' firms in these regions are re-organising the organisational and spatial structures of production systems, decentralising much of the material transformation stages of the production process to other locations. As a result, the home regions of these lead firms are increasingly becoming systems integrators, sites of key decision making, design and marketing within wider, spatially dispersed production systems that link a variety of other firms and places". The internal and external linkages characteristics of the districts models have thus been turned upside down by the increased global competition and evolving organisational design of firms.

The success of the Third Italy has induced to find similar areas in other part of the world. Different territorial organisations apparently equivalent to the districts have so been evidenced in France, in Oyonnax, Roanne, Cholet, based on traditional industries and on local context of interdependent small and medium firms. These areas have exhibited an important economic growth in the seventies. The changes in competition evidenced previously have induced difficulties; but, contrary to the Italian districts, the strategies implemented to face the changes have been more individual than local. The socio-economic structure characteristic of the territorial dynamics of the districts appeared inexistent in France. More than districts, the areas are in fact systems of specialized SMEs (Courraut 2000). The Choletais for example, is specialized in shoes and textile industries. Cholet accounts for a third of the national production of shoes, for roughly 100 firms and 1500 jobs. The development of the local productive capacity has been based on interdependent SMEs and local division of labour. But with the crisis, the Choletais has been the locus of a process of increased internalisation of the activities into the firms, of development of internal flexibility through large investments, and increase in the size of the firms. The same trend has emerged in textile, where the growth had led to the creation of numerous small firms and the increase of interdependent relations between small sub-contractors and local industrial firms. Again, the solution to the crisis has not been searched in some recombination of the existing local capabilities. The industrial firms have lost the local identity and have joined large national or international group, moving themselves to subcontracting and leaving their previous local productive linkages (Peyrache-Gadeau 1997). Some small sub-contractors have built local networks and works for external clients. The Choletais has thus moved towards a sub-contracting area, the coordination of the conception and the production of the final goods is externalised in other areas, certainly because the social dimension of the industrial districts was missing in the French SME-systems.

4.2. Hub-and-Spokes

The areas under the *hub–and–spokes* category of the Markusen taxonomy had also to face major changes with the development of the new organisational designs set up by firms. The hierarchical organisation of the production working under this territorial arrangement is not well designed to meet permanent innovation and to produce the flexibility allowing to cope with the main features of the contemporaneous globalisation. Thus new forms have emerged in the 'sticky' places, towards technological districts or technopoles.

Turin is certainly a paradigmatic case of *hub–and–spokes*, or hierarchical urban organisation driven by large industrial firms. The necessity to develop new organisational design already emerged in the eighties with the project Tecnocity supported by the foundation Agnelli, in a territory built on a triangle Turin, Ivrea, Novara including large firms with an important technological potential (Fiat, Olivetti, Stet). According to the project Tecnocity, the territory met a triple coincidence, a strong and specialized industrial context, an important scientific and technological potential, and driving firms, with the capacity to develop territorial dynamics. Tecnocity has underlain the first definition of technological district, defined by Antonelli (1989), as characterized by the existence of a horizontal coordination of activities, cooperation processes regarding internal transactions, and an important integration of functions and actors. In France, Toulouse can certainly best illustrate the transition of a local system from an *hub–and–spokes* towards other forms.

Toulouse is indeed an example of case, usual in France, of traditional *hub–and–spokes*, with a state-anchored additional dimension. Indeed, different distinctive features can be usually associated to the French economy. A first one is the important role played by the state and the national public firms in the development of industrial activity, even in competitive markets, explaining that the 'hubs' are often state-led. A second feature is the huge concentration of economic activity in Paris, and a decentralisation process which has worked as a regional development policy. Toulouse has benefited from this policy in the civil aerospace industries, and has grown as a major centre in France or even in Europe.

The territorial dimension of this state-led *hub-and-spokes* was not restricted to Toulouse, but concerned its whole region, Midi-Pyrénées. Indeed, the regional development has accompanied the state-led restructuring process of the aeronautic industries in France which has been held according to an 'arsenal logic' (Muller 1988), i.e. a highly centralized industrial process driven by the political sphere, the decisions on the programs being made by the ministries of Defence, Air, Finance, and the head of the Air Force, for defence as well as civil applications. Two main basic goals were entrusted to the national firms – mission-oriented national champions – in charge of the realisation of the programs (Muller 1988, Talbot 2000): first to reach the technological frontier, without consideration of markets or airlines needs (Caravelle and Concorde for instance); secondly the public firms had to be the vectors of the regional development policy planned by the government. Aérospatiale played this role in Toulouse, animating a network of subcontractors in the whole region. The region gained increased productive capacities, on a 'fordist' mode; the subcontractors were not involved in the conception of the elements to be manufactured, but on volumes, and supported the peaks of the market.

Different important events have changed this territorial organisation, towards a radically new system. It will be impossible here to go into details given the general scope of the paper, but the main steps related with globalisation can be underlined. First, the emergence of the spatial industry, whose many of the national actors have been located in the region, has changed the nature of the local relationships. Clearly, resource bases did not exist in manufacturing firms, therefore industry has been created at the European level through the programs designed by the European Space Agency (ESA). The cooperative dimension of the activity is thus born with the industry itself, and Toulouse, as a result of the regional development policy implemented by the French government, appeared rapidly as a node of the networks making this emerging European spatial industry. With aeronautics, the regional development policy allowed the industrial takeoff of the region; with aerospace, it promoted the development of a technopolitan area, defined by the interdependent local links between industry, research and training, and services.

Second, different public policy decisions have changed the socio-economic landscape of Toulouse in the late sixties, the decentralisation from Paris of the main research and education institutions related to aerospace activities, and the induced impetus given to the existing local resources; the decentralisation of a 'collective agent', the CNES (Centre National des Etudes Spatiales), which had a pivotal role to generate positive feedbacks from this accumulation of new resources. A knowledge base has grown from the local linkages established between the different actors of the field. The industrial strategy of Matra Espace for instance has been very influential on the constitution of the milieu, and complemented the action the CNES (Dupuy and Gilly 1999). The firm was organized without central laboratory of research and multiplied the local links with the CNES, the institutes of research and the potential subcontractors to solve the complex technological problem-solving activities raised by the space industry. Matra acted as prime contractor of the projects and specialized in integration of systems, implying the coherent merging of the different knowledge bases involved in the definition of highly complex products like satellites. As underlined by Dupuis and Gilly (1999), these problem-solving activities call for multiple skills and confrontations of non-formalized knowledge, which continuously reshape the solution. Proximity appears pivotal: 80 % of the Matra subcontracting has been allocated to local research institutes and firms, essentially in computing services or electronics, but also in firms like Zodiac, for multi-layer insulation equipment for satellites.

Third, the aeronautic industry has faced something like a revolution, with major territorial impact. Different dimensions have combined to reach a radical change: European integration - the development of cooperative programs like Airbus, with a clear market driven strategy -, privatisation of the main French actors first, and constitution of European firms, major organisational change of the production through externalisation.

The development of the Airbus family has induced the restructuring of the activities of Aérospatiale, from an organisation based on largely autonomous sites to a multidivisional organisation (Kechidi 1996). The autonomy of the sites was a heritage of the artisanal past of the activity. The restructuring, started in 1988, has mainly concerned the 'Aircraft Division', in which all the establishments have been integrated through the creation of a 'Direction of Production'. The design and conception departments attached to the different sites have also been merged, and located in Toulouse along with the head offices of the Division. Airbus Industry has in fact 'attracted' all the related divisions of Aérospatiale in Toulouse, the head management staying located in Paris. The design department of Aérospatiale in Toulouse is now the most important in Europe, as it gathers 2200 researchers and engineers in 2002.

The specialisation process induced by the GIE Airbus in the consortium has been internalised by the firm. It obeys the decomposition of the aircraft on subsystems, allocated to the partners depending of their specialization, and the process of standardisation induced by the development of the Airbus family, optimised through flexible factories; accordingly, the division of labour between the sites obeys their technological specialisation. The different components of the aircrafts are thus produced in different sites across Europe, each site offering a particular domain of expertise and a particular specialization. The assembly lines of the A300, A310, A320, A330, A340, and A380 families are located in Toulouse, which is specialized in integration of systems.

This process is gone with the complete redefinition of the subcontracting strategy, from its decentralization by sites to its co-ordination from the Toulouse direction. The new internal principles of specialisation, standardisation, automation, have been applied to the subcontractors, and the internal tools of computer-aided technology developed by Aérospatiale and Airbus extended to the network of subcontractors. The share and the nature of the subcontracting have also evolved. Aérospatiale internalises only the strategic activities, design, cockpit, controls, electronic systems, engine pylons, assembling, but 10 to 40 % of these activities are planned to be subcontracted. The share of the sub-systems based on diffused technologies is planned from 80 to 90 %, and of 100 % for standard technologies (Kechidi 1996). A further consequence of the specialisation is that subcontractors are entrusted with the whole responsibility of sub-systems, from design to production, meaning development of internal capacities of conception, involvement in the financing of programs, in maintenance. A multi-layer organisation of subcontracting is adopted, the first layer firms organising the subsequent levels, with the agreement of the prime contractor; the direct links of the Aérospatiale have fallen from 650 in 1987 to less than 100. The externalisation of sub-systems from design to production has induced new coordination processes between Aérospatiale and the first layer of subcontractors. For example, the Program Meeting Review, i.e. regular bimonthly meetings where the evolution of the plans are discussed and the coherence of the whole process ascertained (Talbot 2000).

The consequence of this reorganisation has been the concentration of the first-layer subcontractors in Toulouse, because of the coordination process going with design activities, and new arrivals of firms, to the detriment of Midi-Pyrénées or other regions, where volume subcontractors are dispersed. Giving the pressure on costs implied by the market-oriented strategy of Airbus, and thus Aérospatiale, these last are indeed more and more under competitive pressure from foreign firms. For example, Lacétoère, first layer firm, subcontracts activities in Poland, Korea, and has acquired firms in Czech Republic. This process is reinforced by the principle of compensation working with the aircraft market. As a consequence, subcontracting covers today the whole countries clients from Airbus; the main partner is obviously the US, up to 40 % of the aircraft is contributed by suppliers from the US.

The competitive and technological levels of firms located in Toulouse have increased. They have been able to diversify their markets; Latécoère, Microturbo, Ratier, Messier, Sextant Avionique, Liebherr Aerospace work also for Boeing or Bombardier. The trend is a transition from a regional system of production to a local system of innovation; only Socata in Tarbes, which produces also light aircrafts, Microturbo in Pau, or Ratier in Figeac, have still a position of important specialized subcontractors of Aérospatiale in Midi-Pyrénées. But most of these subcontractors are located in Toulouse. The position of Aérospatiale and Toulouse as nodes of the Airbus organisation depends on the quality and stability of the local industrial context, and the firm entertains close links with its prime subcontractors. Toulouse is thus the node of global networks characterizing the contemporaneous innovative systems, closely linked with other nodes in Germany, UK, Spain, USA, but with decreasing links with its regional periphery. The privatisation and the creation of E.A.D.S. and other European firms have deepened this process.

Thus in Toulouse, the stickiness of the local system is gone with major changes, from a state-led hub-and-spokes design towards a *technopole*, with strong European or international dimension. This evolution is gone with the *metropolisation* process underlying globalisation; the local system has evolved from a regional dimension (Midi-Pyrénées) to the restricted metropolitan area of

Toulouse. The relations between the centre and its peripheries have changed, and the peripheries themselves have also changed, from the region to international location. The proximity is restricted to the metropolitan area, its design became technopolitan and it is associated to a global network of innovation. The territory has evolved, from the area to the network.

4.3. Satellite Platform

A last category of the Markusen taxonomy that has been turn upside down is the *satellite platform* one. This category covers very different territorial situations, from traditional to high-tech locations. This category is also by definition the most unstable, as the decision centres and the strategic elements of the activities are usually external to the local system. The globalisation has consequently implied major consequences on their activities, whatever the technological situation. Cases as different as Wales and Sophia Antipolis, for example, had to face very similar challenges.

Indeed, Wales can be considered as a *satellite platform*, and the strategy of development set up in Wales to move towards an alternative local organisation is often considered as a benchmark of successful regional policy (Cooke and Morgan 1999). The region has undertaken a process of radical change of its industrial context, mainly led by the Welch Development Agency (WDA) which has precisely measured the necessary conditions to adapt the regional industrial structure to the new economic deal. It has implemented a new strategy of development restructuring first the steel industry though the redefinition of its whole organization (Rees and Morgan 1991). The WDA has also implemented a policy aiming at embedding the FDI in the local context. Though its strategy has always consisted to attract new FDI (in electronics or car industry), making autonomous facilities using unskilled labour, it has moved towards the development of an endogenous industrial context able to enter in specialized relationships with the facilities of the multinationals. This strategy has met the large multinational firms and the organizational changes they were implementing. Sony for example, which has located a largely autonomous establishment in 1974, has moved to 'just in time' organisation, specialized subcontracting, and met the strategy of the WDA. The firm has developed different technological and organisational training programs for its potential subcontractors, inducing the emergence of local industrial capabilities and of local processes innovation. The WDA has been deeply involved in these programs. In the car industry, which has grown as a regional specialization, it has organized linkages between the existing SME and find out their needs in terms of competences to develop. The ACT (Automobile Centre Training) was created to feed this needs (Cooke and Morgan 1999).

The local system has thus been able to move from its satellite platform configuration towards a technological district. Sophia Antipolis started from the same situation of satellite platform, besides build on very different activities, and moved towards a technopole after a deep crisis. Re-combinations can be very costly, but these phases appear in some sense necessary conditions to face changes.

The Sophia Antipolis Park, located in the South of France, on the French Riviera is often presented as a project which initiated a new form of local development, built on the idea of cross-fertilization between research and industry championed by its creator, Pierre Laffitte. In fact the project has grown as a satellite platform, as it has been built on green fields, in a region devoid of industrial or university tradition. The take-off stage for Sophia-Antipolis had thus logically been based predominantly on the location of external organisations on the site which were attracted by the quality of the infrastructure made available to them. There was indeed an infrastructure linked to the tourist industry, the main activity of the area, as the international airport, and the crucial impulse given by the huge public investment in telecommunications. The participation of France Télécom and the creation in Sophia-Antipolis of a 'Zone of Advanced Telecommunications' allowed nodes of a national and international communications network to be located on the site. A welcoming climate and a cosmopolitan tradition made easier the location of high qualified resources.

The implant companies had their own internal resource base but this was but external to Sophia-Antipolis. Resources were elsewhere and were mobilised to provide for new on-site organisations. This form of development resulted in minimal interaction and interdependence between the organisations on the site. Decision centres and industrial strategy making were external to Sophia-Antipolis itself. After the first period where large public sector companies and laboratories were introduced onto the site, linked to the French decentralisation movement, new locations emerged as the outcome of a commercialisation strategy for the science park based on a major international marketing effort, mainly directed at the USA. Large multinational companies, mostly American, adopted Sophia-Antipolis either as their European administrative base or as an R&D centre charged with adapting their products to European markets. The availability of high-quality telecommunication infrastructures able to support hubs and Nice international airport explain most of these location decisions. These international firms have made major investments, establishing self-contained entities able to operate without local linkages.

The mass effect created by the process of accumulation of external activities has obviously resulted in internal dynamics and positive feedbacks in Sophia-Antipolis, which will be analysed later, but basically the project has grown as a system directed from outside, rich in external connections but deprived of internal linkages. Nevertheless, a process reinforcing early expansion set in, as companies chose to locate in Sophia-Antipolis not because resources were available there to mobilise but because of strategic considerations relating to the sitting of European operations. This process drew upon an 'image effect that soon built up around the experiment: high tech image of modernity, collegiality, and enhanced productivity. But mainly Sophia-Antipolis is the result of a cumulative process somewhat without direction, set off by an active commercial policy but without any sound strategy for technological development. The site grew as a periphery, a system directed from outside according to a corporate logic independent of any considerations of economic exchange with other economic actors on the site. The success of the project in terms of numbers of companies and the rapid expansion are wit-

nessed by the success of these corporate strategies, and the eighties are characterized by an important process of growth, feed by new locations. This first phase
will be followed by a severe slowdown to be discussed further. Independently of
the nature of the economic relations characterising the site, the process of accumulation initially resulted in the emergence of three dominant poles of technological
activity which were shaped by the history of the project, by the role of the site in
attracting the first implants and by early investment decisions of the public authorities: the computer science, telecommunications and electronics pole, which
provided the impetus for the growth of the project, the life sciences and health sciences pole, and the natural sciences, environment pole.

Limits to growth in Sophia Antipolis were closely linked to the initial conditions of the project, i.e. lack of a local labour market, lack of endogenous creation
of resources, of high tech SMEs or specialized services, which are often presented
as necessary conditions of technological development. Nevertheless, the accumulation of economic activities on site have triggered positive processes and caught
up effects which smoothed progressively these limits until the beginning of the
nineties, with significant developments like the sitting in Sophia-Antipolis of research institutes and doctoral studies of the University of Nice in 1986. Nevertheless a crisis emerged in the beginning nineties (Longhi 1999).

The shocks that characterized the early 1990s have been of considerable importance for Sophia-Antipolis because of the importance in the area of large multinational firms, which altered corporate strategies in response to new pressures. This
change has been critical for Sophia-Antipolis, as its process of development was
especially influenced by the behaviour of large international firms. The nineties
brought on new forms of globalization we have analysed supra. The crisis of
Sophia-Antipolis in the early 1990s corresponds to this change in the nature of the
process of globalization. The global restructuring of industry was associated with
a substantial down-sizing of the units of large international corporations on the
site, with, at the same time, an interruption in the flow into the industrial park of
new units of large technological firms. The strategy pursued by Sophia Antipolis,
based on the attraction of new resources, was clearly a strategy for coping with the
1980s but one which appeared to have a negative impact in the 1990s. In the eighties, the attractiveness of Sophia Antipolis for inward investments gave it a comparative advantage over alternative locations. Corporations were not concerned
with the specific competencies or capabilities of regions in choosing their location,
but were influenced mainly by general conditions in terms of costs and facilities.
As we have seen, Sophia-Antipolis was well-endowed in this respect. The changes
resulted in the location of more conventional activities without any high-
technology or technological content, and in the depreciation of the park's image. A
new strategy of development, based on local resources and competencies, had to
be generated. The accumulation of resources created during the history of Sophia
Antipolis has resulted in the emergence of local specificities which could allow a
new strategy of development. Recent growth in Sophia-Antipolis based, on activities at the heart of the global innovative process, seems to attest the capability of
adaptation of the local context. Contrary to the original design of the project, these
new trends have emerged without the involvement of a central authority or clearly

defined strategy. In fact the absence of public response to the crisis has induced the emergence of collective initiatives on the industrial park, and of new internal relationships.

Indeed, after three years of instability, different trends have emerged. Mainly, the unexpected consequence of the crises has been a change in the regime of growth, from exogenous to endogenous, and the development of local relations between firms or firms and research institutions, and the emergence of collective learning in some technological activities. A main actor of this process has been the professional associations existing in the park, which stood for the absence of clear public strategy to face the crises. These associations are particularly concerned with technologies and the building of networks and relationships. The Telecom Valley Association for example was the first initiative in this direction; created by Texas Instruments and France Telecom, it now includes all local telecommunication organisations, both public and private, large and small, and aim to promote the development of Sophia-Antipolis as a strategic centre of telecommunications activity in Europe. Indeed, the main institutions defining the European standards for telecommunications (ETSI) and internet (WWW) are located in Sophia-Antipolis, which is thus at the heart of the innovative process and of the information system in these technologies.

The processes of interactions have been tremendously reinforced by the creation of these different professional association and the new goals they set up. The growth potential of Sophia Antipolis certainly lies in the multiplication of such self-organizing processes. The project had certainly reached a threshold after the first phase of growth, and it is through a radical change in the nature of the local agent relationships that this threshold could be cleared. The future of the experiment depends not so much on its capacity to attract new resources – even if this process is important as underlined further – as on its capacity to induce institutional arrangements making it possible to take advantage of the local resources made available by past investment.

Another important trend to be noticed is an important movement of creation of new SMEs, which was lacking in Sophia-Antipolis. As stressed by Keeble et al. (1998), the creation of new high-technology SMEs and spin-offs is a "major process whereby research ideas, technological innovations and expertise are diffused and shared within a region, rather than being confined and internalised within a single, secretive firm". This process is indeed conducive to collective learning and local positive feedback. Paradoxically, the most important movement of creation of new SMEs correspond to the major slowdown of the project in terms of employment growth at the beginning of the nineties, and to the process of downsizing and outsourcing induced by large firms. The number of firms increased significantly during the crisis. Downsizing resulted in the diffusion of capabilities up to there internalized in the large firms through the local labour market, and not in a loss of resources. Indeed despite the weakness of linkages between firms or institutions a strong 'sophipolitan milieu' effect has always existed for the people involved in the project, which have tried to find local solution to the crisis. A lot of 'forced' spin-offs from large firms have emerged, which have helped to diffuse technological capabilities and competences locally. These firms, created by former engineers of large firms (Thomson, Texas Instruments, DEC) reluctant to leave the project when confronted to 'downsizing', have often subcontracting relationships with their parents, and important informal networking relations between them, to share problems and solutions. The fact that most of these SMEs have been able to adapt and grow has enhanced the movement. Recently, numerous local start-ups and spin-offs have emerged in the software industry, multimedia, and telecommunication services. Correspondingly, this process has been helped by the emergence of a local labour market, allowing skilled labour mobility, diffusion of embodied and tacit expertise and technological know-how to feed local development.

The last important change concerns the key actors of the development of Sophia-Antipolis, i.e. the large firms. As we have emphasized, the growth of Sophia Antipolis has resulted from the coincidence of a supply of general advantages (physical infrastructures, climate...) and the needs induced by the *multinationalisation* of large firms aimed at organizing their European operations. The attractiveness is no more only dependent of physical infrastructures, but mainly from specific capabilities and human infrastructures. The location of large firms is nevertheless still crucial to the project, but it takes a different sense, it eventually validate its technological and innovative potential and its position of 'pole of excellence' in some fields, and constitutes opportunities for the existing local labour market. Indeed, the arrival of new firms does not now involve neither huge investments nor simply adaptation of existing products or services. The new firms usually settle in the park as tenants with small units and grow locally drawing on local capabilities and on the existing local labour market to develop their innovative activities.

Connection to markets has always worked as the key for the development of Sophia Antipolis, and crisis has resulted in the local system from a change in the working of these markets in the nineties, inducing a growing discrepancy between the Sophia Antipolis institutional arrangements devoted to innovation and the needs of globalised high tech markets. In the contemporaneous process of innovation, the challenge for Sophia Antipolis was to enter the global networks set up by the firms to sustain their innovative activities, and which links large and small and specialized high tech firms as well as public research institutions. The emergence of a new regime of growth and of new institutional arrangements after a crisis of adaptation show that the resource base accumulated in the eighties was sufficient to face the shocks. Mainly collective initiatives of local actors have supplemented absent public policies, and set off the emergence of an innovative milieu and collective learning. But the shocks of the nineties have resulted in an unbalanced local system, in which information and telecom activities have been able to adapt to the new environment and to regenerate growth while other activities (heath sciences) are still locked into the previous regime and failing to fulfil their potential. But still, the growth of Sophia Antipolis has been very important since its creation, along a logistic curve showing two similar quantitative trends interrupted by the crisis of the nineties. Nevertheless, the economic model feeding these identical quantitative trends are symmetrically opposed: the first is based on a *satellite plat-*

form exogenously driven regime, when the second is organized as a technopolitan area, feed by endogenous process.

5. Conclusions

"As [the] changes have begun to run their course, it has become increasingly apparent that the city on the narrow sense is less an appropriate or viable unit of local social organisation that city-regions or regional networks of cities" (Scott et al. 2001). In a sense, Scott et al. (2001) emphasize that close or self-contained local systems are no more viable in the contemporaneous economic dynamics. These dynamics are indeed built on a generalized local – global interdependence, articulated through global networks of innovation. *Metropolisation* appears as a process embodying this articulation, gathering the strategic functions and the strategic areas through interdependent relations. The established local systems have been challenged by this evolution and the paper shows that in this global reorganisation of the economic activity, 'sticky places' have been those places able to implement huge recombination of their local systems, of the territorial organisation underlying their activity. Implementation has usually been self-organized, with rare exceptions. As underlined by Lundvall (2001), if the contemporaneous economies are effectively characterized as globalised and knowledge-based, the more important point is not the intensive use of knowledge, but rather that knowledge becomes obsolete more rapidly than before. The acceleration of the rate of change going with permanent innovation implies that knowledge and capabilities are exposed to rapid depreciation. Learning, recombination of the local systems to generate or gain access to new capabilities is thus the key of local development.

In this process, the perimeter of the local systems has been reduced. In terms of economic functions first, with a concentration on the strategic functions regarding its specificity. In terms of territory second, the system being more and more restricted to the metropolitan or centre areas, when in the past it fed and worked as an engine of growth for the whole regions including these strategic areas. The result is a dramatic change in the relations centres – peripheries, which call for a renewal of regional policies.

References

Antonelli C (1989) Technological district and regional innovative capacity. In *Revue d'Economie Régionale et Urbaine*, 5.

Armstrong J (1995) Convergence among regions of the European Union, 1959-1990. In *Papers in Regional Science*, 74.

Barro R, Sala MX (1991) Convergence across states and regions. In *Brookings Papers on Economic Activity*, 1.

Beccattini G (1990) The Marshallian industrial district as a socio-economic notion. In Pyke F. *et al,. Industrial Districts and Inter-firm Co-operation in Italy*, ILO, Geneva.

Bianchi P (1989) Industrial restructruring within an Italian perspective. In *Laboratorio di Politica Industriale*, W.P. 3, Bologna.

Brusco S (1982) The emilian model: productive decentralisation and social integration. In *Cambridge Journal of Economics*, vol. 6, pp. 167-184.

Cairncross F (1997) The Death of Distance, HBS Press, Boston

Camagni R (1991) Local 'milieu', uncertainty and innovation networks : towards a new dynamic theory of economic space. In Camagni R ed., *Innovation networks : spatial perspective*, Belhaven Press, London.

Camagni R (1995) High-technology milieux in Italy and new reflections about the concept of "milieu innovateur". Paper presented at European Workshop on High-Technology Enterprise and Innovative Regional Milieux, Cambridge, March 3-4, 1995

Commission Européenne (1999) Sixième rapport périodique sur la situation et l'évolution socio-économique des régions de l'Union européenne, Luxembourg.

Cooke P, Morgan K (1998) The associational economy. Oxford, Oxford University Press.

Courault B (2000) Districts italiens et PME-systèmes français. Centre d'Etudes de l'Emploi, Lettre 61.

De Bandt J, Gadrey J ed. (1994) Relations de services, marchés de services. Edition du CNRS, Paris.

Dupuy C, Gilly JP (1999) Industrial groups and territories : the case of Matra-Marconi-Space in Toulouse. In *Cambridge Journal of Economics*, 23.

Fagerberg J, Verspagen B, Caniëls M (1997) Technology, Growth and Unemployment across European Regions. In *Regional Studies*, 31 (5): 457-466.

Feldman M (2001) The entrepreneurial spark : individual agents and the formation of innovative clusters. In Quadrio Curzio A and Fortis M eds., *Complexity and industrial clusters*, Physica-Verlag, Heidelberg.

Fujita M, Thisse JF (1997) Economie géographique, problèmes anciens et nouvelles perspectives. In *Annales d'Economie et de Statistique*, n°45.

Garnsey E (1998) The Genesis of the High Technology Milieu. In *International Journal of Urban and Regional Research*, Vol 22 n° 3.

Garnsey E, Longhi C (1999) Auto-organisation et émergence des milieux innovateurs. In *Revue d'Economie Régionale et Urbaine*, 3, Juillet.

Gordon R (1990) Global networks and the innovation process in high technology SMEs: the case of Silicon Valley. Working Paper, Silicon Valley Research Group, University of California.

Gordon R (1996) Industrial districts and the globalization of innovation : Regions and Networks in the new economic space. In Vence-Deza X and Metcalfe JS *Wealth from Diversity*, Dordrecht, Kluwer Academic Press.

Graham B, Hart M (1999) Cohesion and diversity in the European Union. In *Regional Studies*, 33.3.

Greffe X (1999) Le chantier permanent des milieux innovateurs. In *Revue d'Economie Régionale et Urbaine*, 3.

Herrigel G (2000) Large firms and industrial districts in Europe: De-regionalization, re-regionalization and the transformation of manufacturing flexibility. In Dunning JH (2000) *Regions, Globalization and the Knowledge-Based Economy*, Oxford University Press, Oxford: pp 286 – 302.

Hudson R (2002) Global production systems and European integration, ESRC "One Europe or Several?" Programme Working Paper 43/02

Imai K, Baba Y (1989) Systemic innovation and cross-border networks. Paper presented at International Seminar on Science, Technology and Economic Growth, OECD, Paris

Kechidi M, (1996) Coordination inter-entreprises et relations de sous-traitance: le cas d'Aérospatiale. In *Revue d'Economie Régionale et Urbaine*, 1.

Keeble D et al. (1998) Collective learning processes and inter-firm networking in innovative high-technology regions, ESRC Centre for Business Research, WP 86, March.

Krugman P (1991) Geography and trade, MIT Press.

Lazerson MH, Lorenzoni G (1999) The firms that feed industrial districts, a return to the Italian source. In *Industrial and Corporate Change*, 8.2.

Longhi C (1999) Networks, collective learning and technology development in innovative high- technology regions: the case of Sophia Antipolis. In *Regional Studies*, Vol.33.4.

Longhi C (2001) Intégration Européenne et Dynamiques Régionales. In D Torre, E Tosi (eds), *Intégration européenne et institutions économiques*, De Boeck, Paris.

Longhi C (2001) From exogenous to endogenous local development: The cases of Toulouse and Sophia Antipolis technopoles. In Quadrio Curzio A and Fortis M eds., *Complexity and industrial clusters*, Physica-Verlag, Heidelberg.

Longhi C, Keeble D (2000) European regional clusters of high tech SMEs: evolutionary trajectories in the 1990s. In Keeble D, Wilkinson F eds. *High-Technology Clusters, Networking and Collective Learning in Europe*, Ashgate.

Longhi C, Quéré M (1993) Systèmes de production et d'innovation, et dynamique des territoires. In *Revue Economique*, n°4.

Longhi C, Spindler J (2000) Le développement local. LGDJ, Paris.

Luger MI (2001) Science and technology parks at the millennium: concept, history, and metrics.

Lundvall BA (2001) Innovation and learning in a national system, in industries and firms. ECIS conference, Eindhoven, September.

Malecki EJ (2001) Hard and Soft Networks for Urban Competitiveness. ESRC Cities Programme Research Workshop, Innovation and Competitive Cities in the Global Economy, Worcester College, Oxford, March.

Markusen A (1996) Sticky places in slippery space: a typology of industrial districts. In *Economic Geography*, 72, 3, 293-313

Maskell P, Malmberg A (1999) Localised learning and industrial competitiveness. In *Cambridge Journal of Economics*, vol. 23:2.

Morgan K (1997) The learning region : institutions, innovation, and regional renewal. In *Regional Studies*, 31.5.

Muller P (1988) Airbus, l'ambition européenne. Logique d'Etat, logique de marché. L'Harmattan, Paris.

OECD (1996) The knowledge–based economy. In *Science, Technology and Industry Outlook*, 229-256, Paris.

Peyrache-Gadeau V (1997) Dynamic and structural change of localised production systems. In *The dynamics of innovative milieu*, R. Ratti et al. eds, Ashgate, Aldershot.

Porter ME (1990) L'avantage concurrentiel des nations. Inter Editions, Paris (traduction 1993).

Scott AJ (1988) New industrial spaces: flexible production and regional development in North America and Western Europe. Pion, Londres.

Scott AJ, Agnew J, Storper M (2001) Global-City Regions. In *Global-City Regions - Trends, Theory, Policy,* Scott A.J. ed., Oxford, O.U.P.

Storper M (1993) Regional 'worlds' of production: learning and innovation in the technology districts of France, Italy and the USA. In *Regional Studies* , 27, 433-455

Storper M (1997) The regional world. Guilford Press, New York.

Talbot D (2000) Institutional dynamics and localized inter-firms relations. The case of Aerospatiale and its subcontractors in Toulouse. In *European Urban and Regional Studies*, 7(3).

Veltz P (1993) D'une géographie des coûts et une géographie de l'organisation. Quelques théses sur l'évolution des rapports entreprises/territories. In *Revue Economique*, no 4.

Veltz P (2000) Mondialisation, villes et territoires: l'économie d'archipel. PUF, Paris.

The Dynamics of High-Tech Clusters: Competition, Predation, Synergies[1]

Mario A. Maggioni

Department of International Economics, Institutions and Development,
Faculty of Political Science, Catholic University, Milan, Italy
mario.maggioni@unicatt.it

"Precisely why particular technologies cluster is not well understood. Innovations often occur in more than one location at about the same time; largely because of different environmental conditions, however, commercial exploitation flourishes in a much smaller number of places. Powerful agglomeration advantages develop in the specialised technopolis. Supplier and service firms arise to serve the growing industry (...). Firms that represent downstream markets join the cluster. A specialised labour market forms, which reinforces the growth of the industry (which, in turn, attracts more specialised labour). Local educational and research institution collaborate with industry to develop programs to meet the need of the industry. University thus develop national and international reputation for excellence in the specialised field of the regional industry. In mature technopolises, diversification of the industrial base occurs (as) a natural consequence of the agglomeration process and linkages among certain technologies. (...) The large technical labour force attracts other industries that demand skills similar to those needed by the core industry. (...) Service industries that arose to meet the demand of local industry find export markets and become an independent source of growth for the technopolis. Universities and other research institutions sometimes broaden their areas of specialisation and generate new growth in new fields."
R.W. Preer (1992), *The Emergence of Technopolis*, Praeger, New York

[1] This paper is a reprinting already published in Atti dei Convegni *Reti. Italia ed Europa* (Roma, 8-9 aprile 2003), Accademia N... Thanks are due to M. Feldman, P. Swann, and C. Longhi... Uberti provided inestimable research assistance for the econ... cial support from PRIN-MIUR (2003131274_001 *«Dinamic...* *nizzazioni, istituzioni»*, is gratefully acknowledged.

1. Introduction

The causes and effects of the spatial clustering of firms within a given industry have been suggested as a research question to economists by Marshall (1920) but later forgotten by the economic profession. Seventy years later, Krugman (1991) gave new emphasis on the spatial aspect of firm behaviours and his contribution spurred a new surge in what has been defined as the "New Economic Geography" literature.

Aim of this paper is to apply an original theoretical framework, derived from population ecology, to the analysis of the development of high-tech cluster in the US in order to underline the interplay of agglomeration economies and diseconomies in the growth process of a cluster and to stress the complex and different (i.e. synergic, competitive, etc.) interactions which exists between different high-tech industries, within the same states, and between different states within the same industry. The formal model is able to identify and discuss the existence and stability conditions of long run equilibria through a graphical analysis (phase diagrams).

2. The Population Ecology Approach

While we refer to previous works (Maggioni 1993, 1994, 2002a) for the discussion of the micro-foundation of population ecology models applied to firms' location decision and clustering dynamics, here we will briefly illustrate a number of possible different patterns of interactions which may emerge between two "populations" of firms with special emphasis on long-run dynamics and to the stability/instability of equilibria.

According to the population ecology approach, the development pattern of an industrial cluster is jointly determined by two distinct but interrelated processes: an inner dynamics (driven by the number of firms already located in the cluster) and an external dynamics (driven by the spatial and industrial interaction between and within clusters).

2.1. Clusters' Growth and Size

In the population ecology literature, a generic modelling framework describes the growth process of a given population (in our case of firms belonging to a certain industry and locating in a given area) as a differential equation (or, more often, a system of differential equations) which describes the changes over time of a variable (i.e. the population net growth) as function of: the level of the same variable (the size of the population) at each moment in time; a ceiling level (which takes into account the limit imposed by the available amount of resources); and the level of other variables (which represent the interacting populations).

Despite their analytical simplicity, these models are able to take into account a series of typical processes and stylised facts which characterise the clustering phenomenon and dynamics and their underlining forces:

- Often new firms in a cluster are started either by people which were previously employed by other local firms willing to try the entrepreneurial venture (spin-off) or by local resident willing to emulate successful entrepreneurs (imitation);
- In an uncertain environment, where there are information asymmetries between insiders (resident firms) and outsiders (external and "potential" firms): 1) the number of located firms signals to the potential entrant the profitability (which in turns depend on the availability and quality of: labour force, intermediate inputs, and specialized services; on the industrial relation and business "climate"; etc.); 2) by locating into an established cluster a firm signals his quality to potential customers by showing it's ability to survive to harm's length competition in inputs markets (i.e. skilled labour, venture capital/bank funding, etc.)
- Each new entrant increases the locational benefits to each and every incumbents (agglomeration economies, which develop through the marshallian externalities channels: labour market pooling, specialized intermediate inputs, technological externalities and knowledge spillovers) only up to a point, then it decreases them (agglomeration diseconomies) when congestion and competition prevail.The model we are using in this paper explains firms' entry in the cluster as a function of the average locational benefits available in each moment in time. Thus these models describe the growth of the cluster's industrial mass as a S-shaped path with a slow start (when locational benefits are still low), an 'explosive' central period of rapid increase (when the average net benefits in the cluster are highest) and a final part when the cluster gradually reaches and then settles to its "equilibrium"[2] size. Such a development pattern is shown in figure 1 and compared with real data on the development of firms producing 'computers and office equipments' in California in the period 1956-2000[3] (as shown in figure 2).

---

[2] It should be bore in mind, however, that this notion of equilibrium value can be changed in the long run by radical innovations, exogenous demand shocks and appropriate regional policies.

[3] The more remarkable difference between figures 1 and 2 lies in the decreasing part of the curve, depicted in figure 2, after 1980. This can be explained by referring to a more general model which takes into account the contemporary evolution of other clusters (i.e. other US states) in the same industry and of other industries in the same cluster (i.e. California), to the general industrial trend, and to the macroeconomic condition. Spatial and industrial interactions will be dealt with in the next sections.

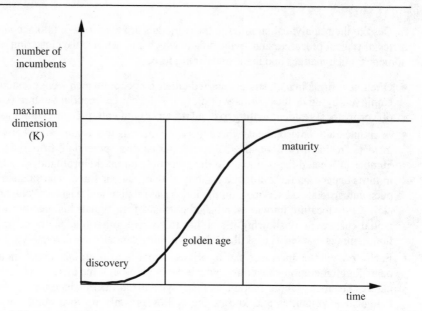

Fig. 1. The Theoretical Development Path of an Industrial Cluster

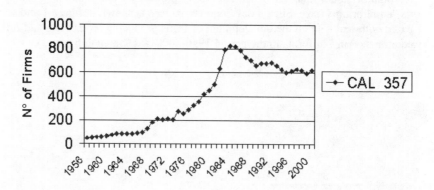

Fig. 2. The Actual Development Path of an Industrial Cluster. Computer and Office Equipment Firms (SIC 357) in California (1956-2000)

2.2. A Logistic Growth Model 'In Isolation'

The simplest growth model for an industrial cluster q - which stresses the relevance of firms spatial interactions - can be expressed in the following format: "the rate of growth of the industrial mass equals the product of the individual firm's contribution[4] to the regional population's growth and the number of firms already in the cluster" (Maggioni, 1993, 1999).

If congestion and competition effects are taken into account as well as agglomeration economies and positive spillovers, then some 'density dependent' factors have to be included in the exponential growth model to progressively depress the level of locational benefits and to slow down the process of industrial growth of the cluster. A simple dynamic model, which takes into account these features is the logistic equation[5], which can be written as (1a):

$$\frac{dn_q}{dt} = r_q n_q(t)\left(1 - \frac{n_q(t)}{K_q}\right) \tag{1a}$$

where r_q is the incipient (or maximum) rate of increase and $K_q = \lim_{t \to \infty} n_q(t)$, is called the cluster "equilibrium" level[6]. Solving for $n^j(t) = e^{rt} n^j(0)$ one obtains (1b):

$$n_q(t) = \frac{K_q n_q(0)e^{r_q(t)}}{K_q + n_q(0)\left(e^{r_q(t)} - 1\right)} \tag{1b}$$

Which describes an S-shaped curve (described in figure 1) due to the counteracting roles played by r_q and K_q. The higher r_q, the steeper the curve; the higher K_q the higher the ceiling level of the function (and the equilibrium size of the cluster).

In this first formulation, the number of located firms directly generates (through agglomeration and congestion dynamics) the level of locational benefits; since the entry rate is assumed to be proportional to the level of locational benefits, it also indirectly determines the location of new firms into the cluster.

---

[4] In terms of changes in the average locational net benefits, due to the interactions of agglomeration economies and diseconomies.

[5] The logistic equation - firstly developed by Verhulst (1845) and Pearl - Reed (1920) for demographic studies, then adopted by the ecological literature since Lotka (1925) - "is the simplest model containing negative density dependence interaction. Further, it is the first two terms in a power series expansion of a more general growth model where the growth is a function of the actual size of the population" (Dendrinos - Mullally, 1985, p. 38).

[6] K in the original ecological jargon is called *carrying capacity*: "a measure of the amount of renewable resources in the environment in units of the number of organisms these resources can support" (Roughgarden, 1979, p. 305).

However this formulation suffers from two main limits. The first refers to the exogeneity ot the cluster's maximum dimension K_q; the second refers to the 'isolation hypothesis' (i.e. the fact that there is only one possible site for location available to potential entrants and that the choice variable is the mere timing of the entry).

The first limit can be addressed by re-writing equation (1a) in the following way (1c) where the cluster growth rate depends solely on the cluster dimension[7].

$$\frac{dn_q}{dt} = \left(a_q - a_{qq}\, n_q\right)n_q \tag{1c}$$

The second limit may be solved through the explicit formulation of industrial and spatial interactions. The following sections extend the simple logistic growth path to take into account bilateral interactions.

2.3. A Logistic Growth Model with Spatial Competition

The simplest way to extend the growth model 'in isolation' is to consider each bilateral interaction one at the time. Through a system of two differential equations (as in 2a) one may deal with competitive dynamics between two alternative locations (US states) for the same population of firms and with (synergistic a/o predatory) industrial interactions arising within the same area (state).

Formally, the spatial competition between two US states[8] can be described through the following system of equations which directly recalls the mono-cluster development process of equation (1a):

$$\begin{cases} \dfrac{dn_1}{dt} = r_1 n_1(t)\left[1 - \dfrac{n_1(t) + c_{12} n_2(t)}{K_1}\right] \\[3mm] \dfrac{dn_2}{dt} = r_2 n_2(t)\left[1 - \dfrac{n_2(t) + c_{21} n_1(t)}{K_2}\right] \end{cases} \tag{2a}$$

where r_1 and K_1 are respectively cluster 1 incipient growth rate and equilibrium levels and c_{12}, is the "competition coefficient" which measures the extent to which cluster 2 competes as an alternative location to cluster 1.

However – in order to endogenise the equilibrium levels of different clusters - it is more convenient to replace this formulation (which underlines the similarities between the two-clusters case and the model of development of an isolated cluster) with an alternative formalisation which is able to model different multire-

---

[7] Where a_q is the intrinsic growth rate (previously: r_q) and a_q/a_{qq} the maximum cluster dimension (previously: K_q).

[8] The same analytical framework can be used to describe the interaction between two industries in the same cluster which compete on a given pool of local limited resources (land, workers, bank credit etc.).

gional interactions through simple differences in the sign of parameters. We thus replace (2a) by (2b), where time references are dropped for the sake of clarity:

$$\begin{cases} \dfrac{dn_1}{dt} = \left(a_1 - a_{11}n_1 - a_{12}n_2\right)n_1 \\[2ex] \dfrac{dn_2}{dt} = \left(a_2 - a_{22}n_2 - a_{21}n_1\right)n_2 \end{cases} \tag{2b}$$

In system (2b), n_1 and n_2 are the 'economic masses' (number of incumbents) of each cluster, a_1 and a_2 are the intrinsic rates of increase of each cluster in isolation, a_{11} and a_{22} - the parameters on the quadratic terms which reflect the concavity of the net agglomeration benefits function - i.e. that reflect the inhibiting effects that a firm's entry has on the growth rate of the same cluster[9] (intra-cluster competition parameters); a_{12} and a_{21} show the inhibiting effects that one firm - locating in a cluster - has on the growth of the other cluster[10] (inter-clusters competition parameters).

Expression (2b) may be analytically solved as such in order to find the exact roots. However, for the purpose of this paper is better to use phase diagram in order to study its qualitative structure.

Phase diagrams are useful tools to describe systems of differential equations. At any moment in time the state of the system is fully described by the number of firms located in each cluster (n_1 and n_2). Within the phase plane one can further draw for each cluster the locus of points (i.e. combination of n_1 and n_2), which is called the isocline, where the cluster's industrial mass does not change (i.e. where $\dfrac{dn_1}{dt} = 0$ and $\dfrac{dn_2}{dt} = 0$). Non trivial equilibria (such as the axes origin) are thus identified by the intersections of one isocline with either the axes or the other isocline[11]. The arrows in the phase planes indicate the direction in which the system, at that point, will move; the colours and shapes of the dots show whether an equi-

---

[9] $\dfrac{a_1}{a_{11}}$ and $\dfrac{a_2}{a_{22}}$ in this formulations are the clusters' maximum size or isolated equilibrium values (K_1 and K_2).

[10] Different interpretations for these parameters are possible: the simplest relates the values of inter-regional competition parameters to the fact that - given a certain number of potential entrants - each firm that locates in cluster 1 does not locate in cluster 2. Then the inter-clusters coefficients should be equal, i.e. $a_{12} = a_{21}$. Another interpretation explicitly relates to the possible differences in the logistic growth path of the two clusters in isolation (which reflect differences in the net benefits function). In this case inter-clusters competition coefficients may be different.

[11] The intersection of an isocline with an axis is an equilibrium point since one cluster is deserted and the other does not change its industrial mass, the intersection of two isoclines is an equilibrium point since both clusters do not register any changes in the number of located firms.

librium is either stable (black circle) or unstable (white circle) or a saddle point (white square).

Figure 3 (explained with greater details in Maggioni – Fortis, 2001) shows all possible outcomes of a bilateral competitive spatial interaction between two areas which may result in persistent coexistence of two clusters (3a: steady equilibrium); the coexistence of two clusters as an unstable equilibrium, which is extremely vulnerable to local perturbations and initial biases (3b); the total exclusion of one cluster from the location process (that occurs only in the other cluster, irrespective of the initial state) which reaches its carrying capacity leaving the opponent deserted [12]. (3c and 3d). This last situation is labeled: 'strong competition'.

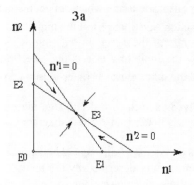
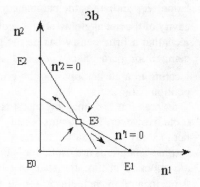
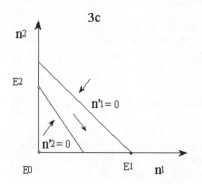
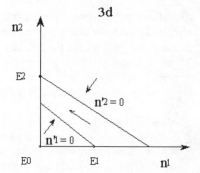

Fig. 3. Spatial Competition

---

[12] This case includes two opposite situations of only cluster 1 surviving and only cluster 2 surviving.

2.4. Logistic Growth Model with Mutualistic and Predatory Interactions

The analytical representation, used in equation (2b) to describe the location decisions of a set of potential entrants between two alternative locations, can be easily encompassed to describe other significant interactions which may arise during the development process of two different industries within the same industrial cluster.

Table 1 shows, in the first column, a subset of all possible interactions which may arise between two different industries and, in the second column the signs of the inter-regional coefficients a_{12} and a_{21} in expression (2b).

Table 1. Selected Types of Bilateral Interactions

Types of interactions	Sign of interaction coefficients a_{12} and a_{21}	
Competition	−	−
Mutualism	+	+
Predation	+	−

Mutualistic interactions – which describe the development of two interrelated industries – may be modelled through an expression similar to (2b) in which both interaction coefficients are positive. Formally:

$$\begin{cases} \dfrac{dn_1}{dt} = \left(a_1 - a_{11}n_1 + a_{12}n_2\right)n_1 \\ \dfrac{dn_2}{dt} = \left(a_2 - a_{22}n_2 + a_{21}n_1\right)n_2 \end{cases} \qquad (2c)$$

In this model each industry in isolation would follow a logistic growth pattern, but the presence of one industry in the same cluster has a positive influence on the rate of growth of the other one. The system's dynamics - which is described through a phase diagram in figure 4 - always displays three trivial unstable equilibria: the origin (corresponding to the underdevelopment of both industries) and each industry's isolated maximum dimension (4a). However, under certain assumptions concerning the slope of isoclines (4b), a fourth stable equilibrium (E3) emerges which enables both industries to reach a higher level in the cluster. The coexistence of two industries in the same cluster allows both industries to grow larger than would have been possible in the isolated case, but intra-industry competition effects prevent the system from experiencing explosive growth.

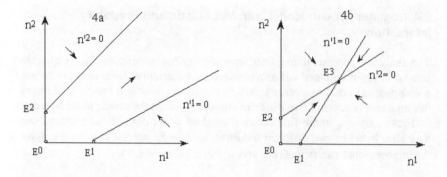

Fig. 4. Inter-Industry Mutualism

Both the economic literature (from Jacobs, 1969 to Swann et Al., 1998), and the empirical evidence, presented in section 3, show that inter-industry mutualism (i.e. technological linkages and knowledge spillovers) is one of the main engine of clusters growth in the long run. However, alternative types of inter-industry relations may develop in situation where the development of one industry hinders the development of the other one (prey-predation).

The interaction between hardware and software production in California is the best example of this kind of predatory relations. A well developed industry produces, through a sort of indirect spin-off process, the birth, within the very same cluster, of another (technologically related) industry which acts as supplier of intermediate inputs or complementary goods. If the derived industry has a higher value added per worker (or, more generally, if firms in this sectors are more productive and profitable) then it may well happen that the development of the second industry determines endogenously the crisis of the first one since it may cause the rise of local inputs prices (skilled workers' wages; land rents, interest rate on loans) to such a level which is not sustainable for the original industry.

Analytically one may model a prey-predator system as a mix of systems (2b) and (2c) since its essence lies in the combination of a competitive with a synergetic relationship.

$$\begin{cases} \dfrac{dn_1}{dt} = \left(a_1 - a_{11}n_1 - a_{12}n_2\right)n_1 \\ \dfrac{dn_2}{dt} = \left(a_2 - a_{22}n_2 + a_{21}n_1\right)n_2 \end{cases} \tag{2d}$$

Where n_1 is the prey (or the older and currently declining industry) and n_2 is the predator (or the younger and rising one).

Predatory interactions typically display oscillatory dynamics. A phase diagram (see figure 5) illustrates two possible configurations: case (5a) where the coexistence of both population is a stable equilibrium surrounded by a converging spiral, case (5b) where the coexistence of both population is an unstable equilibrium surrounded by a diverging spiral.

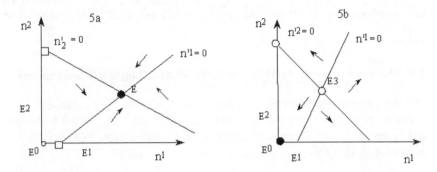

Fig. 5. Inter-Industry Predation within the Same State

The qualitative identification of such interactions and the quantitative measurement of their effect on the growth rate of industries are thus left to the empirical analysis of section 3.

3. Empirical Analysis

3.1. The Data

Data used in this section refer to the number of establishments of 16 selected high-tech industries[13] localized within some US states[14] for the period 1948-2000[15]. This sample accounts for about 63% of the total number of high-tech establishments at the beginning of the period and for about 49% in 2000[16].

Original data were collected from the database "County Business Patterns" of the US Census Bureau. The empirical identification of a state as a geographical

---

[13] The original sample, developed in Maggioni 2002a and extended to more recent dates for this paper, contained data for 7 high–tech industries defined at 3 digit SIC: 283 Pharmaceuticals, 357 Computers and office equipment, 367 Electronic components, 372 Aircrafts, 376 Missiles, 380 Scientific instruments, 737 Computer services and data processing.

[14] The original sample referred to 16 US states (Arizona, California, Colorado, Connecticut, Florida, Illinois, Kansas, Massachusetts, Michigan, New Jersey, New York, Ohio, Pennsylvania, Texas, Utah, Washington) which were obtained as the union of two subsets: the most developed high-tech states at the beginning or at the end of the considered period.

[15] For certain industries (which were not defined in the SIC classification until 1959) the period is slightly shorter (i.e. 1959-2000).

[16] The reduction in the share of total US high-tech establishments is a first sign of the spatial diffusion of high-tech industries throughout the whole of the US.

counterpart of the spatial dimension of a cluster is not optimal. However alternative solutions, such as the county, would have increased the complexity of the empirical analysis and reduced the time span of the data series. For these reason we followed Swann et. Al. (1989) who developed their empirical analysis at the state level.

3.2. The Econometric Analysis and the Phase Diagram Construction

The econometric analysis runs as follows: one has to estimate expression (3) – which is the empirical version of models (2b), (2c) and (2d) – to get both signs and values of the interaction coefficients $\hat{a}_{12}$ e $\hat{a}_{21}$ and compare them to table 1 in order to classify the interaction types[17].

$$
\begin{cases}
n_{1(t)} - n_{1(t-1)} = \hat{a}_1 n_{1(t-1)} + \hat{a}_{11} n_1^2{}_{(t-1)} + \hat{a}_{12} n_{1(t-1)} n_{2(t-1)} + \varepsilon_{1(t-1)} \\
n_{2(t)} - n_{2(t-1)} = \hat{a}_2 n_{2(t-1)} + \hat{a}_{22} n_2^2{}_{(t-1)} + \hat{a}_{21} n_{2(t-1)} n_{1(t-1)} + \eta_{2(t-1)}
\end{cases}
\tag{3}
$$

where $n_{1(t-1)}$ e $n_{2(t-1)}$ are the 'industrial masses' (number of establishments belonging to a given industry a/o state); $\hat{a}_1$ e $\hat{a}_2$ are the estimated parameters of the intrinsic growth rate of each cluster 'in isolation'; $\hat{a}_1/\hat{a}_{11}$ e $\hat{a}_2/\hat{a}_{22}$ are the estimated parameters of intra-specific competition (i.e. within the same population); $\hat{a}_{12}$ e $\hat{a}_{21}$ are the estimated parameters of inter-specific competition (i.e. between two different populations); ε_1 and η_2 are two white noise error terms.

Once all parameters have been estimated, it is possible to calculate the isoclines' equations by equating to zero the left hand side of equations (3) (i.e. $\dfrac{dn_1}{dt} = 0$ and $\dfrac{dn_2}{dt} = 0$). In this way it is possible to look for the isoclines intersections and to identify all equilibria.

In the competitive case, the isoclines equations are as follows:

$$
\frac{dn_1}{dt} = 0 \text{ for } n_2 = \frac{a_1}{a_{12}} - \frac{a_{11}}{a_{12}} n_1 \text{ and } \frac{dn_2}{dt} = 0 \text{ for } n_2 = \frac{a_2}{a_{22}} - \frac{a_{21}}{a_{22}} n_1 \; ;
$$

In the mutualistic case, the isoclines equations are as follows:

$$
\frac{dn_1}{dt} = 0 \text{ for } n_2 = -\frac{a_1}{a_{12}} + \frac{a_{11}}{a_{12}} n_1 \text{ and } \frac{dn_2}{dt} = 0 \text{ for } n_2 = \frac{a_2}{a_{22}} + \frac{a_{21}}{a_{22}} n_1
$$

In the predatory case, the isoclines equations are as follows:

---

[17] OLS estimation may give biased results due to endogenity problems and non stationarity Instrumental variables did confirm the result. Further refinements of the analysis will deal with co-integration techniques.

$$\frac{dn_1}{dt} = 0 \text{ for } n_2 = -\frac{a_1}{a_{12}} + \frac{a_{11}}{a_{12}} n_1 \text{ and } \frac{dn_2}{dt} = 0 \text{ for } n_2 = \frac{a_2}{a_{22}} - \frac{a_{21}}{a_{22}} n_1$$

3.3. Empirical Results

Table 2 shows a summary of all estimated parameters (columns 4, 5, 6 e 7), which have been used to draw the isoclines in the phase space.[18]. Column 1 identifies the interaction environment, column 2 and 3 describe the different firm populations and column 8 labels the appropriate type of interaction and the actual state of the system.

Table 2. Isocline Coefficients and Type of Interactions

Interaction environment (industry/state)	n_1	n_2	$\dfrac{\hat{a}_1}{\hat{a}_{12}}$	$\dfrac{\hat{a}_{11}}{\hat{a}_{12}}$	$\dfrac{\hat{a}_2}{\hat{a}_{22}}$	$\dfrac{\hat{a}_2}{\hat{a}_{22}}$	Interaction type Predator's name (state of the system in year 2000)
367 (E'tronics)	Tex	Pen	-663,34	0,82	-190,11	-0,37	Competition (285, 367)
Florida	372	380	-156,05	3,65	-282,38	-6,64	Mutualism (132, 579)
California	357	737	-134927,49	-126,11	113839,13	108,20	Competition (624, 21118)
Massachusetts	367	357	477,08	0,43	-91,43	1,84	367 Predator (342, 113)

Isoclines' intersection determines the existence of long run equilibria. Isoclines' slope determines the number and nature (stability/instability) of equilibria.

By comparing the actual (year 2000) state of the system and the long run equilibria, one may further infer the long run dynamics which will be followed by the cluster according to the arrows in the phase diagram.

In particular one may note a predatory relationship within the electronic component industry (SIC 367) between Pennsylvania and Texas, where Pennsylvania acts as predator (figure 6). Such a relationship will determine a stable long run equilibrium which will be approached by the system through a dampened oscillatory dynamics (as it is shown in figure 7). Other interesting results of spatial interaction (within the same industry) did not pass the econometric test of significance and robustness.

---

[18] Out of more than 30 cases only few yielded econometrically significant results (by using both OLS and instrumental variables). Here we present a restricted sub-sample of 4 cases which display a higher representativity of the different interactions.

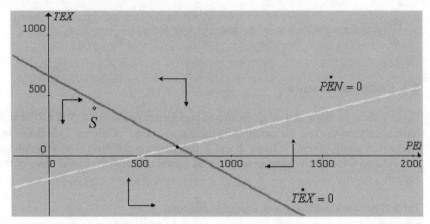

Fig. 6. Interstate Predation within Electronics Components Industry (367 PEN-TEX). Point *S* Represents Situation in 2000.

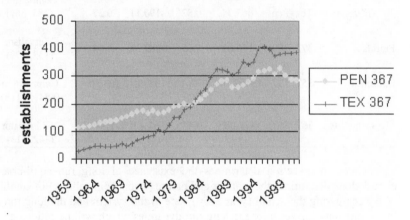

Fig. 7. Electronics Components Development in Pennsylvania and Texas (1959-2000)

Stronger results have been obtained by looking at different industries in the same state. In particular Aerospace industry (SIC 372) and Instruments industry (SIC 380) show mutualistic relationships in Florida leading to a stable equilibrium in which each industry develops well beyond its own equilibrium level in isolation (figure 8). Figure 9 illustrates the evolution of both industries and the stronger growth of Instruments industry.

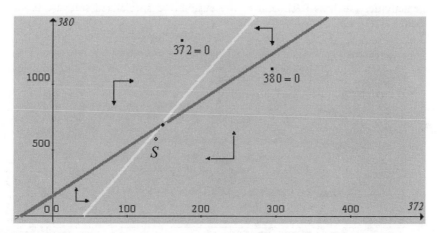

Fig. 8. Inter-Industry Mutualism in Florida (FLO 372-380). Point S Represents Situation in 2000.

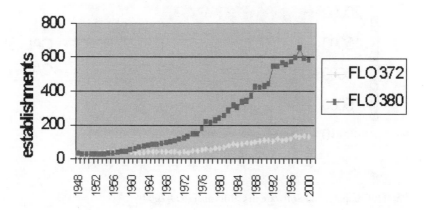

Fig. 9. Aerospace and Instruments in Florida (1948-2000)

Computer production (SIC 357) and software production and related services (SIC 737) are strongly competing for local resources in California (figure 10). The econometric analysis confirms the anecdotic evidence and the long run trends (figure 11) seem to suggest a near future in which no more hardware production will take place in California which will specialize in higher value added industries or activities (such as R&D and highly customized specialized software production).

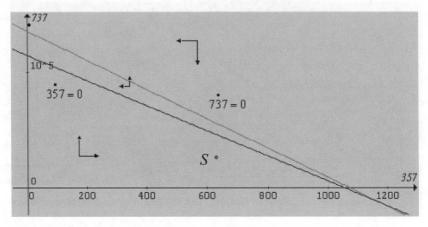

Fig. 10. Inter Industry Strong Competition in California (CAL 357-737). Point S Represents Situation in 2000.

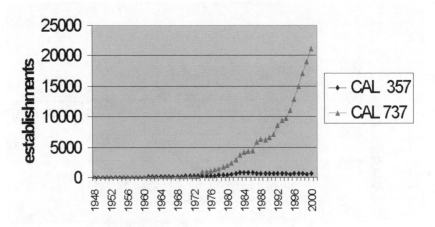

Fig. 11. Computer and Software in California (1959-2000)

Computer production (SIC 357) and electronic components production (SIC 367) in Massachusetts show clear sign of a predatory dynamics (figure 12) which is oscillating around a stable equilibrium in which the relative weight of the two industries will get back to a more balanced equilibrium as the most likely outcome to the long crisis of the computer started in the middle 80s (figure 13).

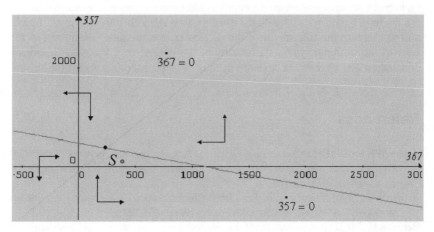

Fig. 12. Inter Industry Predation in Massachusetts (MAS 367-357). Point S Represents Situation in 2000.

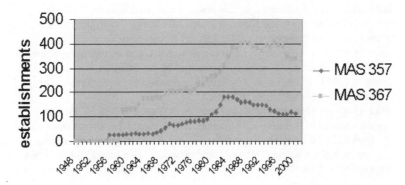

Fig. 13. Computers and Electronic Components in Massachusetts (1959-2000)

4. Conclusions

This paper has shown that population ecology model is a powerful tool to analyze the co-evolution of different industries in the same area and the spatial competition and predation in the same industry both from a theoretical and an empirical perspective.

The empirical evidence provided about some US high-tech clusters demonstrates the explanatory and the 'forecasting' power of such techniques.

Further research is needed in order to enlarge the scope of the models (allowing for declining dynamics of isolated clusters through a 3rd order logistic function) and to increase the robustness of the econometric estimations (with special reference to the stationarity/non stationarity of the data series). For these reasons this conclusion acts as a sort of research agenda to be pursued in the next future.

References

Arthur WB (1988) Urban System and Historical Path Dependency, in Ausubel JH, Herman R (eds.) *Cities and Their Vital Systems*, National Academy Press, Washington D.C., pp. 85-97.

Arthur WB (1990) Silicon Valley Locational Clusters: when Do Increasing Returns Imply Monopoly?, *Mathematical Social Sciences*, 19, pp. 235-251.

Beltrami E (1987) *Mathematics for Dynamic Modelling*, Academic Press, Boston.

Capelo AC (1989) *Modelli matematici in biologia*, Decibel, Padova.

Dendrinos DS, Mullally H (1985) *Urban Evolution. Studies in the Mathematical Ecology of Cities*, Oxford University Press, Oxford.

Gambarotto F, Maggioni MA (1998) Regional Development Strategies in Changing Environments: an Ecological Approach, *Regional Studies*, 32, pp. 49-61.

Gause GF (1934) *The Struggle for Existence*, Williams & Wilkins, Baltimore.

Isard W (1956) *Location and Space-economy*, MIT Press, Cambridge (Mass.).

Jacobs (1969) *The Economy of Cities*, Random House, New York.

Levin SA (1970) Community Equilibria and Stability, and an Extension of the Competitive Exclusion Principle, *American Naturalist*, 108, pp. 207-228.

Levins R (1968) *Evolution in Changing Environments: Some Theoretical Explorations*, Princeton University Press, Princeton.

Lotka AJ (1925) *Elements of Physical Biology*, Williams & Wilkins, Baltimore.

Maggioni MA (1993) *Ecological Dynamics and Critical Mass Processes in the Location of High Tech Firms*, paper presented at the 40th RSAI (Regional Sciences Association International) Conference, North American Section, Houston, 11-14 November.

Maggioni MA (1994) Modelli ecologici per l'analisi della dinamica industriale regionale, in Pasquini F, Pompili T, Secondini P (eds.) *Modelli d'analisi e d'intervento per un nuovo regionalismo*, Angeli, Milano, pp. 79-105.

Maggioni MA (2002a) *Clustering Dynamics and the Location of High-Tech Firms*, Springer Verlag, Heidelberg and New York.

Maggioni MA (2002b) The Development of High-Tech Clusters: Theoretical Insights and Policy Implications in Feldman M, Massard N, (eds.) *Institutions and Systems in the Geography of Innovation*, Kluwer, Dordrecht, pp. 309-340

Maggioni MA, Fortis M (2001) Competitive and synergic behaviors in the development of industrial clusters. Ecological modeling and empirical evidence, in Quadrio Curzio A, Fortis M (eds) Complexity and Industrial Clusters, Springer Verlag, Heidelberg and New York.

Maggioni MA, Gambarotto F (1997) Sviluppo locale, dinamiche globali e ruolo dell'operatore pubblico: un modello ecologico, in Bramanti A, Maggioni MA (eds.) *La dinamica dei sistemi produttivi territoriali: teorie, tecniche, politiche*, Angeli, Milano, pp. 280-306.

Maggioni MA, Porro G (1994) Dinamiche di crescita regionale: il ruolo delle aspettative in modelli di tipo ecologico, *Quaderno della ricerca di base "Modelli di sviluppo e regional competition"*, 6, Università Bocconi, Milano.

Maino R (1989) Aree interne ed interdipendenze settoriali. Uno schema interpretativo fondato su modelli dinamici del tipo preda-predatore, in Becchi Collidà A, Ciciotti E, Mela A *Aree interne, tutela del territorio e valorizzazione delle risorse*, Angeli, Milano, pp. 81-110.

May RM (1974) *Stability and Complexity in Model Ecosystems*, Princeton University Press, Princeton.

May RM (1976) *Theoretical Ecology, Principles and Applications*, Saunders, Philadelphia.

Marshall A. (1920), *Principles of Economics*, McMillan, London.

Marshall A . (1921), *Industry and Trade*, McMillan, London.

Metcalfe JS (1994) Competition, Fisher's Principle and Increasing Returns in the Selection Process, *Journal of Evolutionary Economics*, 4 (4), pp. 327-346.

Miyao T, Kanemoto Y (1987) *Urban Dynamics and Urban Externalities*, Harwood Academic Publishers, London.

Nijkamp P, Reggiani A (1998) *The Economics of Complex Spatial Systems*, Elsevier, Amsterdam.

Papageorgiou YY (1979) Agglomerations, *Regional Science and Urban Economics*, 9, pp. 41-49.

Pearl R, Reed LJ (1925) Skew-Growth Curves, *Proceeding of the National Academy of Natural Sciences of the USA*, 11, pp. 16-22.

Preer RW (1992) *The Emergence of Technopolis, Knowedge-intensive Technologies and Regional Development*, Praeger, New York.

Richardson HW (1978) *Regional and Urban Economics*, Penguin Books, Harmondsworth.

Roughgarden J (1979) *Theory of Population Genetics and Evolutionary Ecology: an Introduction*, MacMillan, New York-London.

Storper M, Walker R (1984) The Spatial Division of Labour: Labour and the Location of Industries, in Sawers L, Tabb WK (eds.) *Sunbelt/Snowbelt: Urban Development and Regional Restructuring*, Oxford University Press, Oxford, pp. 19-47.

Swann GMP (1998) Towards a Model of Clustering in High-Technology Industries, in Swann GMP, Prevezer M, Stout D (eds.) *The Dynamics of Industrial Clustering*, Oxford University Press, Oxford, pp. 52-76.

Tauchen H, Witte AD (1983) An Equilibrium Model of Office Location and Contact Patterns, *Environment and Planning A*, 15, pp. 1311-1326.

Verhulst PF (1845) Recherches Mathématique sur la loi d'accroissement de la population, *Nouveaux Mémoires de l'Académie Royale des Sciences et Belles-Lettres de Bruxelles*, 18 (2), pp. 3-38.

Volterra V (1926) Variazioni e fluttuazioni del numero di individui in specie di animali conviventi, *Memorie Accademia dei Lincei*, 2, pp. 31-113.

Weber (1929) *Theory of the Location of Industry*, Chicago, Chicago University Press.

High-Technology Clusters: Specialisation and Interaction[1]

G. M. Peter Swann

Professor of Industrial Economics, Nottingham University Business School
Jubilee Campus, Wollaton Road, Nottingham NG8 1BB, UK
peter.swann@nottingham.ac.uk

1. Introduction

One of the interesting dynamic features of many high-technology clusters is an increase in the division of labour, and hence an increasing fragmentation of production. One striking example of this is in the manufacture of personal computers (PCs), where it has become almost meaningless to ask in what country a PC is manufactured. The various components of a PC are manufactured in many different countries, assembly may be done in more than one country, and the final "badge" may be added somewhere else again. Particular companies (and indeed particular clusters) may become specialised in just one particular activity within the overall process of PC manufacture. This specialisation and fragmentation of production depends on interaction between the different activities, and hence on cost-effective communication and transportation.

The objective of this paper is to describe and analyse a simple model of the comparative efficiency of several different industrial structures. At one end we examine the co-location of all production with final consumption; at the other, we examine the emergence of specialised clusters each focusing on just one stage of production. The model shows how this comparative efficiency depends on economies of scale and scope, economies of agglomeration and congestion cost~ and on costs of communication and transportation. The model also explai~ the degree of codification of the production process influences this ~

[1] This paper is a reprinting already published in Atti dei Convegr~
Reti. Italia ed Europa (Roma, 8-9 aprile 2003), Accademi~

efficiency, and hence explains why we may see a marked change in clustering over a product life cycle.

The paper is relevant to the process of clustering in many European countries, but especially relevant to issues arising in the United Kingdom. The British government has adopted clustering as a major instrument of industrial policy, and believes it has a role in helping to revive the economies of poorer regions. Unfortunately however, much of the clustering observed in practice is a further concentration of activity into the over-heated South East of England. The paper concludes by asking if there are any components of cluster policy that might enhance regional prospects and slow down the over-heating of the South East.

The rest of the paper is arranged as follows. Section 2 describes in a very cursory way some of the key ideas in the literature about the interplay between the emergence of clusters and the growth of specialisation. It makes no claim to comprehensiveness, but identifies the main ideas used in this paper. Section 3 then sets out our basic model of clustering, interaction and specialisation. This model is in two parts: a model of production costs (depending on scale, scope, and agglomeration economies) and a model of transportation and communication costs. Section 4 illustrates the workings of this model by considering the case of a production process that can be split into four parts. Demand is inelastic, and is dispersed over a wide geographical area, with customers grouped into cities, towns and villages, and we consider five industrial structures for producing the necessary output required to satisfy demand. Sections 5 and 6 explore how the efficiency of different industrial structures depends on the various parameters identified in Section 3. This relationship is summarised by means of two different diagrams - a simple 'map' in Section 5 and a 'radar' chart in Section 6. Section 7 concludes with some observations about the implications of this model for industrial policy towards clusters, with special reference to the UK.

2. Underlying Ideas

In relating this paper to the wide literature on clusters, a few main points need to be made. As Martin and Sunley (2003) show, the use of the term 'cluster' is not standardised in the literature, and this can lead to considerable confusion. For example, some definitions imply rich interaction between those companies in the cluster while other definitions imply little more than co-location, without any necessary interaction between companies. Moreover, while there is general agreement that a high-tech cluster contains a disproportionately high concentration of particular high-tech industrial sub-sectors, the exact breadth of this portfolio is not defined.

In this paper, we are concerned with one specific aspect of clustering: the tendency for production in a particular industry to become vertically disaggregated, with particular companies and particular clusters specialising in a particular part of the value chain. As such, an essential building block for our analysis is the division of labour and those factors that influence it.

Smith's (1776) classic analysis of the division of labour saw it as one of the main routes to promoting productivity and therefore growth. Smith recognised that the division of labour was limited by the extent of the market. Any process that increases the extent of the market would provide greater incentives for a further sub-division of labour. The clustering process we observe in this paper is one where a cluster or collection of clusters supplies the demand originating from a wide geographical area, whereas the dispersed (or non-clustered) outcome, is where demand at each location is supplied by production at that same location. For that reason, it is clear that the clusters emerge alongside an increase in the extent of the market.

Babbage (1835) built on Smith's analysis to show the importance of interchangeable parts (and hence standards) in the division of labour.[2] That feature plays an important role in this paper. Here one specialized cluster sources its inputs from another specialised cluster, but the identity of the firm from which it sources these inputs does not matter since the inputs are assumed to be standardised and interchangeable. This feature also means that companies only require a limited face-to-face contact with their suppliers and customers: since they are dealing in standardised parts, the product description is clearly codified, and hence much of the necessary communication can be done online.

However, it is equally well known - notably from the work of Pavitt (1987) - that some of the most important knowledge exchanged in high-tech clusters is tacit knowledge, not codified knowledge. It is generally agreed that tacit knowledge is much harder to communicate online, in part because it requires richer social interaction in order to tease out relevant pieces of tacit knowledge. For that reason, the model in this paper allows that a proportion of communication between different stages of the production process must be done face-to-face, and that proportion can change over time, and over the product life cycle.

In particular, product life cycle theory recognises that while tacit knowledge may be very important in the introductory phase, production tends to become more codified as the life cycle progresses. At the start of the life cycle, the importance of tacit knowledge exchange means that different vertical stages of production need to be co-located because of the necessity of frequent face-to-face meetings to facilitate this exchange of tacit knowledge. As a result, the clustering patterns observed at that time involve the co-location of several production stages. Later on in the life cycle, however, the importance of the tacit component declines (relatively speaking) and this co-location of different vertical stages is no longer essential. Indeed, under some circumstances we observe vertical fragmentation of production, with a collection of clusters each specialising in one particular stage of the production process.[3]

---

[2] One of the outstanding historical cases of how standards and accurate measurement can be used to achieve interchangeable parts and the division of labour, is to be found in the work of Whitworth (see Hyman, 1982, pp. 230-233).

[3] Again the history of PC manufacture illustrates this. In the early stages of the life cycle, Langlois (1992) described how early "network firms" (such as Apple) could be highly

A number of econometric studies have examined the relationship between company performance and the strength of the cluster within which it is located. Some of these (and their methodology) are described in Swann et al (1998) and in Beaudry and Swann (2001). At the simplest, these studies find some evidence that companies can perform better when located in clusters. In particular, companies can grow faster and may be more innovative, and also there are more successful entrants into strong clusters. These studies also find occasional evidence that company performance may decline when co-located with companies from other sectors. These findings are consistent with the assumptions of this paper that companies in clusters can enjoy economies of scale, scope and agglomeration, but also that congestion costs can dominate in large clusters when economies of scale and scope are weak.

Several popular accounts of the role of transportation networks in economic development see transport having a potentially benign on less developed regions. Transport allows those in the villages to take advantage of market opportunities in the city. While that is true, as far as it goes, it is regrettably only one half of the story. Equally, transport makes it even easier for the city to dominate the village. Transport increases the extent of the market and therefore allows large-scale producers to further exploit economies of scale, scope and agglomeration, and hence to undercut small suppliers in the regions. The model of this paper brings out this tension very clearly. We shall see that when transport costs are high, an industrial structure where production is dispersed alongside demand is not in danger of being undercut by large scale clustered production. Conversely, when transport costs are low, clustering is the most efficient structure - whether in a single city cluster or in distinct and specialised industrial clusters.

A final strand of the literature is relevant here. While many have focused on the good side of clustering, there is also inevitably a bad side. Swann (2002) emphasises that this process of specialisation in clusters in turn depends on a cost effective transportation and communication infrastructure. Without that either the clusters do not form critical mass, or all activity tends to pile into the most concentrated clusters leading to high congestion in the biggest cities, and decline of other regions. But while an enhanced transportation infrastructure can help the development of specialised clusters, this development will proceed until all additional transportation capacity is used up. In short, progress in clustering appears to imply congestion in transportation. New capacity is soon exhausted. Swann also reflects on what is implied by relaxation of planning controls. These may help the

---

specialised in a small part of the value chain, but the key is that they would source their inputs from other Silicon Valley firms. By the later stages, as already remarked, the value chain was broken up across many different clusters, and indeed different countries. The Cambridge Phenomenon shows some similar features. Segal, Quince and Wicksteed's (1985) original work found that in the introductory phase of their industry's life cycle, many startups located near Cambridge to maintain proximity to the science base. Interviewed later in the life cycle, these companies indicated that proximity was much less important to them, and their essential commercial linkages were spread much more widely.

progress in clustering, but usually at the expense of ever-greater concentration of economic activity in a few highly congested areas. We shall revisit some of these themes in Section 7.

3. Basic Model

This section sets out a model of how the comparative efficiency of different industrial/geographical structures depends on various production parameters (including scale economies, scope economies and agglomeration economies), on congestion costs, and on the costs of communication and transportation. There are two basic elements to this model: a model of production costs and a model of interaction costs.

3.1. Production Costs

We start with the model of production costs. First, take a single part of a production process (j) viewed on its own, where there are economies of scale in that process (j) at a given location (i). Production costs are equal to:

$$PC_{ij} = X_{ij}\, exp\left\{-\alpha_j X_{ij}\right\} \tag{3.1}$$

In what follows, we shall call the α_j 'scale economy' parameters. In principle the values of these parameters are specific to each particular production stage, but in the simple implementation of Sections 4-6, these scale economy parameters are assumed equal to each other. We can compute total costs at location i across all the component parts of the process ($j = 1, ..., N$) by aggregating over j:

$$PC_i = \sum_{j=1}^{N} PC_{ij} = \sum_{j=1}^{N} X_{ij}\, exp\left\{-\alpha_j X_{ij}\right\} \tag{3.2}$$

In addition to these scale economies, we also allow for the possibility that different activities (j) clustering together in the same location i enjoy economies of scope. These are defined by:

$$PC_i' = PC_i\, exp\left\{-\beta \sum_{j=1}^{N} X_{ij}\right\} \tag{3.3}$$

Note that the term on the left-hand side of (3.3) has a mark ($'$) to distinguish it from the term in the left-hand side of (3.2). In what follows, we shall call β the 'scope economy' parameter. Now, thirdly, we allow for the possibility that production benefits from clustering together with other activities that are not part of this particular production process. In short we posit economies of agglomeration from co-locating with other distinct businesses. In addition, we allow that in very large conurbations, congestion costs may start to exceed economies of agglomeration. For that reason we posit a quadratic relationship in the exponent.

$$PC_i'' = PC_i' . exp\left\{-\gamma_1\left[Z_i + \sum_{j=1}^{N} X_{ij}\right] + \gamma_2\left[Z_i + \sum_{j=1}^{N} X_{ij}\right]^2\right\} \qquad (3.4)$$

Again, note that the term on the left-hand side of (3.4) has a double mark ($''$) to distinguish it from the term in the left-hand side of (3.3). In what follows, we shall call γ_1 the 'agglomeration economy' parameter, and γ_2 the 'congestion cost' parameter.[4] We can compute total production costs (counting all scale, scope and agglomeration economies, and also any congestion costs) by aggregating over all locations (1,...,K):

$$PC'' = \sum_{i=1}^{K} PC_i'' \qquad (3.5)$$

3.2. Interaction Costs

Now we turn to the definition of interaction costs (IC), which comprise communication costs (CC) and transportation costs (TC). Let the input-output matrix Φ^C describe the communication intensity between the different activities and let the input-output matrix Φ^T describe the transportation intensity between the different activities. The cost of this communication and transportation depends on intensity and the distance between the different activities. Let the function $i(p,h)$ define the location (i) of a particular production activity (p) as carried out for a particular supply chain (h). Suppose that in a particular supply chain, h, activity p is located in cluster $i(p,h)$ and activity q is located in cluster $i(q,h)$, and define $d[i(p,h),i(q,h)]$ as the distance between these two locations, and hence the two activities in a particular supply chain. Then, assuming for simplicity that communications and transportation costs are both a linear function of distance, communications costs are as follows:

$$CC^h_{pq} = \Phi^C_{pq}\left\{e_C + f_C.d\left[i(p,h),i(q,h)\right]\right\} \qquad (3.6)$$

and transportation costs as follows:

$$TC^h_{pq} = \Phi^T_{pq}\left\{e_T + f_T.d\left[i(p,h),i(q,h)\right]\right\} \qquad (3.7)$$

---

[4] That is not strictly accurate, since agglomeration economies depend on both γ parameters, but will simplify some of the discussion below.

Below we shall work with a simplified form of these where the intensity of interaction is given by the input-output matrix Φ, and the parameter $0 \le \theta_{pq} \le 1$ describes the extent to which that interaction between activities p and q can only be achieved face-to-face (or *offline*). If $\theta_{pq} = 0$, then the entire interaction can be achieved online, and none requires face-to-face (offline) interaction. By contrast, if $\theta_{pq} = 1$, then no interaction can be achieve online, and all requires face-to-face (offline) interaction. Hence in this case:

$$CC^h{}_{pq} = \left(1 - \theta_{pq}\right)\Phi_{pq}\left\{e_C + f_C.d\left[i(p,h),i(q,h)\right]\right\} \tag{3.8}$$

$$TC^h{}_{pq} = \theta_{pq}\Phi_{pq}\left\{e_T + f_T.d\left[i(p,h),i(q,h)\right]\right\} \tag{3.9}$$

Adding these two, we obtain the following for interaction costs:

$$IC^h{}_{pq} = \Phi_{pq}\left\{\left[\theta_{pq}e_T + \left(1 - \theta_{pq}\right)e_C\right] + \left[\theta_{pq}f_T + \left(1 - \theta_{pq}\right)f_C\right].d\left[i(p,h),i(q,h)\right]\right\} \tag{3.10}$$

To compute total interaction costs for a given industrial structure we need to aggregate these across all pairs (p,q) in a given supply chain, h, and then across all supply chains. For simplicity we concentrate on the case where there are no economies of scale in communication and transportation.[5]

$$IC = \sum_{h=1}^{H}\sum_{p=1}^{N}\sum_{q=1}^{N}IC^h{}_{pq} \tag{3.11}$$

Total costs comprise the production costs defined in equation (3.5) and interaction costs defined in equation (3.11):

$$Total\ C = PC'' + IC \tag{3.12}$$

4. Interaction, Communication and Transportation

To illustrate this model, we consider a production process that can in principle be split into four distinct stages (A, B, C, D). For simplicity, we shall assume that these follow a vertical progression, so that the output of A is an input to stage B, the output of B is an input to stage C, and the output of C is an input to stage D. The output of stage D is the finished product, which is sold to the final customer (Fc). Again, for simplicity, we shall assume that the only necessary interactions

---

[5] That is quite a strong assumption for online communications, though perhaps less so for transportation. However, allowing for economies of scale in interaction makes the algebra rather messy. We shall attend to this point in a revision of this paper.

(whether online communication or involving travel/transportation) are between successive stages: A↔B, B↔C, C↔D, D↔Fc. This last assumption simplifies the structure of the Φ matrix to:[6]

$$\Phi = \begin{bmatrix} \Phi_{AA} & \Phi_{AB} & 0 & 0 & 0 \\ \Phi_{BA} & \Phi_{BB} & \Phi_{BC} & 0 & 0 \\ 0 & \Phi_{CB} & \Phi_{CC} & \Phi_{CD} & 0 \\ 0 & 0 & \Phi_{DC} & \Phi_{DD} & \Phi_{DFc} \\ 0 & 0 & 0 & \Phi_{FcD} & \Phi_{FcFc} \end{bmatrix} \qquad (4.1)$$

We shall illustrate the model with reference to the geographical and industrial structure described in Figure 1. This grid describes a simplified economy where each square describes a city (large square), town (medium sized square) or village (small square). The lines describe roads between adjacent conurbations (and communication networks), and all roads form a grid structure. The white areas represent pure countryside. The vertical or horizontal distance between any adjacent squares is 2 units. The largest distance in the map is therefore 16 units - from top left to bottom right, or from top right to bottom left.

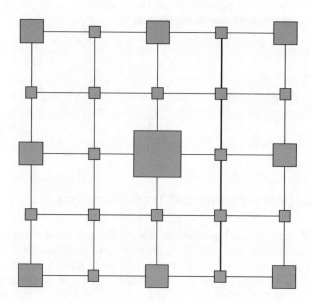

Fig. 1. Geographical Map of City, Towns, Villages and Roads

---

[6] In fact we simplify this further for the exploration in Sections 4-6. Elements on the principal diagonal represent interaction within a particular activity, and there is therefore no relevant distance metric here.

Demand for the final product is inelastic and is assumed proportional to the density of population in each conurbation. The demand from each village is 1, from each town 4, and from the city 16, giving total demand of 64. The paper now explores the efficiency of different industrial/geographical structures in supplying this final demand. In this introductory version of the paper we consider just five such structures, illustrated in Figure 2 (parts 1-5). In Figure 2, the outline squares denote the different conurbations from Figure 1, while the squares in different grey tones indicate the presence of productive capacity to supply each stage of production (dark grey=A, light grey=B, grey=C, black=D).

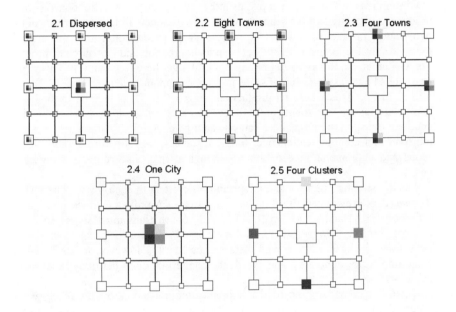

Fig 2. Five Industrial/Geographical Structures

Structure (2.1) is where production is dispersed across the map, and co-located with demand. All the productive capacity necessary to supply each conurbation (for each stage A to D) is located within the conurbation. In this structure, all interaction is localised within a small area: no interactions ever need transcend the boundaries of the conurbation. In particular, no production is transported outside the region. We could call this a *mediaeval economy*, since there is no need for communication or transportation over distance. Such a structure obviously saves on communication and transportation costs, but does not exploit the economies of scale, scope and agglomeration that can be found in some other structures.

Structure (2.2) is where production is located in 8 equal-sized industrial towns around the periphery. Each of these industrial towns contains capacity in each stage (A-D), but each town supplies a wider area than just its indigenous population. Each village satisfies demand from the nearest industrial town(s), and the large city sources its product from the towns in the same way. The largest distance between any conurbation and its source of supply is 4 units. Such a structure is economical on long-distance communication and transportation, but again does not fully exploit economies of scale, scope and agglomeration that can be found in some other structures - though it does this better than structure (2.1).

Structure (2.3) is where production is located in four equal sized industrial towns. Of the 8 towns, these four are the *best located* in the sense that they are nearest to the centre of the map, and not the towns at the four corners of the map. Each of these industrial towns contains capacity in each stage (A-D), but each town supplies a wider area than just its indigenous population. The towns without production capacity and the villages source their products from one or other of the two nearest productive towns. The city sources production equally from each town. Again the largest distance between a conurbation and its source of production is 4 units, but the average journey is a bit longer here (see below). This structure offers better exploitation of scale and scope economies than (2.1) or (2.2).

Structure (2.4) is where all production (stages A to D) is located in the city - one giant cluster. All towns and villages source their production from the city, and here transportation distances can rise as high as 8 units. Although it requires transport and communication over longer distances, this structure exploits scale, scope and agglomeration economies - though it may also run into congestion costs.

Finally, structure (2.5) is one of specialised clusters in each town. There is an *A-town* (dark grey), specialised in the production of A only, a *B-town* (light grey), a *C-town* (grey) and a *D-town* (black). All conurbations must source the final product from the *D-town* (black), so this structure involves the greatest amount of long-distance transportation, with distances up to 12. However, it is efficient at exploiting scale economies, and avoids the congestion costs that may beset structure (2.4).

Table 1 summarises the total communication/transportation distances, while Figure 3 illustrates the frequency of different transportation distances between stage D and the final customer for each of the five structures.

Table 1. Total Communication/Transportation Distances, by Industrial Structure

Industrial/Geographical Structures	A→B	B→C	C→D	D→Fc
4 Specialised Clusters	512	512	512	388
1 Vertically Integrated City	0	0	0	264
4 Vertically Integrated Towns	0	0	0	168
8 Vertically Integrated Towns	0	0	0	104
Dispersed Production Co-located with Customers	0	0	0	0

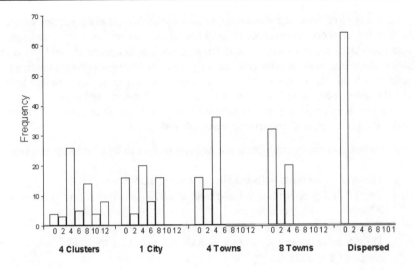

Fig 3. Transportation to Customers – Frequency by Length of Journey (by Industrial Structure)

It is clear that the two clustered structures (4 specialised clusters, and the single-cluster city) require the greatest communication and transportation over distance. As a result, their efficiency must decline as transport and communications costs increase. In the next two sections, we see how the relative efficiency of these different structures depends on the parameters set out in Section 3.

5. Outcomes and Parameters (a)

In this section, we shall draw a simple diagram that gives a rough idea of the comparative efficiency of the five different structures defined above. Each of the structures has its place, and the aim is to show what configuration of the parameters in Section 3 will favour each structure. We should stress, however, that we are not asserting that the observed outcome will necessarily correspond to the most efficient outcome. It is likely that some forms of inertia may mean that an economy may temporarily show a structure that is not the most efficient. Or it is possible that longer-term lock-in to sub-optimal structures may persist. Moreover, we stress that these efficiency measures just measure internal costs - they do not attempt to quantify the social cost of uneven development, or any externalities from transportation.

The model of Section 3 has seven parameters, describing: economies of scale,[7] economies of scope, economies of agglomeration, congestion costs, communication costs per unit distance, transportation costs per unit distance and the online share of all interactions. To provide an exhaustive mapping from parameters to outcomes would therefore require a seven-dimensional map, easy enough to construct inside a computer, but not easy to represent on the printed page.

We produce below a two-dimensional mapping from parameters to outcomes, under the following six simplifying assumptions:

1. Online communication costs are negligible, so can be treated as zero ($e_C = f_C = 0$)
2. Transportation costs within a cluster are negligible, so $e_T = 0$
3. The offline proportion (θ) is *fixed* at 10% (and the online proportion at 90%)[8]
4. The congestion cost parameter (γ_2) is *fixed* at 0.00006
5. The scope economy parameter is *half* the value of the scale economy parameter ($\beta = \alpha/2$)
6. The agglomeration economy parameter is *one tenth* of the scale economy parameter ($\gamma_1 = \alpha/10$)

These assumptions are arbitrary, except that they offer a compact way to illustrate the different parameter zones in which each different structure finds its place. Using these six assumptions, we can capture the parameter variability in two dimensions:

- The transportation cost per unit distance (f_T)
- The scale economy parameter, from which scope and agglomeration economy parameters follow (α, β, γ_1)

Figure 4 illustrates how the most efficient structure depends on parameters, in this simplified schema. The horizontal axis shows the scale economy parameter (on a linear scale), while the vertical axis shows the transport cost parameter (on a log scale).

---

[7] There are in fact four scale economy parameters, one for each production activity. But here we shall assume that these are all equal: $\alpha_1 = \alpha_2 = \alpha_3 = \alpha_4 = \alpha$.

[8] As noted above, θ is in principle specific to each pair of activities, but for simplicity we shall assume that all these different θ have the same value.

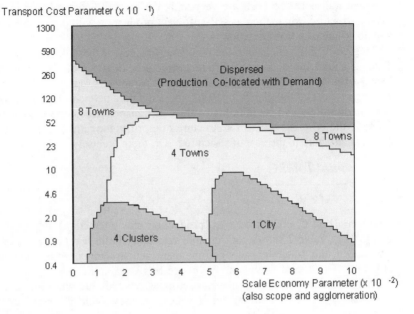

Fig 4. Model Parameters and Structural Outcomes

When scale economies are very low (and so also scope and agglomeration economies), the 8-town structure is the most efficient, except at very high transportation costs. This makes good intuitive sense. If there are no scale, scope or agglomeration economies, then we lose nothing by fragmenting production into a large number of smallish units.[9] As the scale economy parameter increases, however, it is not long before one of the other structures becomes the most efficient.

If transportation costs are very low, then the most efficient structure at intermediate values of scale economy is the specialised cluster structure. When scale economies are very large however, the single city cluster is even more efficient. However, the 4 cluster or single city cluster solutions are only viable if transportation costs remain low - we saw above (Table 1) that transportation costs are highest for these two structures. As transportation costs rise, however, the most efficient solution is no longer the 4 cluster or single city cluster, but rather the 4 (vertically integrated) town structure. This may enjoy smaller scale economies than the 4 cluster or the single city cluster, but does not suffer from such large transportation costs.

---

[9] In this far left hand part of the diagram, we can see the optimist's perspective (noted in Section 2) that reducing transportation costs favours the small players in the regions, by opening up large city markets to these small producers. But when there are important economies of scale, that optimism is misplaced.

When transportation costs are very high, the most efficient solution is the dispersed structure, where there is self-sufficient production within each conurbation, and no reliance on transportation.

To give further insight into the relative efficiency of these different structures, Table 2 shows the ranking of different structures in terms of efficiency, for selected different parameter values. This grid of parameters represents low, medium and high values of the scale/scope/agglomeration parameters in Figure 4, and very low, medium-low and medium-high values of transportation costs in Figure 4. In Table 2, the efficiency score for structure t describes the ratio of the cost of most efficient structure to the cost of structure t. Or, more precisely:

$$E_t = \frac{min\left(Total\ C_s\right)}{Total\ C_t} * 100\% \tag{5.1}$$

Where *Total C_t* is the total cost (production plus interaction) defined in equation (3.12). Table 2 shows considerable variability in these rankings. The single city cluster, the 4-town-clusters and the dispersed structures can be most or least efficient. The 4- and 8-town structures are less variable in their rankings, essentially because they avoid the transport costs associated with clustering and make some use of scale economies, but also because they avoid the high congestion costs of the single city cluster.

Table 2. Ranking of Different Industrial Structures by Efficiency, for Certain Parameter Values

	Scale (α) = 0 Scope (β) = 0 Agglomeration (γ_1) = 0 Congestion (γ_2) = 0.00006	Scale (α) = 0.05 Scope (β) = 0.25 Agglomeration (γ_1) = 0.005 Congestion (γ_2) = 0.00006	Scale (α) = 0.1 Scope (β) = 0.05 Agglomeration (γ_1) = 0.01 Congestion (γ_2) = 0.00006
Offline (θ) = 10% **Comm Cost ($e_C = f_C$) = 0** **Transp Cost (f_T) = 26**	8 Towns (100%) Dispersed (75%) 4 Towns (68%) 4 Clusters (11%) 1 City (0%)	Dispersed (100%) 8 Towns (40%) 4 Towns (29%) 1 City (19%) 4 Clusters (3%)	Dispersed (100%) 8 Towns (25%) 4 Towns (16%) 1 City (10%) 4 Clusters (1%)
Offline (θ) = 10% **Comm Cost ($e_C = f_C$) = 0** **Transp Cost (f_T) = 1**	8 Towns (100%) 4 Towns (73%) 4 Clusters (53%) Dispersed (43%) 1 City (0%)	4 Towns (100%) 1 City (95%) 8 Towns (51%) Dispersed (31%) 4 Clusters (21%)	4 Towns (100%) 8 Towns (69%) 1 City (69%) Dispersed (26%) 4 Clusters (9%)
Offline (θ) = 10% **Comm Cost ($e_C = f_C$) = 0** **Transp Cost (f_T) = 0.04**	8 Towns (100%) 4 Towns (74%) 4 Clusters (73%) Dispersed (41%) 1 City (0%)	4 Clusters (100%) 1 City (53%) 4 Towns (39%) 8 Towns (14%) Dispersed (7%)	1 City (100%) 4 Towns (52%) 4 Clusters (14%) 8 Towns (7%) Dispersed (2%)

6. Outcomes and Parameters (b)

The diagram in the previous section showed the mapping from parameters to the efficiency of different structures under some quite strong assumptions. As noted at the start of that section, the ideal might be to evaluate the model over a large grid of values for each parameter, though that would create a large-dimensional map. Here we use a different way to summarise just such a large grid of parameter values.

We have evaluated the model at each of four possible values for each parameter (apart from the communication cost, which is held at zero). These parameter values are as follows:

Table 3. Grid of Parameter Values

	Value 1	Value 2	Value 3	Value 4
Scale Economy (α)	0.006	0.024	0.042	0.06
Scope Economy (β)	0.0006	0.0024	0.0042	0.006
Agglomeration Economy (γ_1)	0.00006	0.00024	0.00042	0.0006
Congestion Costs (γ_2)	0.000006	0.000024	0.000042	0.00006
Offline % (θ)	10%	40%	70%	100%
Transportation Costs (f_T)	0.3	1.2	2.1	3.0

This creates a grid of $4^6 = 2^{12} = 4096$ different parameter combinations and outcomes. Then for each of the outcomes (i.e. for all combinations in which a particular structure is most efficient) we compute the average value of each parameter. These are plotted on a radar-graph, as in Figure 5. The scale of each axis here runs from 0% to 100%, since each parameter average is expressed relative to the maximum value for that parameter in Table 3.

First, consider the average transportation cost parameter. Amongst those simulations where the dispersed outcome (red) is the most efficient, the average transportation cost parameter is rather high. At the opposite extreme, amongst those simulations where the 4-cluster structure is most efficient, the average transportation cost parameter is very low. This all makes sense, because as we said before, specialised clusters depend on low transportation and communications costs, while the dispersed outcome (where production is co-located with final demand) does not.

Next, consider the average offline percentage parameter. Again, amongst those simulations where the dispersed solution is most efficient, the average offline percentage is high. But amongst those simulations where the 4-cluster structure is most efficient, the average offline percentage is very low. Again, this all makes sense, because offline communication is not expensive when production and consumption are co-located; it becomes expensive when (as in specialised clusters) one part of the supply chain is distant from another.

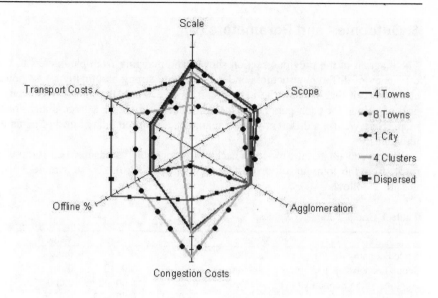

Fig. 5. Mean Parameter Values for Simulations with Different Outcomes

This offline percentage parameter is an indirect measure of the effects of codi-fication. Why is that? It is generally recognised that it is relatively easy to ex-change codified knowledge online, but the exchange of tacit knowledge is much easier when done face-to-face (or offline). Now, the higher the required offline percentage of interaction, the greater the tacit component of the knowledge to be exchanged. Basic product life cycle theory asserts that in the early stage of the life-cycle, much of the knowledge to be exchanged between adjacent production activities is tacit, so requires a high face-to-face (or offline) component. By con-trast, by the later stages of the life cycle, much of the knowledge to be exchanged between adjacent production activities is now codified, and hence exchange can be achieved online.

Hence we can deduce from the above how the degree of codification of the production process influences this comparative efficiency. When codification is low, as in the initial stages of a product life cycle, then the face-to-face percentage of interactions is high, and hence a dispersed solution, where production is collo-cated with consumption, or a single-city cluster is more likely than a collection of specialised (vertically fragmented) clusters. But when codification is high, as in the mature stages of a product life cycle, then the offline percentage of interactions can be quite low, and then a four specialised cluster solution is likely. These ob-servations can be used to offer an interpretation of why we often see a marked change in the geographical pattern of production over a product life cycle. The geographical fragmentation of production into specialised clusters - as noted above in our discussion of the personal computer industry - is more likely in the later growth and maturity stages of the life cycle.

Turning to the congestion cost parameter, we see that amongst the simulations where the 8-town structure is most efficient, this congestion cost parameter is relatively high. But amongst those simulations where the single city cluster is most efficient, this congestion cost parameter is low. Again, this makes good sense. High congestion costs do not afflict the 8-town structure, but do badly affect the single city cluster. The latter is only likely to be the most efficient structure when congestion costs are low. Again, in terms of our PC industry example, the Silicon Valley cluster started to fragment when that cluster became very large, and production of standardised parts would be spread out to lower cost locations.

Turning to the scale economy parameter, we see that the average values do not vary very much, except that these average values are low amongst those simulations where the 8-town structure is most efficient. That makes good sense, because the 8-town solution is (as we saw in Figure 4) most likely to be efficient when scale economies are not large. The same sort of argument applies to the scope economy parameter, though the differences in Figure 5 are small. And finally, there are no differences of significance in terms of the average values for the agglomeration economy parameter.

7. Conclusions and Policy

The main arguments of this paper are that the development of specialised and vertically-fragmented production clusters tends to occur during the later stages of a product life cycle, where a large proportion of interaction between different stages can be done online. In addition, such specialised and fragmented clusters also depend on cheap transportation and communication, because these structures are transportation-intensive. The fragmented and specialised structure (4 clusters) tends to be at its most efficient when transport costs and the offline proportion are both low, when congestion costs are high and scope economies are not especially high. The single city cluster is at its most efficient when scale and scope economies are high and congestion costs are low.

The paper is relevant to the process of clustering in many European countries, but especially relevant to issues arising in the United Kingdom. The British government has adopted clustering as a major instrument of industrial policy, and believes it has a role in helping to revive the economies of poorer regions. Unfortunately however, much of the clustering observed in practice is a further concentration of activity into the over-heated South East of England. Why is that?

In terms of the model in this paper, there are two reasons. The first relates to the effect of the reduction of transport costs and (more especially) the cheapening of high-bandwidth communications within Figure 4. Optimists perhaps believe that these effects lead us from the top middle to the bottom middle. However, the direction of transition is probably from top middle to bottom-middle right. This is partly because reductions in communications costs have not been matched by reductions in transport costs.[10] In addition, several components of government policy seem to have been directed at reducing congestion costs in the South East of the UK (e.g. the relaxation in planning controls), or reinforcing economies of agglomeration by locating public facilities[11] in the *Golden Triangle* of London, Cambridge and Oxford.

If transportation is too expensive for the fragmented/specialised cluster structure, then a single city cluster may be more viable, but is it desirable? The latter experiences high congestion costs, and indeed the true costs of the congestion may be higher still if full social costs are not captured in market prices - see below. Moreover, the single city cluster reinforces an unbalanced pattern of regional development, which is socially dysfunctional. Moreover, while this single city cluster may be attractive from the perspective of international competitiveness, it is not attractive when the true social cost of transportation exceeds the market price. The fact that aircraft fuel is not taxed must be leading to an excessive amount of clustering and transportation.[12]

Are there any components of cluster policy that might enhance regional prospects and slow down the over-heating of the South-East UK? Difficult as it seems, a policy that sincerely seeks to correct overheating in the Southeast and correct regional imbalance must stop trying to alleviate congestion costs in the South-East. All that does is add further fuel to the overheating, and further reinforce the pattern of single-city clustering that is taking over so much of the UK economy. Moreover, from this point of view, governments should not take a lax attitude to planning controls on green-field sites in the South-East. But they can be lax about planning controls on brownfield sites in the North. Finally, a fragmented/specialised cluster structure would be more plausible if the public transportation infrastructure were in better condition, and cheaper. In this respect the high price of peak time rail travel and the underused capacity on 'peak time' trains cannot be helpful.

References

Arthur WB (1990) Silicon Valley Locational Clusters: Do Increasing Returns Imply Monopoly? *Mathematical Social Sciences*, 19, 235-51

Babbage C (1835) *On the Economy of Machinery and Manufactures,* 4th Edition, London: Charles Knight

Beaudry C, Swann GMP (2001) Growth in Industrial Clusters: A Bird's Eye View of the UK, *SIEPR Working Paper* 00-38, Stanford University

---

[10] It is interesting, for example, to compare the (quite high) cost of train travel in UK with that in Italy and France.

[11] For example, the controversial decision to locate a key laboratory in Oxford rather than Daresbury (between Manchester and Liverpool).

[12] Fuel tax protests in the UK in 2000 made it clear that tax of car fuel is highly unpopular amongst some segments of society.

David PA, Rosenbloom JL (1990) Marshallian Factor Market Externalities and the Dynamics of Industrial Localisation. In *Journal of Urban Economics*, 28, 349-70

Department for Transport, Local Government and the Regions (2001a) Planning: Delivering a Fundamental Change, Green Paper, available at:
http://www.planning.dtlr.gov.uk/consult/greenpap/index.htm

Department for Transport, Local Government and the Regions (2001b) New Parliamentary Procedures for Processing Major Infrastructure Projects, available at:
http://www.planning.dtlr.gov.uk/consult/majinfra/index.htm

Herbig P, Golden JE (1993) How to Keep that Innovative Spirit Alive: An Examination of Evolving Innovative Hot Spots. In *Technological Forecasting and Social Change*, 43, 75-90

Hyman A (1982) Charles Babbage: Pioneer of the Computer, Oxford: Oxford University Press

Jacobs J (1961) The Death and Life of Great American Cities. New York

Joseph Rowntree Foundation (2002) Land for Housing; Current Practice and Future Options, York Publishing Services Ltd/Joseph Rowntree Foundation

Krugman P (1991) Geography and Trade, Cambridge, Mass: MIT Press

Langlois RN (1992) External Economies and Economic Progress: The Case of the Microcomputer Industry, *Business History Review*, 66, 1-50

McCann P, Arita T (2000) Industrial Alliances and Firm Location Behaviour: Some Evidence from the US Semiconductor Industry, *Applied Economics*, 32, 1391-1403

Martin R, Sunley P (2003) Deconstructing clusters: chaotic concept or policy panacea?, *Journal of Economic Geography*, 3: 5-35

Mumford L (1961) The City in History, London: Penguin Books

Pavitt K (1987) On the Nature of Technology, Brighton: University of Sussex, SPRU

Porter M (1990) The Competitive Advantage of Nations, London: MacMillan

Quadrio Curzio A, Fortis M (eds. 2002) Complexity and Industrial Clusters: Dynamics and Models in Theory and Practice, Heidelberg: Physica-Verlag

Saxenian A (1994) Regional Advantage: Culture and Competition in Silicon Valley and Route 128, Cambridge, Mass: Harvard University Press

Segal Quince Wicksteed (1985) The Cambridge Phenomenon, Cambridge: Segal Quince Wicksteed

Smith A (1776/1910) The Wealth of Nations, Everyman Edition, London: J. M. Dent and Sons

Swann GMP (2002) The Implications of Clustering: Some Reflections, *CREIM Conference on Clusters*, Manchester Business School (April)

Swann GMP, Prevezer M, Stout D (eds. 1998) The Dynamics of Industrial Clustering, Oxford: Oxford University Press

II. New Industry, European Framework and National Success Stories

New Science, New Industry and New Institutions? Second Thoughts on Innovation and Europe's Universities[1]

Paul A. David

Stanford University, California (USA)
Oxford Internet Institute, University of Oxford, Oxford, UK
pad@stanford.edu
pdavid@herald.ox.ac.uk

1. Introduction

When discussing the goals and strategies for enhancing the European region's international economic competitiveness - specifically those announced at the Meeting of EU Council of Ministers in Lisbon - several are the themes that can be analyzed. For example the relationship between fundamental advances in scientific understanding and technological innovation that is complicated and multivalent, and probabilistic; the incentives for discovery and invention, entrepreneurship and finance, the formation of managerial expertise and workforce skills, the diffusion of new processes and products, and a multiplicity of expectational effects and dynamic feedbacks that interconnect all of the foregoing processes. There is also to be considered the roles played by public institutions involved in training and research, particularly the universities.

[1] This essay has been developed from my presentation to the Conference organized by the Accademia Nazionale dei Lincei and the Fondazione Edison on New Science, New Industry held in Rome, Italy on 13-14 October 2004. It draws upon material in "Innovation in the Past and Future of Europe's Universities," presented to the Coimbra General Assembly of the Historical European Universities, convened in Siena, Italy, 14-16th April 2004, and my "Lectio Magistralis" delivered at the University of Torino, 12th May 2003. I wish to express my gratitude to each of the institutions that have invited me to speak on this important subject, and to the participants in those events from whose comments and suggestions this work has benefited.

I intend to limit my focus to the nexus of issues raised by the Commission of the European Communities' *Communication* (of February 2003) on "the role of the universities in the Europe of knowledge".[2] That document assessed Europe's critical needs in the epoch of "knowledge-driven economic growth" and the means to meeting those needs. Beyond its specifics, I regard the general thrust of that text to be both influential and emblematic of the wider stream of thinking that has been shaping the policies of both EU agencies and the ministries of national governments on science, technology and innovation in recent years.

The EC's *Communication* identifies the university as the institution uniquely suited to meeting Europe's needs to become more effective in generating and exploiting science-based innovation, and it goes on to call for debate on the means by which the conditions prevailing among the region's universities can be changed in order to better satisfy the requirements of the new societal role for which the Commission those institutions to be destined. Underlying that belief about Europe's path to a brighter economic future, as far as I can discern, is the arresting assessment that the leading institutions of higher education in the EU possess the potential to be more effective at commercially successful technological innovation than are the mass of business firms comprising the economy's private sector. At the same time, along with other recent pronouncements by representatives of the governments of the member states, the Commission finds fault with the universities' researchers and administrators for failing to make the realization of their "innovation-potential" an institutional priority. From this it follows that what is needed is a program of institutional reform and reorientation that would mobilize of that latent capability in order to meet a two key requirements for faster productivity growth and greater competitiveness: paying for the cost of expanding public education and training at the tertiary level, and raising the share of EU gross domestic product invested in R&D – a 50% increase, from the 2 percentage point to the 3 percentage point level, being a major strategic "target" announced by the Lisbon Meeting.

I am persuaded that university adaptations and institutional innovation are both possible and desirable as steps towards reinvigorating the performance of the so-called European Research Area. Nevertheless, the premises upon which the EC's proposed programs of university redirection and reform are grounded, and the basic economic logic of this aspect of the innovation strategy for Europe should be re-submitted for a more careful, indeed, more sceptical examination that they have generally been receiving. I want approach that argument a little indirectly – envisaging the dawning of a new, innovative epoch in the development of higher education institutions for Europe.

---

[2] European Commission, *Communication from the Commission: The role of the university in the Europe of knowledge*, COM(2003) 58 final. Brussels: Commission of the European Communities (5 February), 2003.

2. An Innovative Epoch in the European University System

2.1. Institutional Creativity Envisaged

Communities of scholars and students from distant parts of the continent have assembled collectively to form centres of learning of unprecedented size, and by adapting pre-existing organizational forms to create novel governance structures, have given rise to numerous new and *more efficient* nodes for knowledge-creation and knowledge dissemination. The resulting radically new institutional model lends itself readily for imitation, and soon is being replicated widely throughout the entire region of Western Europe, and eventually far beyond. Moreover, the academic life carried on within these new organizations is *infused with much infectious dedication, which makes possible the highest intellectual standards*, especially in those institutions that succeed in their struggles to free themselves from the repressive constraints imposed by various regulatory authorities. A movement is underway, with the active encouragement and the sanctions granted by a pan-European authority, to bring into being *an international university system…a European-wide academic commonwealth which would transcend race and provincialism in the collective pursuit and dissemination of learning.*

The profound departure from previous traditions and formal arrangements in higher education just depicted has been conceived during a period of intense and eclectic intellectual activity, featuring efforts to synthesize old and new systems of thought. This has required mastering and further developing what for many of the participants is a powerful but unaccustomed set of analytical tools. The resulting new analytical mode finds many trans-disciplinary applications, and has *advanced with such meteoric pace that it is displacing the established, classical norms of education*. It is destined to achieve intellectual dominance as *the centerpiece of the university curriculum*, thus marking *a radical transition* in pedagogy: from an educational *system founded on a passive attachment to an inherited culture*, to one in which an investigative and *questioning approach to all sources of knowledge is in the ascendant.*

These dramatic alterations in the cognitive and institutional structures of higher education in Europe are nonetheless firmly *rooted in utilitarian soil*. They are responses to the need to harness the expanding intellectual forces of the era to the increasingly demanding knowledge requirements of the surrounding society and economy. While pursuit of advanced inquiry by an intellectual elite -- as a contribution to fundamental understanding of an ordered universe and the place of human-kind within it – is held to be one of the universities' perennial functions, these institutions also are seen *as service agencies catering for a hierarchy of social needs*.

The surrounding societies, with which these organizations soon develop increasingly strong symbiotic relationships, have at their disposal only limited finances for the purposes of higher education. Returns of a concrete nature are expected from investment in university concerns. Scarce resources are not made

available for the subsistence of ivory towers. Instead, the society of this era ex-
pects its universities to be vocational institutions responding to vocational needs.
Reciprocally, new arrangements are introduced by other institutions to facilitate
the provision of finance for the continuing education of certain cadres of specialized workers who engage in knowledge-intensive service activities that the community at large deems to be particularly important. Thus, by mobilizing and ra-
tionally deploying Europe's intellectual and pedagogical resources on a hitherto
unprecedented scale, the new system manages - despite the constraints of its situation - to meet the professional expectations of a broad spectrum of contemporary
society; and its constituent institutions are judged to have achieved this without
becoming the monopolistic agencies of any one privileged section of the community.

The preceding evocation of the emergence of a vibrant, innovating and socially
responsive university system reflects the assessment by modern historians of the
rise the Europe's medieval universities in the epoch stretching from the 12th to the
15th century – an epoch which saw the founding of the venerable institutions of
Bologna and Padua, Paris and Montepellier, Oxford and Cambridge, Prague and
many others. Indeed, I constructed my text by piecing together direct quotations
and close paraphrasing of the works of Professor A. B. Cobban, a leading British
historian of the origins and early development of the remarkably successful medieval institutional innovations.[3]

2.2. The 'Vision' Deciphered

I make no apologies for the benign deception entailed my relating modern historians' views of salient developments in the early medieval university scene, masked
in the language of our contemporary discussions of university research and training policies in Europe. 'The medieval university' has been receiving an unwar-
ranted amount of bad press in recent times, in Britain, most notably in the public
utterances of the Labour Government's present Minister of Education and Skills,
Charles Clarke: in urging universities to think more about how they benefit the
economy, Mr. Clarke argued that "a medieval concept of a community of scholars
seeking truth is not in itself a justification for the state to put money into that. We
might do it at, say, a level of one hundredth of what we do now and have one university of medieval seekers after truth...as an adornment to our society."[4] Thus,
there is some value simply in reminding ourselves from time to time, and reminding the makers of public policy, too, that to propose that the university community
should serve the 'utilitarian' needs of society hardly is a modern thought. The me-

---

[3] The portions of the text in the preceding section that appear in italics are direct quotations
drawn from A.B. Cobban, *Europe's Medieval Universities*, Oxford: Oxford University
Press, 1988. Ch.1, which provides citations to numerous sources – including recent historical studies by other.

[4] *The Guardian*, May 10 2003, p.3, reports these statements as taken from a transcript, re-
leased by the Department of Education and Skills, of the Minister's remarks made earlier
in that week at a gathering at University College, Worcester.

dieval roots of this remarkable institutional form, as Professor Cobban says, were firmly planted 'in utilitarian soil'. Greater awareness of this fact would be useful especially in drawing attention to the difference between the principle of 'service' – about which there is no real debate -- and the question of how best the modern university can serve the societies on which it ultimately must rely for its support.

Nevertheless, for the benefit of those who wish to complete their decoding of my 'vision', I should perhaps quickly identify the most salient among the historical details to which I was alluding, before coming back to the future vision of the university's role in 'the Europe of knowledge' – as the European Commission would have it.

The medieval idea of the *studium generale* was indeed a major institutional innovation. That was the term by which the medieval universities were first described, distinguishing them from *studium particulare* --institutions offering instruction in the arts by local scholars for local students. Although thought to require endorsement of the Pope or the Holy Roman Emperor, the status of *studium generale* was of a customary rather than legal nature until the late 13th and 14th centuries, when Italian jurists devised the term *studium generale ex consuetudine*, and applied it to long established centers such as Paris, Bologna, Montpellier, Padua, Oxford, and Cambridge.

By adapting pre-existing organizational forms -- notably, corporate guild organization-- the masters and students created novel governance structures for a rapidly increasing number of these new and *more efficient nodes* – or as we economists would say, agglomerations or 'clusters' that generated economies of scale and scope for knowledge-creation and knowledge dissemination. Only by accident did the Latin term *universitas –which in common usage denoted several types of corporate bodies, e.g., craft guilds or municipal councils* -- come to be specifically associated with university institutions. Before the 15th century *universitas* referred to guilds of students (as in the case of Bologna) or of the masters (in case of Paris), -- the personnel rather than the university structure as a whole.

The 'New Logic' of Aristotle, rediscovered and made available in Latin (c. 1150 – 1250) emerged as the characteristic analytical mode associated with these novel institutions of learning, *advancing with such meteoric pace that it soon displaced established classical norms of education and found many transdisciplinary applications*. Logic, or dialectic, was the indispensable instrument for deep penetration of all branches of learning – including theology, law, medicine, the natural sciences and grammar; it soon achieved intellectual dominance as *the centerpiece of the new university curriculum, the quintessence of all that was forward-looking and creative*. Logic's rise thus marked *a radical transition* in pedagogy: from an educational *system founded on a passive attachment to an inherited culture* (namely that associated with studies of classical literature), to one that was committed to an investigative and *questioning approach to all sources of knowledge*.

These alterations in the cognitive and institutional structures of higher education in Europe were *rooted in utilitarian soil;* their respective societies expected its universities *to be vocational institutions responding to vocational needs*. The *studium generale* featured a regime offering graduate training in at least one of the 'superior faculties' of law (canon or civil or both), theology, and medicine. Training in logic and the art of disputation was the prescribed general preparation for most professional activities. Allied to knowledge of the relevant procedures, dialectical training could be applied successfully over a wide range of intricate administrative, litigious, educational, and diplomatic affairs.

Reciprocally, new arrangements were introduced by other institutions (namely, the Church) in order to facilitate the provision of finance for the continuing education of certain cadres in specialized knowledge-intensive service activities whose work was held to be socially important. The specific financing arrangements to which I thus referred were those permitting beneficed members of the clergy to receive the incomes of their benefices whilst absent from their parish and attending university as students or teachers.

By the 13th century a movement was underway with the encouragement and sanction of pan-European authorities (namely, that of the Pope and the Holy Roman Emperor) that aimed to create *an international university system...a European-wide academic commonwealth which would transcend race and provincialism in the collective pursuit and dissemination of learning*. This advanced the theoretical notion of the *ius ubique docendi* – the right of a graduate of one university to teach in another without undergoing examination. By the 14th century possession of this right by holders of a master's degree from the institution was a cardinal legal hallmark of the status of *studium generale* – normally included in the foundation charters. In practice, however, university particularism (and job-protection for the masters) tended to prevail against the supranational (and leveling) implications of the *ius ubique docendi*. The dream of the *ius ubique docendi* is one that continues today to haunt the European Commission when it contemplates the advantages of creating a truly integrated labor market for science and engineering researchers that would embrace the entire European Research Area.

2.3. The Evolving Legacy of Medieval Institutional Innovation

That was not the only business left 'unfinished' by the medieval institutional innovators. It is glaring the absence – both in the cryptic and the decoded versions of my 'vision' of the medieval university system – of any explicit references to scientific or technological research, indeed to organized research activities of all kinds. Resistance to the new mechanical philosophy of the 16th and 17th centuries by the entrenched university faculties meant that the fusion of mathematics with experimentalism which created the epistemological foundations of the Scientific Revolution was not carried forward within that institutional setting, even though many of the great names associated with the movement (including Copernicus, and Galileo) held university posts at some points in their careers. Instead, those pioneering the emerging experimental and observational sciences managed to insinuate their new methods and style of discourse into the proceedings of the independent humanistic academies that had flourished during the late Renaissance era. At the end of the 16th century they had begun to form more specialized scientific societies, such as Della Porta's *Accademia Secretorum Naturae* (founded in Napoli, 1589), the *Accademia dei Cacciatore* (inVenezia, 1596) and, of course, Federico Cesi's *Accademia dei Lincei* (Roma, 1603). Only subsequently, toward the latter part of the 17th century did mechanical philosophy, and the associated behavioural precepts of the equally novel social structure of 'open science,' became institutionalized under state patronage – in the Royal Society of London (1662), and the *Académie royale des Sciences* (1666).

There ensued a further delay of almost two centuries duration before 'research' as we know it became established alongside teaching as a central activity of the faculties of Europe's higher education institutions – on the model of Wilhem von Humbolt's proposed reform of the German university. That development, and the subsequent importation of the Humboltian model into American universities during the two closing decades of the 19th century, belongs to the longer story into the details of which it will be neither possible nor necessary for me to enter on this occasion. It is nevertheless worth noting that this second great institutional innovation led relatively swiftly to the experiment of closely coupling of graduate instruction and faculty research activities, a pedagogical shift that was fully embraced in the U.S. university setting; it has proved to be so effective a means of forming large cadres of productive researchers in the physical, engineering and life sciences, that today one observes it being taken up by countries (including France, and Japan) where science and engineering research formerly had been largely conducted in government laboratories and public institutes, in isolation from their universities' instructional activities.

With the progressive integration of advanced instruction with research in universities, the institutionalization of open science throughout the modern world, albeit to a different degree in different places, was reinforced and its normative structure was imparted to successive cohorts of academics and public sector researchers. Generation after generation of graduate students were thereby exposed to, and inculcated with the ethos of open science that became more and more clearly articulated in the democratic societies of the West from the late nineteenth century onwards. This was a potent means of reinforcing the informal behavioural norms of cooperation in pursuit of knowledge, meritocratic universalism, and uninhibited intellectual scepticism. It promoted conditions in which the responsibility of faculty-researchers teachers to impart their knowledge fully to graduate students was well aligned with the open pursuit of scientific enquiry, rather than trammelled by secrecy, restrictions on the usage new research methods, and potential conflicts arising from organizations' and individuals' ambitions to create economically valuable intellectual property from which they would benefit directly. Furthermore, it reinforced and sustained the ability of the universities in many parts of the work to continuing to function effectively as open nodes in an international information network that transmitted, received and validated claims to discoveries and inventions that represented advances in knowledge, and upon which further advances in knowledge could be based. In this way, the universalist promise of the original, medieval European institutional innovation came to be realized throughout a far more extensive and culturally diverse domain: the global domain of the Republic of Science.[5]

The ethos of open science – as much as formal institutional regulations designed to avoid conflicts of interest and the misuse of public resources for purely private gain – formed an effective bulwark in the democratic societies against the more subtle distorting pressures that commercial and political interests could bring to bear upon the conduct of university-based research and the reporting of its outcomes. Upon this and kindred fragile structures of institutionalized behaviour came to rest the public trust that once was more or less automatically accorded to 'disinterestedness' academic research; and consequently to the reliability of universities as the loci of enquiries that could, more than any other, impartially ascertain and report on the meaning and implications of new discoveries and devices for human knowledge, individual well-being and the vitality of society.

3. Back to the Future: the Quest for the 'Wealth-Creating' University Reconsidered

These qualities, achievements and potentialities of Europe's universities should be borne regarded as unique societal assets that would in all likelihood be placed at risk by a concerted effort to develop commercially-oriented 'knowledge management enterprises' within those institutions. Yet that is what appears to be contemplated today in Britain, where the Board of Trade and Industry speaks of the need to expand a 'third stream' – in addition to the traditional channels of teaching and research – through which the university can contribute to national and regional 'wealth creation', specifically by creating and exploiting intellectual property rights, by offering the services of its faculty as consultants to private firms, by introducing specialized degree courses tailored to the needs of industrial sponsors who would be able to select candidates for instruction, by developing 'distance learning' services that could be marketed to the public both at home and overseas via the Internet, and so forth.

Such a program constitutes perhaps the leading edge of reformist policy initiatives intended to re-animate the universities with an entrepreneurial spirit of 'wealth creation'. Certainly it envisages a much wider array of university profit-seeking activities than those proposed for discussion and debate by the EC (2003) *Communication*. The latter, more conservatively, focuses attention upon the remaining changes in national regulations that would be needed not only to enable the universities to patent discoveries and inventions resulting from publicly funded research, and to increase the incentives for those working in public research or-

---

[5] On the economics of the ethos and institutions of open science, see P. Dasgupta and P A. David, Towards a New Economics of Science. In *Research Policy*, 23 (1994):pp.487-521; P. A. David, The Economic Logic of 'Open Science' and the Balance Between Private Property Rights and the Public Domain in Scientific Data and Information. in *The Role of Scientific and Technical Data and Information in the Public Domain*, eds. J. M. Esau and P. F. Uhlir, Washington, D.C.: National Academies Press, 2003.

ganizations to engage in more applied, commercially-oriented projects – by permitting them to share along with their institutions in the income derived from the exploitation of their findings. In this regard, the position presented by the Commission is hardly a radical one; it reflects policy initiatives that already were being actively considered and in some cases have been implemented by a number of OECD member nations, apparently in emulation of the experiment undertaken by the U.S. under the term of the Bayh-Dole Act and the Stevenson-Wydler Act, legislation passed by the Congress in 1980 to simply and codify the terms on which institutions conducting federally sponsored research could seek intellectual property rights in the results.[6] In Italy, for example, legislation was adopted in 2001 to shift ownership of intellectual property based upon university research from the institution to individual researchers. In Japanese universities the allocation of ownership of IPR from publicly funded research is determined by a committee in each institution, and these bodies on occasion award title to individual researchers. In Britain there has been a trend to transfer ownership rights to patents (and electronic copyrights) on publicly supported research results from the funding agencies to the universities, and a variety of arrangements exist among the institutions for distributing royalties between individual researchers and their institutions. Professors in the university systems of Germany and Sweden long held ownership of intellectual property resulting from the activities of their laboratories, and while debate about shifting ownership to the university continues in Sweden, recent legislation has accomplished that change in Germany. In each of the countries mentioned, in addition, as well as in France, governments have encouraged the formation of external 'technology licensing organizations' which may be affiliated with a given university—as is the norm in Britain, and in the U.S.--or be an independent entity. Overall, there has been an evident trend toward engaging university faculty researchers in 'patentable' research, and toward involving their respective institutions in the ownership and licensing of intellectual property based upon publicly funded research results.

The scale on which these institutional innovations are being promoted is, in my view, and that of other economists and science and technology analysts, a matter of concern. For these policy initiatives to succeed will require a significant reorientation of university-based research, pushing it away from areas in which these institutions have a demonstrable comparative advantage. Within the familiar context of academic, 'open science' norms and governance structures, the comparative advantage of university-based researchers' lies in conducting fundamental,

---

[6] The Bayh-Dole Act was passed as Pub. L No. 96-517, Section 6(a) 3015, 3019-28 and codified as amended ast 34 U.S.C. Sections 200-212 (1994); the Stevenson-Wydler Technology Innovation Act of 1980, Publ. L. No. 96-480, 94 Stat. 2311-2320 (codified as amended at 15 U.S.C., Sections 3701-2714) pertained to the assignment of title to federal research institutes and national laboratories, and they complemented, whereas Bayh-Dole pertained to vesting title to IPR in universities. On international emulation, see OECD, *Benchmarking Science-Industry Relationships*, Paris: OCED, 2002, and the discussion by D.C. Mowery and B. Sampat, The Bayh-Dole Act of 1980 and University-Industry Technology Transfer: A Model for Other OECD Governments?. U.C. Berkeley Haas School of Business Working Paper. 2003.

exploratory enquiries that in many cases will turn out to have laid the foundations for subsequently fruitful investment in applications-oriented R&D. It is also the case that in some new, frontier areas of science physical effects are discovered and new research techniques are devised that quite readily can be translated – even before the fundamental underlying phenomena are thoroughly understood – into devices which provide prototypes for valuable commercial innovations. One may think in this connection of contemporary fields as diverse as proteomics, nanotechnology, or the connection between advanced number theory and cryptographic algorithms; just as the exploratory, academic research of an earlier era in molecular chemistry, solid state physics, and photo-optics rather unexpectedly opened pathways for the industrial development of new synthetic materials, microwave devices and transistor technologies, and lasers.

But such passages from exploratory science to commercially profitable R&D as a rule do not occur in a tightly-coupled, highly predictable fashion that attract the attention of research-intensive companies, whose managers seek identifiable and dependable payoffs streams from portfolios of new product development projects. Moreover, for university administrators to encourage (or even permit) political leaders to entertain the hope that the energies of their faculties and students could be harnesses to yield accelerated productivity growth, showers of better quality products, enlarged export earnings, and local job creation – all within the brief time frame that will make a difference in the coming elections – is not simply deceptive. It is reckless in risking the almost certain disappointment of unrealistic expectations, and so bring public disaffection and damage to the university.

I believe it would be irresponsible not to question whether the prospects of gain can justify the potential costs of redirecting the energies of Europe's university communities in ways that surely must complicate, even if they do not seriously jeopardize their ability to perform the social functions that traditionally have brought these institutions public respect, material support and a considerable measure of insulation from political inference in the conduct of their special educational and research missions.

There are only three main classes of questions in this vein that I can hope to address here:

1. Is there really a problem arising from a failure of European scientific expertise in the academic sphere to respond to industry's innovation needs, a problem for which the proposed redirection of university research activities toward commercial goals would be at least an important part of the solution?
2. Does the example of the U.S. experience with the Bayh-Dole Act (1980) indicate that, by imitating this institutional innovation the EU's member countries can expect to stimulate university researchers to develop and patent technological innovations which will provide that basis for new industrial products, private investment and job creation?
3. Is there a empirical evidence to support the expectation that by becoming better at 'knowledge management' and accumulating intellectual property rights on the basis of the research of their faculty and students, Europe's universities individually and collectively will be able to contribute signifi-

cantly to defraying the rising costs of public sector science and university education?

To come to the point immediately, my answer to these questions is simply: 'No':

1. The problem of the innovation gap in Europe, if it exists, is not attributable to the supposed failure on the part of the professoriate to patent inventions and discoveries in which industry would take an interest. Such statistical data as is recently being produced confirms a different picture: academic researchers in Europe are active in patenting, but the title to the intellectual property in their inventions tends – in contrast to the U.S. situation—to be assigned to industrial firms rather than to their universities.

2. The Bayh-Dole regime is not an appropriate model for emulation: its apparently positive effects upon the rise of science-based technological innovation, and university patenting activity in the U.S. during the past two decades has been widely mis-perceived in European policy circles. Other factors, which may not be operative elsewhere under currently prevailing conditions, played a major role in those ostensibly positive developments during the 1980's and 1990's. On the other hand, the Bayh-Dole legislation interacted with features of the American university and legal systems to produce a number of unintended consequences that have been quiet perverse in their effects upon the some areas of scientific and technological research and the social benefits derived therefore, as well as creating new and costly issues with which universities have been obliged to contend.

3. It is thoroughly misleading to suppose on the basis of the only reasonably well-documented experience with a regime of extensive university patenting activity, namely the recent American case, that the fiscal burden upon taxpayers of supporting research and human capital formation in institutions of higher education can be significantly reduced by creating institutional incentives for faculty to disclose potentially patentable inventions, and for university technology managers to file for patent protection and then seek to exploit whatever intellectual property rights the institution thereby acquires.

It should be appreciated that the questions I have just posed are not so simple when considered in all their ramifications. Consequently, the evidence and arguments that is available to support my bald conclusions in each instance are more intricate, and more subject to important qualifications that the foregoing unnuanced assertions would suggest. A brief elaboration of my answers under the three headings will have to suffice to indicate the nature of the complicating issues, without – I hope – reducing the persuasiveness of my argument that Europe should be building new elements of an organizational infrastructure for science-based innovation, rather than setting new and inappropriate tasks for its existing academic institutions.

4. Towards 'Evidence-Based Policies' for Science and Technology in the ERA

4.1. Is There a Problem, and Where Does It Lie?

Is the problem of the Europe's so-called 'innovation gap' - the alleged failure to fully apply the region's scientific research capabilities to the generation of profitable innovations - one that should be laid first at the door of the universities? We know that the proximate source of the shortfall in Europe's relative R&D expenditure level vis-à-vis other industrial nation's like Japan and the U.S. is not the lower rate of public sector research investment, but, rather, the comparative shortfall in private business investment in R&D as proportion of GDP.

Economists can think of two reasons why the private R&D rate is low: either the supply of potential innovations is very restricted, or the demand for inventions is weak for reasons having to do with market conditions, or financing costs, or lack of expertise on the part of industrial managers in perceiving existing opportunities, or all of these deficiencies. It is difficult to clearly disentangle the two main sets of forces, but it is possible to dispel the mistaken impression that researcher at Europe's universities are not inventive, or fail to generate inventions that are relevant to the needs of industry. Recent empirical studies show that there is a big difference between institutional patenting of inventions by universities in Europe and successful involvement of university faculty researchers in patentable inventions that are taken up by industry. For example, during 1978-1999 there were only 40 patents filed by Italian universities at the European Patent Office, whereas during the same period the EPO issued 1,475 patents – mostly in the areas of biotechnology, drugs and organic chemistry – to Italian university faculty.[7] In the case of a single French institution, the University Louis Pasteur in Strasbourg, during 1993-2000 the EPO issued 463 patents to members of the faculty (mainly in the fields of genetics, biology and physics), but only 62 patents to the university itself. Of course, it is well known that until the recent change of the law in Germany, the professoriate received and could retain the rights to all patents – some 1800 of which were issued to them between 1986 and 2000, principally for inventions in scientific instruments, telecommunications, and biotechnology and pharmaceuticals.[8]

---

[7] See M. Balconi, S. Breschi, and F. Lissoni, Il trasferimento di conoscenze tecnologiche dall'università all'industria in Italia: Nuove evidenze sui brevetti dei docenti, in A. Bonacorse, ed., Il sistema della ricera pubblica in Italia, Milano: Franco Angeli, 2003; M. Balconi, S. Breschi, and F. Lissoni, Networks of inventors and the role of academia: An exploration of Italian patent data, Research Policy, 2004.

[8] The French and German statistics, as well as data for Belgium and Sweden are presented by A. Geuna and L. Nesta, University patenting and its effects on academic research: The emerging European evidence, (SPRU Working Paper, University of Sussex January 2004), forthcoming in Research Policy [Special Issue on Property and the Pursuit of Knowledge: Impacts of IPR on Scientific Research, eds., P. A. David and B. H. Hall].

Table 1. European University-Owned vs University-Invented Patents

	Owned	Invented	Time Period	Areas
Italy	40 EPO	1,475 EPO	1978-1999	Biotechnology, Drugs, Organic Chemistry
Finland	36 USPTO	530 USPTO	1986-2000	TLC, Instruments, Pharmaceuticals/Biotechnology
Germany		200 (1970) 1800 (2000)	1970-2000	
Belgium	153 EPO	Between 35% and 78% EPO	1985-1999	Biotechnology
France Univ of Strasbourg	62 Various	463 Various	1993-2000	Genetics, Biology, Physics

Source: Geuna and Nesta (2004)

What would it mean, then, to seek to fix the European innovation gap by administrative measures designed to raise the rates of university originated applications for patents?

It would displace some part of the assignment of patents on faculty investments to industrial firms, without necessarily increasing the total flow of patentable inventions arising from university research.

There is nothing to assure that the resulting shift in the initial ownership of patent rights from firms to universities would enhance the value of patent portfolios in the economy. Indeed, the outcome might well work in the opposite direction because university patent holdings would provide government authorities with a convenient 'indicator' of institutions comparative performance in meeting 'targets' for commercially relevant research. The trouble with the use of patents for monitoring the universities is that their value to the institution in negotiations for research funding from government ministries may well make its administrators loath to part with them; by contrast, a private firm is less likely to consider the symbolic value that the patent has in some administrative transaction, and so will be ready to the rights assigned to them by their employees to be exploited by other firms, for whom their market-based value is higher. It would oblige firms that are interested in further developing those inventions and making them the basis for new products and new processes to negotiate for patent (or copyright) licenses with university technology managers; and it is likely to complicate some of the directly consultative relationships for knowledge transfer that would otherwise be concluded between faculty researchers and the companies to which they assign the patents on their inventions.

The views of large R&D-intensive corporations in the U.S. regarding the experience in trying to negotiate with universities over the intellectual property rights arising from collaborative research should be instructive in the foregoing connections.[9] As one may see they are hardly flattering about the performance of university technology management offices.

4.2. Does the Bayh-Dole Regime Offer a Suitable Model for European Adoption?

Ideas for European institutional reform and regeneration along those lines clearly have been inspired by perceptions of vigorous university-industry research partnerships, rising patenting activity and the flourishing of academic entrepreneurship in the U.S. during the two closing decades of the past century. As those years followed immediately upon the date of the passage of the Bayh-Dole Act (1980), the latter has been accepted as a model for emulation. This is dangerously simplistic. Closer examination of the available record leads one to doubt that the Bayh-Dole regime offers an appropriate paradigm for the European Research Area, and indeed, a growing number of observers of the U.S. university scene have recently voiced doubts about the wisdom of the experiment.

The Act initially was justified as a measure that would promote the transfer of university inventions to the business sector for further development and job creation, and therefore contained provisions that allowed universities to license their patents only to small and medium size firms; it was not intended as a stimulus to university applied research. Originally, universities were restricted to granting exclusive licenses on their patents to small businesses, on the grounds that such rights would be needed to enable them obtain an attractive rate of return on their investment in developing new products; the encouragement of small business at the time was very much driven by government concerns for job-creation and the then fashionable belief that small business formation was disproportionately responsible for generating increases in employment. Only in the course of the 1980's, as worries about competition from Japanese firm's penetration of the U.S. domestic and foreign markets hitherto held by large manufacturing companies, did the rationale for the institutional experiment undergo a transformation. The transfer of technological discoveries from universities to the private sector became subservient to the stimulation of university-research based businesses in the new scientific fields where – it was hoped – the U.S. was less likely to face immediate challenges from either Europe or the new industrial nations.[10]

---

[9] The following is drawn from H.R. Hertzfeld, A.N Link, and N.S. Vonortas, Intellectual Property Protection Mechanisms in Research Partnerships, (Working Paper, George Washington University, January 2004) forthcoming in *Research Policy* [Special Issue on Property and the Pursuit of Knowledge: Impacts of IPR on Scientific Research, eds., P. A. David and B. H. Hall].

[10] On this background, see B. N. Sampat, Patenting and U.S. academic research in the twentieth century: The world before and after Bayh-Dole, (Working Paper, University of Michigan, Janury 2004), forthcoming in *Research Policy* [Special Issue on Property and the Pursuit of Knowledge: Impacts of IPR on Scientific Research, eds., P. A. David and B. H. Hall].

The rise of university patenting and start-ups are traceable in significant part to factors other than to the U.S. congressional initiative, particularly to the antecedent emergence of biotechnology and new foundational breakthroughs in the biomedical sciences more generally. The available data show that university patenting was rising in the 1970's, in advance of the Bayh-Dole Act, and in significant measure the impetus for the drafting of the legislation derived from the concern on the part of a small number of universities active in the biomedical research area about a possible reversal of the policies of the funding agencies that had enabled them to secure patent rights under individually negotiated Intellectual Property Agreements (the so-called called 'IPA's').

A number of factors quite distinct from the legislative innovation of the Bayh-Dole Act underlay the emergence of university research as a driver of patented inventions in the U.S. What the quantitative evidence shows, first, is that the rapid growth of patent citations to scientific papers in U.S. was not an unprecedented development, having begun during the 1970's. The trend certainly has become more salient since the mid-1980's, an 8-fold increase having occurred in the number of such citations in a random sample of utility patents during 1987-1997. But, rather than being a reflection of an across the board tightening of the connection between advances in academic science and technological invention, it reflected a number of features that were more specific to the participation of university researchers in the biotechnology revolution:[11]

- A 3.4-fold rise in the number of university-industry research centres during 1985-1995 brought firms' researchers into closer contact with academic research publications: the 'general propensity' of patent applications of all kinds (mainly by firms) to cite scientific publications surged in the 1980's.
- A 3.5-fold increase in patenting by research universities during 1985-1995 contributed disproportionately: university-assigned patents (in the aggregate and in every major technical field) cite scientific papers more frequently than other patents.
- The rise of biotechnology - promoted by the shift of federal R&D funding toward the life sciences - is the main factor behind the aggregate trend of patent citations to scientific publications: drug & medicine patents are 260-times more likely to cite science than mechanical patents; biomedical research paper are 38 times more likely to be cited than biology papers.

Thus, with regard to the Commission's strategic vision of the existence of an easy path to renewed industrial innovativeness via university research, the burden of evidence on the factors underlying the rising trend of patent citations to university science suggests that this strategy could be tantamount to 'betting the farm on the future of biotech'. Moreover, even were one to suppose that the concentration of citations in the 'bioscience-biotech nexus' reflects the actual underlying distribution of knowledge 'spillovers', rather than the peculiarities of citation practices

---

[11] The following draws on L. Branstetter, Measuring the Impact of Academic Science on Industrial Innovation: The Case of California's Research Universities, Working Paper, Columbia University, NY. August 2003; B. N. Sampat, op.cit., 2004.

in this particular research area, the clearest positive lesson to be drawn from the U.S. data points to a rather different policy than the emulation of the Bayh-Dole regime. The massive shift of U.S. public funding towards the life sciences laid foundations for expanded industry R&D expenditures in the biomedical field, and a rising stream of product innovations. That 'payoff', however, required matching increases in levels of private sector investment. Perhaps the right lesson for Europe to draw from this experience, therefore, is to emulate the U.S. focused public funding approach in a newly emerging area of science, and to prepare its private sector firms to take advantage of the expected 'spillovers'.

4.3. Could the Exploitation of Intellectual Property Really Offset Universities' Costs?

The results of universities' attempts to exploit IPR, whether by licensing or by faculty 'start-ups', are likely to bring significant financial gains for only a very few institutions at best, whereas the increased administrative problems and the private and social costs almost inevitably will be quite widespread and represented an added distraction (and expense) that will deflect resources from the perform- ance of the institutions main social missions.

The plain truth is that most of the OTL's (offices of technology licensing) at American universities do not produce enough revenue to cover their own costs. Only for a very few institutions it is likely that the net income from their intellec- tual property rights will be substantial enough to materially contribute to solution of the universities' funding problems. There is a pronounced skew in the distribu- tion of patent income receivers, as there is in the distribution of public R&D fund- ing. In 1993, for example, 50% of public R&D funding for university based re- search in the US went to the top 25% of the 200 research universities. The skew in the returns to patenting are more pronounced than that: just 3 institutions (the University of California, Stanford, and Columbia) received one-third of all the royalties earned by U.S. university patent licenses in 1995. The top 10 royalty- earners garnered far more than two-thirds of university patent licensing revenues; whereas roughly 45% of the institutions with OTL's received no royalty income at all in 1997.[12]

Nor have the institutions that subsidize the operations of technology licensing offices been willing to bear the adverse publicity and, in the case of state universi- ties, pay the possible political costs of shutting them down. What president of a state university wants to explain to the institution's politically appointed Regents, and ultimately to the legislators, that her budget cannot afford to go on paying for patenting inventions that might be of interest to local businesses, and might be the basis for regional job growth – just because there hasn't been any noticeable reve- nue from any of the past patents its technology managers have managed to obtain?

---

[12] See D.C. Mowery et al., *Ivory Tower and Industrial Innovation*, Stanford CA: Stanford U.P., 2004, for further statistics.

Patenting for profit is a lottery. The business of lotteries thrives on hope. It is politically costly to deny hope, even when doing so would favour the public interest.

Besides, the political economy of university patenting has made the collective commitment to this institutional experiment more and more difficult to reverse. Even if a core of university administrators at leading institutions became convinced that the Bayh-Dole regime require significant reforms, they would need to contend with vigorous public opposition in defence of the *status quo*. Another unintended consequence of the federal legislation has been the fostering of a new profession, and the building of a new professional organization: the Association of University Technology Managers. With its nearly 3000 members, newsletter, and conference program, the AUTM now constitutes a well-organized and vocal professional lobby, a vested interest whose very survival is dependent upon the perpetuation of university patenting activity.

And so we have had all this in exchange for $1.4 billion in annual licensing revenues,[13] which amounts to well less than a tenth of U.S. expenditures on university research, and roughly one-hundredth of the costs of operating the nation's 200-odd research universities.

If major revenue generating patents have not been induced by the promise of returns to academic inventors and their institutions, programs modelled upon the U.S. Bayh-Dole Act – which the EC's 'Communication' much admires – what then is their effect? From the economist's perspective the patenting outcomes of research that would in any case have been undertaken under public or private foundation sponsorship is tantamount to permitting universities to levy a tax on users of the new knowledge. The tax falls first upon the business firms that wish to invest in exploiting those discoveries and inventions, but, by granting exclusive licenses, the universities can sell private parties a chance to collect the tax in the form of monopoly profits (rents) extracted from the ultimate users of their new, knowledge-based goods and services.[14]

The sale of monopoly rights to private parties was utilized by Europe's kings and princes assiduously as a mechanism of financing various purposes of the state which, in the political theory of the day, generally were not distinguishable from their own purposes. But that took place in the epoch before the modern state acquired its extensive fiscal powers. Quite apart from the political troubles that historically ensued on more than one occasion from a sovereign's grants of such rights to favourites, and the high leakage of revenues gathered by 'tax-farming', this means of arranging what are in effect transfer payments has long been eschewed for sound economic reasons. As a government device *for financing uni-*

---

[13] See AUTM, *Licensing Survey: FY 2002*, Norwalk, CT: Association of University Technology Managers, Inc., 2003.

[14] One might cite as particularly appropriate the supporting statement by Niels Reimers, formerly the director of the Office of Technology Licensing at Stanford University, and in a sense the modern founder of the profession of university technology managers, to the effect that university patenting is simply "a tax" whenever the ability to grant an exclusive license for commercial development of the innovation does not induce further, complementary R&D investment from industry. See N. Riemers, Tiger by the Tail, Chemtech, August 1987, 17 (8), pp. 464-471.

versity activities, even the most visible successes of the Bayh-Dole university-patenting regime stand indicted as involving a doubly inefficient allocation of society's resources: firstly, because monopoly pricing imposes a restraint on the use made of new knowledge, and secondly, because in the situation considered, the university research was publicly subsidized and its outcomes can not reasonably be ascribed the effects of prospects of eventual financial rewards deriving from commercial exploitation of the results.

5. Developing Institutional Innovations for Innovative Europe

The proposal for today's public universities (along with the state-subsidized private institutions of higher education) to help support themselves financially by owning and exploiting intellectual property is a bad idea. It is a misuse of the economic rationale for the system of intellectual property protection, namely that the granting of legally enforceable monopoly rights is justifiable as a means of providing incentives for undertaking investment in intellectually creative activities.

The modern university form, having fused pedagogy and research, has been privileged and supported by tax-paying members of society at large because it provides a home and haven, and a social institution with distinctive internal incentives and norms governing the activities of individuals who independently are motivated to engage in creative activities.

Asking, let alone demanding, that those responsible for university administration to attend to the profit-potentialities of their faculties,' has turned out to be pernicious in its unintended side effects. If pursued rigorously, it is likely to be destructive of the very qualities for which these institutions rightly have come to be admired and maintained by open societies – however grudging and inadequate their support may be at the present time. Although not in the habit of appealing to Papal Authority to reinforce my economic arguments, the occasion calls for an exception: I will quote here the following thoughtful passage in a letter to the apostolic nuncio in Poland on 25th March, 2002, in which John Paul II decried the "overriding financial interests" that had become particularly manifest in the areas of biomedical and pharmaceutical research:[15]

> "[T]he pre-eminence of the profit motive in conducting scientific research ultimately means that science is deprived of its epistemological character, according to which its primary goal is discovery of the truth. The risk is that when research takes a utilitarian turn, its speculative dimension, which is the inner dynamic of man's intellectual journey, will be diminished or stifled."

Moreover, as has been amply demonstrated by the experience of U.S. universities with institutionalized technology licensing under the terms permitted by the Bayh-Dole legislation, it offers no realistic solution to the problems of university

---

[15] This passage is reproduced as quoted in Richard Horton, The Dawn of McScience, The New York Review of Books (vol. 1.1, no. 4), March 11, 2004, p. 7.

finance. At best, and for a very few institutions, direct and indirect licensing of patents returns only a small portion of the costs of research performed by university personnel; whereas, for the overwhelming majority the activities of their technology licensing offices represent a net financial burden.

5.1. Hopeful Monsters, and Plain Monsters

The Bayh-Dole regime in the U.S. has developed into something rather different than that which its creators intended. They argued that socially useful innovations often could not be derived immediately from publicly-funded discoveries and inventions, but that the additional R&D investments which were needed would be forthcoming from business firms if only they could be assigned exclusive rights exploit those university research findings that proved to be patentable. Installing the profit-making impulse into the body of the research university was not the original intention, although that outcome - surely the creature of a Frankenstein experiment, if ever such a thing could be conceived of in the area of institutional reform - has been celebrated by some enthusiasts for the emerging 'entrepreneurial university'. There was never a reason to believe that throwing opening the doors of university offices and laboratories to commercial entrepreneurship was a proposition entirely different in its ability to yield unwanted consequences than was another particularly American higher education innovation, the idea of having universities meet the cost of their athletic programs (and why not operating expenses in general?) by the commercial exploitation of admission and media broadcast rights to college football, basketball, and other sports events.

Earlier in this essay I alluded to the European medieval university innovation in metaphoric, evolutionary terms, as one of those 'hopeful monsters', a mutant form of the Cathedral schools, so to speak, which turned out to be not only viable but marvellously adaptable, and socially productive. Nevertheless, as widely as this innovation has propagated itself, the individual organizations carrying the germ of the 'university idea' remain fragile bequests from the past, and history has shown that whole populations of such institutions are terribly vulnerable to shocks from alterations in the political climate, as well as to adverse trends in their economic environment. The proposed transformation of the university into a knowledge-management business would undoubtedly constitute a further innovative enterprise. Even if it is advocated with the best of intentions by political leaders and their policy advisors, we would do well to protect this remarkable institutional heritage from pressures to embrace new and potentially self-debilitating missions.

Innovation, as a human activity is good. It carries risks, but modern societies are right to give it encouragement, for without the novelty that regenerates diversity, the possibilities of learning and selecting new social and cultural ways eventually would be exhausted. By the same token, we must be prepared to accept the reality that even the best-intended innovations may turn out not be 'good enough'. Society must be ready to experiment, and even to experiment in more radical ways than thinking up new purposes to be tackled with familiar devices. But it must also recognize and act decisively on the difference between a 'hopeful monster', and an attempted hybrid such as the proprietary research university, which can be seen to be 'a hopeless monster'.

It is not just a matter of preserving the cultural legacies that are 'the historical Universities of Europe', and freeing those who wish to work therein from the distractions and tensions of managing, or trying to manage multiple and mutually conflicting missions. Another purpose is served by my sceptical examination of European policy makers' too-ready surmise that the U.S. has discovered the secret of universal institutional 'best practice' in the organization of its innovation system. Not only is the Bayh-Dole regime a dubious paradigm for Europe to emulate, a growing number of my fellow economists now argue that the legislation and the system it has spawned stands in need of significant reform in the very place where it has become entrenched. What Europe needs, in my view, and what Europe has to offer the knowledge society and the knowledge-driven economy, is a new surge of institutional innovation, complementing its universities and institutions of higher education with novel organizations that are better suited to fostering the generation of commercially successful innovations based upon the results of publicly supported research.

If latter is accepted as a truly important and enduring societal priority, then the attention of creative people and the necessary public resources should be liberated from the distraction of tinkering with inherited institutional forms that are ill-suited for that mission, however well they serve society in other vital respects. It is clearly a job for talented individuals with a wide variety of public and private sector experience with various aspects of the worlds of R&D-based enterprise and 'open science' throughout western Europe - and why not also in the accession states of the EU?

It is not as though there were no experiments from which to learn, and on which it might be possible to build: there are bridge institutions like the Fraunhofer Gesellschaft, independent research consortia operating under sponsorship of business firms and public foundations, such as IMEC, regional incubators linked to universities and to research parks. But rather than being peripheral, and rather marginal, the development of novel institutional forms and procedures to populate the organizational terrain situated between the university, the state agency and the business corporation, now should be brought to the centre of the stage, promoted, and accordingly resourced. It calls for a commensurately serious response if the European Research Area is to become more than a wishful conceptualization - a suitably symbolic gesture with which to usher in a new millennium - that the European Commission was able to persuade the national leaders of the EU member states to embrace on the occasion of their meeting in Lisbon in October of 2000. In my vision of the future, the creative task of enriching the institutional infrastructure for scientific and technological advance in a way that protects and sustains the vital heritage of the universities within that structure, is the critical challenge that should and can be met by an 'innovative Europe'.

6. A Summing Up

This essay has been framed as a response to the February 2003 *Communication on the role of the universities in the Europe of knowledge,* issued by the Commission of the European Communities. That thought-provoking document assessed Europe's critical needs in the epoch of 'knowledge-driven economic growth', and identified the university as the institution uniquely suited to meeting those needs. It called for debate on the means by which the conditions of European universities can be changed to satisfy the requirements of the new societal role for which the Commission believes them to be destined. Reduced to its essence, this presented a view of Europe's institutions of higher education as possessing the potential to be more effective than its industry at the business of technological innovation. But, it also faulted the university researchers and administrators for failing to make the realization of that potential a priority. What is being advocated, therefore, is tantamount to a program of institutional reforms intended to mobilize of that capability in order to meet a dual societal problem: financing the rising costs of public education and research, and enlarging the share of EU gross domestic product that is devoted to public and private investment in R&D.

This approach to fostering what the Commission referred to as 'a Europe of knowledge' aims to harness the energies of university professors, students and administrators to a new and highly instrumental goal, the advancement of knowledge for national and regional 'wealth creation'. But the likely costs, as well as the promised benefits of this proposal deserve more careful consideration than they have been receiving from enthusiasts for the grand goal. With regard to the costs, it is apparent that many of the features of universities that have rendered them particularly effective when called upon to perform in their historical societal role as 'nodes' in the international dissemination of knowledge and, since Humboldt, as generators of fundamental advances in scientific understanding, might have to be sacrificed in order to effectively carry through the institutional reforms suggested by the EC's *Communication.* Within the familiar context of academic, 'open science' norms and governance structures, the comparative advantage of university-based researchers' lies in conducting inquiries that may provide the foundations for valuable commercial innovations. But the best way to do this is precisely not the closely managed, tightly-coupled search for discoveries and inventions that fires the imaginations of many political leaders, policy-advisors and financially hard-pressed university administrators who are seeking predictable and readily identifiable near-term payoffs.

Turning to the supposed benefits, it is equally apparent that the EC's *Communication* (and many similar policy pronouncements of national government ministries) has failed to show that there is an adequate evidentiary basis for supposing that the envisaged societal gains will be substantial enough to justify attempting to transform Europe's most prestigious academic institutions into 'knowledge-management enterprises'. It is not plausible to suppose that more than a few among Europe's research universities would, by exploiting the intellectual property created by the people who study and work there, be enabled to contribute materially to the costs of their own upkeep. Ideas for European institutional reform and regeneration along those lines clearly have been inspired by perceptions of vigorous university-industry research partnerships, rising patenting activity and the flourishing of academic entrepreneurship in the U.S. during the two closing decades of the past century. As those years followed immediately upon the date of the passage of the Bayh-Dole Act (1980), the latter has been accepted as a model for emulation. This has been seen to be dangerously simplistic in several respects.

Firstly, closer examination of the available record leads one to doubt that the Bayh-Dole regime offers an appropriate paradigm for the European Research Area. The rise of university patenting and start-ups are traceable in significant part to factors other than that U.S. congressional initiative, and particularly the advances in biomedical knowledge driven by the rise of massive public research funding pre-dating 1980. Secondly, the universities' attempts to exploit IPR, whether by licensing or by faculty 'start-ups', has brought significant financial gains for only a very few U.S. institutions, whereas the increased administrative problems, and the private and social costs of patenting – especially in the biomedical areas are widely felt. Thirdly, there have been unforeseen and somewhat perverse consequences of this institutional experiment. The highly decentralized approach of the Bayh-Dole Act, in giving every university and public research institute the responsibility for securing and exploiting its intellectual property portfolio, has imposed significant 'learning costs' on the system as a whole and brought into existence a new professional group – university technology managers – who have personal and collective interests in the perpetuation of these arrangements. Concomitantly, there are few if any large, R&D intensive firms in the U.S. that now express general enthusiasm for the Bayh-Dole regime, and, many of their executive now speak in very critical terms about the performance of most of the universities' technology licensing offices.

In sum, then, European policy-makers concerned with the scientific and technological foundations for business innovation and economic growth should be considering reforms and revitalizing measures that build upon the region's own rich and diverse institutional foundations, rather than risking doing damage to them by blindly imitating a dubious American experiment.

References

AUTM (2003), *Licensing Survey: FY 2002*, Norwalk, CT: Association of University Technology Managers.

Balconi M, Breschi S, Dissoni F (2003), Il trasferimento di conoscenze tecnologiche dall'università all'industria in Italia: Nuove evidenze sui brevetti dei docenti. In Bonacorse A, ed., *Il sistema della ricera pubblica in Italia*, Milano: Franco Angeli, 2003

Balconi M, Breschi S, Lissoni F (2004), Networks of inventors and the role of academia: An exploration of Italian patent data, *Research Policy*.

Branstetter L (2003), Measuring the Impact of Academic Science on Industrial Innovation: The Case of California's Research Universities, Working Paper, Columbia University, NY.

Cobban AB (1998), Europe's Medieval Universities, Oxford: Oxford University Press.

Dasgupta P, David PA (1994), Towards a New Economics of Science. In *Research Policy*, 23: pp.487-521.

David PA (2003), The Economic Logic of 'Open Science' and the Balance Between Private Property Rights and the Public Domain in Scientific Data and Information. In *The Role of Scientific and Technical Data and Information in the Public Domain*, eds. Esau JM and Uhlir PF, Washington, D.C.: National Academies Press.

Geuna A, Nesta L (2004), University patenting and its effects on academic research: The emerging European evidence, SPRU Working Paper, University of Sussex and forthcoming in *Research Policy* [Special Issue on Property and the Pursuit of Knowledge: Impacts of IPR on Scientific Research, eds., David PA and Hall BH].

Hertzfeld HR, Link AN, Vonortas NS (2004), Intellectual Property Protection Mechanisms in Research Partnerships, Working Paper, George Washington University and forthcoming in *Research Policy* [Special Issue on Property and the Pursuit of Knowledge: Impacts of IPR on Scientific Research, eds., David PA and Hall BH].

Horton R (2004), The Dawn of McScience, The New York Review of Books (vol. 1.1, no. 4), March 11.

European Commission (2003), *Communication from the Commission: The role of the university in the Europe of knowledge*, COM 58 final. Brussels: Commission of the European Communities.

Mowery DC, Sampat B (2003), The Bayh-Dole Act of 1980 and University-Industry Technology Transfer: A Model for Other OECD Governments?. U.C. Berkeley Haas School of Business Working Paper.

Mowery DC, Sampat B (2004), Ivory Tower and Industrial Innovation, Stanford CA: Stanford U.P.

OECD (2002), Benchmarking Science-Industry Relationships, Paris

Riemers N (1987), Tiger by the Tail, Chemtech.

Sampat BN (2004), Patenting and U.S. academic research in the twentieth century: The world before and after Bayh-Dole, Working Paper, University of Michigan and forthcoming in *Research Policy* [Special Issue on Property and the Pursuit of Knowledge: Impacts of IPR on Scientific Research, eds., David PA and Hall BH].

EU Strategies for Research and Development

Ezio Andreta

Direction Générale de la Recherche
Direction Technologies industrielles MO75 6/26
European Commission – Rue Montoyer, 75 - 1049 Bruxelles, Belgium
ezio.andreta@cec.eu.int

1. Introduction

The purpose of this paper is not so much to describe the EU directives and Regulations, i.e. the tools that Brussels has designed in the field of research and innovation, as to go upstream and discuss the problems so as to understand why certain objectives and tools have been set.

The central point is that of industrial mutation. The debate on industrial mutation is a lively one, one that worries the European Ministers and a problem that is on the agenda of all Councils.

It is interesting to notice that in this decline there are some really worrying, but also some encouraging symptoms.

The three worrying symptoms are:

- the loss of foreign markets; Europe, which is the first exporting area in the world, still holds this position, but it has lost some market share;
- the loss of jobs, mainly due to the relocation of production;
- excessive automation of the production system, which has been leading to further job losses.

Though the picture is not positive there are signs of recovery and evolution towards a positive mutation, which is necessary and above all urgent, and even more importantly, is closely linked to research and innovation. This is the critical point: research/innovation, because innovation without research is likely to be not only insufficient, but even harmful.

2. The Mutation of the Economic System

What is the meaning of 'mutation'? In order to understand mutation one needs clear pictures of the starting and arrival points.

Today at the global level there are two perfectly active economic systems that, though having different basic characteristics, do co-exist and our challenge is exactly the change-over from one to the other. It is the change-over from traditional industry to a new industry, i.e. from a resource-based to a knowledge-based economy.

Traditional industry is predominant in Europe, where 80% of industry is traditional, therefore old, and adapted to an old pattern that is now changing. Its characteristics are clear: the first and most visible one is that of low value-added mass production. It is about low added-value mass products involving large physical investments, plants, assembly lines, and a lot of manpower, energy and pollution, but clearly based on the principle of Taylorism, i.e. on linearity.

All this is changing towards a new economy, with a different organisation, completely different production processes, different products, a completely different type of manpower and, above all, a different approach.

It is a very big revolution, where the real 'driver' of the new economy is an intelligent product that completes a service, a high value-added product that meets the consumers' needs and provides them with a service, because the real added value is in the service itself. Few industries follow this reasoning because, if they did, they would immediately re-organise their whole production system, their logistics and all their procedures: they would radically change their production patterns, abandoning the linear system and starting a totally new system where the number of products is limited but the added value is very high, and where the organisation is flexible and global. In fact, the big industries are dismantling their manufacturing plants to keep only assembly centres. The manufacturing system is no longer based on the assembly line, but on a network of sub-suppliers, thus causing terrible problems to the small and medium-sized European businesses because they lose their points of reference. To those that were in Fiat's supply chain or assembly line, the loss of Fiat as a reference point creates problems and practical difficulties in finding new reference points at a global level.

Large products are no longer manufactured but small ones. The trend is towards micro-products and micro-motors, where more know-how and less material are required.

It is interesting to have a look at statistical figures: in 1945 the know-how content of products was 5%, today it is 16% and the target is to reach 20-25% by 2010, which means that know-how has an increasingly large share in the products.

Where does this come from? From people who produce know-how and do not work with their hands because the big difference between the previous and the new system is the utilisation of man: man is a part of the system, totally deprived of any responsibility, and the faults of Taylorism should be analysed. Taylorism has taken all responsibility away from individuals and has made it impossible for them to have a global system view, which is today's winning approach, requiring different people with different cultures capable of producing know-how. But what can be seen behind these differences?

In my opinion, very important changes are emerging that constitute system shake-ups and could, I dare day, be described as Copernican revolutions that should be thought about and worked on carefully.

3. System Changes

The first change is based on the fact that linearity is no longer a winner, but complexity is a winner. The complex approach prevails. We have been brought up in linearity, all our education was linear, and we have not learned how to approach a problem in a complex way. We can make excellent linear analyses, but, when we put them together, we find that the dynamics of the system is different. Linear addition does not lead to an exact result, mathematics is not suitable for complexity, which means that education in complexity is a problem that not only needs to be considered seriously, but that should become an educational goal; right from primary school upwards, there is no education in complexity and we keep educating people in linearity.

Another very important element is that individual competitiveness is no longer relevant. Nobody in the globalised world has the critical mass to be the main player and the leader alone. The co-operation of others is needed because today the competitiveness of a system is much more important than individual competitiveness and it is clear that relocation of production is actually relocation to a more competitive system; this means that I have to look for conditions where I can create at a global level my own system where I am competitive. However, the interesting thing is that system competitiveness is not the sum of the competition capabilities of the system's players – because we are moving within complexity - but it is something more and different, which means that without a continuous dialogue, without 'governance' among the system players, it is very difficult to obtain system competitiveness. Just think of something very interesting: in the traditional system the competitiveness of small and medium-sized companies is tied to the competitiveness of the leading company: if the leader sells, all sell and all are competitive. Nowadays it is the contrary: the leader's competitiveness is subject to the competitiveness of the suppliers' network and this is the reason why big industry looks for the component it needs anywhere in the world where sufficient quality and cost conditions are available to allow it find it's equilibrium This is a complete turn-around and a major revolution.

The third and most important element is economic, because a radical change is involved: from an economy based on the three classical factors, i.e. capital, raw materials and labour, there is a switch to two factors, i.e. capital and know-how. It is a formidable dematerialization process. One could object that science has always helped industrial production. Certainly, it has always allowed a better engineering to emerge, but it has never reached the core of products and this is the revolution: knowledge enters the core of the product and becomes itself the product, which envelops the knowledge, in an extremely intelligent and extremely simplified way.

The revolution is taking place also at the economic actor's level because the figure of the entrepreneur increasingly emerges.

Fourthly, a significant trend from macro to micro is emerging. Biotechnology and Microelectronics lead the trend, but the latter has almost reached the micro limit and is triggering the biggest of all industrial revolutions; that generated by Nano-technologies, because it involves a reversal of production methods. We are producing in a linear way and 'top down', from big to small, in successive steps. We fell a tree to make a toothpick, throwing away a lot of waste and then using the toothpick to consume a mozzarella, that has been produced in another way, and so forth. It is therefore an entirely linear system from big to small, with a great deal of waste. What is important is that today Nanotechnologies allow us to turnaround and imitate nature: the ability to control and put together atoms and molecules to make structures and, with these structures, to make small bricks, with which we can play and on which we can build bigger structures. It is a sweeping innovation because it involves a radical change in the production system. It is certainly more sustainable; it is certainly a method that requires new competencies and is the latest revolution, but it is very important. Nanotechnologies, just as micro and bio-technologies previously, have triggered a convergent technologies process, i.e. the practice of Microelectronics and Biotechnology requires a movement towards convergence of technologies, but with Nanotechnologies the three factors become really disruptive because they change the whole production system, the way products are made and the products themselves. We may be still in the textiles sector, or still in the pharmaceuticals sector, but the products are made and have a totally different valence.

Another major point – the fifth one – is the need to leave monodisciplinarity and enter not multi-disciplinarity but interdisciplinarity, which is even more important. This is a problem faced by all educators because none of the university reforms carried out anywhere in the world are based on interdisciplinarity. Just as quantitative production is a feature of the obsolescent traditional system, innovation without research belongs to that system, exactly like monodisciplinarity. This does not mean that people should no longer be educated in monodisciplinarity, because thorough scientific education and progress beyond the frontiers are necessary, but it is also necessary to educate people who can use different types of knowledge and are able to cross-fertilise all these disciplines, because this is the key to the future.

The process of managing change is complex. 'Governance' is required to help those who do make the conversion step and to make others do so. However, 'governance' is not only useful, but also necessary because without a governance approach we cannot speed up this mutation and push it as far as we want to. The 'governance' system focuses on the ability to produce know-how in a competitive way.

Finally, one of the changes to take into consideration is that of relocation of production due to the fact that industry is old; therefore it is an industry that in order to cut costs relocates to where they are lower for ecological reasons or due to low wages.

The real problem, however, that Europe is already facing and that the US may have to face too, is the relocation of high value-added production to countries where competitive knowledge production systems have been put in place.

The latest data is alarming. California has lost 400 thousand jobs due to relocations to India and China; Europe is running the same risk vis-a-vis Malaysia in high-tech business sector and in particular in the entire information technology sector. Impressive investments are being made in China, not as absolute, but as relative values: very huge human and financial resources are being concentrated in some centres, such as the Shanghai and the North Hong-Kong areas, with all the biomedical business in the former and all micro-electronics in the latter. Today China manufactures 50% of the mobile phones produced in the world. 80% of the world's colour TV sets are manufactured in China and packaged elsewhere.

China is therefore not only an example of low-cost industrial relocation, but also an example of industrial relocation to areas where the ability to produce knowledge is actually competitive, and this is the big challenge. However, it is not enough to produce knowledge competitively: it is necessary to be able to transform it to the advantage of the end customer, who now returns to the centre of the system.

4. The Pillars of World Competition

There are five pillars of global economic competition: three of them: education, research and infrastructures are inseparable. It is not possible to invest in one of them without investing in the others.

Innovation is the fourth pillar and has peculiar, but interesting characteristics: the major one being that it is always a local feature and resembles karst rivers, that come to the surface when they find appropriate morphological conditions. These conditions are sketched out here.

I wish to simply underline the decisive roles of at least three of them: patents, standards and regulations, and then importantly, demand. If there is no demand for high value-added products, there can be no value-added production, but there can be no demand unless regulations exist that create a market and protect the consumers and there cannot even be knowledge protection unless patents are recognised everywhere. China has no patent system and this is one of a number of reasons why industries are migrating to China, but the patent system is too fractionalised and heterogeneous. In our globalised world there is no single patent system, not only meaning that the system is not run by a single organisation, but because the contents of the products to be patented are not the same.

In Europe we rarely patent knowledge. In the US, by contrast, they can patent the know-how contained in the products more easily than we do and here the debate is wide open.

The last of the pillars of this integrated approach is the science-citizens relationship. The separation between science and society dates back to 1600, it may have been Galilei that started it, with a beneficial outcome, because talking about science and theology meant immobilism at that time. The dissociation of science led to dramatic developments, the first and second industrial revolutions, but what is hugely significant is that the third cannot take place without the reintegration of science with the so-called humanities disciplines.

Some people produce knowledge, others use it, engineer it, industrialise it and some others criticise it from the outside with religious-philosophical or cultural approaches.

This is a mistake as in the era of globalisation and of the complex approach it is necessary to reintegrate all these types of knowledge with their origins and make sure that the man of the future is transdisciplinary or interdisciplinary, able to synthesise and realise knowledge.

5. A Few European Innovation Indicators

Let's look at the European system. Not only does Europe invest only 2%, or 170 billion euro per year, compared to. 280 per year in the US, which means an absolute-value gap of 110 billion, or a 33% difference, and the absolute value is important because of the critical mass it moves but the problem is also that in the US 70% of the investment is private and industrial and 30% public. In Europe, 55% is private and 45% public. In Japan 80% is private and very little public.

In the research sector, Europe has 5.7 researchers per 1000 workers, compared to 8 in the US and as many as 10 in Japan. However, the interesting point coming out of these indicators is the public-to-private relationship: Europe has 1 private researcher to almost 5 public, while the US has exactly the opposite, 1 public to 7 private researchers the same as in Japan.

What does this mean? It means that European industry is old, traditional and does not feel the need to use knowledge not only as its core business, but not even as a tool, as a production factor.

Patents and scientific publications are also a part of the past, because Europe publishes a great deal and holds many meetings, but following the dissemination type of culture. The Italian and European professors boast that they can disseminate what they know: this is because they have not yet discovered the economic value behind it. They don't go to a lawyer before holding a lecture to ask: "Can I say these things? Am I protected or not?"

This type of culture does not exist in Europe, there is a culture of dissemination and this is the reason why Europe has the largest number of scientific publications, even in the most advanced sectors. On the other hand, Europe has the smallest number of patents. What is more interesting, however, is to see that the European patents are registered in the US, i.e. the Europeans patent in the US because the system is different over there.

If a small or medium-sized biotech business, a small or medium-sized firm in the biomedical sector wants to expand its business, it patents its results and its products in the US, not in Europe.

6. European Strategies

A problem that does not exist either in the US or in Japan is fragmentation and the lack of resources for rational utilisation. Europe consisted of 15 countries that have now increased to 25, hence 25 systems, 25 different resources that are used according to strategies that are not always co-ordinated, though they are better co-ordinated now through the EU instruments. But it is clear that there is a risk of overlapping, and therefore of a lack of a critical mass.

It is therefore necessary to get rid of this fragmentation and these obstacles and try to have one single entity, Europe. The only playing ground for science and research is Europe. Faced with these problems, how has Europe reacted?

In the year 2000, the heads of State took an important step in Lisbon and decided to make Europe the most dynamic economy in the world, but based on knowledge, by 2010 (in 10 years). This important change pivots not on being 'most dynamic' but on being 'based on knowledge'.

The goal, therefore, is to transform a resource-based economy into a knowledge-based one. This was a very important statement that, though devoid of any legal value, has a huge political and economic value because this declaration and its signature gave rise to a movement towards convergence to using all the available EU instruments in this direction.

After a few months the Lisbon Declaration was completed with the setting up of the European Research Area. Europe became aware that no knowledge market existed and created one.

Looking at the history of the European Union, one can see that it has always been built upon goods around which solidarity was required: coal, steel, nuclear energy, food – which is ultimately agriculture – the Euro, and, now with a very interesting dematerialization process, knowledge.

With the creation of the European Research Area, knowledge becomes a solidarity good, which is an extraordinary turn-around that can be seen in the European Constitution.

Article 163 of the Treaty of Rome, later to become the Single treaty, says: "The goal of European research aims at strengthening the scientific and technological bases of the European industry to make it more competitive in the world".

Article 248 Ter says clearly: "The goal of European research is the strengthening of Europe's scientific and technological bases through the setting up of the European area for the competitiveness of the European system", which includes industrial competitiveness.

This is revolutionary in terms of the concept of individual competitiveness, which had clearly marked the Treaty of Rome and therefore the Single Act, because we are discovering that individual competitiveness is no longer significant. It is the system's competitiveness that counts.

The interesting point is that there is a convergence of instruments because, directly beyond this European area, there is a 3% target, but this 3% is a difficult target, because in order to reach 3% of the GDP by 2010 an annual incremental growth of 8.5% is required, of which 9.9% from the private sector – which is behind schedule – and 6.5% public. The efforts should therefore be concentrated more in the private than in the public sector, because it is the private sector that needs to change. The public administration should also change through an intelligent targeting of its resources. However, even if we reached 3%, we would still face a gap: the number of research workers.

Europe has 960 thousand researchers. 700 thousand more are required to reach 3% for RTD expanses of GDP, but they must have a new, not an old profile.

400 thousand European researchers are working in the US, 120 thousand in research and the others in industry.

This is not a defeat, but a privilege. Europe has always been open, the Europeans are culturally open. It is not a question of making them come back, I would say that the challenge is different and it is the same for the Americans, the Europeans, the Japanese and for everyone else, i.e. the availability of competitive production systems is the only condition to attract researchers. Without this we cannot attract and there is no hope of reversing the declining trend.

Competition policy, structural funds and agriculture fall within this convergence of utilisation of the tools. The competition authorities have decided that State aids to small and medium-sized firms will not have to be notified if they concern research. On the contrary, no departure from the regulations is allowed in connection with innovation because the latter consists of mere state aids.

The trend of structural funds is towards two priorities: the production of knowledge, hence infrastructure and education, and the aspect of sustainability, hence ecological.

This turnaround is interesting also in the agricultural world. It is a hard world because it is quantitative, based on measurable output, but the mechanism is reversing, quality has become important with the protection of niche production, which is a trend toward quality. It is a difficult process because very complex balances have to be changed: big industries are behind quantity, whereas small industries are behind quality.

All of this is important because behind it there is a 'governance' with a trend towards the utilisation of all the European resources and instruments, towards a knowledge-based society, hence towards a knowledge-based economy.

The knowledge-based society is our society, with an awareness that knowledge is the centre of the 'village', which becomes the driver of development, the driver of a new type of system and values.

The Framework Programme is the tool with which Europe finances research and even this Programme has been re-oriented because the Sixth Framework programme already uses the tools not only to support the 'driver' priorities, i.e. Nanotechnologies, Genomics and Micro-electronics – to name a few applications – but it has also used two new instruments that caused quite a lot of preoccupation on the part of participants. These are Integrated projects and Networks of excellence, where the goal was exactly that of reaching a critical mass on a given topic in a new and different way.

In addition, a new very elementary concept is being tested; that of 'technological platforms'. We have actually launched a series of technological platforms, which are nothing other than a governance tool: groupings of all the 'stake holders' have emerged in a 'bottom up' and spontaneous fashion, in various key sectors. They include big and small industry, universities, research centres, public and private authorities, and all have agreed to define a long-term vision, and then to set a long-term plan to identify an agenda of actions that should take account of the obstacles – which are not only of a technological nature but concern also innovation, infrastructures and research on the one hand and should provide a sort of scheduled 'road map' on the other.

These types of technological platforms will be one of the major features of the new Framework Programme because they will provide the method of governing the mutation in various industrial sectors in a relatively simple way but in real time, and with a systems approach.

This type of technological platform is certainly not a universal tool that can be used to govern other types of mutation, but it is in our opinion the most appropriate.

A last piece of information: the new Framework Programme that should start in 2006 will introduce a new activity; 'blue sky', 'curiosity driven' research, i.e. Europe is discovering that it also has an interest in investing in the future, by providing resources to people who are not aiming at immediate products or targets.

Aiming at the Barcelona Target: Best Practices and National Performances. The EASAC Perspective[1]

Uno Lindberg

Stockholm University
Arrheniuslab ES – 10691 Stockholm – Sweden
uno@cellbio.su.se

1. Introduction

The objective of this paper is to discuss the Barcelona 3% target and to analyze the situation in Finland and Sweden, the two countries in Europe which already appear to be operating at this level of R&D.

2. The Barcelona Declaration

The European Union is committed to becoming an economically competitive player at the global level, and it is realized that to reach this position, it must be globally competitive in science and technology. These ambitions are enshrined in the declarations of the European Council at the March 2000 Summit in Lisbon and the March 2002 Summit in Barcelona, and are endorsed by the European Parliament. They signify direct recognition at the highest political level of the central role of science and technology in economic prosperity.

More specifically, the Lisbon Summit set 'a new strategic goal for the next decade: to become the most competitive and dynamic knowledge-based economy in the world, capable of sustainable economic growth with more and better jobs and greater social cohesion'.

The Barcelona Summit spelt out that in order to close the gap between the EU and its major competitors, there must be a significant boost of the overall R&D and innovative efforts in the Union, with a particular emphasis on frontier tech-

---

[1] This article is based on the EASAC report 01, April 2004

nologies. The European Council therefore agrees that overall spending on R&D and innovation in the Union should be increased towards 3% of GDP by 2010. Two-thirds of this new investment should come from the private sector. The Summit also stressed the urgent need to strengthen arrangements for intellectual property. Tables 1, 2 and 3 summarize the situation for the previous years.

The challenging targets decided upon in Barcelona in 2002 are indeed worth achieving, but will it be possible to reach the goals considering the limited time allotted to reach them.

The 3% target challenges national governments and the European Union itself as the channels of public funds to S&T – even more, it challenges industry and commerce as the channels of private funds to S&T (To reach 3% GDP by 2010 from current levels implies an overall annual growth of 8% in real terms, with public R&D expenditure growing at 6%pa and private expenditure at 9%pa).

It will not be easy to reach these goals – many say impossible before 2010. It challenges the educational system and the research community to make good use of the funding it receives, and industry to work much more closely with academe. This does not mean that academic research has to be focused on narrow goals of immediate applicability, but it does mean a relentless pursuit of excellence and an awareness of factors that promote interaction between those who create new knowledge (basic as well as applied research) and (where different) those who put it to use.

Table 1. R&D Input in Some OECD Countries (% of GDP)

	1990	1991	1992	1993	1994	1995	1996	1997	1998	1999	2000	2001	2002
Austria	1.42	1.5	1.48	1.49	1.56	1.55	1.60	1.71	1.79	1.85	1.86	1.92	1.93
Canada	1.47	1.52	1.55	1.63	1.67	1.64	1.69	1.71	1.79	1.81	1.92	2.03	1.91
Denmark	1.63	1.7	1.74	1.74	1.80	1.84	1.85	1.94	2.06	2.19	2.25	2.4	2.52
France	2.41	2.41	2.42	2.40	2.34	2.31	2.30	2.22	2.17	2.18	2.18	2.23	2.2
Germany	2.75	2.61	2.48	2.37	2.28	2.26	2.26	2.29	2.31	2.44	2.49	2.51	2.52
Japan	2.85	2.82	2.76	2.68	2.63	2.77	2.77	2.83	2.94	2.94	2.99	3.07	3.12
Norway	-	1.65	1.70	1.73	1.72	1.71	1.65	1.64	1.64	1.65	1.63	1.6	1.67
Sweden	-	**2.89**	**3.00**	**3.27**	**3.30**	**3.46**	**3.60**	**3.67**	**3.70**	**3.78**	**4.00**	**4.27**	**4.00**
UK	2.16	2.08	2.09	2.12	2.07	1.98	1.88	1.81	1.80	1.88	1.84	1.86	1.88
USA	2.69	2.71	2.64	2.52	2.42	2.5	2.55	2.58	2.60	2.65	2.72	2.74	2.67
OECD	2.32	2.24	2.20	2.15	2.10	2.11	2.13	2.15	2.17	2.2	2.24	2.28	2.26
Finland	**1.91**	**2.04**	**2.18**	**2.16**	**2.29**	**2.28**	**2.54**	**2.71**	**2.88**	**3.23**	**3.40**	**3.41**	**3.46**
Israel	-	2.5	2.57	2.68	2.68	2.74	2.92	3.16	3.35	3.83	4.72	5.04	4.72
Iceland	1.17	1.18	1.27	1.36	1.45	1.57	1.70	1.88	2.07	2.39	2.75	3.06	3.09
South Korea	90	1.92	2.03	2.22	2.44	2.5	2.60	2.69	2.55	2.47	2.65	2.92	2.91
China	1.42	0.74	0.74	0.72	0.65	0.6	0.60	0.68	0.70	0.83	1.00	1.07	1.23
Singapore	1.47	-	-	-	1.10	1.16	1.40	1.53	1.82	1.9	1.88	2.1	2.15

Source: OECD, Main Science and Technology Indicators; National Statistics Authorities Finland; Tekes.

Table 2. Share of R&D Activities Funded by the Public Sector in OECD Countries (%)

	1990	1991	1992	1993	1994	1995	1996	1997	1998	1999	2000	2001	2002
Norway	-	49.5	49.3	49.1	46.6	44.0	43.5	42.9	42.8	42.6	39.8	40.0	-
Austria	44.6	46.5	47.4	48.0	49.4	47.3	43.7	41.5	39.6	39.7	38.8	41.0	40.9
France	48.3	48.8	43.5	43.5	41.6	41.9	41.5	38.8	37.3	36.9	38.7	36.9	36.9
Netherlands	48.3	48.6	48.9	48.5	43.8	42.2	41.5	39.1	37.9	35.7	35.9	36.1	36.2
Denmark	42.3	39.7	38.6	37.7	38.7	39.6	35.7	36.1	34.4	32.6	31.0	27.8	28.0
Germany	33.8	35.7	35.7	36.1	36.5	36.8	36.9	35.9	34.9	32.5	31.6	31.5	32.1
Canada	44.2	43.9	43.2	40.7	38.0	35.8	33.7	32.0	30.5	32.3	30.8	33.3	34.0
USA	40.8	38.7	37.9	37.7	37.2	35.5	33.2	31.6	30.5	28.8	26.0	26.9	28.7
UK	35.5	35.0	33.4	32.5	33.2	33.2	31.9	31.1	31.0	29.2	28.9	30.2	26.9
Sweden	**36.1**	**34.0**	**33.5**	**33.0**	**30.9**	**28.8**	**27.3**	**25.8**	**25.2**	**24.5**	**21.0**	**21.0**	**-**
Japan	16.1	16.4	17.5	21.6	21.5	22.8	18.7	18.2	19.3	19.6	19.6	18.5	18.2
Ireland	30.1	27.8	25.2	27.9	20.9	21.4	22.6	22.2	23.1	21.8	22.6	25.2	-
OECD	37.8	35.5	34.9	35.1	34.4	33.8	32.1	30.6	29.6	29.8	28.4	28.9	29.9
EU	40.8	41.2	39.7	39.7	39.0	38.8	38.1	36.7	35.9	35.0	34.5	34.4	34.7
Finland	**38.1**	**40.9**	**40.4**	**39.8**	**37.5**	**35.1**	**33.0**	**30.9**	**30.0**	**29.2**	**26.2**	**25.5**	**26.1**

Source: OECD, Main Science and Technology Indicators; Tekes.

Table 3. Share of Corporate R&D Activities Funded by the Public Sector (%)

	1990	1991	1992	1993	1994	1995	1996	1997	1998	1999	2000	2001	2002
UK	16.7	14.6	13.8	12.4	11.8	11.3	9.9	10.4	11.6	10.2	8.8	8.9	6.8
USA	25.6	22.5	20.8	19.4	18.8	17.8	16.3	15.2	14.3	12.3	9.6	9.4	9.9
Norway	-	15.9	16.0	16.0	14.0	11.9	11.5	11.0	10.4	9.7	10.0	10.3	-
France	19.8	22.3	16.4	15.3	13.0	12.7	13.1	10.4	9.0	10.0	9.9	8.4	-
EU	14.5	13.5	11.9	11.3	10.3	10.3	9.7	9.2	8.8	8.6	7.8	8.0	-
OECD	16.6	14.7	13.4	12.6	11.9	11.5	10.7	10.1	9.8	8.9	7.5	7.2	7.1
Germany	10.7	10.0	9.8	9.0	9.0	8.8	9.0	9.2	8.6	7.6	7.2	6.7	6.2
Sweden	**11.5**	**10.3**	**10.6**	**10.8**	**10.2**	**9.5**	**8.6**	**7.6**	**7.7**	**7.8**	**5.8**	**5.8**	**-**
Netherlands	11.9	7.5	7.2	7.8	8.4	6.6	5.6	5.4	4.4	5.1	5.3	5.2	-
Denmark	9.6	7.9	6.8	5.8	6.0	6.1	5.7	5.3	4.2	4.4	3.8	3.1	-
Ireland	5.2	3.7	3.1	10.6	2.1	4.5	5.3	5.3	5.1	4.0	3.3	2.7	-
Finland	**4.3**	**5.4**	**5.8**	**6.1**	**5.9**	**5.6**	**4.9**	**4.1**	**4.4**	**4.2**	**3.5**	**3.4**	**3.2**
Canada	9.2	9.7	9.8	9.8	7.5	6.2	4.9	5.0	3.4	3.7	2.4	3.2	3.2
Japan	1.3	1.4	1.1	1.4	1.2	1.6	1.1	1.3	2.1	1.8	1.7	0.8	0.1

Source: OECD, Main Science and Technology Indicators; Tekes.

These issues demand attention from us all. As a contribution to this, the Industry, External Trade, Research and Energy Committee of the European Parliament commissioned European Academies Science Advisory Council (EASAC;

http://www.easac.org/) to undertake short case studies of R&D expenditure trends in Sweden and Finland, the two countries which appeared to have the highest and most rapidly growing R&D spends in the EU.

EASAC provides a means for the national Academies of Europe to work together to inject high quality science into EU policy-making. EASAC task is building science into policy at EU level by providing independent, expert, credible advice about the scientific aspects of public policy issues to those who make or influence policy for the European Union. EASAC ultimate target is being recognized by EU policy-makers as the place to go for reliable, timely advice that reflects the best that the European scientific community can deliver. EASAC is designed to combine ease and speed of operation, with the unrivalled prestige and authority of the national Academies of science and with the opportunities that come from ready access to the networks of members and colleagues that constitute Academies.

The case studies were carried out by small teams of experts selected by EASAC over a two-month period. The results of the analysis were presented during a workshop in Brussels, together with three related topics identified by the Industry Committee.

The additional topics concerned "The role of R&D in Hungary", "Benchmarking R&D investment: a perspective from the USA", and "Intellectual property and investment in research". The EASAC report was also presented at the European Science Congress held in Brussels April 6, 2004.

3. The Finnish 3.6% of GDP

I will highlight some aspects described in the report, trying to identify possible instruments that might be valuable in the process of strengthening R&D in Europe.

In terms of the size of the economy, structure of industry, educational level (Fig. 1) and other variables, Finland and Sweden are quite similar, although there are significant differences in tax load and in many indicators measuring the size of the economy.

There are also differences in soft indicators. On the positive side for Finland is the apparent trust that the business sector has in the economic policy and knowledge infrastructure (Fig. 2). This trust would seem to be related to the functioning of a Science and Technology Policy Council (STPC) in Finland.

Clearly, this council is playing a major role in shaping the economic policy of Finland, where Nokia has been of particular importance (Fig. 3).

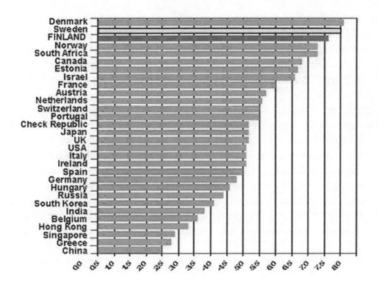

Fig. 1. Education Spending as Percentage of GDP in 1998
Sources: Tekes; OECD, Main Science and Technology Indicators; National Statistics.

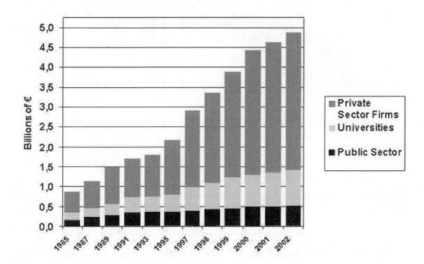

Fig. 2. R&D Investment in Finland (Billions of €).
Sources: Tekes; OECD, Main Science and Technology Indicators; National Statistics.

The success of Nokia, with its positive effects on literally thousands of other companies, has influenced the entire economic policy in a favorable way. The telecom and IT businesses owe their success to the economic policy, which has built on ideas of cluster formation and innovation systems. These concepts have been popularized in the Academic debate during the last decade, and the Finnish business policy, with its emphasis on system perspective, has become a role model internationally.

The International Monetary Fund provided excellent proof of the strong competitiveness of Finland (http://www.imf.org/external/). As a complement to the STPC, the technology development centre (The National Technology Agency of Finland, TEKES) was established in 1983 to finance applied and industrial R&D. It has been pointed out that, although Ericsson of Sweden has been successful, Nokia appears to have had a comparatively greater influence on the economy of Finland (Swedish long-term analysis - LU, 2003 part 6). Nokia became the nucleus of an IT cluster that was almost equal in importance to other basic business activities in Finland and it has had a big influence on the economic-political debate in Finland.

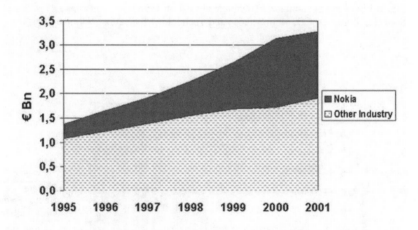

Fig. 3. Industrial R&D Spending in Finland and the Estimated Share of Nokia (€ Bn)
Sources: Tekes; OECD, Main Science and Technology Indicators; National Statistics.

The Finnish system-thinking gradually led to an attempt to strengthen the business environment by introducing different reforms. The TEKES, and STPC became increasingly important. Since 1983, when TEKES was formed, it has administered between 75% and 89% of public R&D spending targeted towards the manufacturing industry. It is important to realize that in a typical project, TEKES has been financing 30-40% of the R&D of the projects, but the share has often been higher if the receiving part is a university or a research institute. The projects still require cooperation between the private sector and the university, and are aimed at facilitating the spread of technology and internationalization by the involvement of many actors also outside Finland.

In year 2000, 2400 companies and a large number of research institutes participated in the different TEKES technology programs: a large part of R&D and production takes place in networks of companies and research institutes. It is obvious that TEKES' demand for cooperation and spreading of the research results has had the desired effects.

It is noteworthy that Finland during 1990-1993 did not abandon its then 2% target in R&D, despite the financial crisis and the collapse of the Soviet Union, which threatened the structural changes in Finland. If anything, the Finns were strengthened by the crises. The structural reorganization was continued to retain the income level, especially since it was obvious that entry into the EU and EMU would eliminate the possibilities to create competitiveness through adaptations of the Finnish mark to developments in the surrounding world (Fig. 4).

The emphasis on technical development and upgrading was retained, and R&D was one of the few areas protected against financial cuts during the crisis. So it is clearly valuable to incorporate the strategy of forming industrial clusters and cluster policy into plans for industrial development. Cooperation between different actors in the innovation system should be facilitated.

The lesson learnt from the Finnish case is that it is favorable if different ministries, public and private research institutes, companies and consumer organizations can cooperate, and keep a close contact also with higher education in universities and research institutes. This is what STPC facilitates. It is a reviewing organization with an advising function. It has greatly influenced Finnish research and technology politics. Its success as a rather independent think-tank depends on having representation from almost all important actors and a strong backing from the government. It is led by the prime minister. Among the members of STPC you find the ministers of business and industry, finance, education, communication, defense and culture, and representatives of the private sector, industrial organizations, TEKES, Academy of Finland and environment.

Horizontal communications between business, research and authorities have the capacity to identify the weakest links in the system rapidly, to initiate a broad debate, and to take immediate actions. With the rather wide fluctuations that can occur in the competitive business world today, it is important to be able to react swiftly.

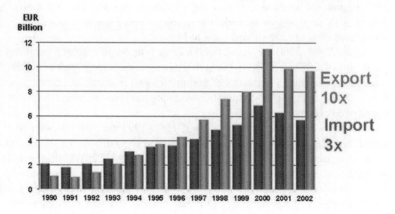

Fig. 4. Finnish Trade on High-Tech Products. Exports of Finnish High-Tech Products Totalled € 9.7 Billion and Imports 5.7 Billion in 2002
Source: National Board of Customs, Finland.

A cluster strategy in research policy appears to be important for the efficient use of available national financial resources for R&D. If the conditions are favorable, the clusters allow knowledge, created within the cluster R&D activities to be spread to many companies for the benefit of an entire industry.

However, the spread of knowledge depends on close contacts between an innovative company and other actors, and on the capacity of companies that are not carrying out R&D to receive the knowledge. To strengthen the capacity to receive knowledge in small and medium-sized enterprises, it may be wise to direct public R&D-financing to companies and industries carrying out publicly financed R&D projects (often dominated by multinational enterprises, MNEs - like NOKIA), thereby supporting the cluster rather than a specific enterprise.

4. The Swedish 4.3% of GDP

Since the days of industrialization, Sweden has gone through many phases in its development. To create a good educational system in parallel with industrial development has been a part of the will of the Swedish political establishment. Sweden is among the first countries within the OECD group for fractions of people having academic education and also for fractions of people having longer and research education (Fig. 5).

The period from 1950 to 1960 was characterized by a consensus policy referred to as the 'spirit of Saltsjöbaden' ('The Swedish Model'), allowing piecemeal social engineering. This resembles the relation between political forces and industrialists developed in Finland during recent years. This consensus policy was abandoned in Sweden in the early 1970s, after which the situation on the market became rather chaotic with strikes and lock-outs.

An interesting analysis of the economic development in Sweden since industrialization was recently published by Deiaco, Giertz and Reitenberger (Vinnova, 2002). These authors have analyzed the role of techno-parks and clusters in the Swedish innovation system. Their conclusions are in agreement with what we have learnt from the Finnish case, emphasizing the importance of cooperation between companies, society and research organizations, cluster formation, and regional innovation systems. These analysts point out that clusters may develop an internal competence - a silent, experienced-based knowledge, which develops over time and is difficult to reproduce. Nursing the clusters strengthens the competitiveness of the innovative environment, and the presence of big companies forces the development of SMEs.

Close contacts with universities and institutes for higher education and research is considered to be important.

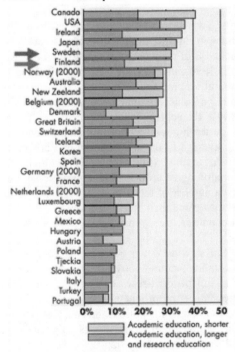

Fig. 5. Part of the Population Having Academic Education 2001, Age 25-64
Source: OECD, Education at a Glance, 2002

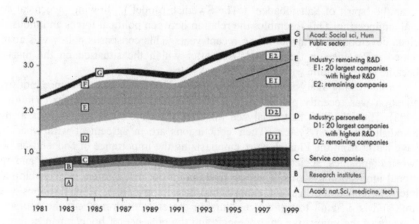

Fig.6. R&D Expenditures in % of GDP in Sweden
Source: Deiaco, Giertz, Reitberger (Vinnova, 2002)

Since the beginning of the 1990s, Sweden has been investing more in R&D relative to GDP than any other country in Europe. In 2001, the total R&D expenditures amounted to €11 billion. About 1% of the workforce was involved in R&D activities. During the latter half of the 1990s, investments were made in education on different levels, especially in natural science and technology. However, there was no real increase in expenditures on basic research in Academe, something which has been pointed out repeatedly in the general debate.

Although the R&D investments are the highest, production, income and competitiveness in Sweden are closer to average in the western part of Europe. This has been referred to as the 'Swedish paradox' (See OECD STI-outlook 2002, country response to policy questionnaire, and European Trend Chart on Innovation; Country report, Sweden). Since a number of the largest Swedish and foreign multinational companies have chosen to place their R&D in Sweden, but a large part of their production in low-cost countries, there would seem to be a 'Swedish problem' rather than a paradox.

The above mentioned fact has been slowing down economic development in Sweden, but there are certainly also other factors contributing to the stagnating economic development. A number of independent researchers and governmental institutes are involved in analyzing whether the problems concern the education system, taxes, the function of the market and its institutions, driving forces for entrepreneurship, availability of venture capital etc. It would also be of great interest to know exactly what the Swedish 4.3% R&D actually stands for. Many analysts believe that today the figure 4.3% is significantly lower (perhaps below 4%), despite the fact that there are known R&D activities that cannot be included in the statistics because of lack of information.

The R&D consists of basic research, target-oriented research carried out by the company, and development of processes and products. By far the largest share of the R&D expenditure is accounted for by activities in the 20 largest companies, and a significant part of the R&D spending reported may represent costs for consulting carried out for the large companies, and it is not clear to what extent this influences the R&D. As seen in Figure 6, the estimated spending on basic research is not impressive. It is particularly alarming that the expenditures on basic research have not increased during the period 1981-1999.

The message is that efforts in the coming years in the different EU countries to reach the 3% target must be evaluated carefully to see what expenditures directly benefit the development towards a knowledge-based society in Europe.

In addition to the Long-Term Evaluations made directly for the Swedish Department of Finance, there are a number of institutes, linked in various ways to the government, evaluating the performance of different sectors, assessing education and research, growth, and innovation strength in Sweden. There is no question that these evaluations provide important information about the development of Sweden in their respective areas, and, collectively, their results constitute a valuable basis for forming a policy for the future development of the country, but it is debatable whether their results are influencing the planning of the future of Sweden to the same extent as those of the Finnish STPC.

5. Research in the European Union

The European Union needs a holistic growth vision including both traditional and new industries. It needs to be focused, to support initiators and protect ownerships. In addition to this, due attention must be given to the environment and to social situation of the people of Europe.

The adjoining illustration (figure 7) is aimed at showing the relationship between the different actors and targets in the innovation chain. The S-formed connects the different actors in basic research at the Academes all the way through to the final products

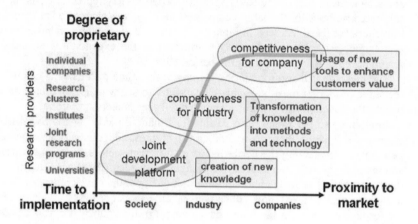

Fig.7. Actors and Targets in R&D and Innovation Chain
Source: Adapted from an Illustration by Ingve Stade, Stora Enso and CEPS.

Universities must focus on higher education and free, fundamental research (research aimed at solving central problems concerning our understanding of the material world). Therefore, EU must support world class institutions and world class research institutes to create an industrial goal-oriented approach. Alliances, networking and joint 'ventures' within the Academe and between universities and institutes are fruitful if properly nursed and dearly needed.

It should be noted that since the 1970s important developments come from so many discoveries made in basic research. In fact 5 of the thematic areas supported by the 6th Framework Program are based on such discoveries:

1. Genomics and biotechnology for health
2. Information Society technologies
3. Nanotechnologies
4. Aeronautics and space
5. Food Safety and health risks
6. Sustainable development and global change
7. Citizens and governance in the European knowledge-based society
8. Anticipating the EU's scientific and technological needs

Thus it seems safe to conclude that for the long-term development of Europe into the most competitive and dynamic knowledge-based economy in the world, there is a need for the development of continued highly competitive basic research. In this enterprise the role of the governments is to provide the consistent and sustained support at the base of development. Industrial joint funding could be an efficient and rational means to extract the basic understanding and knowledge at universities and institutes. Growth industry has often had a well developed competitive edge. What is lacking are breakthroughs in product innovation to create a competitive edge, i.e. there is a need for improved commercialization link. In order to get the adequate public/political support there is a need for understanding of the factors that drive development.

During the last couple of years a lot of effort has been put into convincing the European Union that it must allocate substantial financial means to support basic research, not only research that has the immediate added value. These plans to create a European Research Council have come a long way now, and the goal seems to be within reach. The European Research Council Expert Group has delivered its report, and this is now under debate. The hope is that the EU shall find the legal solution to creating such a research council. The important point is to create a funding body at the European level, supporting the very best research in Europe, funded by the European Union and being an autonomous body built on the research community of Europe.

6. Education in the European Union

It seems appropriate in this context finally to make a statement concerning education. As a consequence of research and development in a number of areas since the 1970s all of us have to learn to live in, and handle, an increasingly more difficult world. It is in this world of innovations and high density of information that the young have to find their place and make their living. All of us will need an improved all round knowledge, including natural science and technology, and for those who are to engage in R&D in the future the educational system has to be excellent.

It seems clear that the educational system has to be revolutionized. The situation for teachers at work has to be improved and the teaching of science to those who are choosing to become teachers and teaching of the young have to be modernized to allow everybody to use their cognitive ability to its limits. Efforts are being made in Sweden and in France to introduce systematic inquiry-based science and technology teaching in schools with the intention to contribute to eradicating science illiteracy. Performing experiments is the instrument used in these efforts. In Sweden there is a program run by the Royal Swedish Academy of Sciences (RSAS) called Natural Science and Technology for All (NTA; http://www.nta.nu/). It is based on a program created by the National Science Resource Center (NSRC), USA supported by the National Academy of Sciences and the Smithsonian Institution, USA, in the 1980-ties, and implemented in Sweden in 1996/97.

This program is comprised of a number of parts, including, in addition to materials for experiments, manuals for teachers and pupils, and not the least important, involvement of politicians in the municipalities, teaching of teachers, creating networks, continuous evaluations and development of new experiment. The NTA program has gone through a far-reaching adaptation to Swedish education culture, meaning bottom up development of the activity (not top down, as in the US). Today there are more than 2000 teachers and 40 000 children in more than 40 municipalities involved in NTA.

In 2003 the municipalities formed a special organization called NTA Production and Service (NTA PoS) for supplying the municipalities with the products and service. A second organization called NTA-U is taking care of continued evaluation of the results of the program and of research in science education in connection with NTA. The hope is that the NTA-program will reach all 287 municipalities in a period of 5-10 years. The introduction of the program has been financed by the Department of Education and a large number of private funds.

Recently, the Nobel laureate George Charpak of the Académie des Sciences, France took the initiative to form an alliance with the RSAS and academies in Estonia, Hungary and Portugal to produce an application to the EU FP6 called March 2003 – Science and Society, European Science Education Initiative, for the introduction of inquiry-based science education. A grant was given to the alliance, but compared to the grant given to Excite for the implementation of ICT, it was a small grant.

This international cooperation aimed at strengthening the general knowledge in science and technology is important. However, eradication of science illiteracy requires a major effort in the years to come. It will have to become a central issue for European Union in the making of a knowledge-based society, where the citizens understand the material world and participate in the democratic decision process. This was expressed clearly by Busquin, the EU General Director of Research at the time of launching the FP6. 'The way we teach today, tomorrow will be' (Peter Medawar). Building science into policy is another important task.

7. Conclusions

Thus, to reach the Barcelona 3% target as quickly as asked for, there is a need for close cooperation at all levels in society, i.e. cooperation involving the political leadership, educational organizations, research institutions and institutes, as well as the industry. Each country will have its own problems in finding the best practice. Each country will have to carry out a system analysis with the aim at reaching a consensus over what the possibilities are, to prioritize, and to show willingness to direct public and private funds to where they might have the greatest effect with regard to R&D, and finally efficient exploitation of innovations. Thus, SWOT analyses will have to be carried out at each level, and prioritization will have to be stringent.

Education has to be reformed. Formal education in science and technology must be carried out such that the growing generation becomes comfortable with scientific reasoning. It would seem to be important to introduce more of inquiry-based education in science and technology based on experimentation and it is important to start already in the *kindergarten*. The time has come to transform teaching/learning through ICT in schools with the aim at reaching science literacy. Eventually, all Europeans should have acquired a good understanding of the structure and function of the material world and an adequate science literacy.

The Locational Dynamics of the U.S. Biotech Industry: Knowledge Externalities and the Anchor Hypothesis[1]

Maryann Feldman

Rotman School of Management, University of Toronto,
105 St. George St., Toronto, ON M5S 3E6, Canada
maryann.feldman@rotman.utoronto.ca

1. Introduction

One of the important motivations in economic geography is to understand the forces that contribute to the agglomeration of innovative activity and affect the growth potential of the firms and cities. A significant body of research examines this question in light of the concept of knowledge spillovers (see Feldman 2000 for a review). More recent work highlights the importance of industry life cycle (Duranton and Puga 2001), the composition of activities within an agglomeration (Glaeser et al. 1992; Henderson et al. 1995, Feldman and Audretsch 1999) and the influence of existing industrial structure (Klepper 2001; Rosenthal and Strange 2002). Together this work suggests a more nuanced understanding of the nature

---

[1] This paper is a reprinting already published in Atti dei Convegni Lincei, *Distretti Pilastri Reti. Italia ed Europa* (Roma, 8-9 aprile 2003), Accademia Nazionale dei Lincei, 2004. An earlier version of this paper was prepared for the Danish Research Unit for Industrial Dynamics (DRUID) 2002 meetings. Thanks to Morris Teubal, Mark Lorenzen and the audience for comments. Thanks are due to the anonymous referees and to Jens Christensen Frøslev for suggestions. This paper has benefited from discussions with David Audretsch, Iain Cockburn, Johanna Francis and Elaine Romanelli. Invaluable research assistance in the preparation of the database was provided by Ivar Strand, Nathaniel Deines, Tom West and Johanna Francis. This work is part of a larger ongoing project. Comments and suggestions are appreciated.

of agglomeration economies and the way in which the fortunes of firms and regional clusters are intertwined.

Biotechnology presents an opportunity to study the emergence and growth of a new industry. Biotechnology is the commercialization of scientific discoveries related to genetic engineering. The industry has captured the imagination of government officials who hope to garner the potential economic rents of the next important general purpose technology. Biotech, however, is still at an early stage of development and there are many competing hypotheses about its future development. While significant resources are spent trying to promote new firm formation and the development of biotech clusters, we have a limited understanding of the process by which clusters are formed, how new industries become anchored in a local economy and, as a result, how locations may reap the resulting economic rewards.

This paper uses a panel of firms to explore the locational patterns and place-specific evolution in the U.S. biotech industry. As predicted from prior studies of knowledge-intensive industries, the biotech industry is becoming more geographically concentrated and highly specialized in certain locations. While the existence of knowledge externalities contributes to geographic concentration the larger question of how regional specialization is determined and how this affects firm survival and growth and subsequently the viability of the regional cluster is relatively unexplored.

One answer may be that existing firms serve as anchors that attract skilled labor pools, specialized intermediate industries and provide knowledge spillovers that benefit new technology intensive firms in the region. Established firms may provide expertise and knowledge about specific applications, product markets, and technical developmental trajectories that move generic scientific innovations in a particular direction, which, over time, may distinguish the specialization of the industrial cluster. For example, if there is a regional anchor with a sophisticated expertise in vaccines, new start-up firms may be likely to specialize in that same or a related trajectory. Once the region is noted to have developed an expertise, others that work on the application or in the product market may be encouraged to start firms in the region. Over time, a cluster may develop around that specialized expertise. This implies a regional path dependency that stems from the existence of the anchor firm to the specialization of new entrepreneurial start-ups that enter the industry in that location. As a result, the fortunes of technologies, firms, and regions are jointly determined.

Section Two of the paper examines the historical development of the biotech industry while Section Three sets out some of the empirical patterns of geographic location and specialization in the biotech industry. Section Four considers this descriptive analysis in the context of the literature. Section Five develops the concept of the Anchor firm as an agglomerative force and provides hypotheses about the Anchors' relationship to the formation of new dedicated biotechnology firms, their growth and the technical specialization of clusters. Section Six concludes with some reflective conclusions and future areas of research.

2. Biotechnology as an Emerging Industry in a Regional Context

The biotechnology industry is a collection of firms that focus on the application of recombinant DNA (rDNA) and its related technologies. This industry is based on a series of scientific advances in the twentieth century that provided key insights into the biological basis of life (Kenney 1986:9-27).[2] This technology may be conceptualized as a radical scientific breakthrough that creates a platform for revolutionary economic growth (Rifkin 1998). Just as our understanding of chemistry in the prior century revolutionized products and production processes in such diverse industries as the dye industry, pharmaceuticals, agriculture and fuel, biotechnology displaces the focus from chemistry to molecular biology in applications across a variety of industries.

The birth of the biotechnology industry may be dated to 1973 with a series of patent applications that were filed by Professors Stan Cohen of Stanford University and Herb Boyer of the University of California at San Francisco.[3] The patents provided a technique for moving genes between organisms and transformed the basic science of molecular biology into commercially useful knowledge. The timing of these discoveries coincided with a new era of active technology transfer by American research universities that relied on patenting scientific discoveries and then licensing the right to use these patents to firms to increase the commercialization of academic research.[4] Many new dedicated biotechnology firms (DBFs) have been formed around licenses of university patents (Powell and Brantley 1992) and maintain strong ties with academic researchers (Zucker and Darby 1996; Audretsch and Stephan 1996).

From its embryonic beginnings the biotech industry is now about thirty years old. As a new industry, biotechnology is not part of the standard industrial classification system that economists usually use to study an industry.[5] As a result,

---

[2] Modern biotechnology traces its origins to the discovery of the molecular structure of the basic building block of genetic material, deoxyribonucleic acid or DNA, by James Watson and Francis Crick in the 1950s. This work made it possible to identify the genes that make specific proteins. James Watson and Francis Crick were awarded the Nobel Prize in Medicine in 1962 for this work. See Watson (1981) for an account of the discovery process.

[3] Hall et al. (2001) argue that the patent application date should be used to date inventive activity as the lag between application and grant dates reflects administrative policies at the U.S. Patent Office.

[4] For example, in licensing the Cohen-Boyer patents on recombinant DNA technology, Stanford University asked for a one-time licensing fee of $10,000 and royalty rates ranging from 0.5% on sales of end products such as insulin to 10% on sales of research vectors and enzymes (Scherer 1999: 55).

[5] Toole (forthcoming) relies on SIC code 283 and SIC code 8731 to capture the human therapeutics and diagnostics segments of the biotechnology industry. However, it is not a clean measure because SIC 283 includes traditional pharmaceutical firms and SIC 8731 includes commercial physical research companies.

studies have used a variety of proprietary data to study biotechnology. Unfortunately, most biotech firms are small and publicly held. Biotech firms are noted to have faced greater difficulties at initial public offering (IPO) due to the embryonic stage of development of their technology and the potential for long regulatory delays in bio-medical applications and public skepticism in agricultural and environmental applications.

This paper examines data from BioAbility (formerly known as the Institute for Biotechnology Information), which maintains a proprietary database of U.S. biotechnology companies. The database provides company profiles on more than 1,700 biotechnology and biotechnology-related corporations in the United States, including company location, year of founding, product areas, technology used, and number of employees, annual revenues, and type of financing and corporate associations. The data are updated frequently using various sources including, but not limited to, company press releases, company web pages, numerous periodicals and journals, Security and Exchange Commission (SEC) reports, company annual reports, and direct contact with company officials.[6] These data are described as a "complete information source on biotechnology in the United States" and is primarily sold to companies who are interested in marketing and competitive intelligence.[7] These data have been used extensively by other researchers (Greis *et al.* 1995; Prevezer 1997; Zucker and Darby, 1996, 1997, and their colleagues 1997, 1998, 2002, Baptista and Swann 1996; Feldman and Ronzio 2001; Hall 2001) and offer a snapshot of the industry at a specific point in time. The BioAbility data will be used here to examine the locational patterns of the industry.[8]

3. Regional Distribution of the Industry

Knowledge-intensive, early stage industries are expected to be geographically concentrated. Prevezer (1997) reports that there were 849 DBFs in the biotech industry in 1991, with 63 percent (536 firms) located in 8 (out of a total of 50) states. In 1997, there were 1,478 DBFs and 1,497 firms in 2001.[9] It should be

---

[6] See the BioAbility company web page for more information (http://www. bioability.com/Database.htm).

[7] To check these data, Feldman and Ronzio (2001) cross-referenced companies in Maryland identified by BioAbility with companies identified by other sources. The BioAbility data missed a total of 55 companies that were identified by the CorpTech Directory and Maryland Technology Resource Council. However, IBI identified 20 companies that the other two references missed. There does not appear to be any discernable bias in the companies that are included by the various sources and this fact only serves to illustrate the difficulty in defining an emerging industry.

[8] The data presented here have been checked for accuracy and cleaned (see Appendix).

[9] There are two distinct types of firms in the biotech industry and in the BioAbility data. Dedicated biotech firms (DBFs) are young firms that have biotechnology as their focus. The biotech industry began in the early 1970s and the analysis excludes firms that were

noted that 47 of the 50 states had at least one biotech firm (the exceptions were South Dakota, Wyoming and Alaska), perhaps reflecting incentives targeted to encourage the development of the biotechnology industry within their borders (Biotechnology Industry Organization 2001).[10]

Table 1. Proportion of Dedicated Biotech Firms in Top Eight States: 1991, 1997, 2001

	1991		1997		2001	
	N of Firms	Share	N of Firms	Share	N of Firms	Share
California	197	23.2%	354	24.0%	363	24.3%
Massachusetts	68	8%	157	10.6%	162	10.8%
New Jersey	58	6.8%	78	5.3%	82	5.5%
Maryland	57	6.7%	81	5.5%	86	5.7%
Texas	41	4.8%	59	4.0%	54	3.6%
New York	39	4.5%	64	4.3%	66	4.4%
North Carolina	39	4.6%	82	5.6%	98	6.6%
Pennsylvania	37	4.4%	67	4.5%	68	4.5%
Total of Above	**536**	**63.1%**	**942**	**63.7%**	**979**	**65.4%**
Out of	849		1478		1497	
Total of Top 3	323	38.0%	592	40.1%	623	41.2%

Source: 1991 is from Dibner (1991) as reported by Prevezer (1997); 1997 and 2001 from IBI, author's calculations.

Table 1 demonstrates that while the concentration of DBFs in the top states increased slightly from 1991 to 2001, the relative ordering of states changed with New Jersey losing ranking while Maryland and North Carolina moved forward with a greater number of firms. What is most surprising is that the top three states

---

founded prior to 1970. In addition, there are many larger and more established entities that have only a small interest in biotech are not considered as dedicated biotech firms.

[10] Forty-eight out of fifty states have programs aimed at spurring development of the life sciences, according to the 2001 Biotechnology Industry Organization study. For example, Wisconsin has directed that about $65 million of its public employee pension funds be invested in young life-sciences companies. Michigan is spending $50 million a year for 20 years, or $1 billion, from the state's share of the tobacco settlement to nurture a life sciences corridor from Detroit to Grand Rapids. Kentucky has been trying to lure academic stars to the universities by supplementing their salaries with its "Bucks for Brains" program. New York State this year allocated $225 million for the Gen*NY*sis program to promote commercializing biotech research and to fund business incubators to attempt to compensate for the expensive real estate near New York City leading medical research centers.

(California, Massachusetts and New Jersey) accounted for 38 percent of the industry in 1991, 40 percent in 1997 and 42 percent in 2001 (California, Massachusetts and North Carolina). Thus, there is somewhat of a paradox. The industry is simultaneously becoming more distributed to a variety of locations. At the same time, the industry is becoming more geographically concentrated in a few locations. Moreover, the relative ranking of these locations is not static.

Table 2. Distribution of Dedicated Biotech Firms by City

Geographic Entity	State	1997		2001	
		N of Firms	Share	N of Firms	Share
Boston PMSA	MA	142	9.6%	142	9.5%
San Diego MSA	CA	107	7.2%	109	7.3%
San Francisco PMSA	CA	76	5.1%	70	4.7%
Washington, DC PMSA	MD/DC/VA	74	5.0%	77	5.1%
Raleigh--Durham MSA	NC	69	4.7%	88	5.9%
Philadelphia PMSA	PA/NJ	56	3.8%	47	3.1%
San Jose PMSA	CA	53	3.6%	50	3.3%
Seattle--Bellevue PMSA	WA	45	3.0%	42	2.8%
Oakland PMSA	CA	44	3.0%	55	3.7%
Minneapolis--St. Paul	MN	31	2.1%	27	1.8%
Orange County	CA	30	2.0%	28	1.9%
Houston PMSA	TX	29	2.0%	23	1.5%
Madison MSA	WI	28	1.9%	24	1.6%
Middlesex--Somerset MSA	NJ	26	1.8%	30	2.0%
Chicago PMSA	IL	25	1.7%	29	1.9%
New York, NY PMSA	NY	25	1.7%	27	1.8%
Baltimore, MD PMSA	MD	22	1.5%	25	1.7%

Source: Authors Calculations, 2000 Census Geography definitions used

Table 2 provides the sub-state distribution of the industry in 1997 and 2001 for those cities that had the largest concentrations of firms.[11] The largest number of DBFs were located in the Boston area (142 firms or 10 percent of the industry), followed second by San Diego (107 firms or 7 percent of the industry) and San Francisco (76 firms or 5 percent of the industry). In sum, these 17 cities account for 60 percent of the biotech firms. The top four cities accounted for about 28 percent of the firms. Only about 4 percent of the firms were not located in an urban

---

[11] Geographic assignment is based on the address of the firm and is allocated to the geographic unit, Primary Metropolitan Statistical Area (PMSA).

area in 1997 or in 2001, consistent with other analyses of innovative activity that finds that innovation is an urban phenomenon (Feldman and Audretsch 1999).

Table 3. Within City Concentration of Firms and Degree of Specialization

N	% of City Firms	Location Quotient	Product Category
Boston, Massachusetts: Total of 142 firms			
67	42.41%	155.00	Therapeutics: 557 or 30.44%
28	17.72%	93.72	Clinical Diagnostics: 385 firms or 21.04%
14	8.86%	128.04	Cell Culture: 141 firms or 7.70%
9	5.70%	77.29	Immunological Products: 150 firms or 8.20%
8	5.06%	90.43	Medical Devices: 114 companies or 6.23%
5	3.16%	59.68	Environmental Testing: 108 firms or 5.90%
4	2.53%	35.66	Plant Agriculture: 145 firms or 7.92%
San Diego, California: Total of 107 firms			
53	49.53%	162.72%	Therapeutics: 557 or 30.44%
30	28.04%	133.26%	Clinical Diagnostics: 385 firms or 21.04%
13	12.15%	200.16%	Drug Delivery Systems: 111 Companies or 6.07%
12	11.21%	136.77%	Immunological Products: 150 firms or 8.20%
10	9.35%	121.37%	Cell Culture: 141 firms or 7.70%
10	9.35%	150.01%	Medical Devices: 114 companies or 6.23%
San Francisco, CA: Total of 76 Firms			
34	44.74%	146.97%	Therapeutics: 557 or 30.44%
20	26.32%	125.08%	Clinical Diagnostics: 385 firms or 21.04%
8	10.53%	128.37%	Immunological Products: 150 firms or 8.20%
7	9.21%	119.62%	Cell Culture: 141 firms or 7.70%
5	6.58%	108.38%	Drug Delivery Systems: 111 Companies or 6.07%
Washington, DC: Total of 74 Firms			
22	29.73%	97.67%	Therapeutics: 557 or 30.44%
17	22.97%	109.19%	Clinical Diagnostics: 385 firms or 21.04%
10	13.51%	175.50%	Cell Culture: 141 firms or 7.70%
10	13.51%	164.80%	Immunological Products: 150 firms or 8.20%
8	10.81%	178.10%	Analytical Testing Services: 111 companies 6.07%

N	% of City Firms	Location Quotient	Product Category
		Raleigh—Durham, North Carolina: Total of 69 Firms	
25	36.23%	119.03%	Therapeutics: 557 or 30.44%
17	24.64%	117.10%	Clinical Diagnostics: 385 firms or 21.04%
9	13.04%	209.37%	Medical Devices: 114 companies or 6.23%
8	11.59%	191.01%	Drug Delivery Systems: 111 companies or 6.07%
8	11.59%	191.01%	Analytical Testing Services: 111 comp or 06.07%
8	11.59%	184.62%	Veterinary Products: 115 firms or 6.28%
7	10.14%	131.75%	Cell Culture: 141 firms or 7.70%
6	8.70%	109.79%	Plant Agriculture: 145 firms or 7.92%
6	8.70%	106.04%	Immunological Products: 150 firms or 8.20%
5	7.25%	122.82%	Environmental Testing: 108 firms or 5.90%
		Philadelphia, Pennsylvania: Total of 56 firms	
29	51.79%	170.12%	Therapeutics: 557 or 30.44%
9	16.07%	76.39%	Clinical Diagnostics: 385 firms or 21.04%
7	12.50%	211.86%	Environmental Testing: 108 firms or 5.90%
6	10.71%	176.51%	Drug Delivery Systems: 111 Companies or 6.07%
6	10.71%	135.28%	Plant Agriculture: 145 firms or 7.92%
4	7.14%	87.11%	Immunological Products: 150 firms or 8.20%
4	7.14%	140.61%	Animal Agriculture: 93 firms or 5.08%
3	5.36%	377.26%	Biomaterials: 26 Firms or 1.42%

The rank-order of cities in terms of the distribution of firms is not static over this four year time period. The Boston and San Francisco areas, where the industry is noted to have had its origins in the 1970s are among the leaders (Cortright and Mayer 2002). The industry in Boston is substantially concentrated in Cambridge while the Northern California industry is spread between San Francisco's neighboring jurisdictions of Oakland and San Jose. San Diego, Seattle and Raleigh-Durham are typically seen as concentrations that emerged later but have developed substantial industries. Raleigh-Durham, the city associated with Research Triangle Park, had the greatest increase in the number of firms and moved from fifth to third in the rankings between 1997 and 2001. The Washington, D.C. cluster is frequently cited as benefiting from proximity to the U.S. National Institutes of Health which accounts for $25 billion in intramural research funding. Conversely, New York and Philadelphia are two cities that are historically prominent headquarters for the pharmaceutical industry. In contrast, Los Angeles and Orange County in Southern California is noted to be the home of Amgen, one of the earliest and currently the world's largest biotech company.[12] Thus, the geographic location of the industry appears to be anchored by some large institutions, related firms and successful early entrants to the industry.

3.1. Technological Specialization

Biotechnology is a scientific knowledge base that has economically valuable applications in such diverse industries as pharmaceuticals, medical diagnostics, food production and agriculture, bio-environmental remediation and chemical processing. We analyzed the regional concentration of product categories by city for the cities with the largest number of DBFs in Table 3. There is evidence of regional specialization in biotech products and technological sub-fields that suggest there are unique and regionally defined centers of expertise. For example, Boston, Massachusetts was the site for 142 firms in 1997. Of these 142 firms, 67 firms had an active interest in therapeutics. This represents 42.4 percent of the firms within the city. The location quotient measures the degree of specialization of the firms within a city relative to the nation.[13] A location quotient of 100 indicates that the city has the same proportion of companies specialising in a certain product category as the national industry. In Boston, the location quotient for therapeutics is 155, indicating that the industry concentration in therapeutics is 55 percent greater than if firms specializing in therapeutics were evenly distributed throughout the country. These results suggest that the industry is developing differentiated and unique capabilities in specific locations.[14].

In contrast, Table 4 presents location quotients for cities that do not have a prominent presence for the industry overall but exhibit a high degree of specialization. It is most surprising that the cities listed are not typically considered as hot beds for technology and lack many of the prerequisites for science-based industry development, notably prominent research universities. For example, Des Moines, Iowa does not have a major university. It does have a set of large established firms with a reputation for R&D in animal products such as Garst Seed Company (established in 1930; 450 employees); Hy-Line International (established in 1936; 300 employees) and Pioneer Hi-bred International (established 1926; 5,025 em-

---

[12] Amgen's web site (http://www.amgen.com/corporate/AboutAmgen/backgrounder. html) indicates that the company chose Thousand Oaks, California as its location to be near such major research centers as the University of California at Los Angeles, the University of California at Santa Barbara and the California Institute of Technology.

[13] It is calculated as the ratio of the percentage of the state's biotech firm with a specific specialization divided by the percentage of the nation's biotech firms with that specialization.

[14] These data are based on firms' reports of their research and product development areas. No measure of firm effort or success in these fields is provided.

ployees). These firms are part of the BioAbility database because they have activity in biotechnology.[15]

Table 4. Location Quotients for Non-Prominent Cities, All Firms, by Product Type

	N	% of City Firms	Location Quotient	Product Category
Des Moines, IA	4	50.00%	984.25%	Animal Agriculture
Kansas City, MO	4	36.36%	579.04%	Veterinary Products
Atlanta, GA	4	22.22%	356.70%	Medical Devices
Nassau—Suffolk, NY	6	28.57%	348.43%	Immunological Products
Milwaukee, WI	4	17.39%	342.35%	Animal Agriculture
Portland, OR	4	20.00%	338.98%	Environmental Testing
Miami, FL	4	21.05%	337.92%	Medical Devices
Bergen--Passaic, NJ	4	19.05%	313.80%	Drug Delivery Systems
Baltimore, MD	6	23.08%	299.70%	Cell Culture
Salt Lake City, UT	4	22.22%	280.58%	Plant Agriculture
Middlesex—Somerset, NJ	6	13.95%	229.88%	Drug Delivery Systems
Houston, TX	4	12.90%	212.57%	Drug Delivery Systems
Orange County, CA	4	11.76%	193.82%	Drug Delivery Systems
Orange County, CA	4	11.76%	192.86%	Analytical Testing Services
Minneapolis--St. Paul	5	11.90%	191.09%	Medical Devices
Portland—Vancouver	8	40.00%	190.11%	Clinical Diagnostics
Bergen—Passaic, NJ	12	57.14%	187.72%	Therapeutics
Madison, WI	5	14.29%	180.38%	Plant Agriculture
New Haven, CN	6	54.55%	179.19%	Therapeutics
Chicago, IL	4	9.09%	178.95%	Animal Agriculture
Los Angeles, CA	7	36.84%	175.11%	Clinical Diagnostics

While the term biotechnology is used to describe an entire industry, it is really a set of many different product applications noted in Table 3 and 4. Following the path of most generic platform technologies, genetic engineering DNA replication and the other scientific techniques that define biotechnology are adapted to spe-

---

[15] These firms are included in the BioAbility database have a product development agenda in biotechnology and are potential clients for firms who use the U.S. Company Database as a marketing tool.

cific commercial uses. While market forces will decide what applications are pursued, we may expect that a geographic pattern of technology specialization reflects the localized nature of knowledge spillovers. Existing expertise in a region may define the transformation of generic scientific discoveries into specific specialized technological trajectories. Orlando (2000) and Autant-Bernard (2000) provide evidence that the ability to benefit from knowledge spillovers is conditioned on technological proximity: the effects of knowledge spillovers are greater for similar applications. This suggests that firms working on applications for which the region is specialized will realize a locational premium that will aid their growth.

Most analysis considers biotechnology as a homogeneous industry. Kenney and Von Berg (1999) note that early discussions of the computer industry relied on an aggregation of mainframe computers and personal computers. Yet, in retrospect there was substantial regional differentiation between these two sub-sectors which subsequently manifested in widely divergent growth trajectories. In sum, we may expect that the regional growth trajectory is endogenous to the technology trajectory. Thus the specific technological tools and the applications the firm develops is a function of regional capability. The growth of the cluster and the region, in turn, may be a function of the technology chosen.

Table 5. Comparison of Characteristics of Dedicated Biotechnology Firms in Prominent Cities

				Corporate Organization		City-Industry Demography			
	DBF Characteristics					Event / Firms in 1997			
		Year Founded	N° of Employees	Public (%)	Sub-sidiary (%)	Death Rate	Merger Rate	Birth Rate	DBF / Anchor
Boston	Mean	1988 (5.8)	107 (346.0)	41.5%	15.5%	0.070	0.141	0.197	142/ 19
	Me-dian	1989	35						
Minneapolis	Mean	1984 (6.8)	61 (87.8)	61.3%	6.5%	0.032	0.129	0.032	31/ 11
	Me-dian	1985	20						

| | | DBF Characteristics | | Corporate Organization | | City-Industry Demography | | | |
| | | | | | | Event / Firms in 1997 | | | |
		Year Founded	N° of Employees	Public (%)	Subsidiary (%)	Death Rate	Merger Rate	Birth Rate	DBF / Anchor
Oakland	Mean	1987 (5.7)	258 (1141.3)	43.2%	11.4%	0.045	0.114	0.136	44/ 5
	Median	1988	35						
Philadelphia	Mean	1987 (7.9)	64 (115.1)	12.5%	19.6%	0.125	0.107	0.143	56/ 14
	Median	1987	28						
Raleigh-Durham	Mean	1990 (5.2)	20 (23.4)	14.5%	7.2%	0.145	0.072	0.478	69/ 23
	Median	1992	10						
San Diego	Mean	1988 (5.3)	89 (127.2)	39.3%	11.2%	0.056	0.047	0.215	107/ 7
	Median	1988	47						
San Francisco	Mean	1989 (5.2)	96 (363.0)	35.5%	11.1%	0.118	0.118	0.184	76/ 4
	Median	1990	25						

	DBF Characteristics			Corporate Organization		City-Industry Demography			
						Event / Firms in 1997			
	Year Founded		N° of Employees	Public (%)	Subsidiary (%)	Death Rate	Merger Rate	Birth Rate	DBF / Anchor
San Jose	Mean	1989 (4.8)	89 (101.7)	43.4%	17%	0.075	0.075	0.151	53/ 6
	Median	1990	50						
Seattle	Mean	1987 (6.3)	92 (158.3)	37.8%	20%	0.067	0.156	0.111	45/ 1
	Median	1987	29						
Washington	Mean	1985 (7.6)	83 (220.6)	29.7%	16.2%	0.068	0.054	0.135	74/ 6
	Median	1985	25						
National	Mean	1987 (7.1)	79 (309.9)	31.5%	13.3%	0.079	0.087	0.158	1491 /356
	Median	1987	25						

3.2. Differences in Industry Composition

Table 5 presents more descriptive statistics on the characteristics of biotechnology firms and the industrial concentrations in the ten most prominent cities. Column 1 provides the average year founded for all the DBFs, both in terms of mean (with standard deviation) and median. While we date the beginning of the industry to the early 1970s, these data suggest that the industry is in different stages of development in different locations. Column 2 presents average number of employees.

Again, there is great variation, reflecting not only the age of firms but also the success of a few firms. Column 3 presents the fraction of DBFs that are either publicly traded or subsidiaries of other firms. The number of firms that are independently privately held is the residual fraction.

City-industry demographic data are provided for the time period 1997-2001: death rate, the number of firms that failed during the time period relative to the total number of firms in 1997; the merger rate: the number of firms that merged or were acquired over the time period relative to the population, and: the birth rate or the rate at which new firms were started relative to the 1997 existing base of firms.

Finally, the last column in Table 5 presents the ratio of DBFs to what we term Anchor Firms in the city.[16.] For example, nationally, there were 1,491 DBFs in 1997 and 356 Anchor Firms using biotechnology in their existing product lines, for a ratio of 4.2. This contrasts to a ratio of 3 in Raleigh-Durham and 45 in Seattle.

In sum, this descriptive analysis presents a detailed picture of a geographically concentrated emerging industry. The American biotech industry is dominated by a large number of new start-up firms, as others have noted (Zucker and Darby 1996). In addition, a number of larger, more established firms apply biotechnology tools to their existing product lines and these firms are part of the biotech industry as they advance the technology by adaptation to serve their established markets. Next, the data demonstrate that firms are specialized in terms of product applications that fall under the umbrella term biotechnology. There is a high degree of product application specialization within geographic locations. This indicates that firms within the biotech industry are developing in diverse ways in different locations: biotech as a platform technology is adapted differentially within locations. Finally, firm demography is heterogeneous between clusters. There is great variation in the biotech industry-city clusters in terms of the number of firms, their size, age and type of financial backing.

4. Descriptive Analysis in Context

Much of the empirical investigation of the biotech industry has focused on academic research and linkages to university activity with mixed results. The work of Zucker et al. examined the influence of academic star scientists prior to 1990 and concludes that the location of biotechnology start-ups is influenced by the location of these star scientists.[17] Toole (forthcoming) notes that the focus on star scientists

---

[16] As noted previously, the Anchor Firms are more established firms with product lines that predate the biotechnology revolution but have current efforts involving biotechnology. More generally, regional anchors may encompass other institutions such as universities, government labs, research institutes and other entities.

[17] Biotechnology star scientists are defined as those scientists with more than 40 genetic sequence discoveries in GenBank, the National Institutes of Health (NIH) genetic sequence database, through April 1990.

is due to the observation that early biotechnology discoveries were characterized by tacit knowledge that is best communicated through face-to-face contact. Zucker, Darby and Armstrong (1998: 152) interpret their findings to suggest that market mechanisms rather than knowledge spillovers account for the geographic concentration of the industry. But, they qualify their conclusions: "We suspect that more or better screens would identify top scientists in other aspects of modern biotechnology, which are not captured by genetic sequence discoveries, and would reduce or even eliminate the separate significance of top-quality universities and federally supported university researchers" (Zucker and Darby 1997). This suggests that the findings may reflect the very beginning of the industry, which coincided with aggressive intellectual property licensing on the part of universities and a series of initiatives to leverage universities for local economic development. We may question the importance of universities to the continuing development of the industry, especially as the industry moves to specialized commercial applications. Thus while knowledge spillovers from universities may be important to early stage innovative activity, universities alone may not be sufficient to anchor a developing industry in a location.

Dasgupta and David (1987) highlight the distinction between the social organization of science and the more practical concerns of technology. Science, the pursuit of new knowledge, occurs primarily within the domain of the research university and is characterized by a priority-based reward system that emphasizes scientific publication. Technology, on the other hand, develops ideas from science for commercial markets. It is characterized by the pursuit of economic returns and its venue is rent seeking firms. While it is appropriate to consider patents, publication and the location of star scientists in the earliest stages of firm formation – the science stage- we may expect that as an industry develops and science is translated into commercial applications the locational dynamics may change to emphasize industrial and technological attributes. While science resources may be most important in the earliest stages of the industry development, technology resources may become more important as the industry develops.

Evidence on the location of the biotech industry highlights the importance of the location of the chemical and pharmaceutical industry, especially their headquarters and R&D labs (Gray and Parker 1998; Orsenigo 2001:81-82; Zeller 2001). Orsenigo (2001:86) notes, "The pre-existence of a strong pharmaceutical national industry, with some large internationalized companies may have been a fundamental prerequisite for the rapid adoption of molecular biology" and further, the strength of the local science base is important but may not be the only factor in accounting for the development of the biotech industry. The biotech industry in Italy developed in Milan which did not have the top-rated academic research while Naples, an important academic center, did not develop a biotech industry (Orsenigo 2001:83)." Without the technological and market capabilities developed in prior time periods, the firms in Naples were unable to utilize scientific breakthroughs while the Milanese firms were able to innovate without strong support from local universities. Once the academic knowledge was codified it could be transferred and other types of knowledge became decisive. These results may hold for a broad range of industry life-cycles.

Innovative activity depends on knowledge and spillovers of knowledge are geographically mediated. Certainly, academic knowledge is important to innovative activity however as an industry develops complementary types of knowledge become important. This relationship may not be linear. In some sectors the development of technological resources precedes scientific discovery and firms may subsequently fund academic research as a means to further their business interests. For example, Mansfield (1995) found that industrial R&D is likely to be localized as firms fund nearby universities. Through these inclusive relationships regional expertise is reinforced.

The next step is to develop a theory to understand the dynamics of geographic clusters of innovative firms. After all, local economies are simply geographically bounded collections of firms. A cluster exists when there is a concentrated industrial focus. Given that knowledge about specific applications and product markets resides in industrial firms, it would be useful to specifically consider the role of industrial firms in clusters to account for these empirical observations and provide some testable hypothesis. The next section develops a theoretical model.

5. The Anchor-Tenant Hypothesis

The question is what forces promote the agglomeration of innovative activity and affect the growth potential of firms and clusters? Insights into industrial clusters may borrow from the real estate economics literature, which considers the problem of creating a viable economic unit in the design of the shopping mall (Agrawal and Cockburn 2002). Shopping malls are freestanding groups of retail stores under one roof, accessible primarily by car. They are designed to be self-contained shopping destinations that are isolated from other retail districts. Surrounded by parking space, they may be seen to resemble cities in their geographic isolation and dispersion throughout the landscape. Cities, like shopping malls, are the result of market forces. However, while it is difficult to observe the forces that shape agglomerations, the shopping mall problem is tractable. The problem for the profit-maximizing real estate developer is to rent space to a set of retail store tenants in order to generate a large volume of consumer foot traffic.

The typical shopping mall configuration is at least one large nationally recognized department store with an established clientele and then a diversified set of smaller, lesser known and more specialized stores.[18] The large national department store is known as the anchor tenant. It is termed the anchor as it generates high volume mall traffic that provides a customer base for the shopping mall (Eppli and Shilling 1995; Pashigian and Gould 1998). If the anchor leaves the mall, the viability of the smaller stores is threatened (Gatzlaff et al. 1994).

---

[18] A larger mall, such as the Mall of America in Bloomington, Minnesota, has four national department stores: Nordstroms, Macys, Bloomingdales and Sears. For more information, see, http://www.mallofamerica.com/

The anchor tenant's brand recognition creates an externality for the smaller stores who realize greater sales volume than they would in other locations. The value of this externality is reflected in higher rents the average tenant pays in comparison to the lower rent per square foot paid by the anchor tenant. In this way, the smaller, local stores compensate the anchor for the external benefit they receive from the Anchor (Pashigian and Gould 1998). This form of price discrimination reflects a willingness of the average tenants to pay a premium for location in the mall with the Anchor. Of course, capturing the exact value of the externality is difficult but the presence of higher rents for the average tenant recognizes that a positive externality exists.

A regional economy may similarly benefit from the presence of large, technologically sophisticated entities that anchor local economies. Conceptually, the foot traffic generated in this case would be the volume of ideas. This may have particular importance for small firms in emerging industries which is associated with innovation. An anchor, in the form of a large, established firm may create externalities that contribute to benefit of agglomerations. Other studies have considered large established firms as part of an innovative infrastructure and found that the presence of related industry increases innovative output. In addition, Criscuolo, and Rajneesh (2002) among others adapt the concept of absorptive capacity to the geographic level to account for the ability of a region to benefit from R&D investments. The anchor tenant hypothesis proposes that a large firm may be a better anchor, in terms of economic success, for a developing industry than an equivalent number of small firms. Even if the stock of skilled employees were equal under each regime, the large firm may exert a stronger influence. Organizational theorists have long recognized that there are size advantages to task coordination, efficiencies from internal economies of scale and scope and increased information flows. We can apply this theory to a regional economy to demonstrate how it may benefit from the presence of a large firm.

Certainly, the presence of a large established entity creates some of the well-known advantages of agglomeration economies such as pools of skilled labor and demand for specialized inputs that may benefit smaller start-up firms. In addition, an anchor may provide a pool of potential entrepreneurs who may take ideas out of the established anchor and form new firms (Klepper 2001). One measure of innovation that is important for early stage emerging industries is start-up firms. A stylized fact about entrepreneurship is that individuals do not relocate to start firms but instead use existing local contacts and networks to start their firms (Feldman 2001). This form of locational inertia indicates that regions holding stocks of potential entrepreneurs are more likely to be successful at promoting new firm start-ups and establishing new industries.

> H1: The number of new start-up firms will be positively related to the number of anchor tenants in a city.

Anchor Firms may further increase the viability of local firms through knowledge externalities. Anchors may serve as customers for new start-up firms and as such may engage in local user innovation networks (von Hipple 1994). Another stylized fact about start-up firms is that rather than rely on external financing or venture capital, start-up firms grow by selling services or engaging in procurement contracts for specialized products (Bhide 1999). The presence of an anchor may allow start-up firms to find relatively stable product niches that would allow firms to develop. Of course, in this manner the applications and technological orientation of the anchor would influence the technological trajectory of the start-ups and the specialization of the cluster.

Biotechnology may be conceptualized as the type of general purpose technology that has the potential for pervasive use in a wide variety of applications (Bresnahan and Trajtenberg 1995). The application of general purpose technology requires co-invention or the process of customizing the technological frontier to the unique needs of users in specific markets (Bresnahan and Trajtenberg 1995). Bresnahan and Greenstein (2001) suggest that general purpose technologies in information technologies were adapted to local needs. They conclude that "many of the determinants of co-invention are geographically local, but no authors have identified clear determinants of them (Bresnahan and Greenstein 2001: 112)."

We may expect that Anchor Firms may affect localized co-invention by dictating the demand conditions to which the general purpose technologies are adapted. The distinct geographic patterns of DBFs may reflect the specific technology focus of the Anchor firms and the specialized resources that emerge to support its market applications. This suggests that specialized regional trajectories would develop.

> H2: The technical specialization of the DBFs will be related to the focus of anchor tenants in a city.

The anchor tenant hypothesis suggests that geographic specialization may reflect the technological orientation of the Anchor. At the earliest stages of technology development, we may expect that universities and government labs serve as the source of relevant knowledge and may act as anchors. Certainly this was the case in biotechnology with the many university patents, through licensing agreements, providing the technological underpinning of many start-up firms. However, not all regions with strong research universities have been able to develop biotech industries suggesting that universities appear to be a necessary but not a sufficient condition for the development of knowledge-intensive industries.[19] The presence of Anchor Firms may provide a means to further the translation of the general purpose technologies developed at universities and research institutes into commercial products and may facilitate the growth of individual firms and the development of clusters.

As the industry develops further, we may expect that more established firms focusing on applications related to biotech could serve as anchors. Locations lack-

---

[19] The correlation between university research funding and patents, and company start-ups is weak and not statistically significant (cf. Barnes et al. 1997; Siegel et al. 1999; Raider 1998).

ing these anchors may be able to generate start-up firms but not be able to retain firms as they grow.

> H3: Growth in DBFs will be positively related to the number of anchor tenants in a city.

Anchor Firms may create knowledge externalities that benefit the agglomeration and increase overall innovative output in the region. In the situation of a shopping mall, the market failure is addressed through rents. In the absence of such a transfer mechanism among firms, we may except that smaller firms would benefit from a location premium and this would result in a greater number of new start-ups and better performance.

6. Reflective Conclusions

The development of firms within regions is fundamental to our understanding of economic development, technological change, industrial evolution and economic growth. Firms located in geographically bounded knowledge rich environments are expected to realize higher rates of innovation, increased entrepreneurial activity, and increased productivity due to the localized nature of knowledge creation and deployment. This paper has provided an analysis of the development of the biotech industry, demonstrating increased geographic concentration, specialization and differential growth. The paper borrows from literature on real estate economics to offer some hypothesis about the composition of agglomerations. The concept of the Anchor – a large firm that provides both stability and traffic in ideas is related to the number of start-ups and their growth. While these results are descriptive they suggest that regional industrial structure, product applications and technological orientation matter to innovative activity in an emerging industry. The ability of firms to derive economic value from knowledge is dependent on the firms' capabilities and strategic use of resources but the local environment shapes the firm's competencies, ability to absorb and utilize knowledge in the development of new products. Thus, the capabilities of firms and regions weave a tapestry of knowledge creation and commercial success.

The concept of a regional anchor provides a more detailed examination of the forces of agglomeration with implications for the development of emerging industries and regional specialization. In its earliest years, the biotech industry grew up around university star scientists who licensed innovations to companies. Today, there are many initiatives that attempt to build biotechnology clusters around universities using formal technology transfer mechanisms. Yet universities appear not to be a sufficient condition to promote an industrial cluster. Further, as biotechnology moves out of the lab, out of small single technology based start-ups and into new commercial applications, the location dynamics of the industry are evolving. The emphasis on star scientists is based on the observation that biotechnology discoveries are characterized by tacit knowledge that is best communicated through face-to-face contact. There is little doubt that this natural excludability played a role in the evolution of biotechnology, however, it depends on the specific discovery in question and it is likely to hold true for a relatively short period of time as valuable ideas and methods spread quickly (Toole, forthcoming). Industrial expertise and know-how are equally relevant and appear to be stickier and less easily transferred. The presence of Anchor Firms may affect the specialized development of the industry within a region, a topic that requires further investigation.

Appendix: Description of the Data

BioAbility creates snapshots of the industry at specific points in time. It is a proprietary database that is market to companies who seek to sell products to the industry or conduct competitive intelligence. It is primarily a marketing tool.

The data do provide a comprehensive list of companies that participate in the industry at a specific point in time. One copy of the U.S. Company Database was purchased in July 1997. Another copy was purchased in July 2001. Company names were matched to create a panel. This simple statement underestimates the difficulty of creating a two-time period panel because this industry is very fluid and many firms change their names, merge or exit the industry. Verifying the data and status of the companies was a time consuming effort.

First, firms were classified as either dedicated biotech firms or Anchors. The criteria for an Anchor was that:

1. the company was started before 1970;
2. the company was a positive revenue stream from non-biotech product lines or
3. the firm was a wholly owned subsidiary or division of a non-biotech company.

To reiterate, these firms are included in the BioAbility database, have a product development agenda in biotechnology and are potential clients for firms who use the U.S. Company Database as a marketing tool.

For Dedicated Biotech .Firms (DBFs) there were several outcomes:

- Firm is in continuous existence
  - accounted for 18 name changes
  - firms may relocate
- New Entrants to the industry: these are counted as births
- Exits from the industry
  - Bankruptcies
  - Movement out of biotechnology
  - Mergers/Acquisitions

These data form the basis of the investigation.

References

Adams J, Chiang E, Starkey K (2001) Industry-University Cooperative Research Centers. *Journal of Technology Transfer* 26: 73-86.

Agrawal A, Cockburn I (2002) University Research, Industrial R&D, and the Anchor Tenant Hypothesis

Almeida P, Kogut B (1997) The Exploration of Technological Diversity and the Geographic Localization of Innovation. *Small Business Economics* 9 (1): 21-31.

Audretsch D, Feldman M (1996) R&D Spillovers and the Geography of Innovation and Production. *American Economic Review* 86 (4): 253-273.

Audretsch D, Stephan P (1996) Company-Scientist Locational Links: The Case of Biotechnology. *American Economic Review* 86 (4): 641-652.

Autant-Bernard CP (2000) Science and Knowledge Flows: Evidence from the French Case. *Research Policy* 30: 1069-1078.

Baptista R, Swann P (1996) A comparison of clustering dynamics in the US and UK computer industries. Paper presented at the 6th International Joseph A. Schumpeter Conference, Stockholm, June, and at the 23rd EARIE Conference, Vienna, September.

Barnes M, Mowery DC, Ziedonis AA (1997) The Geographic Reach of Market and Non-market Channels of Technology Transfer: Comparing Citations and Licenses of University Patents. Paper presented at the Academy of Management.

Beardsell M, Henderson V (1999) Spatial evolution of the computer industry. *European Economic Review* 43: 431-56.

Bhide AV (1999) The Origin and Evolution of New Businesses. Oxford University Press, Oxford.

Biotechnology Industry Organization (2001) State Government Initiatives in Biotechnology 2001, Washington, D.C. http://www.bio.org/tax/battelle.pdf.

Bresnahan TF, Greenstein S (1996) Technical Progress and Co-invention in Computing and in the Uses of Computers. Brookings-Papers-on-Economic-Activity. Microeconomics 1996: 1-77.

Bresnahan TF, Greenstein S (2001) The Economic Contribution of Information Technology: Towards Comparative and User Studies. Journal-of-Evolutionary-Economics 11: 95-118.

Bresnahan TF, Trajtenberg M (1995) General Purpose Technologies: 'Engines of Growth'? *Journal-of-Econometrics* 65: 83-108

Caniëls M, Verspagen B (2001) Barriers to knowledge spillovers and regional convergence in an evolutionary model. *Journal of Evolutionary Economics* 11: 307-329.

Cohen W, Levinthal D (1989) Innovation and Learning: The Two Faces of R&D. *The Economic Journal* 99: 569-596.

Cortright J, Mayer H (2002) Signs of Life: The Growth of Biotechnology Centers in the U.S. The Brookings Institution; Washington, DC.

Criscuolo P, Rajneesh N (2002) A novel Approach to National Technological Accumulation and Absorptive Capacity: Aggregating Cohen and Levinthal. Conference Paper for DRUID's New Economy Conference, June.

Dalum B, Laursen K, Verspagen B (1999) Does Specialization Matter for Growth?. *Industrial and Corporate Change* 8:2:267-288.

Dasgupta P, David P (1987) Information Disclosure and the Economics of Science and Technology. In: *Arrow and the ascent of modern economic theory.* Ed: George R. Feiwel. New York: New York University Press, pp. 519-94.

Durnaton G, Puga D (2001) Nursery Cities: Urban Diversity, Process Innovation and the Life Cycle of Products. *American Economic Review* 91:5:1454-1477.

Eppli MJ, Shilling JD (1995) Large-Scale Shopping Center Development Opportunities. *Land-Economics* 71:1:35-41 (February).

Feldman M (2000) Location and Innovation: The new economics of innovation, spillovers and agglomeration. In: Clark G, Feldman M, Gertler M (eds), *The Oxford Handbook of Economic Geography.* Oxford: Oxford University Press, 373-394.

Feldman M (2001) The Entrepreneurial Event Revisited: Firm Formation in a Regional Context. *Industrial and Corporate Change* 10(4):861-891.

Feldman M, Audretsch D (1999) Innovation in Cities: Science-Based Diversity, Specialization and Localized Competition. *European Economic Review* 43: 409-429

Feldman M, Francis J (2002) The Biotech Capitol Cluster. (August)

Feldman M, Ronzio CR (2001) Closing the innovative loop: Moving from the lab to the shop floor in biotech. *Innovation and Entrepreneurship* 13: 1-16.

Gatzlaf DH, Sirmans S, Diskin B (1994) The Effect of Anchor Tenant Loss on Shopping Center Rents. *Journal-of-Real-Estate-Research* 9 (1): 99-110 (Winter).

Geiger R, Feller I (1995) The Dispersion of Academic Research in the 1980s. *Journal of Higher Education* 66 (3): 336-360.

Glaeser E, Kallal H, Scheinkman J, Shleifer A (1992) Growth of Cities. *Journal of Political Economy* 100: 1126-1152.

Goetz SJ, Morgan RS (1995) State Level Locational Determinants of Biotechnology Firms. *Economic Development Quarterly* 9 (2): 174-85.

Gray M, Parker E (1998) Industrial change and regional development: The case of the U.S. pharmaceutical industries. *Environment and Planning* 30 (10): 1757-1774.

Greis N, Dibner M, Bean A (1995) External partnering as a response to innovation barriers and global competition in biotechnology. *Research Policy* 24: 609-630.

Hall BH, Jaffe AB, Trajenberg M (2001) The NBER Patent Citation Data File: Lessons, Insights and Methodological Tools. NBER Working Paper 8498.

Hall L (2001) An Analysis of R&D, Innovation, and Business Performance in the U.S. Biotechnology Industry. *International Journal of Biotechnology* 3 (3): 1-10.

Henderson V, Kuncoro A, Turner M (1995) Industrial Development in Cities. *Journal of Political Economy* 103 (5): 1067-1090.

Kenney MP (1986) Biotechnology: The University-Industrial Complex. Yale University Press: New Haven, CT, pp: 9-27.

Kenney M, Von Burg U (1999) Technology and path dependence: the divergence between Silicon Valley and Route 128. *Industrial and Corporate Change* 8 (1): 67-103.

Klepper S (2001) The Evolution of the U.S. Automobile Industry and Detroit as its Capital. (November).

Mansfield, Edwin (1995) Academic Research Underlying Industrial Innovations: Sources, Characteristics, and Financing *Review-of-Economics-and-Statistics, 77: 55-65.*

Orlando MP (2000) On the Importance of Geographic and Technological Proximity for R&D Spillover: An Empirical Investigation. *Federal Reserve Bank of Kansas City.*

Orsenigo L (2001) The (Failed) Development of a Biotechnology Cluster: The Case of Lombardy. *Small Business Economics*, 17: 81-82.

Pashigan P, Gould E (1998) Internalizing Externalities: The Pricing of Space in Shopping Malls. *Journal of Law and Economics*, XLI: 115-142.

Powell W, Brantley P (1992) Competitive cooperation in biotechnology: learning through networks?. In: Nohria N, Eccles RG (eds), Networks and Organizations: Structure, Form and Action. Harvard Business School Press: Boston, MA, pp: 366-394.

Prevezer M (1997) The dynamics of industrial clustering in biotechnology, *Small Business Economics* 9: 255-271.

Prevezer M, Toker S (1996) The degree of integration in strategic alliances in biotechnology. *Technology Analysis & Strategic Management* 8 (2): 117-133.

Raider H (1998) Repeated Exchange and Evidence of Trust in the Substance Contract. Working paper, Columbia University.

Rifkin J (1998) The Biotech Century: Harnessing the Gene and Remaking the World. Jeremy Tarcher Putnam, New York, NY.

Rosenthal S, Strange W Geography, Industrial Organization, and Agglomeration. *Review of Economics and Statistics* (forthcoming).

Scherer FM (1999) New Perspectives on economic Growth and Technological Innovation. Washington: Brookings Institution Press.

Siegel D, Waldman D, Link A (1999) Assessing the Impact of Organizational Practices on the Productivity of University Technology Transfer Offices: An Exploratory Study. Working Paper 7256. Cambridge, MA: National Bureau of Economic Research.

Sorenson O, Audia P (2000) The Social Structure of Entrepreneurial Activity: Geographic Concentration of Footwear Production in the United States, 1940-1989. *American Journal of Sociology* 106 (2): 324-362.

Stephan PE (1996) The Economics of Science. *Journal of Economic Literature* 34:3.

Swann P, Prevezer M (1996) A Comparison of the Dynamics of Industrial Clustering in Computing and Biotechnology. *Research Policy* 25: 1139 – 1157.

Toole A (forthcoming) Understanding Entrepreneurship in U.S. Biotechnology: What are its characteristics, facilitating factors, and policy challenges?. In: David Hart ed. The Emergence of Entrepreneurship Policy: Governance, Start-Ups, and Growth in the Knowledge Economy. Cambridge, U.K.: Cambridge University Press (forthcoming).

Von Hippel E (1994) Sticky Information and the Locus of Problem Solving: Implications for Innovation. *Management Science* 40: 429-439.

Watson JP (1981) The Double Helix: A Personal Account of the Discovery of the Structure of DNA. Norton; New York, NY

Zeller C (2001) Clustering Biotech: A Recipe for Success? Spatial Patterns of Growth of Biotechnology in Munich, Rhineland and Hamburg. *Small Business Economics* 17: 123-141.

Zucker LG, Darby MR (1996) Star scientists and institutional transformation: Patterns of invention and innovation in the formation of the biotechnology industry. *Proceedings of the National Academy of Science* 93: 12709-12716 (November).

Zucker LG, Darby MR (1997) The Economist's Case for Biomedical Research. In: The Future of Biomedical Research, Claude E. Barfield and Bruce L. R. Smith (editors), Washington: D.C.: American Enterprise Institute and The Brookings Institution.

Zucker LG, Darby MR, Brewer MB (1997) Intellectual human capital and the birth of U.S. biotechnology enterprises. *American Economic Review* 88 (1): 290-306.

Zucker LG, Darby MR, Armstrong J (1998) Intellectual Capital and the Firm: The Technology of Geographically Localized Knowledge Spillovers. *Economic Inquiry* 36: 65-86.

Zucker LG, Darby MR, Armstrong J (2002) Commercializing Knowledge: University Science, Knowledge Capture and Firm Performance in Biotechnology. *Management Science* 48 (1): 138-153.

The Cambridge Phenomenon[1]

John Eatwell

Financial Policy Professor, University of Cambridge
Queens' College President, Cambridge, CB3 9ET, UK
president@quns.cam.ac.uk

1. Introduction

Over the past 30 years the economy of the City of Cambridge and of the surrounding area (Greater Cambridge) has been transformed by the growth of predominantly high-technology industry. This transformation, often referred to as the "Cambridge Phenomenon" has produced the largest concentration of high-technology research and production in Europe (the leading rival being, probably, Munich). This brief essay will examine the history of that phenomenon, its impact on the British economy, and the changing nature of the technological basis of that phenomenon as the engine of growth moves from electronics towards biotechnology. Emerging constraints on the growth of new industries in Cambridge will also be considered in the light of policies now being developed to attempt to overcome those constraints. Some comparisons will be made with other concentrations of high-technology industrial growth (in a global context the competition to Cambridge), such as Silicon Valley, Munich or Sophia Antipolis, seeking lessons from the policies that have been adopted there, and assessing their relevance for the Cambridge region.

---

[1] This paper is a reprinting already published in Atti dei Convegni Lincei, *Distretti Pilastri Reti. Italia ed Europa* (Roma, 8-9 aprile 2003), Accademia Nazionale dei Lincei, 2004. This paper is based on the work of my colleague Barry Moore, of Downing College, Cambridge.

2. History

High-technology growth in the Cambridge area did not arise from any conscious plan or even any set of broadly coherent policies. Instead it came from very informal structures, very modest local financing and essentially organic growth from small, existing independent companies. There have been scientific companies operating in Cambridge for many years. The Cambridge Scientific Instruments Company (now Cambridge Instruments) was founded in 1881 to serve the needs of the University's expanding new laboratories. The Pye Group, an electronics company, was founded in 1896. These companies first served the growing scientific University and, having done that, they expanded to providing electronic and scientific products to the world market.

The key event in the modern era occurred in 1969 when a Cambridge University report recommended the establishment of a 'science park' for science-based industry "accessible to the University of Cambridge". The Cambridge Science Park was established the next year, in 1970, by Trinity College (the wealthiest of the Cambridge colleges), on land that had been owned by Trinity for hundreds of years. Not very much had happened at first. It was only after 1979, nine years later, that there emerge the first signs of a dynamic relationship between high-technology companies and the university. This important beginning took the form of what was called the 'Cambridge Computer Group', a group of small companies who gathered together to promote their mutual interests and which attracted the attention of one of Britain's biggest banks, Barclays Bank, which actually provided the premises and the secretariat for this group. Barclays Bank later provided significant financing for small start-ups. (It is worth noting the Cambridge branch of Barclays Bank acted in a way that was not typical of the major British banks. The initiatives taken by Barclays at the time are attributable to the foresight of one particular local manager, a crucial figure who has since left Barclays).

Early growth was characterised by two sorts of companies: *first* those created by people leaving existing companies or the research laboratories of the University to form new start-ups, *secondly* subsidiaries of existing companies in the area, like Cambridge Instruments and Pye, that were started and operated as independent companies. There was a significant movement of people between these companies, the university and the research laboratories, providing very high quality technology transfer right from the beginning. However, only 17% of new companies were actually started by people coming straight from the university. More of the new companies were spin-offs from existing companies.

Typically the new firms were very small. They used little external finance. Many people, for example, borrowed money against the value of their houses to start their small company, although (as noted above) the local branch of Barclays Bank was very supportive with overdraft facilities, loans and business advice.

Such were the beginnings of high-technology growth in so-called Greater Cambridge. This is a geographical region (i.e. not a political or administrative region) with the City of Cambridge and the University at its centre, with a population of about 635,000.

3. Economic Structure of Greater Cambridge

Despite 30 years of high technology development, the economic structure of that area is not, at first sight, notably dissimilar to the economic structure of the eastern region or indeed the rest of the UK (see Figure 1).

The only extraordinary sector is 'public services', and that is of course because of the very large impact on employment of the university itself as a public university. But in general, the growth of Cambridge has been very broad based. This is an important point. When there are high-technology companies, people who work in them will still need leisure facilities, hospitals, laundries, and restaurants and so on. The dynamism that has derived from the high-tech sector has manifested itself across all sectors in the local economy.

But there is no doubt that the Cambridge economy is a knowledge economy. About a third of the 350,000 jobs in Greater Cambridge are defined as knowledge economy jobs. In most 'knowledge economy' sectors, such as computing services, electronic instruments and design, the concentration in Greater Cambridge is around 50% greater than in the UK as a whole. In research and development (7,000 jobs) the concentration is 600% higher, and in bio-sciences (13,000 jobs) 800% higher.

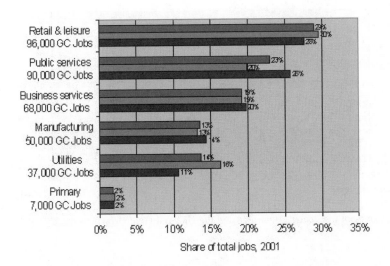

Fig 1. Greater Cambridge (GC - *Black*) Economic Structure, Compared with that of the United Kingdom *(Dark Grey)* and the Eastern Region (ER – *Light grey*), 2001. Distribution of a Total of 348,000 Jobs.

The dynamism of this knowledge economy has resulted in the total level of employment increasing from 151,000 to 348,000 over the past thirty years. This is illustrated in Figure 2 - the solid line indicates the jobs growth in Greater Cambridge, in thousands, while the dotted line indicates the jobs growth in the UK as a whole, in millions. It is clear that employment in Greater Cambridge has grown much more quickly than in the UK economy as a whole. Recently in the mid 1990s, whilst the British economy grew at about 3% a year, Greater Cambridge grew at 5% per year.

In the high-tech sector employment growth has even been more dramatic. There are roughly 42,000 jobs in Greater Cambridge that are defined as not just knowledge economy, but high-technology. This figure has more than doubled over the last 30 years, whilst in the UK as a whole there has not been any significant growth of high-tech jobs (see Figure 3). This latter statistic may be surprising. But it should be remembered that high-tech employment in the 1960s and 1970s included several of the large manufacturing sectors such as aerospace, aero engines, and the high-tech part of the automotive industry. These sectors have declined in the UK, to be replaced by computing, bio-sciences and so on.

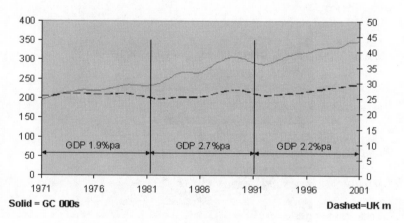

Fig 2. Employment in Greater Cambridge and the UK, and GDP Growth in the UK, 1971-2001.

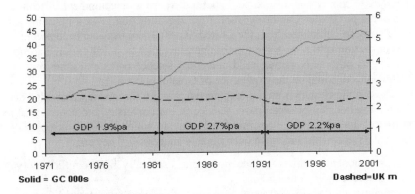

Fig 3. Growth of High-Technology Employment in Greater Cambridge and the UK, 1971-2001.

In Greater Cambridge growth in employment has not been high in the 'traditional' high-tech sectors - pharmaceuticals, instruments, electronics and telecommunications - the number of jobs being roughly the same in 2001 as it was in 1971. Growth has been in the 'new' industries - computing, research and development, design and the very new sector of bio-science which has seen very rapid expansion in recent years. Cambridge has preserved its old high-tech sectors, such as pharmaceuticals and telecoms, but has grown the dramatically new sectors of computing, research and development, design and so on. If instead of considering employment, we consider the number of high-tech businesses, computing services dominate. They are the main component of high-tech businesses in Cambridge, with about 1,800 high-tech businesses whereas the new field of bio-sciences area comprises just 230 businesses so far. But already there are more jobs in bio-sciences than there are in computing. The dramatic growth of computing has been overtaken equally dramatically in the last 5 years by biological sciences.

Cambridge businesses are typically very small. The vast majority of the high-tech businesses within the Cambridge area have only 1 to 4 employees. Only 30 businesses have more than 200 employees. Interestingly, the largest companies are often the very new ones. These are the bio-sciences companies that tend to operate on a larger scale than do computer businesses.

4. Benefits to the UK Economy as a Whole

The UK economy has, of course, benefited from the development of technology and skills in Greater Cambridge, and from the attraction inward investment from the European Union and from the United States. There has also been an important demonstration effect, with the Cambridge phenomenon being imitated around the country as other universities build university science parks and other regions develop policies based on the experience of Greater Cambridge.

Those policies start from the recognition that the success of Cambridge derives from a relationship between basic science in the university and commercial technological developments. Four major areas are in which the basic science – commercial development link have been notably successful. They are:

1. components, which include polymers, especially light emitting polymers, print technology and so on;
2. computing, major software innovations that have characterized Cambridge's success;
3. environmental science;
4. the new growth area of the bio sciences.

In the University the major developments in basic science are now taking place in material sciences, especially polymers, genetics and bio sciences, and nanotechnology, as well as the sustained innovation in computing. An interesting development is the interrelationship between all of these. For example, the process of miniaturisation in electronics using current technologies ('photographing' circuits onto silicon chips) is limited by the wavelength of light or of X-rays. However, using the new techniques of nanotechnology, chips may be 'grown' from their molecular basis rather than trying to photograph them down. So nanotechnologies and bio-sciences are interacting with the demands of computing.

5. New Technologies and the Constraints on Future Growth

When it comes to the commercial exploitation of these new scientific developments the scale on which these new industries must operate, as noted above, is much greater than the early computer industries. The emerging technologies are not just 'more of the same'. There are emerging business problems associated with these changes: the business demands for developing downstream production, actually not just doing the scientific research but moving on to production, and a shifting university/industry relationship with new technologies demanding closer relationships between the universities and companies than has been the case up to now. There is undoubtedly a fear that there may be a failure to capitalise on the new science base, with discoveries being made in the UK but developed in the US. For, whilst Cambridge has been an extraordinary success as an example of the relationship between a university and business research, in a very important sense it has been a commercial failure. Cambridge has not grown a single world-class company. Not one. There is no Polaroid, there is no Raytheon, there is no Microsoft growing out of Cambridge. There has not been the transition from the development of small-scale commercial research into large-scale commercial exploitation. Why not? What are the implications of this past failure for the exploitation of the new sciences?

First, in harnessing technologies, there has been insufficient commercial orientation in Cambridge. Business developments have been seen very much as a spin-off of the university. The people who work in research firms around Cambridge lead a life very similar to that of academics, with the same personal goals. There is still a significant perception of barriers between the university and real commercial exploitation. If firms are asked what the barriers to growth might be within Cambridge, the key elements are ranked as follows: first, marketing, actually selling their product, then the availability of skilled labour, the availability and cost of finance for expansion and, to some degree, increasing competition. If, however, banks and the financial sector are asked what the problems are the picture is rather different. The major problem is deemed to be lack of management skill, then, in order, the availability and cost of equity finance, marketing, and other financial problems. This ordering of problems is recognition that there has been a failure to move from small-medium scale to large scale and to mobilize the sort of finance which would enable that to be done, and that failure is itself traced to a lack of management skills.

Second, there are serious infrastructure problems that are limiting growth within Greater Cambridge. There is a great shortage of housing, for example. Accommodation has become very expensive and consequently it is very difficult to attract bright young people to live in the area, indeed even to come to the university. The region also has severe transportation problems. Both housing and transport difficulties seem to stem in part from political problems in organising the planning and development of the region.

So these are the major constraints on the future development of Cambridge: finance, management, and environmental-infrastructure problems in the region. In assessing the significance of these constraints it may be helpful to consider the experience of other major concentrations of high-technology industries.

6. Competitors

The main regions that Cambridge competes with are Silicon Valley where there are 780,000 high-tech jobs, North Carolina with 150,000, Taiwan with 150,000. In Europe, Cambridge, with 42,000 high-tech jobs, is followed by Munich, Ile de France, Sophia Antipolis near Nice, Stockholm and so on. These competing centres display a diverse range of driving forces. In some of them, for example, military and defence expenditure has been hugely important. This is especially important in the United States. The US Dept. of Defence invests very heavily in the development of new technologies even those in which do not have immediate, obvious military significance. And there is no doubt that Silicon Valley has depended enormously on US military expenditures. Other regions benefit from public sector research and procurement. This has been particularly important in Germany and France.

With respect to technology transfer in the major areas, the US has a very active technology transfer policy both in the universities, as indeed does Singapore and as does the emerging area around Dresden in eastern Germany. In all these areas technology transfer is very much associated with government procurement. This is not so important in the UK and it is a weakness in the Cambridge model. Cambridge does not have the backing of long-term government high-tech expenditure that is found in the United States, Germany and Sweden.

As far as finance is concerned, there is no doubt that venture capital in the United States has been much more effective than it has been in Britain. Venture capital firms in the United States tend to stick with a firm and help it commercialise its products much more intensively than do venture capital firms in the UK. UK venture firms tend to see there responsibility as securing the sale of the enterprise on the stock market, rather than the internal long-term development of the firm that is more characteristic of US venture capital. In Germany there is a greater public orientation in finance. Soft loans for bio science companies have played a very important part in the development of bio sciences, particularly when linked with strategies to attract young scientists.

As far as networking is concerned, again the US has had much more success in developing networking between companies and universities. This has also been an important characteristic of the success of Sophia Antipolis which was set up as a new university and new science area in which networking has been the characteristic of the region from the very start, whilst in the UK there is still a cultural barrier.

Finally, Cambridge clearly suffers from the lack of single political authority to tackle its environmental and infrastructure problems. Greater Cambridge has to contend with a number of political authorities – the City of Cambridge, South Cambridgeshire County Council, and the East Anglian Development Authority. In contrast, the high-technology development around Munich has been aided by the commitment of the government of Bavaria to ensure that the necessary infrastructure is developed.

So despite the success of Cambridge up until now, it now faces new constraints. Its problems include maintaining the quality of the science base, continuing to attract first-class scientists to the University of Cambridge and not lose first-class scientists to the United States. There is a need to overcome technology transfer problems especially in these new bio sciences and nanotechnology, where the scale is going to be necessarily much greater than was the case with earlier developments. Technology transfer cannot be 'personal', it must now be institutional. The critical mass of companies able to tackle the new technologies has not yet been established in Cambridge. In addition there are severe environmental problems in housing and transport.

7. Three Possible Futures

Given these constraints, Cambridge faces three possible futures:

1. The first may be labelled 'creative catalyst'. Cambridge could stay a small scale, very high-tech region benefiting from the interrelationship between small quasi-academic firms and university laboratories.

2. Secondly, the companies that are already operating in Greater Cambridge could grow to larger scale. There could be a development of some larger companies, some development of specialist services as companies grow and the development of skill and innovation base. Cambridge would become a mature sub-region of the global economy.

3. Or thirdly, the Cambridge region could become a global player with integration into the global economy. It would become a key location for global research. The location of Microsoft European laboratories in Cambridge to take advantage of encryption technology developed in Cambridge university computer labs is this sort of development. A growing number of multinational corporations might locate in Cambridge with greater scale and diversity and a greater geographic reach.

Those are three futures which do face Cambridge today. How the area moves, from the very small scale success combined with the large scale failure, into a larger scale success, with a range of small, medium and global firms working in Cambridge is the challenge for the future. It is a financial challenge. It is a managerial challenge. It is a government challenge. It is a technology transfer challenge. All these dimensions, both supply side and demand side, will determine which of those three futures Cambridge actually enjoys.

Knowledge Capital and Economic Growth: Sweden as an Emblematic Example[1]

Pontus Braunerhjelm

Linköping University and
The Center for Business and Policy Studies
Sköldungagatan 2, Box 5629, 11486, Stockholm, Sweden
pontus.braunerhjelm@sns.se.

1. Introduction

Sweden is often taken as an example of a knowledge driven economy: a leading R&D spender since at least a couple of decades, top rankings in scientific publications, universities with a solid international reputation – particularly in the medical and technological fields. In addition, Swedish industry endorses a disproportional large share of successful multinational corporations (MNCs) with a strong global position: AstraZeneca, Atlas Copco, Ericsson Gambro, Sandvik, Scania and Volvo, to mention a few.[2] In the latter part of the 1990s, when Sweden seemed to be on the brink of entering the so called 'new economy', these established and well-known MNCs were complemented by a seemingly vibrant technology-based entrepreneurship, foremost in the information- and communication technologies (ICT). Hence, there are a plenty of indications pointing at Sweden being an advanced and highly knowledge intensive economy.

According to contemporary growth theory, such comparatively strong knowledge endowment should show up in strong growth performance (Romer 1986,

---

[1] I am grateful to Göran Marklund, Vinnova, who generously provided me with data used in the report "The Swedish National Innovation System 1970-2003" (2004), from which the current study has benefited.
[2] The Swedish firm Astra merged with British Zeneca in 1998 to become AstraZeneca. The Swedish part of Volvo primarily produces heavy trucks and buses, while the car division has been acquired by Ford.

1990). In fact, based on knowledge endowments Sweden's growth rate could be expected to outpace most other countries. Still, emblematic features of a comparatively strong knowledge base do not automatically translate into positive real economy effects. A striking, and intriguing, feature of the Swedish economy is the relatively poor growth performance in recent decades, and a marked slowdown as compared to the golden years 1870 to 1950.

The issue I raise in this chapter concerns the evolutionary contradiction between these two paths; on the one hand an impressive augmentation of the knowledge stock but on the other a growth pattern that has remained below the OECD-average for a long time. How do we explain 'growth-less' knowledge augmentation in an economy? To resolve this puzzle we have to examine the extent to which economic policies are designed to foster accumulation and upgrading of knowledge, as compared to creating incentives to exploit and convert knowledge into commercial products and services. Sweden has been successful in knowledge creation; however, less attention has been directed towards the mechanisms that promote knowledge exploitation. Doubtlessly Swedish economic policies have managed to provide a more stable macroeconomic setting; rather the weaknesses seem to pertain to microeconomic policy failures in providing a business environment predominantly geared towards knowledge intensive production.

The remaining of the chapter is organized in the following way. The first section contains a brief overview of growth theory. The next section discusses measurement problems as regards knowledge variables, followed by an international comparison of the Swedish knowledge base and growth performance. The subsequent section brings forward conceivable reasons for the Swedish growth performance and stresses the policy implications. The final section summarizes and concludes.

2. Growth: From Neoclassical to Endogenous Growth Models

To achieve sustainable growth, policies have to embrace different but complementary parts of an economy. In particular, growth cannot be disentangled from the legal and institutional context of an economy (North and Thomas 1973, Rosenberg and Birdzell, 1986). The remarkable growth in Sweden between 1870 and 1950 was preceded by a number of important institutional changes; compulsory schooling was initiated in 1842, local monopolies (guilds) were abolished in 1846, whereas a new law for firms with limited liabilities was passed in 1847, followed 1862 by freedom of trade. Hence, the Swedish case illustrates the significance of the institutional set-up.

A major leap forward in understanding growth stems from the work by Solow (1956) and Swan (1956). In the neo-classical model steady state growth was attained as capital accumulated at a rate determined by the increase in the labour force and consumers' rate of time preferences (i.e. the interest rate).[3] The problem was that this did not conform to the observed increases of long-run growth during the last centuries. Growth accounting exercises revealed that something else was also taking place. As shown by Solow (1957), after accounting for the contributions provided by additional labor and capital, there remained a sizeable part of growth to be explained. Solow attributed that unexplained effect to technical progress and knowledge-enhancing processes in general, and the effect became known as Solow's 'technical residual'. However, the mechanisms that resulted in technical progress and knowledge accumulation were still unspecified. Therefore Romer's (1986) proposed method to incorporate knowledge into a model of economic growth revitalized – and initiated a new wave of – growth research.

The knowledge based (or endogenous) growth theory took off in the later part of the 1980s. Romer (1986, 1990) and Lucas (1988) are the standard references. Basically Romer extended the neo-classical growth theory by inserting Arrow's (1962) knowledge externalities into the production function. More precisely, firms undertake inter-temporally profit maximizing investments in knowledge in order to differentiate their products from those of their competitors. Only part of the knowledge investment can however be appropriated by the firms, implying that there is a 'leakage' – or spillover - to a common pool of societal knowledge. This common knowledge stock is then assumed to positively influence the future productivity of all firms within a nation or a region. Hence, even though labour and capital remain constant, productivity and growth may continue to increase. The assumption of partial excludability and non-rivalry thus suggested an important role for technology in augmenting growth, thereby explaining Solow's 'technical residual'. Since knowledge-production was explicitly modelled, and privately financed, there was also scope for growth-enhancing economic policies to correct externalities due to underinvestment in knowledge R&D.[4]

2.1. Why Growth May Fail to Substantiate? The Missing Link

In the first wave of endogenous growth models, emphasis was on the influence of knowledge spillovers on growth without specifying *how* knowledge spills over. Yet, the critical issue in modelling knowledge-based growth rests on the spillover of knowledge. This was to some extent remedied in the second generation of endogenous growth models.[5] These so called neo-Schumpeterian models design entry of new firms as the outcome of an R&D race. Only a fraction of R&D-investments turns into successful innovations, leading to temporary monopoly power for the winner of the race. While this implies a step forward, the essence of

---

[3] See Rostow (1990) and Barro and Sala-i-Martin (1995) for a survey. See also Kaldor (1961) and Denison (1967).

[4] See Acs et al (2004).

[5] See Schmitz 1989, Segerstrom, Anant and Dinopoulos 1990, Aghion and Howitt 1992 and 1998, and Grossman & Helpman (1991).

the Schumpeterian entrepreneur is missed. The innovation and entry process stretches far beyond R&D races that predominantly involve large incumbents and concern quality improvements of existing goods (compare pharmaceuticals).

The key issue – often disregarded – is that even though new knowledge leads to opportunities that can be exploited commercially, it has to be converted into commercial applications. Such opportunities rarely present themselves in neat packages; rather they have to be discovered and applied commercially (Shane and Eckhardt, 2003). In particular, the uncertainty, asymmetries and high transaction costs inherent in knowledge generate a divergence in the assessment and evaluation of the expected value of new ideas (Knight 1921, von Hayek 1945, Arrow 1962). It means that ability to commercialize knowledge – to become entrepreneurs – also vary across individuals (Acs et al, 2004). As Schumpeter (1937) puts it, to understand growth we have to reintroduce "...the source of energy within the economic system which would itself disrupt any equilibrium"; that is, the entrepreneur.[6]

Hence, knowledge by itself is only a necessary condition for the exercise of successful enterprise in a growth model. The emerging empirical literature suggests that entrepreneurial start-ups are important links between knowledge creation and the commercialization of such knowledge, particularly at the early stage when knowledge is still fluid.

By serving as a conduit for the spillover of knowledge that might not otherwise be commercialized, entrepreneurship is *one* mechanism that links knowledge to commercialization and economic growth. A mobile working force may be another mechanism. From that perspective there are undoubtedly many mechanisms that may also impede the commercialization of knowledge – and growth – which opens up a new field of economic policies as compared to the traditional growth instruments of taxes and subsidies.

3. Knowledge Capital and Growth: The Emblematic Case of Sweden

3.1. How to Define Knowledge

Knowledge, and knowledge capital, is a multi-dimensional concept that stretches from basic education to individuals' capacity to upgrade their competence, outlays on R&D, managerial and organisational know-how.[7] The knowledge space is in it-

---

[6] This is essentially the entrepreneur of early Schumpeter (1911). See also Schumpeter 1939 where economic development is explained as the outcome of three parallel economic cycles; the long-run Kondratieff cycle, the medium-run Juglar cycle and the short- to medium-run Kitchin cycle.

[7] As Eliasson (1991) points out, a firm's ability to coordinate and select information is its key asset and decisive in choosing the "appropriate" knowledge. Similarly, the firm's

self unbounded, implying that decisions are made under 'bounded rationality' (Simon 1959). Hence, partiality and subjectivity always influence decisions.

Another typical characteristic of knowledge is its partial non-excludability, implying that only part can be appropriated while part of knowledge diffuse to an indefinite number of users. Low costs in transmitting codified knowledge, together with considerable fixed costs in acquiring and compiling knowledge, points to the difficulties in knowledge producing activities. To solve the opposing interest of firms that wants to recoup their costs on R&D, and the societal objective to enable widespread use of innovations at lowest possible prices, temporary monopolies are granted to innovators through patents.[8]

Even though part of knowledge can be observed, codified and patented, a considerable part of knowledge remains 'tacit' and non-codifiable (Polyani, 1967). Hence, it is embodied in individuals and organizations. Individual competence may have little or no value in isolation, but combined with other competencies in an organization it may constitute an important part of the organization's knowledge capital. [9]

Obviously the specific features associated with knowledge imply difficulties in measuring countries knowledge capital. Such measures will always be subject to criticism. No matter what scale that is applied, measurement difficulties will to a various extent distort the values related to knowledge. Some frequently implemented knowledge variables are likely to miss essential parts, while others tend to exaggerate the knowledge content. Here I will focus on the most frequently applied measurements of knowledge, such as the stock or flow values of R&D and human capital. But also other variables will be used to approximate a country's knowledge stock.

3.2. Sweden's Knowledge Base

The most commonly implemented measure of knowledge is probably a country's outlays on R&D in relation to GDP. By that standard, Sweden has been ranked among the top R&D-investors for several decades. In fact, in the last 20 years Sweden has – with a few exceptions - been the most R&D-intensive country within the developed world. As shown in Figure 1 the major part of R&D-expenditure can be attributed to the business sector, a fact that cuts through all

---

success is dependent on its ability to filter up the right talents to its management (Eliasson 1990)

[8] The patent institution is presently under a vivid debate. It is claimed that the protection granted by patents have become too strong and the legal procedures associated with obtaining or defending a patent too costly.

[9] For instance, for Swedish firms in the engineering sector knowledge capital has been shown to positively influence profits. An increase in a firm's knowledge capital by ten per cent on average increases a firm's profitability with two percent. In addition, the firm's international competitiveness – measured as export share – increases in knowledge capital (Braunerhjelm 1996, 1999).

countries (except New Zealand and Italy). It is also in the business sector where the increase in R&D-intensity has been most pronounced.

In the case of Sweden, this is clearly illustrated in Figure 2 where R&D-outlays are broken down on different subcategories over the period 1981 to 2001. In relative terms, university based R&D increased in the 1980s with a peak in 1989. Thereafter R&D-resources available to the Swedish university sector have not kept up with GDP-growth.

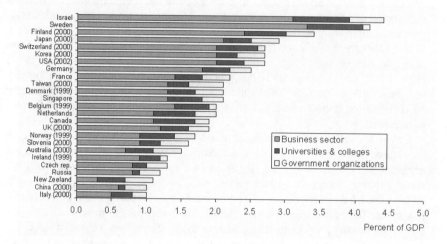

Fig 1. R&D Expenditure in Relation to GDP, 2001
Source: OECD, MSTI

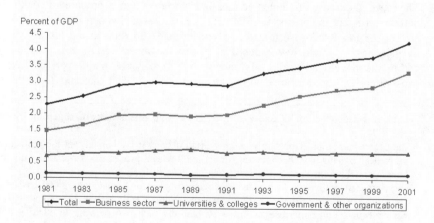

Fig 2. Swedish R&D Expenditures in Different Sectors in Relation to GDP, 1981-2001
Source: OECD, MSTI

Sweden also fares well when we look at scientific publications, having more publications per capita then any other country, with the exception of Switzerland (Figure 3). Also here the high ranking has been stable for the last decades. When it comes to engineering and medical sciences, the Swedish position is even stronger (National Science Indicators, 2003).

A somewhat different picture emerges when we look at citations. As shown in Table 1, Sweden has not been able to maintain its high ranking in the early 1980s, contradicting the evolution in for instance Switzerland, USA, Denmark and Netherlands. This suggests that the impact of Swedish research has diminished, particularly in the 1990s.

A comparatively weak part (in terms of allotted resources) of the Swedish R&D-system, when compared with other countries, seems to be institute based R&D.[10] The institute system dates back to the 1940s and is heavily geared towards traditional industries. R&D undertaken by research institutes (public and private), merely accounts for about three percent of overall R&D, i.e. considerably less then in other countries and the share of public funding is at a much lower level.[11]

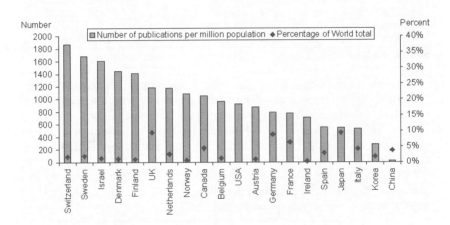

Fig 3. Scientific Publications in Internationally Acknowledged Journals
Source: National Science Indicators (NSI) Database, 2002.

---

[10] Also mission-oriented R&D (outside the business sector) seems to be much lower in Sweden. According to survey data, about 50 percent of innovations originate from sources within the firm themselves in Sweden, compared with a share around 35-45 percent in most other countries. However, at the same time Swedish firms claim that universities are their most crucial external source for innovation. Sweden also spends comparatively large sums on R&D in higher education as compared to other countries (Marklund et al, 2004).

[11] Technopolis & INNO (2004). The future forms of institute based R&D in Sweden is presently subject to a governmental investigation.

Table 1. International Citations of Scientific Publications in Internationally Acknowledged Journals, 1981-2001

1981-1985		1986-1990		1991-1995		1996-2000		2001	
Switzerland	1.23	Switzerland	1.27	Switzerland	1.29	Switzerland	1.34	Switzerland	1.43
Sweden	**1.23**	USA	1.20	USA	1.17	USA	1.17	USA	1.18
USA	1.18	**Sweden**	**1.13**	**Sweden**	**1.10**	Netherlands	1.11	Denmark	1.15
Denmark	1.10	Denmark	1.05	Denmark	1.09	Denmark	1.09	Netherlands	1.09
Netherlands	1.06	Netherlands	1.03	Netherlands	1.07	**Sweden**	**1.04**	UK	1.08
UK	1.00	UK	0.98	UK	0.99	UK	1.00	Israel	1.03
Canada	0.90	Canada	0.87	Finland	0.98	Finland	0.99	Germany	1.01
Israel	0.84	Belgium	0.87	Belgium	0.95	Belgium	0.98	**Sweden**	**0.97**
Finland	0.83	Finland	0.84	Canada	0.91	Germany	0.96	Canada	0.96
Norway	0.83	Norway	0.83	France	0.87	Canada	0.95	Belgium	0.95
Belgium	0.82	France	0.81	Germany	0.87	Austria	0.91	Finland	0.94
France	0.77	Israel	0.78	Austria	0.86	Italy	0.90	France	0.91
Japan	0.74	Germany	0.77	Israel	0.85	France	0.90	Austria	0.91
Germany	0.71	Japan	0.75	Norway	0.84	Israel	0.87	Italy	0.89
Italy	0.70	Italy	0.74	Italy	0.83	Norway	0.85	Norway	0.86
Austria	0.58	Austria	0.73	Japan	0.74	Ireland	0.79	Japan	0.76
Ireland	0.54	Ireland	0.62	Ireland	0.71	Japan	0.76	Spain	0.76
South Korea	0.49	Spain	0.52	Spain	0.66	Spain	0.76	Ireland	0.76
Spain	0.43	S Korea	0.44	S Korea	0.48	S Korea	0.50	S Korea	0.48
China	0.32	China	0.34	China	0.38	China	0.42	China	0.43

Source: Marklund et al., 2004

In terms of human capital, Sweden holds a middle position among the OECD-countries when we look at the share of the population with a tertiary education (Figure 4). Over time a clear improvement can be discerned. However, it was only with the generation born in 1970-1980 that the share of population with a three year university education surpassed the share of those born in the 1940s and the 1950s (SCB 2003). In 2003 a record share of 23 percent of the population born in 1970s had a tertiary education of at least three years. This is however partly explained by the fact that education previously outside the university system has been redefined to qualify as university degrees.

Looking at research graduates in the age between 25 and 34, Sweden has the highest share among the OECD-countries (Marklund et al, 2004). This encouraging development is partly explained by institutional change that put pressure on the universities to increase the speed of examination, partly by the weak Swedish labour market in the aftermath of the 1991-1993 recessions which made continued university studies an attractive option. As regards the distribution of human capital over sectors, about 50 percent of PhDs and licentiates are employed in the public sector (not including universities) which represents about 30 percent of the economy. If universities are included, the public sector employment share grows to approximately 85-90 percent. Hence, the major brunt of research graduates end up in the public sector. Still, an increase in employment of research graduates in the business sector can be observed in the late 1990s, predominantly within knowledge intensive business services and large manufacturing firms.[12]

As regards the knowledge intensity of the private sector of the Swedish economy, the manufacturing industry is characterized by a diversified structure. A high specialization in raw material intensive industries – such as forestry, paper and pulp, and extraction of ore – is paralleled with an advanced manufacturing sector, spearheaded by ICT and pharmaceutical industries. As shown in Figure 5, Sweden has a relatively large percentage share of employees in high- and medium-technology manufacturing industries, albeit dominated by the medium-technology sectors. Together with Germany and Japan, Sweden stands out as being most specialized in those sectors. Sweden's specialization in knowledge intensive service industries is less apparent, rather it seems to belong to the lower end. Here the dominant position of the U.S. is obvious. In all countries the share of the labour force occupied in the knowledge intensive service sector exceeds the share employed in knowledge intensive manufacturing industries.

A recently – and increasingly – used yardstick for knowledge capital refer to investments in ICT where only the U.S. and UK are ranked ahead of Sweden (Figure 6). Since a few years back OECD also presents data on accumulated investments in 'soft assets'; R&D, marketing, software and education. Normally these calculations are based on the simple adding up over the years of current costs on the respective item. Extended to comprise also these knowledge assets, Sweden is shown to be ranked as the largest investor among the OECD-countries (OECD 1999).

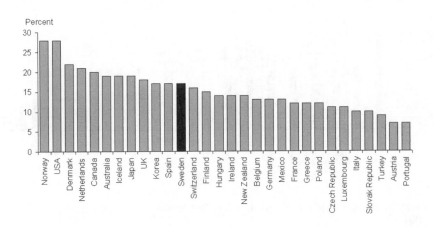

Fig 4. Percentage of Active Population, 25-64 Years Old, with a Tertiary Education, 2002
Source: OECD, Education at a Glance, 2003

---

[12] See Marklund et al (2004).

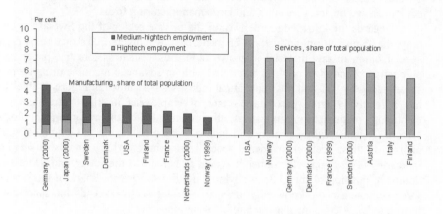

Fig. 5 .Relative Weight of High and Medium High-Technology Employment, Manufacturing and Services, 2001
Source: OECD, STAN, MSTI and MEI, 2003.

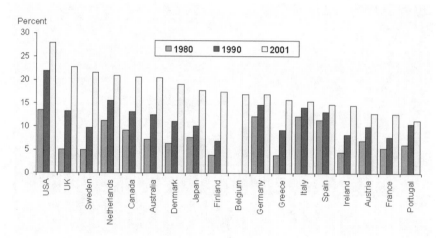

Fig 6. Investment in ICT in Relation to Non-Residential Fixed Capital Formation, 1980-2001
Source: OECD, Science Technology and Industry Score board, 2003.

These above described measures of knowledge intensity in the commercial sector emanate from the input side of the economy; R&D, educated labour and knowledge capital. An alternative approach is to embark from the output side of the commercial sector. The most frequently used measure is patent data.[13] In relation to the population, Sweden has among the highest number of patent within the OECD. Since the beginnings of the 1990s, only Germany is ahead of Sweden (Table 2).

On an aggregate level knowledge content is also reflected in the value-added produced in an economy. In Figure 7 the growth of value-added in different sectors and countries is revealed. Sweden is doing quite well in the manufacturing sector, with an average annual growth in value-added around five percent in the 1990s, while the business service sector growth is much weaker (about three percent). Sweden's international ranking is also lower in the service sector, which nevertheless does much better than the public sector where the weakest performance can be observed (even though a caveat must be thrown in as regards the reliability of these numbers). The emerging picture suggests that it is the service sectors – public but also private – that primarily have reduced the overall Swedish productivity figures.

Table 2. Number of Patents per 100,000 Inhabitants, 1981, 1991 and 2001

1981		1991		2001	
Germany	2.39	Germany	8.23	Germany	10.08
France	0.79	**Sweden**	**6.12**	**Sweden**	**8.20**
Netherlands	0.75	Netherlands	5.50	Finland	6.73
Austria	0.75	France	4.62	Netherlands	5.48
Belgium	0.50	Austria	4.59	Austria	5.39
UK	0.40	Japan	3.93	Japan	5.18
Sweden	**0.38**	UK	2.89	France	4.82
USA	0.26	Belgium	2.77	Denmark	4.70
Denmark	0.22	Finland	2.42	Belgium	4.30
Australia	0.07	USA	2.32	USA	2.88
Norway	0.07	Denmark	2.17	UK	2.85
Japan	0.07	Italy	1.66	Italy	2.27
Italy	0.04	Norway	1.12	Norway	2.02
Canada	0.04	Ireland	0.77	Ireland	1.17
Finland	0.04	Canada	0.77	Canada	1.17
Ireland	0.03	Australia	0.76	Australia	0.82
Spain	0.01	New Zealand	0.39	New Zealand	0.67
New Zealand		Spain	0.16	Spain	0.50
Portugal		Portugal	0.03	Portugal	0.07

Source: OECD, 2003

---

[13] Citations could also be viewed as an output measure, see Table 1.

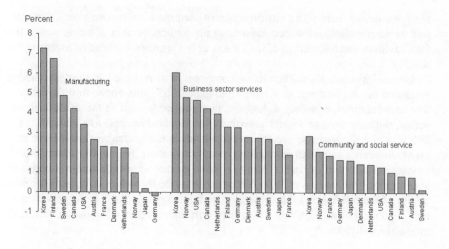

Fig 7. Real Percentage Growth in Value Added, 1991-2001
Source: ESF Nine-Country Project and VINNOVA, 2003

4. Growth Performance – From Tiger to Tortoise?

As evident from the preceding section, Sweden's knowledge base has increased over time and looks highly competitive in an international comparison. The question is whether it also manifests itself in higher growth?

The Swedish industrialization process took off in the second half of the 19th century, which was relatively late. But from then on, Sweden was doubtlessly one of the fastest growing countries in the world up to 1950, perhaps the fastest (Maddison 1982). A slight slowdown could be observed in the 1950s and 1960s as Sweden's productivity growth approached the OECD average (or, rather the war-torn countries after 1945 started to catch-up with Sweden). The main explanations of the almost century long boom in Swedish growth is attributed to international openness, favourable terms of trade, vibrant entrepreneurial achievements in the late 19th century, a modern infrastructure, human capital investments and transparent and stable 'rules of the game' (Lindbeck 1975, 1997, Glete 1994, Myhrman 1994). In addition, a critical event in that process seems to have been the institutional changes – mentioned above - that served to increase human capital (compulsory schooling 1842) but also spurred competition and industrial dynamics (abolishing of guilds and freedom to trade and establish firms, 1846 and 1862, respectively).

This impressive period of sustainable high growth came to an end in the 1970s, and was replaced by a performance below the OECD-average.[14] As pointed out by Lindbeck (1997), the year 1970 is a reasonable starting point since at that time Sweden began to pursue a much more ambitious and expansionary welfare state policy. Basically, a systematic deviation in growth performance as compared to other countries can be discerned from mid 1970s (Figure 8). Growth performance was particularly weak in 1976-1978 and in 1991-1993. In the latter period Sweden experienced its deepest recession since the 1930s when GDP fell for three consecutive years. Something of a catch-up effect occurred in the latter part of 1990s as the economy was picking up the slack in production capacity that resulted from the crisis of 1991-1993. In addition some important structural reforms in previously highly regulated areas also helped to spur growth (Braunerhjelm et al, 2002). However, the higher growth rate in that period turned out to be temporary and since 1999/2000 Sweden is – by and large - on par with the OECD-average growth rate.

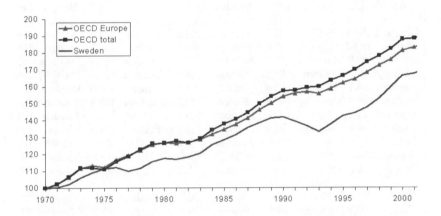

Fig 8. GDP Per Capita 1970-2002, 1995 Year's Prices and PPPs (Index 1970 = 100)
Source: OECD, National Accounts

Also if we look at the development of real GDP per capita, Sweden's growth lag in the period 1970-2002 becomes apparent. In Table 3 it is shown how Sweden's position has gradually decreased from rank four in 1970. In the aftermath of the ICT-boom, where Sweden happened to have a relatively strong specialization, there was a slight recovery in the Swedish position; from rank 13 in 1995 to rank 11 in 2000. The improvement was however not lasting for long, and a few years

---

[14] There has been an intensive debate whether growth in Sweden actually did deviate from other countries. Among economists few would challenge the fact that Sweden did indeed embark on a lower growth trajectory from mid 1970s up to 1995 (see Lindbeck 1997).

later the Swedish slide continued downward to rank 15. If we let out Mexico and Turkey, Sweden would fall below the OECD average by 9 percent in 2002. Over the entire period 1970 to 2002, the average annual GDP-increase per capita among the OECD-countries where two percent, while the corresponding figure was only 1.7 for Sweden. That amounts to 20 percentage points lower GDP in Sweden per capita in that time interval as compared to the OECD average.

Table 3. GDP per Capita, Current Prices and PPP's, OECD = 100

1970		1980		1990		2000		2002	
Switzerl	168.3	Switzerl	147.7	LUX	146.8	LUX	193.9	LUX	187.5
USA	136.2	USA	133.5	Switzerl	139.5	Norway	143.4	USA	137.8
Denmark	123.4	Iceland	123.4	USA	134.7	USA	138.5	Norway	135.4
LUX	123.3	Canada	118.8	Iceland	117.4	Switzerl	116.7	Ireland	124.5
Sweden	**120.4**	LUX	117.1	Canada	111.8	Canada	113.6	Canada	115.6
Canada	115.0	Denmark	113.5	Japan	109.6	Denmark	112.8	Switzerl	114.2
Australia	114.6	**Sweden**	**111.8**	Austria	109.5	Ireland	112.3	Denmark	111.9
NDL	112.3	Austria	109.3	**Sweden**	**109.3**	Iceland	111.9	Nether-lands	110.7
N Zealand	108.1	NDL	108.9	Denmark	107.2	Austria	111.6	Austria	110.1
France	102.7	Belgium	107.6	Finland	105.3	NDL	108.0	Iceland	108.3
Belgium	99.9	Australia	106.8	Belgium	105.0	**Sweden**	**106.4**	Australia	107.1
Germany	99.8	France	105.8	Norway	104.8	Australia	105.0	UK	106.7
Austria	98.1	Norway	103.8	NDL	104.3	Japan	104.0	Belgium	105.7
UK	97.7	Germany	102.8	France	103.7	Belgium	103.8	France	103.8
Iceland	94.4	Italy	100.8	Germany	103.2	Finland	101.5	**Sweden**	**103.8**
Italy	93.8	Finland	100.4	Italy	101.7	France	101.3	Japan	102.8
Finland	91.9	Japan	95.8	Australia	97.6	Germany	99.5	Finland	101.0
Japan	88.2	UK	92.6	UK	95.2	UK	99.5	Germany	98.9
Norway	86.6	N Zea-land	91.1	N Zealand	81.9	Italy	98.8	Italy	97.5
Spain	71.6	Greece	78.7	Spain	76.2	N Zealand	81.7	Spain	85.5
Greece	69.7	Spain	72.9	Ireland	75.5	Spain	81.3	N Zealand	83.1
Ireland	61.8	Ireland	67.3	Greece	64.8	Portugal	68.6	Greece	70.3
Portugal	51.3	Portugal	57.5	Portugal	63.3	Greece	64.4	Portugal	70.2
Mexico	42.7	Mexico	46.7	Mexico	36.8	Mexico	36.5	Mexico	35.2
Turkey	26.4	Turkey	24.9	Turkey	26.5	Turkey	26.9	Turkey	24.4

Source: OECD, 2003

The two pronounced down-turns in the mid 1970s and the beginning of the 1990s have particularly influenced the performance. Still, that does not explain the Swedish drop in relation to other OECD-countries since also these suffered similar macro-economic shocks, albeit without the same long-run effects on growth (Lindbeck 1997). Rather the explanations seem to originate in the radical shifts in economic policies that emerged in the early 1970s. The effect of an expanding welfare state – and the ensuing increase in taxes - on growth is debated and a non-linear relationship is likely to prevail.

More recently a series of articles have advanced evidence of a detrimental effect of too expansionary expenditures, inserting tax wedges, strongly negative marginal effects and a distorted incentive structure.[15] The malfunctioning economy showed up in lower productivity and staggering competitiveness. Given that nominal wage increases could not be matched by productivity increases, the standard policy prescription has been to devaluate the Swedish currency. Between 1976 and 1982 the krona was devaluated five times and in 1992 the krona was floated against other currencies. In relation to its main trading partners the Swedish krona depreciated with about 28 percent.

It is noteworthy that during the period of recurrent depreciations, the Swedish market share to other OECD-countries has also decreased trend-wise. Since most nations have increased their exports in knowledge intensive products, the loss in Swedish market shares suggests a specialization in medium- or low-technology products, spurred by the continuous devaluations (OECD 2003). Paired with policy induced rigidities, the result was to hinder a re-allocation of resources which prevented a shift in specialization towards more knowledge intensive segments.

How does that fit with the image of Sweden as a leading ICT-country? A conceivable explanation is that in the latter part of the 1990s, production of telecommunication products was completely dominated by one firm; Ericsson. The share of telecommunication products in total exports was around 18 percent, however, Ericsson alone accounted for about 16 percent. As the market collapsed in late 1990s and early 2000, the export share of telecommunication products fell back to somewhere around six to eight percent. Instead paper and pulp, and medium knowledge intensive products in the engineering sectors, have expanded.

Another compelling fact is that the depreciating krona 'over-compensated' the nominal wage increases, i.e. the depreciation was larger than motivated by difference between nominal wage increase and the productivity increase. That is likely to have further cemented the traditional industrial structure by facilitating production of price sensitive production at the expense of knowledge intensive production. This is a likely explanation to the falling terms-of-trade since the 1970s, particularly evident after the substantial depreciation of the Swedish krona in the 1990s (Figure 9).

Multi-factor productivity growth is the part of growth that remains after we controlled for the contributions that can be attributed to increases in the supply of labour and capital. A bold interpretation is that multifactor productivity captures the growth effects of technological progress, i.e. advances in knowledge. From Figure 10 is evident that Sweden's performance improved in the 1990s as compared to the 1980s. In the 1980s only four countries were behind Sweden in terms of multifactor productivity, whereas the number had risen to 11 in the 1990s. Still, in an international perspective, Sweden is in a middle position when ranked according to multifactor productivity.

---

[15] Fölster and Henrekson (2001). See DuRietz (2002) for a survey of the recent literature on taxes and growth.

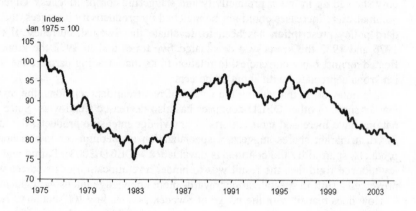

Fig 9. Swedish Terms of Trade, 1975-2004
Source: Statistics Sweden (SCB)

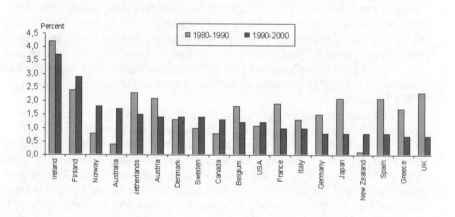

Fig 10. Multi-Factor Productivity Growth Estimates 1980-2000, Average Annual Growth Rates, Adjusted for Hours Worked.
Source: OECD, The Sources of Economic Growth in the OECD Countries.

To summarize, for almost a century Sweden enjoyed growth rates similar to a 'tiger economy'. But from 1970 and onwards that successful track record was replaced by rates of growth that lagged behind the OECD-average. A puzzling fact is that the slowdown in growth coincided with massive increases in knowledge investments, private and public. This challenges the conventional view of knowledge driven growth. In the proceeding section we will discuss some conceivable explanations to this apparent paradox, arguing that microeconomic policies prevented exploitation of the opportunities provided by knowledge investments. The relatively low growth rate in Sweden thus captures a disharmony between micro- and macroeconomic policies.

5. A 'Growth-Less' Knowledge Economy?

A number of analyses have attempted to explain the relatively poor growth performance of the Swedish economy. To some extent statistics is not properly designed to capture growth – hedonic price indexes (predominantly used in knowledge intensive sectors), difficulties in obtaining appropriate productivity measurements of an enlarged public sector, catch-up effects, etc., influence our measures of productivity and growth.[16] However, as Lindbeck (1997) argues, to claim that such artefacts should explain the performance of Sweden's economy requires Sweden to systematically deviate from other countries, which is not likely.

From a macro point of view the prerequisites for enhanced growth in the Swedish economy ameliorated considerably during the 1990s. Sweden's traditional problems of high inflation, lax financial policies, increasing governmental debt and stagflation were brought to a standstill through radical institutional changes. The deep recession in the early 1990s, which was followed by the Maastricht conditions and later on the Growth and Stability Pact, also helped to reshape the macroeconomic environment in Sweden. Indigenous institutional changes comprised the adoption of fiscal expenditure ceilings, and an independent Central Bank with a distinct objective to stabilize inflation around two percents (within the range of one to three percent).

These reforms - embracing monetary and fiscal policies - seem to have tightened up the previously lax financial policies but also served to discipline the labour market. Lately though there has been a tendency towards more expansionary fiscal policies through 'creative' labelling of new expenditures, taking up loans, etc. Yet, the emergence of a macroeconomic situation that should be more conducive to growth does not suffice. It has to be complemented by appropriate economic policies at the micro-level in order for growth to materialize.

Sweden has since long displayed a preference for governmental interventions over the market mechanism. Commencing with the traditional building blocks of growth - labour and capital augmentation - Sweden has been praised for its active

---

[16] Hedonic price indexes have been shown to exert a strong influence on Swedish growth in the latter part of the 1990s, much stronger then in, for example, Finland despite the two countries having approximately the same industrial structure (Edquist 2004).

labour market policies and low unemployment. That came however to an end in the early 1990s as Swedish unemployment levels by large exceeded those of the US and levelled the average European unemployment rates. In 1996/97 the Swedish unemployment rates peaked above eight percent, levels unprecedented since the 1930s crises. In the latter part of the 1990s unemployment had fallen to about 5-6 percent, i.e. around the US level.

The swings in open (official) unemployment rates reflect mainly two causes: First, the crises in the early 1990s implied large lay-offs, primarily in the private sector, contemporaneously as the public sector expansion stopped (Figure 11). Second, unemployment figures conceal that about 1.2 million individuals – roughly 20 percent of the population in the age 20-64 – are outsiders to the labour market. That includes unemployed, sickness leave and early retired. In autumn 2004, 125,000 individuals had been on sickness leave for more then a year out of a total of approximately 275,000 on sickness leave. This evolution has occurred despite the fact that Sweden's population is among the healthiest in the world. It has stirred an intensive political debate about its causes, but economic analysis is quite unambiguous in allotting a substantial part of the explanation to the design of the governmental transfers to the unemployed and long-term sick.

The biggest group within the 1.2 million are the 550,000 individuals that have become pensioners (early retirement), i.e. they are not to the labour market disposal.[17] Within the first six months of 2004 the number of early retired increased by 56,000. The future discounted cost of early retirement – where the overwhelming part seems to be due to labour market reasons – is presently calculated to 640 billion Swedish krona (about 75 percent of current governmental expenditure), and it increased by 140 billion between 2002 and 2003. The current cost (estimated for 2004) is around 60 billion krona. Neither of the above mentioned categories is recorded in the unemployment statistics. There is also a relationship between the group of early retired and those on sickness leave; when a decrease in sickness leave – particularly long-term – can be recorded, a corresponding increase is noted in early retirement (Figure 12).[18] Ultimately this is a failure for the Swedish active labour market policies and it also implies that this source for growth basically is exhausted.

---

[17] Early retirement was meant to take care of disabled people. However, now it is mainly used as a labour market device.

[18] Note that the figure is based on full time equivalent which explains the discrepancy from the number of early retired (550,000). A similar relationship exists between unemployed and long-term sickness leave. See Lindbeck (1995), Johansson and Palme (2002), Henrekson and Persson (2004) and Lindbeck, Persson and Palme (2004).

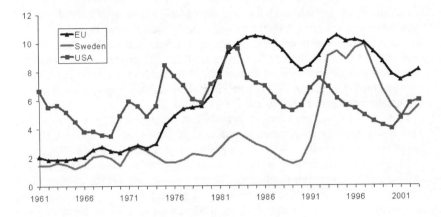

Fig 11. Standardized Unemployment Rate, 1961-2003, Percent
Source: OECD, Main Economic Indicators

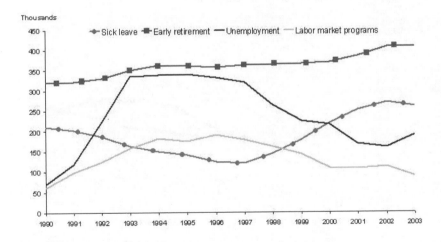

Fig 12. The Development of Full-Time Equivalents in the Ages 20-64 Years, Supported by Social Welfare Systems, 1980-2003.
Source: Statistics Sweden (SCB)

Unemployment figures are hard to compare over time and internationally. If we instead look at employment data, a compelling feature of the Swedish labour market is illustrated in Figure 13. Despite the upturn in the latter part of the 1990s, employment in the private sector has remained constant since the 1970s and even decreased somewhat since 1950. In the mid 1990s, and in the aftermath of the huge depreciation of the Swedish krona in 1992, the private sector began to recover and private employment increased, albeit the level of 1990 has as yet not been retained.[19] This also explains much of the relatively strong growth that Sweden experienced between 1996 and 2000.

Hence, all of the employment increase can be attributed to the public sector. This is mirrored by an increase in public expenditure; as a share of GDP it has risen from 41 in 1970 to 54 percent in 2003, with a peak of almost 70 percent in 1993. Individuals dependent on public sector payment increased by approximately 250 percent between 1960 and 2000. During the same period the number of wage earners in the private sector decreased by 18 percent. Hence, a shrinking share of the population has to generate income sufficient to support an expanding public sector through increased taxes.

The increasing tax pressure implies that the allocative efficiency of the economy has been eroded through the insertion of tax wedges and disincentives, fostering rent seeking, black market activities and other unproductive outcomes. All this is likely to have negatively influenced the supply of labour; Sweden fell from first place in 1981 to tenth in 2001 in terms of the proportion of total population employed among 18 OECD-countries (OECD 2003).

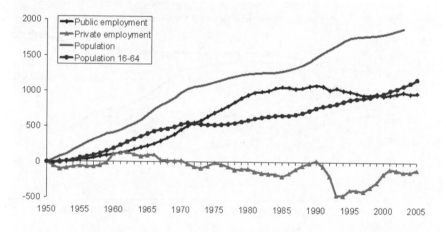

Fig 13. Swedish Population and Employment, 1950-2005 (Cumulative Change in Thousands)
Source: OECD, 2003

---

[19] Demographic characteristics also have an influence, in particular the increasing share of age pensioners.

A worrisome consequence of the labour market development described above is that the so called dependency ratio – the number of individuals dependent on their income from the public sector (through wages and governmental transfers) divided by the number of employees in the private sector - has increased. In 1960 the Swedish dependency ratio was 0.38, i.e. privately employed people outnumbered employees in the public sector and recipients of governmental transfers by almost a factor three. In the mid 1990s the dependency ratio hovered around 1.75 – 1.95, illustrating the rapid expansion of the public sector. As private sector employment picked up after the 1990s crises, the ratio started to fall and by year 2000 it was 1.60. Still, this improvement is only a temporary relief; taking the coming demographic changes into account, the dependency ratio is expected to steadily increase until 2040 (Braunerhjelm 2005). This underlines the importance of mobilizing available labour resources and expanding the private sector of the economy.

Turning to investments, levels remained at a relatively high level for a considerable time, even though the rate of return was quite low. Indeed, the risk premium on investment in real assets, by and large, disappeared between the late 1970s and the mid 1990s (Lindbeck 1997). Still, in the relatively closed Swedish economy at that time it was possible to impact capital accumulation positively through subsidies, low interest rates and foreign exchange controls. The implementation of such devices also became a mean to counteract the profit squeeze that emanated from the solidarity wage policy which had full support by the government. From the 1970s and onward aggregate investments as a share of GDP fell below the OECD average, contrasting a previous pattern of higher Swedish investments as compared to the OECD.[20] In 2003 Sweden's fixed capital gross investment was 12 percent of GDP, which is lower then any other OECD country.

The decrease in return to physical capital was paralleled by lower returns to investments in human capital – it fell from about 12 percent 1960 to 1-3 percent in the early 1980s (Lindbeck 1997). The low return was maintained until the mid 1990s and thereafter a slight increase has been noted (Svensk Handel, 2002). However, levels are still low – much lower then in most other OECD-countries – and the return to education has only marginally increased for those working in Sweden. In real terms average wages have been kept roughly constant since 1970 (Figure 14).

---

[20] This is also an explanation to the high share of ICT-investments in relation to capital investments, see figure 6.

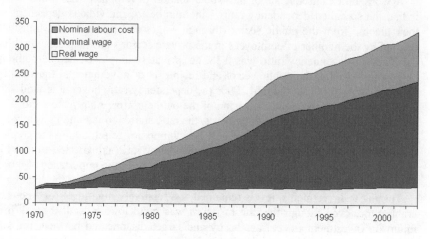

Fig. 14. Labour Cost per Year for Industrial Workers in Sweden, 1970-2003 (Thousands of SEK).
Source: OECD, Labour Market Statistics, 2003

As the prospect for either labour or capital to propel growth is rather bleak, the remaining factor influencing growth is knowledge. A crucial aspect in knowledge based growth concerns the economy's ability to diffuse knowledge across individuals, firms and institutions. One such channel is through labour mobility, i.e. as labour moves between firms and regions they carry and diffuse knowledge. Knowledge diffusion through labour mobility can be expected to be fairly low in the Swedish economy since only 5-10 percent of employees shift between firms in a year. On average an employee spend around 11 years with the same employer (Marklund 2004). The relatively low labour mobility, particularly if compared to the U.S. where an estimated 15-17 percent changes employer annually, is presumably a consequence of strict Swedish labour regulations and the compressed wage structure (particularly taking into account marginal effects of both taxes and income related subsidies).

Another way of diffusing and exploiting knowledge is through entry by new firms. But also here the Swedish performance is less impressive. The share of individuals that either has started a new firm recently or plans to do so is almost negligible in Sweden (Figure 15). Similarly, despite Sweden's larger knowledge base, high-tech spin-offs do not deviate from the other Nordic countries, with the exception of Norway (Figure 16) and there is a low share of researcher participations in start-ups of new technology based firms (Figure 17).

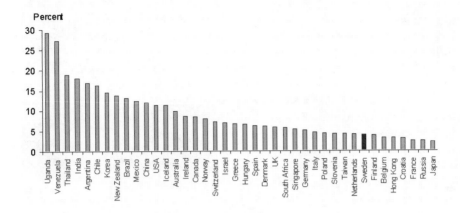

Fig. 15. Percentage of Active Population Engaged in Starting New Firms, 2003
Source: Global Entrepreneurship Monitor (GEM), 2003

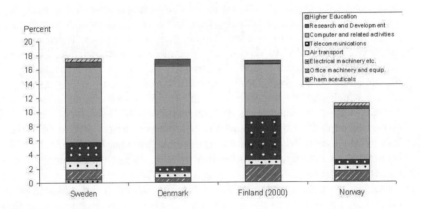

Fig. 16. High-Tech Spin-Offs in the Nordic Countries, 1999-2000 (Percent of All Spin-Offs)
Source: Nas et al, 2004

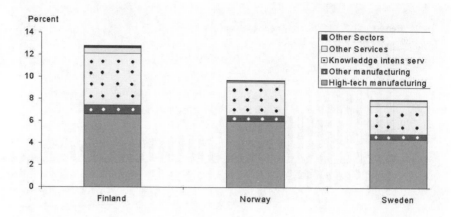

Fig. 17. Researcher Participation in New Firms, 2001
Source: Nas et al, 2004

Finally, a word on the Swedish venture capital market which no doubt saw an impressive increase during the 1990s. Venture capital, supposed to provide firms with both knowledge and capital (equity), has been claimed to be a catalyst by supporting new technology based firms in their initial phases. Thereby it is also a mechanism that helps to diffuse and commercialize knowledge. However, the Swedish venture capital industry is primarily devoted to the later stages, i.e. not the important seed capital stage (Figure 18). At the same time, business angels activities which play an important role in providing seed capital, hardly exists in Sweden.[21] High marginal taxes and internationally high wealth taxes have either driven the capital out of the country or led to investments in less productive – and less risky – assets. Private ownership in small firms has systematically been discriminated as compared to ownership in large firms by institutional investors (Braunerhjelm et al, 2002).

Altogether the reported obstacles to commercialization and diffusion of knowledge show up in a relatively low share of turnover associated with new products (Figure 19). For instance, Sweden's performance is much worse as compared to neighbouring Finland even though several similarities exist between the two countries in terms of industrial structure, but also with regard to the preference for a sizeable public sector.

---

[21] Sweden has a low share of wealthy individuals as compared to other OECD-countries (Pålsson 1998).

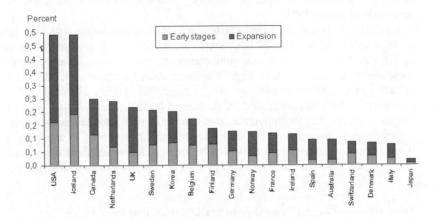

Fig. 18. Venture Capital in Relation to GDP, 1999-2001
Source: OECD, Science Technology and Industry Scoreboard, 2003

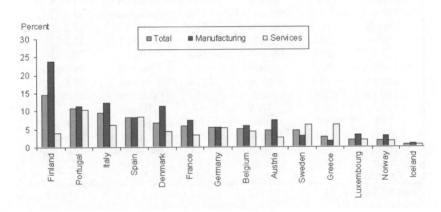

Fig. 19. Economic Turnover Generated by New Products, 2000
Source: Eurostat New Cronos Database, 2003

Hence, there seems to be a discrepancy between economic policies at the macro- and the micro-level. No doubt the macro-economic setting has improved over the last decade. That has been paired with substantial knowledge investments. However, less attention has been directed towards a micro-economic policy conducive to growth. The missing link lies in less favourable conditions for diffusion of knowledge as evident from low labour mobility, low entrepreneurship, and a highly concentrated knowledge industry – about four firms account for 70-80 percent of industrial R&D.

Incentives to engage in entrepreneurial activities, or to take the step from being a wage earner to become entrepreneurs, are basically not present (Henrekson 2003). Taxes on corporations are quite competitive whereas taxes on personal income and wealth still are very high in an international comparison (Table 4). Out of total factor costs for an average income earner (taxes and social costs), 64 percent goes to the government and 36 is retained by the income earner. Moreover, the tax consequences for individuals that contribute with knowledge and equity in a small, newly started firm can be twice as high as compared to investing in a listed company. Firms are thus allowed to become rich, albeit there are less room for owners of firms and entrepreneurs to become wealthy (DuRietz 2002).

Table 4. Personal Income Taxes Divided by GDP, 1981, 1991 and 2001

1981		1991		2001	
Denmark	23.1	Denmark	25.1	Denmark	26.3
New Zealand	20.0	Finland	17.1	**Sweden**	**16.4**
Sweden	**19.0**	**Sweden**	**16.9**	Belgium	14.5
Belgium	15.3	New Zealand	16.1	New Zealand	14.5
Finland	15.3	Canada	14.8	Finland	14.1
Australia	12.7	Belgium	13.5	Canada	13.0
Norway	11.7	Netherlands	11.8	Australia	12.3
Canada	11.3	Australia	11.5	USA	12.2
UK	10.9	Ireland	11.0	UK	11.3
USA	10.9	Norway	10.8	Italy	10.9
Netherlands	10.6	Italy	10.4	Norway	10.5
Ireland	10.2	Germany	10.1	Austria	10.4
Germany	9.9	UK	10.0	Germany	10.0
Austria	9.7	USA	9.8	Ireland	8.9
Italy	8.0	Austria	8.9	France	8.0
Japan	6.4	Japan	8.0	Spain	6.9
France	4.9	Spain	7.8	Netherlands	6.5
Spain	4.9	France	5.8	Portugal	6.0
Portugal		Portugal	5.4	Japan	5.5

Source: OECD, 2003

6. Conclusions

Swedish growth picked up in the latter part of the 1990s, however, largely driven by catch-up effects after the recession in 1991 to 1993. Hence, the relatively strong growth recorded since then is not primarily driven by knowledge. This corroborates with the development of Swedish terms of trade, export market share and GDP per capita.[22] As pointed out by Acs et al (2004), knowledge is a necessary but not sufficient condition for growth.

The policy focus has to shift from emphasis on capital deepening, labour augmenting and knowledge creation. Irrespective of the source of growth, basically the same set of policy instruments has been used (taxes and/or subsidies). The point emphasized in this paper is that a supplementary set of policies focusing on enhancing the conduits of knowledge spill-over also plays a central role in promoting economic growth, such as entrepreneurship and labour market policies. Thus, the data presented above indicates that it is unlikely that Sweden is in the wake of entering a sustainable, knowledge driven, growth path. Knowledge creation has to be matched by incentives to exploit knowledge.

The traditional Swedish policy of solidarity wages, market interventions (through taxes, subsidies and regulations) and devaluation that aimed to push the economy away from low wage activities to more sophisticated segments, achieved precisely the opposite: real wages have not increased in the last decades, there is no distinct shift towards more knowledge intensive production segments and structural adjustments have been deterred by the depreciated Swedish krona.

Policy induced thresholds mirror weak incentives and few channels through which knowledge can be diffused, is likely to impede future growth in Sweden when the effects of the catch-up after the recession in 1991 to 1993 have petered out. Moreover, Sweden's industrial policy is geared towards the creation of internationally competitive innovation systems, which possibly is a step in the right direction. However, without the appropriate incentive structure for labour, entrepreneurs and investors, the potential scope of that policy will not be realized. In general, there is too much emphasis on systems, too little on incentives.

References

Acs Z, Audretsch D, Braunerhjelm P, Carlsson B (2004) The Missing Link. The Knowledge Filter and Entrepreneurship in Endogenous Growth, *CEPR DP 4783*, Stockholm.

Aghion P, Howitt P (1992) A Model of Growth Through Creative Destruction, *Econometrica*, 60, 323-51.

Aghion P, Howitt P (1998), Endogenous Growth Theory, Cambridge, MA: MIT Press.

Arrow K (1962) The Economic Implication of Learning by Doing, *Review of Economics and Statistics*, 80, 155-173.

Barro RJ, Sala-i-Martin X. (1995) Economic Growth, McGraw Hill, New York.

Braunerhjelm P (1996) The Relation Between Firm Specific Intangibles and Exports, *Economic Letters*, 53, 213–219.

Braunerhjelm P (1999) Costs, Firm Size, and Internationalization, *Weltwirtschaftliches Archiv*, Band 135, Heft 4, pp. 657–674.

---

[22] See Jones (1995a, 1995b), Young (1995) and Greenwood and Jovanovic (1998). See Aghion and Howitt (1998) for a discussion of empirical problems.

Braunerhjelm P (2005) Kunskapskapital och ekonomisk tillväxt, *Mimeo*, Linkoping University and SNS, Stockholm.

Braunerhjelm P, Nyberg S, Stennek J, Wahl N (2002) Gränslös konkurrens, SNS Economic Policy Group 2002, SNS, Stockholm.

Denison EF (1967) Why Growth Rates Differ, The Brookings Institution, Washington, D.C.

Domar E (1946) Capital Expansion, Rate of Growth, and Employment, *Econometrica*, 14, 137-47.

DuRietz G (2002) Skatter och den ekonomiska tillväxten, *Utredningsrapport 2002:16*, Skattebetarnas Förening, Stockholm.

Edquist H (2004) The Swedish ICT Miracle – Myth or Reality?, *Information Economics and Policy*, forthcoming.

Eliasson G (1990) The Firm as a Competent Team, *Journal of Economic Behaviour and Economics*, 13, 275-298.

Eliasson G(1991) Modeling the Experimentally Organized Economy, *Journal of Economic Behavior and Economics*, 16, 153-182.

Eurostat, 2003, *New Cronos*.

Fölster S, Henrekson M (2001) Growth Effects of Government Expenditure in Rich Countries, *European Economic Review*, 45, 1501-1520.

Glete J (1994) Nätverk i näringslivet. Ägande och industriell omvandling i det mogna industrisamhället1920-1990, SNS Förlag, Stockholm.

Global Entrepreneurship Monitoring (GEM), 2003, *Global Report 2003* (www.gemconsortium.org)

Greenwood J, Jovanovic B (1998) Accounting for Growth, NBER WP No.6647.

Grossman G, Helpman E (1991) Innovation and Growth in the Global Economy, MIT Press, Cambridge, Ma.

von Hayek F (1945) The Use of Knowledge in Society, *American Economic Review*, 35, 519-530.*l*

Henrekson M (2003) Entreprenörskap – välfärdsstatens svaga länk?, *Ekonomisk Debatt*, 31, 5-18.

Henrekson M, Persson M (2004) The Effects on Sick Leave of Changes in Sickness Insurance System, *Journal of Labor Economics*, 22, 87-113.

Johansson P, Palme M (2002) Assessing the Effects of Public Policies on Worker Absenteeism, *Journal of Human Resources*, 37, 381-409.

Jones CI (1995a) R&D-Based Models of Economic Growth, *Journal of Political Economy*, 103, 759-784.

Jones CI (1995b) Time Series Test of Endogenous Growth Models, *Quarterly Journal of Economics*, 110, 495-525.

Kaldor N (1961) Capital Accumulation and Economic Growth. In Lutz, F.A. and Hague, D.C. (eds.), *The Theory of Capital*, MacMillan, London.

Knight F (1921) Risk, Uncertainty and Profit, Houghton Mifflin, Boston.

Knight F (1944) Diminishing Returns from Investment, *Journal of Political Economy*, 52, 26-47.

Lindbeck A (1975) Swedish Economic Policy, MacMillan, London.

Lindbeck A (1995) Hazardous Welfare State Dynamics, *American Economic Review*, 85, 9-15.

Lindbeck A (1997) The Swedish Experiment, SNS Förlag, Stockholm.

Lindbeck A, Persson M, Palme M (2004) Sjukskrivningar som ett socialt fenomen, *Ekonomisk Debatt*, 32, 50-52.

Lucas R (1988) On the Mechanics of Economic Development, *Journal of Monetary Economics*, 22, 3-39.

Maddison A (1982) Phases of Capitalist Development, Oxford University Press, Oxford.

Marklund G, Nilsson R, Sandgren P, Granat Thorslund J, Ullström J (2004) The Swedish National Innovation System 1970-2003. A quantitative international benchmarking analysis, Vinnova, Stockholm.

Myrhman J (1994) Hur Sverige blev rikt, SNS Förlag, Stockholm.

Nås SO, Sandven T, Eriksson T, Andersson J, Tegsjö B, Lethoranta O, Virtaharju M (2004) High-Tech Spin-Offs in the Nordic Countries, STEP Report 22-2003, SINTEF.

National Science Indicator Database, 2003 (http://www.isinet.com/rsg/nsi/index.html).

North D, Thomas RP (1973) The Rise of the Western World: A New Economic History, Cambridge, Cambridge University Press.

OECD (1999) OECD Science, Technology and Industry Scoreboard 1999, OECD, Paris.

OECD (2002) OECD Science, Technology and Industry Outlook 2002, OECD, Paris.

OECD (2002) Statistical Compendium on CD.

OECD (2003) (www.sourceoecd.org).

OECD (2003) Education at a Glance 2003, OECD, Paris.

OECD (2003) Science, Technology and Industry Scoreboard 2003, OECD, Paris.

OECD (2003) The Sources of Economic Growth, Oecd, Paris.

Pålsson A (1998) De svenska hushållens sparande och förmögenheter, *Mimeo*, Lunds University.

Polyani M (1967) The Tacit Dimension, Doubleday Anchor, Garden City, N.Y.

Romer P (1986) Increasing Returns and Economic Growth, *American Economic Review*, 94, 1002-1037.

Romer P (1990) Endogenous Technical Change, *Journal of Political Economy*, 98, 71-102.

Rosenberg N, Birdzell LE (1986) How the West Grew Rich: The Economic Transformation of the Industrialized World, New York, Basic Books.

Rostow W (1990) Theories of Economic Growth from David Hume to the Present, Oxford University Press, Oxford and New York.

SCB (2003) Official Statistics (www.scb.se)

Schmitz J (1989) Imitation, Entrepreneurship, and Long-Run Growth, *Journal of Political Economy*, 97, 721-739.

Schumpeter J (1911) Theorie der Wirtschaftlichen Entwicklung. English translation: The Theory of Economic Development, Harvard University Press, Cambridge, Ma., 1934.

Schumpeter J (1937) Preface to the 1937 Japanese edition of Theorie der WirtschaftlichenEntwickung. In Schumpeter J (ed.) *Essays on Entrepreneurs, Innovations, Business Cycles, and the Evolution of Capitalism*, Transaction Press, New Brunswick, 1989.

Schumpeter J (1939) Business Cycles: A Theoretical, Historical and Statististical Analysis of the Capitalist Process, McGraw-Hill. New York.

Segerstrom P, Anant TC, Dinopoulos E (1990) A Schumpeterian Model of the Product Life Cycle, *American Economic Review*, 80, 1077-1091.

Simon H (1959) Theories of Decision Making in Economics and Behavioral Science, *American Economic Review*, 49, 253-283.

Shane S, Eckhardt J (2003) The Individual-Opportunity Nexus. In ZJ Acs and D Audretsch, *Handbook of Entrepreneurship Research*, Boston, Kluwer, 161-194.

Shell K (1967) Inventive activity, Industrial Organization, and Economic Activity. In-Mirrlees J and Stern N (eds.) *Models of Economic Growth*, MacMillan, London.

Solow R (1956) A Contribution to Theory of Economic Growth, *Quarterly Journal of Economics*, 70, 65-94.

Solow R (1957) Technical Change and the Aggregate Production Function, *Review of Economics and Statistics*, 39, 312-320.

Svensk Handel (2002) Sveriges län i den nya ekonomin, (www.svenskhandel.se).

Swan TW (1956) Economic Growth and Capital Accumulation, *Economic Record*, 32, 334-361.

Technoplois and INNO (2004) Benchmarking Technology R&D, forthcoming, Vinnova, Stockholm.

Young A (1998) Growth Without Scale Effects, NBER WP No. 5211, Cambridge.

Relationships between Universities, Research Centers and District Firms: the Italian Case

Patrizio Bianchi, Laura Ramaciotti

University of Ferrara
Via del Gregorio, 13/15 – 44100, Ferrara, Italy
rettore@unife.it

1. The Italian Case and the International Competition

Italian system of large firms clearly appears to be today progressively marginalized compared to international competitors (Quadrio Curzio, Fortis 2004). In Italy we have, together with the so called 'Pillars' according to Quadrio Curzio and Fortis terminology to designate large firms that shaped Italian economic history and development, also a district system of firms that allowed, since the 70's, a broad diffusion of industrial production and wealth in the country (Quadrio Curzio, Fortis 2002). Nevertheless also this system appears today to be in serious troubles. For this reason the issue of Italian industrial development must be faced, by now, under a global perspective. This means having a confrontation on the capacity to generate added value within a strongly competitive context in continuous transformation.

The persistent troubles of Italian economy come evidently out when looking at the turnover and export trends in the first years of 2000 (Figure 1). In those years not only industrial production has experienced difficulties in growing, but, above all, exports, that always have represented the real engine of Italian growth, have significantly decreased (Figure 2).

Sectors belonging to the so called 'Made in Italy' have particularly contributed to this result, in spite of the fact that in the past they have pulled Italian industrial innovation and growth. Within the manufacturing sector, in fact, precisely the industries of textile, clothing, shoes, furniture, ceramic tiles, as well as machinery and equipment have slow down while, at the same time, services, particularly state-regulated ones, and the building sector have compensated the difficulties of those industries more exposed to international competition (Figure 3).

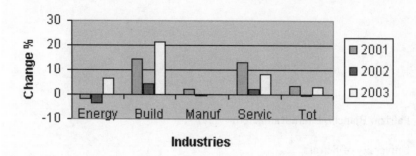

Fig 1. Turnover Yearly Variation in Different Industries (%)
Source: Mediobanca, 2004

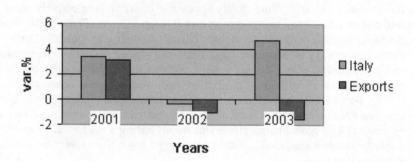

Fig 2. Turnover Variation Italy vs Exports, Years 2001-2003 (%)
Source: Mediobanca, 2004

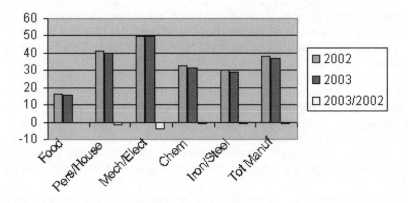

Fig 3. Turnover Variation of 1945 Firms Belonging to Different Sectors (%).
Source: Mediobanca, 2004

This situation is the result of a productive system whose industrial dynamics are not able to fully exploit the national innovation system based on the network of Universities and public research centers. This evident weakness certainly derives from a sort of disconnection between Universities and firms: on one hand Universities have a lot of constraints to overcome, while, on the other one, the productive system is based on two groups of firms both incapable, for different reasons, to express a qualified demand in terms of industrial research.

The Italian industrial system has, at the beginning of the 90's, a limited number of large firms mostly created at the end of the nineteenth century to modernize a country economically backward and politically fragile (Fenoaltea, 2003). This limited group of firms has been redefined in terms of property rights in the 30's through the creation of the IRI institute, the state intervention in the banking sector, the separation between normal credit and investment credit. After having been reconfirmed in the years of postwar reconstruction, the link between public modern enterprises and historical family firms becomes the backbone of the Italian development and of the catching-up process at the opening of European markets. To this group of historical enterprises belong the so called 'pillars' of our productive system that are large firms operating in innovative and modern sectors such as telecommunications, chemicals, iron and steel, automotive (Bianchi 2002).

Those firms, since the beginning of the 70's, have experienced a deep restructuring process with downsizing effects that led between 1980 and 1995 to halve the employment in the Italian big concern. While the new competitive global context was emerging, Italian large firms had to concentrate their resources not on development plans, but on mere survival plans with devastating effects on the existing centers of industrial research that had attained in the past leadership at world level (Gallino, 2003).

Different examples can be cited. There is the case of Montedison laboratory and particularly Donegani center that, in the 50's, have been, with Natta, the leading reference at world level for the chemical of catalysts. There are the laboratories of pharmaceutical firms belonging to Montedison group (Carlo Erba and Farmitalia). There is also the example of Olivetti that in 1955 established, in cooperation with University of Pisa, a research institute in Barbaricina, then a laboratory in Borgomanero and another one in Rho where the Electronic division presented in 1959 the first Italian computer. Nevertheless Olivetti research effort has been punished by the following crisis that finally brought Olivetti to sell the Division in 1964 to General Electric. The industrial research capacity did not survive to that crisis because the firm did not have financial means and organizational competencies adequate to the effort required by that kind of innovation (Giannetti, 1998).

During the years of the crisis for the Italian big concern, a new entrepreneurial class emerged. Through a strong local rooting and a careful focus on the product, it succeeded in compensating the crisis of the large declining firms. It is an entrepreneurial class quite young, located in areas recently industrialized and largely based on the reorganization of traditional sectors (Balloni and Jacobucci, 2001). This new kind of district firm can be associated to an infant industry, growing in traditional sectors characterized by an increasing not formalized type of innovation (Quadrio Curzio and Fortis, 2002).

It comes out the peculiar situation of an industrial system that finds itself in the 90's, when European recovery was starting and world markets were opening, to manage simultaneously the decline of 'old firms in new sectors' and of 'new firms in old sectors'. Both are incapable to express a structured demand in terms of research and particularly of basic research. This last one is very important because it supports the great innovative leaps as is the case of chemical and information technology (Camera dei Deputati, 2003, 2004).

This industrial profile had its correspondence in an educational system characterized by an offer, at University level, substantially not sufficient - in spite of all the attempted reforms - for the needs of a growing country.

2. University in Italy

The number of University students in Italy has experienced a six fold increase since 1960 to 2001 by, from 300,000 to 1,700,000. Enrolled students on the total of 19 aged people, has increased from 9% in 1960 to 26% in 1985 to 52% in 2001 (Treelle, 2003). Nevertheless the fraction of the population aged between 25-34 with a University degree is, in 2001, the lowest in Europe and half of the Spanish one (Figure 4).

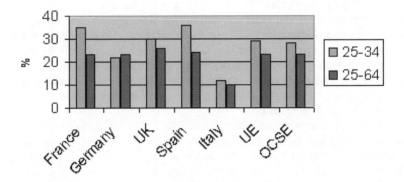

Fig 4. Population with University Degree Divided by Age, 2001.
Source: OCSE, 2002

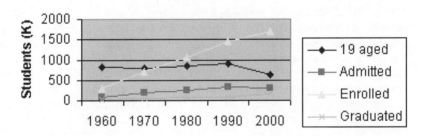

Fig 5. University Attendance.
Source: Trelle, 2003

In the 60's Italy was a country in the middle of the development path. Its industry was still geographically concentrated in the industrial triangle where the first industrialization had begun. Its population was young, with a low degree of education, still working in agricultural or craft sectors, ready to feed the development of a mass industry able to attract a working class with low qualifications. Along with this working class there also was a little group of technicians (mostly engineers) that managed the operations in the large firms, but excluded from property and control, and also a class of professionals (doctors and lawyers) that run local communities, but taking no part in production activities.

In those years the demand for education typical of a growing country added up to the needs of local and technical elites. This phenomenon determined, even if through different adjustments, a continuous increase in the number of enrolled students catching up the levels of developed countries. Nevertheless the number of students graduating within the course legal duration has remained, in absolute terms, similar to that of the 60's. In 2001 the number of students graduating within the course legal duration was 4%, while more than 63% of students graduated with a delay of three or more years.

The direct consequence of this situation is that, in 1999, the yearly cost for each student in Italy was the same as in Spain, Portugal and Greece, the less developed countries in Europe ($ 7,500 against an EU average of $ 9.700). Nevertheless the cost for each student cumulated for the average duration of the degree course was in 1999 of $ 41,000, above France and UK levels (Avveduto, 2003).

The percentage of population with a university degree appeared to be incompatible, in Italy, with the country level of development. In 2001, only 12% of the population aged between 25 and 34 years and only 10% of the population aged between 25 and 64 years had a university degree against European percentages of respectively 29% and 23%. For the Doctorates, the Italian average was only 0,4% for the population aged between 25 and 34 years, placing Italy at the bottom of European rankings, well below Spain and Portugal levels (OCSE, 2002).

University structure was made up, in 2001-2002, by 74 Universities and postgraduate technical colleges and 515 faculties.

Italian universities can be divided into two groups: the 9 biggest universities collect 38% of the enrolled students, while the remaining 62% is spread among the other 65 universities. The first 9 institutes have an average of 70,000 students while the others have an average of 16,000 students. At the beginning of the 80's the first 9 universities counted 57% of the students and the others the remaining 43%. It has therefore taken place a reallocation of students in the territory due to the creation, in the last twenty years, of new academic entities.

Permanent lecturers were 55,000 plus about 15,000 lecturers on contract. In 2001 only 5% of the teachers is younger than 34 years, 24% is between 35 and 45, 33% is between 45 and 54 and 38% is above 55 years. This profile is very different from the European average (CNVSU-MIUR, 2003). The following block in the recruitment has frozen the situation, worsening the comparison in terms of teachers' and researchers' age with the rest of Europe.

The ageing of the University structure in Italy comes out evidently from the age profile of teachers and researchers (Figure 6). In 1985 nearly 50% f the teachers was between 35 and 44 years old. In 1993 the same group is between 45 and 55. In 2001 it is above 55 years.

The average age of researchers in 2001 is nearly 38 years. Associated researchers are on average 44 years old and permanent researchers 50 years. There are big differences according to the research field. For example mathematicians are on average 32 years old while doctors are nearly 42.

It is interesting to compare the different European systems. For example in UK and Germany about half of the lecturers are less than 40 years old (respectively 46% and 54%). In France they are about 25%, while in Italy the percentage is 17%.

Figures 7 and 8 show how the number of researchers in Italy is the lowest in Europe and also how countries such as Greece, Spain and Portugal have increased significantly their endowment (OCSE, 2002).

It is therefore apparent the difficulty of the Italian industrial system characterized by a double regime of 'old firms in new sectors' and 'new firms in old sectors' both unable, for different reasons, to express a suitable and structured demand for research. At the same time it is apparent the difficulty of a university system that copes with the new globalization challenge bearing a previously existing burden of internal problems that prevented it from assuming a leading role in the development process of the country.

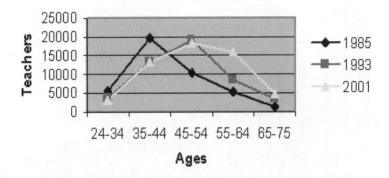

Fig 6. Ages Distribution of Teachers and Researchers.
Source: Trelle, 2003

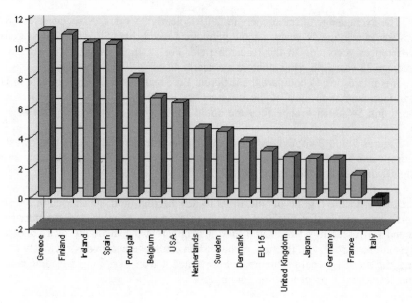

Fig 7. Percentage Variation in the Number of Researchers every 1000 Employees in the Period 1995-2002
Source: EU Key S&T figures, 2002

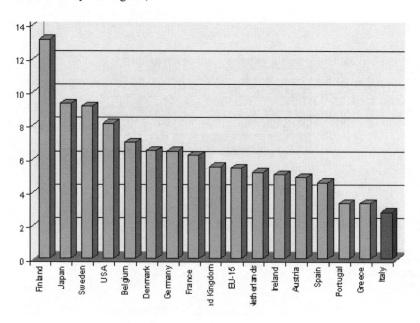

Fig 8. Number of Researchers every 1000 Employees in 2002
Source: EU Key S&T figures, 2002

3. A New International Context

The joint analysis of the evolution of Italian industrial and university systems outlines parallel paths that meet from time to time without defining a proper interdependence trajectory. It is therefore not difficult to foresee the outcome of low investments in research in terms of high-tech content of our exports. The new international competitive context is characterized by a strong reallocation of industrial activities and, at the same time, by a redefinition of the concept of industry itself. A ranking of countries in terms of high-tech content of their exports helps in grasping the Italian international position.

Table 1. Top 25 Exporters of High-Tech Products, 1985 and 1998 (Millions of $)

1985			1998		
Rank	Country	High-Tech Exports	Rank	Country	High-Tech Exports
1	United States	41,859	1	United States	170,513
2	Japan	35,731	2	Japan	109,627
3	German	21,795	3	Germany	83,324
4	UK	13,013	4	UK	68,276
5	France	12,141	5	Singapore	58,678
6	Italy	7,063	6	France	57,025
7	Netherlands	5,195	7	Taiwan	36,944
8	Taiwan	4,480	8	Netherlands	33,390
9	Canada	4,478	9	Korea	32,830
10	Switzerland	4,381	10	Malaysia	30,926
11	Singapore	3,879	11	China	30,518
12	Sweden	3,862	12	Mexico	27,579
13	Korea	3,541	13	Italy	23,023
14	Belgium	2,827	14	Ireland	22,801
15	Honk Kong SAR	2,269	15	Sweden	18,358
16	Ireland	2,123	16	Canada	18,106
17	Austria	1,464	17	Philippines	18,081
18	Denmark	1,356	18	Switzerland	17,331
19	Malaysia	1,277	19	Belgium	14,897
20	Spain	1,255	20	Thailand	12,667
21	Israel	942	21	Finland	9,955
22	Mexico	717	22	Spain	8,696
23	Finland	716	23	Austria	6,519
24	Poland	665	24	Israel	6,247
25	Brazil	599	25	Denmark	5,810
Total for top 25		177,628			922,661
World Total		179,380			952,685
Share of top 25 in World Total		99 %			97 %

Source: Calculated from UN Comtrade Database. Authors elaboration from UNDP, 2002Ref. UNDP (2001), Human Development Report 2001 - Making New Technologies Work for Human Development, Oxford and New York, Oxford University Press

Two groups of countries can be clearly identified. On one hand there are the countries with an old industrial tradition that can use their research structures in order to place themselves at the leading edge of the world market selling goods with high technological content. On the other hand there are the newly industrialized countries that use aggressive industrial policies in order to attract foreign investors to localize high-tech plants in free special areas, the so called 'maquilladoras'.

It is therefore emerging a new economic geography according to the technological clusters that characterize the new industrial development.

The case of China and in particular of Guandong region represents a clear example. In the South of China today a huge production of electronic products is concentrated. All the most important US and European firms have invested there because they can find not only cheap labor, but also increasing benefits in terms of agglomeration and facilities both for manufacturing transformation and for applied research. The same can be said for the Bangalore area in India where an extraordinary concentration of software production increasingly supports R&D activities (Bianchi, Di Tommaso, Paci, Rubini, 2005).

4. The New Concept of Industry and Property Rights

The concept of industry has substantially changed in the last years. Sectors that only a few years ago were considered niches with high research content, but marginal for industrial production, today demonstrate that basic research has become the core of the new industry development. An analysis of the industrial dynamics both in the US and in the UK points out the deep transformation of the industrial profile of those two countries. New firms in sectors related to biotechnologies, nanotechnologies, science of materials are born and have developed. This phenomenon has been possible because of public research investments, a very active market for financing, a favorable set of rules for new firms deriving from basic research.

It is clear that we are facing now an industrial revolution that increasingly shifts the core of new production to the basic research activities. Basic research becomes the real engine that generates value added for productive sectors. This puts barriers to entry for single firms more and more in the access to the country structure of basic research.

The transformation of health sector represents an emblematic example. This sector, seen for years as public expense to cut down, is considered today a sector that generates value added, creates new industrial production and leads the technological change. This is so true that it is possible to define a Health Industry Model (Di Tommaso and Schweitzer, 2005).

New industry is more and more linked to a type of research resulting from the accumulation of knowledge, that includes a significant proportion of public good and that is not more only individual. The invention can not more be realized by a single scientist. The process of scientific discovery requires a debate within the international scientific community and a network of laboratories, services, persons that can be found only within universities. In the development of new industry the university role is essential not only for the basic research, but also for the entrepreneurship of new industrial initiatives, as the US experience demonstrates.

Not only in the recent US experience the role of basic research appears to be dominant, but it has also continuously extended its importance, mostly in the first years of 2000, for the investments made in life sciences that increased significantly compared to all the other sectors.

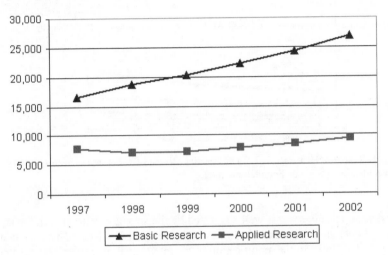

Fig. 9. Research Expenses in US Universities for Basic Research and Applied Research
Source: National Research Foundation, 2002.

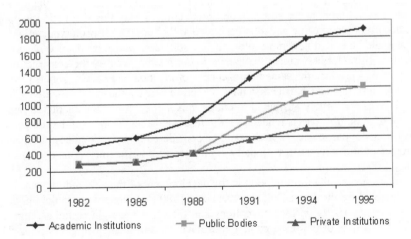

Fig. 10. US Patents Granted in the Period 1982-1995.
Source: US Patent and Trademark Office and National Science Foundation, 2002

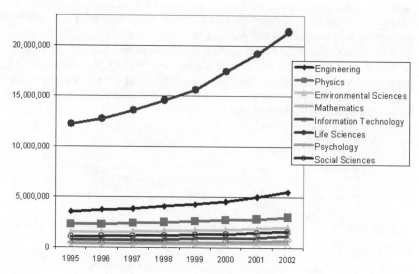

Fig. 11. Research Expenses in US Universities Divided for Scientific Sectors in Millions. **Source**: National Science Foundation, 2002.

The role of university is well suggested by the strong acceleration in the acquisition of patents by academic institutes in the period 1982-1995. This acceleration has been attributed to the modification of the intellectual property rights for the research activities financed by federal funds (Fig. 10).

The concept of industry itself has been redefined. Now the industry organization extends itself up to basic research laboratories. In 'fordist' model there was a clear distinction between research and production. Today this distinction is going to disappear since value added is generated at the moment of prototype definition, that could be both a new molecule or a new software, whose production costs tend to zero. If in 'fordist' model the barrier to entry was given by the construction of the plant to produce the same homogeneous product on large scale, in new productive sectors the real barrier to entry is represented by the basic research whose sunk costs are largely attributed to public universities. Since the economic importance of intangible assets related to basic research becomes more and more evident (while in the past basic research could be considered as a public good), the need to protect public universities property rights grows significantly (Bianchi and Labory, 2004).

In US history the turning point in the development of the new industry has been represented by the Bayh-Dole Act issued in 1980 that recognized to the universities property rights on their inventions and therefore the right to industrially exploit the results of the research activities developed in their own laboratories. The same law also allowed the promotion of spin-offs that now represent the backbone of the new US industry.

This is more evident if we focus our attention on the patents coming from DNA research (Fig. 12). This field clearly shows the combined effect of a worldwide research effort in genetics and of an adequate set of rules that translates the research effort, mostly basic, into property rights and innovation.

A more detailed analysis of the attribution of those patents indicates the presence of traditional pharmaceutical firms, new biotech firms created to this purpose and universities that supported research programs on DNA. The following entities appear on the list: University of California, Federal Government, GlaxoSmith-Kline, Incyte Genomics, Aventis, Chiron, Genentech, Bayer, Wyeth, Novartis, Mercks, Unitex, Human Genomics, Amgen, Johns Hopkins University, Applera, Nova Nordisk, Harvard University Press, Pfizer, Stanford University, Lilly, Salk Institute, Cornell University, Mit, Affimetrix, Columbia University, University of Wisconsin, Washington University, University of Pennsylvania (Pressman, 2004). It is important to remark that new firms such as Incyte Genomics, Genentech, Amgen are university spin-offs. They derive from academic research their original source.

This framework demonstrates how the new health industry has been revived through the extraordinary research effort connected with the DNA program. It also demonstrates that an appropriate law on property rights has allowed universities to lead the re-shaping of the industrial profile of the country.

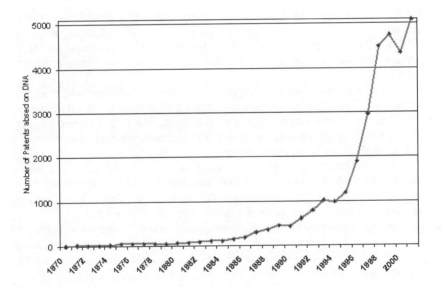

Fig. 12. US Patents based on DNA Research.
Source: LeRoy Walters, 2001; DNA Patent Database, 2001

In the case of health industry a perfect combination has been realized between historical firms and new firms, research institutes and government entities. This combination regenerates the process of knowledge accumulation and translates new science in new industry according to a scheme already tested in the US for electronics and information technology.

In this example the combination between institutions (government, university, historical firms) creates a framework of stability and interrelationship that allows, through specific laws and an adequate financial context, to give birth to an entrepreneurial environment dynamic enough to be able to redefine the industrial profile of a country. In other terms, large firms and district firms become interwoven in a context where universities are the places for the incubation of the new industry.

Undoubtedly after 25 years, the Bayh-Dole Act shows several limits and the debate to overcome it is growing. Nevertheless it has to be underlined the importance of this normative tool that, at the beginning of the 80's, has allowed US universities to have at their disposal property rights deriving from research financed by federal funds and therefore to promote new industrial developments for their research in sectors with high risks of legal disputes.

5. University, Research and Industry in Italy

At this stage of industry transformation, Italy arrives with the heavy burden of a history that has seen university and industry moving with difficulties along parallel lines. The former trying to chase a growing demand for education; the latter remaining constrained between old declining leaders and new firms in traditional sectors.

Also in Italy the cases of spin-offs and exploitation of university research are increasing. Nevertheless laws on property rights and on the legal status of researchers/lecturers are hampering those initiatives. The role of university runs the risk of resulting limited in favor of an individualist approach to firm creation, patenting, exploitation of scientific activities.

The development of a high value added industry is therefore strictly linked to the development of university network and public research institutions. It is required not only to support the demand for research by existing firms, but also to sustain basic research that generates new industry in new sectors.

The idea is not only to encourage industrial research through demand subsidies to firms, but also to reinforce the offer of basic research through an exploitation process that allows universities to finance their development using the outcomes of their own research.

University autonomy and its ability to govern its own resources and organization are to be faced after fifteen years of reforms and three years of blocked recruitment. The role of university in Italy must be seriously and deeply reconsidered because, if it is true that large firms are declining, it is also true that national university is declining. A long term approach to the Italian development and scientific institutions is required. Their autonomy and their ability to become the intellectual and operative engine of civil growth for the country are at stake.

Comparing the development of industrial and university systems, the historical profile of a backward country emerges where the productive development has been accomplished without being supported by an adequate educational organization. The core of modern industry has been for long concentrated in an area protected by the state. After a phase of rapid growing in the postwar period, it has recorded a long decline in employment in its private component, only partially compensated by its public component. Employment growing has been due to small and medium enterprises whose demand in terms of research and higher education qualifications was quite limited. It comes out a scarce stimulus for university that, in the meanwhile, was exploding in terms of enrolled students, but not in terms of educational results.

In the 90's, the acceleration in the process of European integration imposes direct comparisons between productive and educational systems belonging to different countries. At this point the Italian innovative system made up by high-tech industry, industrial research, public research institutes, universities, appears to be evidently not sufficient (Lundvall, 1992).

Regulations on which Italian system is based have been defined in the 30's and reconfirmed in the postwar period. Now they need to be deeply reformed in order to redefine the basic rules for the functioning of the Italian economic and social system.

Reforms have been undertaken in the 90's with privatizations and university autonomy. Nevertheless it is clear that they have not been intended as a turning point for the country. In fact, changing the governments, there was the tendency to bring back firms ownership to the previous family and public owners. Moreover university has suffered a long period of recruitment and transfers blocking, following a complex phase of transformation of the didactic system.

In this context of incomplete reforms, some experiments of connections between universities and firms have emerged. Nevertheless they still not have transformed into a new industrial high-tech profile for the country.

Facing the international competition, there can be different and alternative political choices. There is the option to create a new Italian technology institute, unrelated to the Italian tradition and outside the university network. There is also the proposal for the territorial integration of universities and the creation of a network of university laboratories. This proposal should represent the base for a new approach to districts, whose reference points continue to be the historical universities of the region. Emilia Romagna region, that in the past has been an important place for the development of Italian industrial districts (Pyke, Becattini and Senenberger, 1990) has redefined in these last years a profile of industrial policy aimed at generating new high-technology industrial districts based on public universities.

Regional industrial policies require a redefinition of the normative framework on intellectual property rights. The law 18 October 2001 (Tremonti package) had attributed property rights on innovation exclusively to the individual researcher. This approach has been confirmed by the recent code on intellectual property rights issued by the Ministry for Productive Activities. It poses to the researcher the problem of sustaining and managing patenting costs and leaves the inventor completely in the hands of the corporations willing to finance research. University results marginalized while it should be the main place for research activities and for knowledge accumulation.

6. Emilia Romagna Case

Emilia Romagna region has developed in the last years a new approach aimed at promoting the creation of research and technological transfer networks. In the 70's the region helped the development of industrial districts through the establishment of service centers for firms, the support to the cooperation between firms and local institutions, the promotion of funds to enhance innovation intended, in those years, only as machinery purchase (Leonardi and Nannetti, 1990).

After 30 years, Emilia Romagna proposes different tools to create new high-tech districts. In 2001 the regional government, the four public universities (Bologna, Ferrara, Modena and Reggio, Parma), the research institutes based in the region (CNR and ENEA), signed an agreement to realize a regional network for industrial research, innovation and technological transfer. At the same time the ownership of the regional agency for innovation ASTER has been redefined and it is now shared by the region itself, universities, research institutes and entrepreneurial associations that support innovation. In 2002 regional law n° 7 has been issued. The law promoted a program for the creation of network laboratories, connecting university and research center structures into integrated projects that therefore grow significantly in dimension and are able to attract research activities carried out by private firms.

It is important to highlight that the four public universities based in Emilia Romagna have 4,800 lecturers and researchers (3,200 in scientific departments) that represent the 10.2% of the country total. The region can also count on 800 employees at CNR and 600 at ENEA. To this total of more than 6,000 lecturers and researchers can be added, in 2002, 8,911 employees in private firms carrying out R&D activities (on a country total of 70,228). In 1997 they were 5,185 (on a country total of 61,414). Firms in Emilia Romagna therefore react to lira devaluation (1992-1997) and to euro introduction through an acceleration of the innovation process. This translates in a substantial increase in the number of employees in R&D (+71.9% against a country average of 9% and a Lombardia rate of only 3.6%) and in an increase of the expenses for R&D that rise from 409 millions of euro in 1997 to 856 millions in 2002. This is the highest increase in Italy (109.3%). In fact the country as a whole records a rise in R&D expenses by firms from 5,377 millions of euro in 1997 to 7,056 millions that corresponds to an increase of 24.8%. In 1997 Emilia Romagna had a share of 8.7% on the country total of firm employees in R&D. After five years this share has reached the 12.7% clearly demonstrating the effort made.

This effort is also evident in the framework of actions that the region has undertaken in favor of innovation mainly through the Regional Program for Industrial

Research, Innovation, Technological Transfer (PRRITT) that, on one hand, finances firms' innovative projects to be realized in cooperation with universities and public research entities and, on the other one, promotes the participation of all those actors to focused laboratories that could become, in this way, the place for new district associations.

In addition to the described initiatives, it is also possible to mention:

1. the definition of the Regional TLC Plan, that, basing on the four universities, defines the TLC public network
2. a regional program for innovative actions in the field of health and life sciences
3. a program of services for innovation and research promotion aimed at the creation of new spin-offs and at the boosting of technological transfer. It is named Spinner and is financed by FSE.

Total investments by Emilia Romagna region, in the period 2002-2005, add up to 130 millions of euro.

Having started in 2003, PRRITT program, after one year of activity, has already financed 55 structures integrating 27 laboratories, 22 centers and 4 scientific parks all brought together in the regional network. Through this funding, in addition to the financing of research structures, 313 new researchers have been hired and 236 already active researchers have been paid.

The program HI-MECH can be considered as an example. It puts together laboratories in the field of advanced mechanics and is co-financed by the Ministry of Education, University and Research. This program is coordinated by the University of Modena and Reggio and involves different groups of laboratories. Within the program, a network of laboratories is devoted to acoustics and vibrations (LAV). It is based in Ferrara but involves also other four departments in the other four universities of the region, the CNR institute and 28 firms with their laboratories allowing the construction of large equipments for measurement, research and products certification.

In the above described context, particularly interesting is the case of Ferrara. This province has experienced a substantial delay compared to the other provinces of the region. Moreover since 1996 it has been recognized as an industrial declining area because of the crisis of the chemical plants established here.

Within the PRRITT program, using also the structural funds for areas belonging to Objective 2, 4 network laboratories have been established in Ferrara (LAV – Acoustics and Vibrations Laboratory; LARA – Regional Laboratory for Water; ER GENTECH – Regional Laboratory for Innovation in Genetics and Biotechnology; INSEBALA – Center for Multimedia Integration and Services for Broad Band). Moreover in Ferrara are based the technological virtual park for genetics and health biotechnology and the center for innovation and technological transfer. The latter will take advantage from the Spin Offs Center of Ferrara University that, since 2001, has promoted 14 academic spin-offs participated by the university itself.

7. Final Considerations

The recent development of industrial districts has shown that, when the industrial pillars of the country were in crisis, new productive agglomerations were able to come out in new marginal areas - instead of the traditional developed ones - and to foster the industrial development of the country..

Analyzing Italian districts, David Lane has proposed a theory of complex organizations that demonstrates that network structures, in order to evolve, need to identify not only the single hubs of the system (firms, project groups, individuals), but also the so called 'scaffold' that consist of development rules, interaction places and agents' roles. They function as a support scheme for interactions and make the development paths of the system stable and coherent (Lane, 2002). Lane, following Brusco and Becattini tradition, identifies this 'scaffold' with the social organization of the local context.

Districts allowed the broad diffusion of industrialization on large areas of Italian territory, generating a potential for innovation. Nevertheless they were not able to cumulate knowledge in productive sectors related to new industry and, at the same time, they were unable to transfer knowledge coming from new industry to the districts based on local knowledge.

The essential link between new science and new industry is represented by university. The latter must consist of a network of public universities to be strengthened in their autonomy and capacity.

In this context a possible development path is based on the creation of knowledge networks where firms and universities can work together to project new industrial districts. In this direction region Emilia Romagna has presented its proposal of industrial policy that favors the creation of new districts where public universities work as 'scaffold' to promote new network associations based on the knowledge produced in the universities themselves.

References

Avveduto S (2003) Per una politica delle risorse umane. In volume monografico di Queste Istituzioni, n.129, marzo, *La ricerca scientifica in Italia: quali politiche*.

Balloni V, Iacobucci D (2001) I "nuovi protagonisti" dell'industria italiana. In *L'Industria*, n.s. a.XXII, n.4, ott.dic. pp. 633-675

Banca d'Italia (2003) Relazione Annuale, Roma

Bianchi P (2002) La rincorsa frenata. L'industria italiana dall' unità nazionale alla unificazione europea, Il Mulino, Bologna

Bianchi P (2004) I pilastri dello sviluppo italiano, in *Distretti, pilastri, reti in Italia e Europa* a cura di Quadrio Curzio A e Fortis M, Accademia Nazionale dei Lincei, in corso di pubblicazione

Bianchi P, Labory S (2004) The Economic Importance of Intangible Assets, Ashgate Pu., Hants

Bianchi P, Di Tommaso MR, Paci D, Rubini L (2005) Sistemi di imprese, dinamiche spontanee e interventi pubblici: riflessioni sui paesi in via di sviluppo, Rivista italiana di economia, demografia e statistica, n. 3 (forthcoming)

Camera dei Deputati (2003) Indagine conoscitiva sull'industria dell'automobile, X Commissione Attività produttive, luglio, atti parlamentari, Roma

Camera dei deputati (2004) Indagine conoscitiva sull'industria italiana: tendenze evolutive e politiche di rilancio, X Commissione attività produttive, marzo, atti parlamentari, Roma

Ciocca PL, Toniolo G (2002) Storia economica d'Italia, 3. Industrie, mercati, istituzioni, Laterza, Bari.

Comitato Nazionale per la valutazione del sistema universitario – MIUR (2003) Terzo rapporto sullo stato del sistema universitario, Roma

Di Tommaso M, Schweitzer (2005) Health policy and Hi-Tech Development. Learning from Innovation in the Health Industry, Edward Elgar, London

Fenoaltea S (2002) Lo sviluppo dell'industria dall'unità alla grande guerra: una sintesi provvisoria, in Ciocca e Toniolo, pp137-193

Gallino L (2003) La scomparsa dell'Italia industriale, Einaudi, Torino

Giannetti R (1998) Tecnologia e sviluppo economico italiano 1870-1990, Il Mulino, Bologna

Lane DA (2002) Complessità e interazioni locali. Verso una teoria dei distretti industriali, in Quadrio Curzio A e Fortis M, 2002, pp. 111- 140

Leopardi R, Nannetti RY (1990) The Regions and European Integration. The case of Emilia Romagna, Pinter, London

Lundvall BA (1992) National Systems of Innovation, towards a theory of innovation and interactive learning, Pinter, London

Mediobanca (2004a) Dati Cumulativi di 1945 società italiane, Milano

Mediobanca (2004b) Le principali società italiane, Milano

OCSE (2002) Science and Technology Outlook, Parigi

Quadrio Curzio A, Fortis M (2002) Complessità e distretti industriali. Dinamiche, modelli, casi reali, Il Mulino, Bologna

Quadrio Curzio A, Fortis M (2004) Distretti, pilastri, reti in Italia e in Europa, Accademia nazionale dei Lincei, Fondazione Edison, forthcoming.

Pyke F, Becattini G, Senenberger W (1990) Industrial districts and inter-firm cooperation in Italy, ILO Ginevra

Saraceno P (1978) Irrepetibilità dei modelli di sviluppo, in Economia e direzione dell'impresa industriale, Milano, ISEDI

TreElle (2003) Università italiana, università europea? Dati, proposte e questioni aperte, Quaderno della associazione TreElle, n.3, settembre

List of Authors

Ezio Andreta. He is the Director of the EC Research Directorate G (Industrial Technologies) and he is one of the contributors to the definition and implementation of the 6th European Framework Programme for Research and Technological Development.

He is President of several European Committees in the sectors of coal and steel, nanotechnology and nanosciences, knowledge-based multifunctional materials, new production processes and devices. Since 1999 he is also the UE responsible for the scientific and technological cooperation agreement on material and nanotechnologies with NSF (USA) and for the multilateral agreement 'Intelligent Manufacturing System' (IMS).

In 1973 he contributed to the creation of the International Agency for Energy (AIE-OCSE). As UE Commission representative he has taken part to different committees involved in the sector of oil and energy.

Since 1983 he is the responsible of scientific relations with international organizations in the field of S&T for developing countries contributing to the definition of strategies and priorities with these institutions and countries.

In 1995 he has been appointed Director of the 'Energy' Directorate, in 1999 Director of the 'Competitive and Sustainable Growth' Directorate and he has been called to implement the 5th European Framework Programme.

He wrote many articles on innovation and he has been a Visiting Professor in several Italian universities (Politecnico of Turin, Politecnico of Milan, University of Genova and University of Trento) and foreign universities (Escuela Politecnica de Madrid and IPADE of Mexico City).

Patrizio Bianchi. He is Professor of Applied Economics at University of Ferrara and since 2004 he is the Rector of the University.

After his studies at Bologna University and at London School of Economics and Political Sciences, he became full Professor of Industrial Economics at Bologna University in 1989. In 1996 he is called to establish and direct the new faculty of Economics at the University of Ferrara, where he was elected Rector in 2004.

Patrizio Bianchi worked in several institutions in Italy and abroad (Latin America and China in particular) on issues related to industrial policy, SME development, privatizations. Among his recent works: "International Handbook on Industrial Policy" (with S.Labory), E.Elgar, London, 2005 (forthcoming); "The Economic Importance of Intangible Assets" (with S.Labory), Ashgate, London, 2004; "Technology, Information and Market Dynamics. Topics in Advanced Industrial Organization" (with L.Lambertini), E.Elgar Pu. London, 2003; "Industrial Policies and economic Integration. Learning from the European Experiences", Routledge, London, 1998.

Pontus Braunerhjelm. He earned his Ph D at the Graduate Institute of International Studies, Geneva, Switzerland, in 1994. His has published extensively in journals (*Economics Letters, Weltwirtschaftliches Archiv, Applied Economics, Journal of Evolutionary Economics, Small Business Economics etc.*) and also contributed to several books internationally published. In 2000 he participated in the CEPR Monitoring European Integration report (with co-authors R. Faini, V. Norman, F. Ruane and P. Seabright). Pontus Braunerhjelm is presently heading two larger research projects. One on endogenous growth and entrepreneurship (other participants are David Audretsch, Zoltan Acs, etc.), one on the emergence of agglomerated production structures, clusters (together with Maryann Feldman). Pontus Braunerhjelm has presented papers at the ASSA/AEA-, CEPR-, EEA-. EARIE-, IEA-, WEA-meetings, and also acted referee for EER, EJ, JEBO, JICS, JIO, WWA, etc. Presently Pontus Braunerhjelm share his time between The Center for Business and Policy Studies (SNS), Stockholm, where he is Research Director, and Linköping University.

Paul A. David. He is Professor of Economics and Senior Fellow of the Institute for Economic Policy Research at Stanford University, where he has been a member of the faculty continuously since 1961 and was formerly (in 1977- 1994) the William Robertson Co Professor of American Economic History. From 1994 until 2002 he held a Senior Research Fellowship at All Souls College, Oxford, where presently he is an Emeritus Fellow. Since November 2002 he has been Senior Fellow of the Oxford Internet Institute announced in the University of Oxford.

David is known internationally for his contributions in American economic history, economic and historical demography, and the economics of science and technology. He is the author of more than 145 journal articles and contributions to edited books and several more volumes due to appear under his own name during 2005. He is a founding editor of the international journal *Economics of Innovation and New Technology*, and currently serves on the editorial boards of different scientific-economic journals.

He has been elected as a Fellow of the International Econometrics Society (1975), Fellow of the American Academy of Arts and Sciences (1979), Ordinary Fellow of the British Academy (1995), and Member of the American Philosophical Society (2003). In 1996 the University of Oxford conferred upon him the title of Professor of Economics and Economic History, "in recognition of distinction." He holds a Doctorate *Honoris Causa* from the University of Torino (2003). He has served as elected Vice-President, and President of the Economic History Association (1988-89), and was a Member of Council of the Royal Economics Society (1996-2002).

David has served as a consultant to U. S. government agencies and foundations including the National Academy of Sciences' National Research Council, the National Science Foundation, and the Departments of Commerce, and of Energy; the Rockefeller Foundation, the Sloan Foundation and numerous other public and private organizations.

John Eatwell. He is the President of Queens' College, Cambridge, Director of the Cambridge Endowment for Research in Finance, and Professor of Financial Policy in the Judge Institute of Management, University of Cambridge.

He has been a Visiting Professor at Columbia University, New York, the University of Massachusetts, Amherst, and the University of Amsterdam.
From 1985 to 1992 he served as economic adviser to Neil Kinnock, the then leader of the Labour Party. In 1992 he entered the House of Lords, and from 1993 to 1997 was Principal Opposition Spokesman on Treasury and Economic Affairs.
In 1988, together with Clive Hollick, he set up the Institute for Public Policy Research. He was Chairman from 1997 to 2000, and remains a Trustee.
In 1997 he joined the Board of the Securities and Futures Authority (SFA), Britain's securities markets regulator prior to 30th November 2001, serving on the Enforcement Committee and the Capital Committee. In this position he developed his interest in securities regulation, particularly with respect to risk management in financial institutions. Since the SFA ceased to operate he has been a member of the Regulatory Decisions Committee of the Financial Services Authority.
John Eatwell is a non-executive director of Cambridge Econometrics (an economic research firm) and Rontech Ltd (a producer of management software for the financial services sector), and is an adviser to the private equity firms Warburg Pincus & Company International Ltd and Palamon Capital Partners.
He is also the Chairman of the British Library.

Maryann P. Feldman. She teaches at the Rotman School of Management, University of Toronto, where she is the Jeffery S. Skoll Professor of Innovation and Entrepreneurship. She holds a Ph.D. in economics and management and an M.S. in policy analysis and management from Carnegie Mellon University. She received a B.A. in economics and geography from Ohio State University. She wrote *The Geography of Innovation* (1994), *The Oxford University Handbook of Economic Geography* (ed., 2000), *Innovation Policy in the Knowledge-Based Economy* (ed., 2000) and *Institutions and Systems in the Geography of Innovation* (ed., 2001).

Marco Fortis. He is Director of the Department of Economic Studies of Edison and contract Professor of Industrial Economics at the Faculty of Political Sciences of Catholic University (Milan) since 1989.
He is Member of the Scientific Committee of the Research Centre in Economic Analysis (CRANEC) of Catholic University (Milan), member of the Scientific Committee and Vice-President of the Fondazione Edison, Vice-President of the Fondazione Guido Donegani and member of the Board of Directors of Carlo Erba.
Publications: numerous books and articles in books, journals and newspapers on the subjects of Italian economy, industry and local production systems, technology, development and international trade. Among his main books: "*Prodotti di base e cicli economici*" (Il.Mulino, 1988, Iglesias Prize winner), "*Il made in Italy*" (Il Mulino, 1998) and "*Le imprese multiutility*" (Il Mulino, 2001). With Alberto Quadrio Curzio he edited "*Il made in Italy oltre il 2000*" (Il Mulino, 2000), "*Le liberalizzazioni e le privatizzazioni dei servizi pubblici locali*" (Il Mulino, 2000) and "*Il gruppo Edison 1883-2003. Profili economici e societari*" (Il Mulino, 2003).

Uno Lindberg. He is Professor of Zoological Cell Biology at Stockholm University and Head of the Dept. of Zoological Cell Biology, Wenner-Gren Institute, Stockholm University.

He is member of the Royal Swedish Academy of Sciences and chairman of the European Academies´ Science Advisory Council. He is member of the Committee for a New European Research Policy (CNERP). He is also chairman of the steering group of the committee for the project "Natural Science & Technology for All" (the NTA project).

His field of research in molecular cell biology is concerned with signal transduction, chemo-mechanical transduction, in relation to cell growth and proliferation.

Christian Longhi. He is Senior Researcher at GREDEG (Groupe de Recherche en Droit, Economie et Gestion, CNRS - Centre National de la Recherche Scientifique). Among his publications: 'Networks, Collective Learning and Technology Development in Innovative High-technology Regions: the Case of Sophia-Antipolis' *Regional Studies*, (1999); 'Regional Evolutionary Trends in the 1990's in: D. Keeble and F. Wilkinson (eds) *High Technology Clusters, Networking and Collective Learning in Europe*, (2000); 'Intégration Européenne et Dynamiques Régionales', in: D.Torre, E.Tosi (eds), *Intégration Européenne et Institutions Economiques*, Paris, De Boeck, 2001; 'From Exogenous to Endogenous Local Development : The Cases of Toulouse and Sophia Antipolis Technopoles' (2002), High Technology Locations and Globalization: Converse Paths, Common Processes (with E. Garsney, IJTM 2004).

Mario A. Maggioni. He holds a M.Sc. and a Ph.D. from the University of Warwick, Coventry (UK). Professor of Economics in the Faculty of Political Science at the Catholic University of Milan, he is member of the scientific committee of 'Economia Politica' and associate editor of 'Network and Spatial Economics'.

He is the author of a number of articles and books on; innovation, economic development and technological change; educational systems, human capital and labor markets; genesis and development of high-tech clusters; structure and dynamics of local productive systems. He is member of several Italian and foreign inter-university research groups. His methodological interests span from network analysis to non-linear models simulation, to agent-based modeling, to structural (I-O) analysis.

Joel Mokyr. He is the Robert H. Strotz Professor of Arts and Sciences and Professor of Economics and History at Northwestern University and Sackler Professorial Fellow at the Eitan Berglas School of Economics at the University of Tel Aviv.

He specializes in economic history and the economics of technological change and population change. He is the author of 'Why Ireland Starved: An Analytical and Quantitative Study of the Irish Economy', 'The Lever of Riches: Technological Creativity and Economic Progress', 'The British Industrial Revolution: An Economic Perspective' and his most recent 'The Gifts of Athena: Historical Origins of the Knowledge Economy' and 'The Enlightened Economy'. He has authored over 70 articles and books in his field.

He has served as the senior editor of the Journal of Economic History from 1994 to 1998, and is the editor in chief of the Oxford Encyclopedia of Economic History (2003) and the Princeton University Press Economic History of the Western World. He has served as President of the Economic History Association (2003-04) and is director of the National Bureau of Economic Research and a member of its executive committee. He is a fellow of the American Academy of Arts and Sciences, and a foreign member of the Dutch Royal Academy of Sciences and Accademia Nazionale dei Lincei.

Professor Mokyr has an undergraduate degree from the Hebrew University of Jerusalem and a Ph.D, from Yale University. He has taught at Northwestern since 1974, and has been a visiting Professor at Harvard, the University of Chicago, Stanford, the Hebrew University of Jerusalem, the University of Tel Aviv, University College of Dublin, and the University of Manchester. His books have won a number of important prizes including the Joseph Schumpeter memorial prize (1990), the Rankyi prize for the best book in European Economic history and most recently the Donald Price Prize of the American Political Science Association.

His current research deals with models and historical evidence of the interaction of human knowledge, technology, and economic growth.

Alberto Quadrio Curzio. He is Professor of Political Economy, Dean of the Faculty of Political Sciences and Director of the Research Centre in Economic Analysis (CRANEC), Catholic University (Milan). He is Vice President of Istituto Lombardo - Accademia di Scienze e Lettere and Academic Secretary of the Accademia Nazionale dei Lincei. Chief editor of the journal "Economia Politica", il Mulino and of the Scientific Committee of other journals among which "Structural Change and Economic Dynamics"; "Journal of Policy Modelling".

He has been Dean of the Faculty of Political Sciences of the University of Bologna, Chairman of Società Italiana degli Economisti (1995-98) remaining for twelve years in the Board and he has been elected member of CNR (Italian National Research Council) for ten years. He received many Awards among which the St. Vincent Award for Economics and the international Cortina Ulisse Award. He received from the President of Italian Republic the "Gold Medal Award". He wrote approximately 300 scientific publications, many of which in English. His main subjects of study are: economic theory of scarce resources, income distribution, education, economic development and economic-institutional forms thereof. He is Chairman of the Scientific Committee of the Fondazione Edison.

Laura Ramaciotti. Sheis responsible of the Liaison Office of Ferrara University. She also teaches Economics, firms management and marketing at the faculty of Mathematical, Physical and Natural Sciences of the University of Ferrara.

After her studies at Bologna University, she worked at the National Development Agency. Since 2001 she is responsible of the Spin Off Center of the University of Ferrara, and since 2003 of the network created by the four universities of Emilia Romagna and the regional government to promote new research companies.

She wrote extensively on industrial innovation and policy. She is editing a volume on the Italian experience of research spin offs and university patenting.

G. M. Peter Swann. He is Professor of Industrial Economics at University of Notitngham, UK.

Most of his research is concerned with innovation, and over the last ten years a large part of his research has been concerned with 'innovative clusters'. He has been a Specialist Advisor to the House of Lords Science and Technology Committee, and an Advisor to the British Government's Department of Trade and Industry.

Printing and Binding: Strauss GmbH, Mörlenbach